CONSPIRACY OF SILENCE

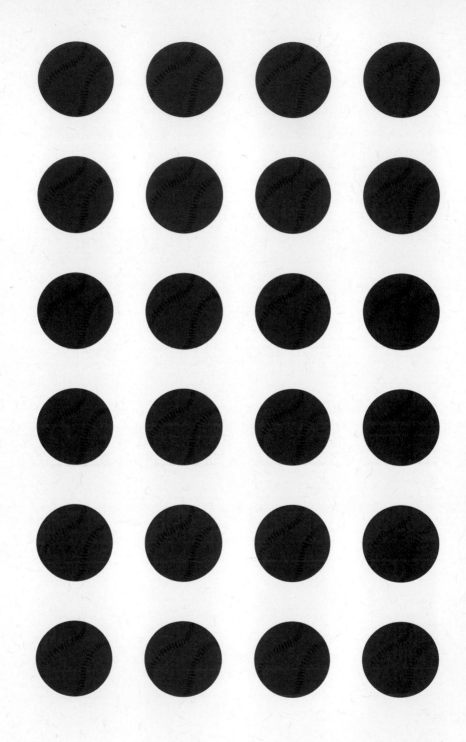

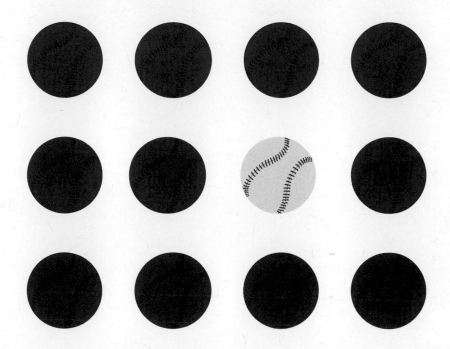

CONSPIRACY OF SILENCE

SPORTSWRITERS AND

THE LONG CAMPAIGN TO

DESEGREGATE BASEBALL

CHRIS LAMB

UNIVERSITY OF NEBRASKA PRESS, LINCOLN AND LONDON

Acknowledgments for the use of
copyrighted material appear on
page xiii, which constitutes an
extension of the copyright page.

Library of Congress Cataloging-
in-Publication Data
Lamb, Chris, 1958–
Conspiracy of silence: sportswriters
and the long campaign to desegregate
baseball / Chris Lamb.
p. cm.
Includes bibliographical references and
index.
ISBN 978-0-8032-1076-9 (cloth: alk.
paper)
1. Baseball—Social aspects—United
States—History—20th century.
2. Discrimination in sports—United
States—History—20th century.
3. Mass media and sports—United
States—History—20th century.
4. Sportswriters—United States—
History—20th century. 5. African
American sportswriters—History—
20th century. 6. Racism—United
States—History—20th century. I. Title.
GV867.64.L36 2012
796.3570973—dc23 2011037503

Set in Minion by Kim Essman.
Designed by Nathan Putens.

TO MY WIFE, LESLY,

AND MY SON, DAVID,

WITH LOVE AND

GRATITUDE

CONTENTS

ACKNOWLEDGMENTS

I am indebted to the late Jules Tygiel, whose book *Baseball's Great Experiment* gave me an appreciation for the human drama and historical importance of the story of the desegregation of baseball. Professor Tygiel's writing took many of us into a world that we had not previously known and inspired us to learn more about the decades of segregated baseball. The story of segregated baseball and how the game finally became desegregated tells us much about segregation in the United States and how the country finally became desegregated. I am also indebted to those other authors and scholars whose works I read and reread, whose work on the press, race, and baseball history laid the foundation for this book: Glen Bleske, Brian Carroll, Richard Crepeau, Ralph Frasca, Timothy Gay, Leslie Heaphy, Jerome Holtzman, John Holway, Sam Lacy, Neil Lanctot, Pamela Laucella, Larry Lester, Lee Lowenfish, Jerry Malloy, Robert Peterson, David Pietrusza, Benjamin Rader, Arnold Rampersad, Jim Reisler, James Riley, Donn Rogosin,

Kelly Rusinack, Harold Seymour, Irwin Silber, William Simons, Glenn Stout, John Thorn, David Voigt, Patrick Washburn, Bill Weaver, David Wiggins, and David Zang. I apologize to those I have neglected to mention.

I am particularly indebted to Brian Carroll, Paul Ashdown, Richard Crepeau, and Larry Lester for taking the time to read drafts of particular chapters. Their suggestions made this a much better book than it otherwise would have been. Brian Carroll's book *When to Stop the Cheering? The Black Press, the Black Community, and the Integration of Baseball* is a must-read for anyone interested in learning more about the black press and the Negro leagues. Professor Carroll's suggestions for improving this book were invaluable. I met Paul Ashdown more than three decades ago when he was my journalism professor at the University of Tennessee. He taught me more about writing than anyone else when I was in college. In the years that have followed, he has continued to give me guidance, advice, and encouragement. I hope one day I can have the kind of influence on one student as he had on untold students. Richard Crepeau's book *Baseball: America's Diamond Mind, 1919–1941* was an excellent source for this book, and his suggestions were helpful in shaping this book's first chapter. I am also indebted to Larry Lester, cofounder of the Negro Leagues Baseball Museum and the most prolific, articulate, and knowledgeable chronicler of black baseball.

I would also like to thank Kelly Rusinack, who wrote her master's thesis on the U.S. Communist Party's campaign to desegregate baseball. Kelly and I collaborated on a chapter in this book. And finally, I would like to express my appreciation to Glen Bleske, who, like me, left newspaper work for academia. He and I collaborated on two journal articles about the desegregation of baseball. One of those articles was on Jackie Robinson's first spring training in professional baseball. This article would serve as the inspiration for my first book, *Blackout: The Untold Story of Jackie Robinson's First Spring Training*.

My interest in the desegregation of baseball began in 1993 when I was working as a columnist for the *Daytona Beach News-Journal* and interviewed retired *Pittsburgh Courier* sportswriter Billy Rowe, who had accompanied Jackie Robinson during the spring training of 1946. Rowe's memories gave that column a voice that would not have been possible if he had not agreed to be interviewed. During the spring of 1946, Rowe was accompanied by the *Courier*'s influential sports editor Wendell Smith, who had crusaded for the desegregation of baseball with other black journalists, including Sam Lacy of the *Baltimore Afro-American*. Both Smith and Lacy were later inducted into the J. G. Taylor Spink baseball writers' wing of the Hall of Fame. I subsequently interviewed Sam Lacy, who provided evocative and painful memories of the racism he faced covering baseball in the years before and then after the signing of Jackie Robinson. I became friends with Mr. Lacy, who died several years ago. I am grateful for the kindness and patience he showed. Until relatively recently, little had been said about the work of the communist newspaper the *Daily Worker* in the campaign to desegregate baseball. One cannot possibly understand this story without an appreciation of the contributions of communist sportswriters, including Lester Rodney, the newspaper's longtime sports editor, and Bill Mardo, who served as sports editor when Rodney was serving in the army during World War II. One day I hope that Lester Rodney, too, will be inducted into the baseball writers' wing of the Hall of Fame for his contributions to the desegregation of baseball. I am indebted to both Mr. Rodney and Mr. Mardo for the opportunity to interview them. Finally, I am grateful for the opportunity to interview the incomparable Shirley Povich, who was one of the relatively few white sportswriters who supported blacks in baseball.

As I worked on *Blackout* and then on this book, *Conspiracy of Silence*, I was fortunate to have had a number of articles published in research journals. Before these articles were accepted, the respective journal editors made suggestions that improved the articles and subsequently improved the content of this book. I would like to express my gratitude to the editors of the following journals: *Journalism and Mass Communication Quarterly*, *Journalism History*, *Western Journal of Black*

Studies, and *Nine: A Journal of Baseball History and Culture*. A longer
version of the article I wrote for *Nine* appears in this book as a separate
chapter. I would like to acknowledge the suggestions and support of
that journal's editor, Trey Strecker.

This book required that I read thousands of articles on microfilm
from newspapers that appeared decades and in some cases more than
a hundred years ago. It would have been impossible for me to do this
without the staffs of the interlibrary loan departments at Bowling Green
State University, where I received my PhD; at Old Dominion University,
where I taught for two years; and then at the College of Charleston,
where I have taught for the past thirteen years. I am thankful for the
kindness and doggedness of those men and women who worked in the
interlibrary loan departments. In addition, I spent many days reading
microfilm at the Library of Congress in Washington DC. I would like to
thank the staff at the reading room at the Library of Congress. I would
also like to acknowledge the respective staffs at the National Baseball Hall of Fame in Cooperstown, New York, and at Ohio Wesleyan
University in Delaware, Ohio. I would like to thank the research and
development committee at the College of Charleston for approving a
summer grant that allowed me the time to work on this book.

I would like to acknowledge the support and patience of my editor
at the University of Nebraska Press, Rob Taylor, and the many people
at the press who turned a manuscript into a book. And finally, I would
like to acknowledge the contributions of friends and colleagues. My
friend Phil Nel, professor of English at Kansas State University, while
doing research on the writer Crockett Johnson, found information for
me on the Committee to End Jim Crow in Baseball. Brian McGee, who
served as my chair for several years at the College of Charleston, was
generous in his support and in the use of the books in his personal
library. I also am thankful to other friends who were patient enough
to listen to me talk about the book and send me stories and articles
I might be able to use, including Randy Norris, Vince Benigni, Lee
Drago, Amy Horwitz, Erik Calonius, and DeForrest Jackson. I also

am thankful for the friendship and companionship of my baseball buddies, who have accompanied me on scores of spring training and regular season Major League games: Marc Bona, Ken Hornack, John Major, and Joe Sharpnack.

I am forever indebted to my family and, in particular, my father, Bob, who instilled in me my love of baseball, and my mother, Jean, the onetime reference librarian, who instilled in me my love of research. I cannot possibly thank them for all they have done for me. I also acknowledge the love for and support of my brothers and sisters, brothers-in-law and sisters-in-law, and nephews and nieces. I am thankful every day for my wife, Lesly, who adds light to my darkness, and my son, David, who reads the box scores every day and loves baseball as much as I do. My wife, son, and I are thankful for my in-laws, Dan and Eleanor, for all they contribute to our lives.

Parts of chapter 1 originally appeared as "'What's Wrong with Baseball?': The *Pittsburgh Courier* and the Beginning of Its Campaign to Integrate Baseball," *Western Journal of Black Studies* 26 (Winter 2002): 189–92.

Parts of chapter 5 originally appeared as "*L'affaire* Jake Powell: The Minority Press Goes to Bat against Segregated Baseball," *Journalism and Mass Communication Quarterly* 76 (Spring 1999): 21–34.

Portions of chapter 6 originally appeared as "Baseball's Whitewash: Sportswriter Wendell Smith Exposes Major League Baseball's Big Lie," *Nine: A Journal of Baseball History and Culture* 18 (Fall 2009): 1–20, with permission from the University of Nebraska Press. Copyright 2009.

Portions of chapter 11 were previously published in *Blackout: The Untold Story of Jackie Robinson's First Spring Training*, by permission of the University of Nebraska Press. Copyright 2004 by the Board of Regents of the University of Nebraska.

CONSPIRACY OF SILENCE

PART 1

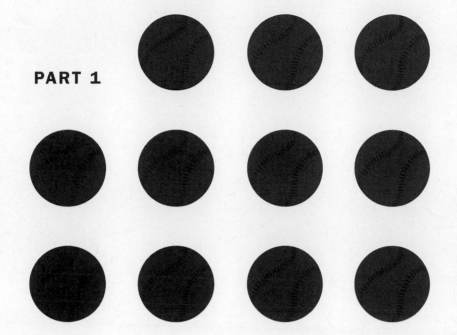

CHAPTER 1

WHITE SPORTSWRITERS
AND MINSTREL SHOWS

On February 5, 1933, the inside of the grand ballroom of New York City's Commodore Hotel crackled with laughter during an evening of songs, skits, and speeches at the tenth annual New York Baseball Writers' Association dinner. Sportswriters took turns spoofing everyone from the guest of honor, retired New York Giants manager John McGraw, to the New York Yankees, who had defeated the Chicago Cubs in the World Series the previous October. In addition, sportswriters performed their annual minstrel show to the delight of the all-white crowd of several hundred. *New York Times* sportswriter John Drebinger called the minstrel show the main entertainment for the evening. "I'm still laughing," Dan Daniel, the president of the association, gushed in his column in the *Sporting News*. Writers, ballplayers, and owners sat together with politicians, judges, businessmen, and ministers to laugh but also to glorify baseball and to honor those who made the game great. New York Yankees pitcher Herb Pennock received the writers' award as the outstanding player of the previous year. John McGraw reflected nostalgically about his long career after receiving the "Outstanding Service to Baseball" award. Other speakers included St. Louis Cardinals vice president Branch Rickey, toastmaster Bugsy Baer, Philadelphia comic Joe Cunningham, and former sportswriter Heywood Broun of the *New York World-Telegram*, who wrote the nationally syndicated column "It Seems to Me."[1]

In his speech Broun responded to a recent editorial in the *New York Daily News* that called for abolishing the color line in baseball. Broun said he saw "no reason" blacks should be prohibited from the Major Leagues.[2] Broun wrote in his February 7 column that his suggestion was "met with no overwhelming roar of approval." Broun, however, added, "It was still a good suggestion." Broun said blacks had proven themselves good athletes. He said Yale University football coach Walter Camp twice had included Paul Robeson of Rutgers University on his All-America team. Broun said that a number of blacks, including sprinter Eddie Tolan, had competed with great success for the United States at the 1932 Olympic Games. If blacks were good enough to represent the United States in the Olympics, Broun said, "it seems a little silly that they cannot participate in a game between the Chicago White Sox and St. Louis Browns." Broun said that nothing, in particular, prevented an owner from signing a black player. "As things stand, I believe there is no set rule barring Negroes from the game. It is merely a tacit agreement," he said, "or possibly custom." If there was no rule, he continued, "Why, in the name of fair play and gate receipts, should professional baseball be so exclusive?" Broun said he had been told players would object to having black teammates. But, as things stood, players already objected to a lot of things in baseball — like being traded, fined, or having their salaries cut — but that did not stop team owners from doing these things. He said blacks would make the game more interesting and also would swell the size of crowds. "And," he added, "it would be a fair and square thing. If baseball is really the national game let the club owners go out and prove it."[3]

New York Daily News columnist Jimmy Powers responded to Broun's speech by asking several baseball executives and ballplayers if they objected to blacks in baseball. National League president John Heydler, New York Yankees owner Jacob Ruppert, and ballplayers such as Pennock, Lou Gehrig, and Frankie Frisch all told him they did not. Only McGraw objected on the record.[4] McGraw's response appeared uncharacteristic, given that he had shown an interest in signing blacks during his long career in baseball. In 1901 McGraw, then managing the Baltimore Orioles of the National League, tried to circumvent the color line by passing a black infielder, Charlie Grant, as a Cherokee Indian. When Grant's real ethnicity was revealed, McGraw released him. When McGraw was managing the New York Giants, he was so impressed with black pitcher "Rube" Foster that he hired him to work with his pitching staff. McGraw later said he would pay fifty thousand dollars for the black Cuban pitcher José Méndez if there had not been a color line. Black teams used the nickname "Giants" as a tribute to McGraw. Black baseball historian Larry Lester said that if black spectators saw the name "Giants" on an advertisement, it meant it was probably a black team.[5]

In his February 8 column, Powers wrote that he was pleased by what he called "a refreshing open-mindedness" from the baseball executives and players he had queried. This, he said, was a sign of progress in race relations. "The bulk of the players then came from the other side of the Mason Dixon line. They brought the Jim Crow . . . ideas into the North with them." Powers said it was only a matter of time before blacks were admitted into the big leagues. "I base this upon the fact that the ball player of today is more liberal than yesterday's leather-necked, tobacco-chewing sharpshooter from the cross roads." Powers agreed with Broun that Major League Baseball should sign black ballplayers. Like Broun, he mentioned that blacks had succeeded in other sports. Powers added that he was not aware of any blacks playing college football who had demonstrated anything but fair play toward whites on the field — not mentioning that the reverse probably was not true. He ended his column by stating that there was little for the black athlete after college. He said the great Marquette University sprinter Ralph Metcalfe had returned from the Olympics to work as a "water boy" on the football team. Metcalfe, Powers suggested, could have been playing professional baseball. "They tell me he is a good outfield prospect and can thump the turnip," Powers said. "College youngsters of his type can play ball for my money any afternoon in the week."[6]

Powers's column appeared in the *Daily News*, which had the highest circulation of any daily newspaper in the country. Broun's column was syndicated to hundreds of newspapers. His speech was heard by a number of New York City journalists, including some of the most influential sportswriters in the country, yet, with the exception of Powers, none responded in print, including neither of Broun's fellow sportswriters on the *World-Telegram*, Tom Meany and Joe Williams. Dan Daniel wrote a lengthy column about the dinner in the *Sporting News* but said nothing about Broun — at least not right away. A year later, on January 18, 1934, Daniel mentioned Broun's speech in a column about how baseball had long served as a point of entry for immigrants to live the American dream. "Baseball," Daniel said, "is as American as America itself." He said the big leagues had players from all over the world but ignored those with black ancestry. "We will not go into the justice of the color line here and at this time, but we do know that there is a color line and that it is adhered to most strictly," Daniel wrote, adding that Broun had once raised the issue. "He wanted to know why Negroes were not permitted to play in the big leagues and he is still asking that same question." Daniel concluded his column by writing, "We all know that the Negroes of America list among their race some of the greatest ballplayers the game has seen and that right now they have a flock of stars who would be eligible for the big show except for the color line."[7]

The *Sporting News* also ignored Broun's comments at the baseball writers' dinner. It did, however, include articles and columns criticizing sportswriter Fred Lieb's widely distributed series, "What's Wrong with Baseball?" The series offered suggestions for reviving interest in the national pastime. Lieb said the game was neither as good nor as colorful as it had been in the past. He said that ticket prices were too high. Lieb also suggested speeding up the pace of the game by encouraging more base stealing and aggressive baserunning. Joe Vila of the *New York Sun*, who had covered baseball for three decades, bristled at Lieb's series in his column in the *Sporting News*. "It is hard to understand how scribes who depend on baseball for a livelihood take delight in belittling it without the slightest idea of fairness, 'What is the matter with baseball?' is an unwarranted question," said Vila, who longed for the good old days when baseball writers "stood loyally by the game."[8]

On February 1 the *Daily News* responded with an editorial with its own suggestions for improving baseball. "Another trouble with major league baseball certainly would seem to be the color line," the editorial said. "There have been good baseball players who were Indians or part Indians, Mexicans, Cubans, etc. A Chinese Hawaiian tried out for the Giants a few years ago, and would have made the team if he had been able to play a little better ball. But good colored ball players aren't eligible." Broun's speech, consequently, had been a response to the *Daily News* editorial. Whereas most sportswriters responded — at least publicly — to Broun with their silence, Vila, a week after criticizing Lieb, chided Broun without identifying him by name for suggesting "in one of the Metropolitan rags . . . Negro players in the big leagues." Vila said that the sportswriter had brought up the idea at the dinner where baseball had honored McGraw. "McGraw," Vila said, "was the only man officially identified with the big leagues who had the guts to say that Negroes should not be permitted to play in teams with white men." Vila wrote that a talented black infielder named Grant had played for Buffalo in the National League in 1887, but that his presence caused such controversy that baseball owners secretly passed a rule forbidding any more blacks.[9] Vila's reference was not to Charlie Grant but to Frank Grant, who played for Buffalo in the International League, a top Minor League, when league officials barred further contracts with black ballplayers.

On February 11 Alvin Moses of a black weekly, the *Pittsburgh Courier*, reported that the *Daily News* had criticized baseball's color line. Moses wrote that "the editorial on fair play" raised hopes for those, like himself, who had long called for blacks in baseball. The editorial, he said, "comes as water to the parched lips of a traveler who has sought in vain for many days." Year after year Moses had yearned for articles like these in white newspapers. Year after year, he added, black Babe Ruths, Lou Gehrigs, Lefty Gomezes, Lefty Groves, and Jimmie Foxxes played in anonymity because of the color of their skin. "Cry out from the shadows of yesteryear against this unholy and un-American idea of fair play to all citizens," Moses wrote. The editorial staff of the *Daily News*, Moses said, "is to be congratulated."[10]

On February 18 a *Courier* editorial praised Broun and Powers, quoting at length from both men's columns. In the editorial's last paragraph, the writer expressed surprise — but not disbelief — that McGraw had opposed the signing of black players because he had attempted to sign Charlie Grant. In a separate column on February 18, sports editor Chester "Ches" Washington called the story the "most significant sports news in many months." Washington praised the *Daily News*, Broun, and Powers for confronting the national pastime. Washington expressed surprise at the "refreshing openness" of those baseball executives and players who said they had no objections to blacks in baseball. Washington said white team owners would now be watching black baseball more closely for players with Major League ability. Washington urged the Negro leagues to prepare for the possibility of integrated baseball. This, he said, might involve adding black teams to the Minor Leagues of "organized professional baseball," as it was called. To prepare for this possibility, Washington called on black baseball to become better organized. This meant creating more uniform rules and better standards of play and conduct for ballplayers and fans. It also meant that ballplayers needed to act more professionally on the field.[11]

In the *Courier*'s next issue Washington announced the beginning of the newspaper's series on baseball and race, which published the views of big league owners, managers, ballplayers, and sportswriters. The series began with an interview with National League president John Heydler, who told the newspaper that the only requirements for the big leagues were good athletic ability and good character. "I do not recall one instance where baseball has allowed either race, creed, or color to enter into the question of the selection of its players," he said. On March 4 *Courier* assistant sports editor Rollo Wilson quoted Gerry Nugent, president of the Philadelphia Phillies, as saying, "Baseball caters to all races and creeds. . . . It is the national game and is played by all groups. Therefore, I see no objections to Negro players in the big leagues." Nugent agreed with Heydler that "ability and conduct" were the primary qualifications for the Major Leagues. Nugent questioned whether there were blacks with big league ability. "It is a long jump from the sandlots to the majors," he said, adding, "I, for one, will be glad to see Negro players in organized baseball if and when that time comes."[12]

Commissioner Kenesaw Mountain Landis did not respond directly to the survey. Leslie O'Connor, the secretary-treasurer of organized baseball, however, spoke for his boss. O'Connor told the *Courier* there was no rule that kept black players out of baseball. He added that any decision to sign blacks would have to come from team owners and not the commissioner's office. Baseball, he said, had no written rule forbidding blacks. When asked if owners had an unwritten law prohibiting blacks, O'Connor "indicated that the subject of Negro ball players had never come up." In the same issue J. Louis Comiskey, president of the Chicago White Sox and the son of the team's late owner, Charles, said, "You can bet your last dime that I'll never refuse to hire a great athlete because he isn't the same color of some other player on my team."[13]

On March 18 Gordon Mackay of the *Philadelphia Record*, a black newspaper, said the addition of blacks into white professional baseball "would be a great thing for baseball if you could prepare for it." Mackay said there would have to be an agreement restricting black players to the Minor Leagues in the North because of segregation laws in the South. Mackay said there were "scores" of black players who could play

in the high Minors and the Major Leagues. Unlike others who clung
to the myth that blacks and white could not share a ball field without
a racial incident, Mackay said blacks and whites were already sharing
ball fields in college football and college baseball. Mackay suggested
that a game be played between the best team in the Major Leagues and
the best team in black baseball for a true national championship.[14] But
such a game would never be played because Landis and team owners
were aware that it would draw attention to the color line. They also
knew that if such a game were played, there was a real possibility the
black team would win.

William Benswanger, president of the Pittsburgh Pirates, responded
by saying he could not give his opinion without first consulting with
owners and league executives. When the Pirates finally responded,
it appeared not only that the team had contacted Heydler but that
the league president had written the response himself. The *Courier*
published the response of Samuel Walters, the team's vice president.
"Exceptional playing ability and proper living habits are the main
attributes and requirements for positions on major league ball clubs,"
Walters said. "And I don't believe that race, creed, or color have ever
entered into the selection of the players on the big league clubs." The
Courier reported that it would continue to include responses "from
notables in baseball's councils." Ches Washington knew baseball had
restricted black players solely on the basis of race for decades, but he
did not challenge this in print, calling Heydler's comment "fair and
open minded." In another column Washington said that the "emphatic
declarations" of Heydler and Nugent "were worthy of commendation."[15]

Whether Washington really believed white baseball executives is
debatable. It is likely he wrote what he did in order to open a dialogue
with the baseball establishment. If this was baseball's argument for why
there were no blacks, then Washington and other black sportswriters
were willing to take baseball executives at their word. Black sportswriters praised the stars of the Negro leagues while lecturing ballplayers
and fans on proper behavior. They sent telegrams to owners of big

league teams, telling them the signing of black stars would improve the quality of their teams as well as put more fans in their stadiums. They urged Negro league officials to standardize rules so that black baseball could be absorbed into white baseball.[16] Black sportswriters would repeat these words year after year with little effect. Neither executives in the Major Leagues nor those in the Negro leagues appeared to pay any attention.

The *Courier* was not the only black newspaper to acknowledge Broun's and Powers's support for blacks in baseball. Romeo Dougherty of the *Amsterdam News*, which was published in Harlem, regretted that "brother" Broun had waited so late in his career to raise the issue. "Better late than never and we hope that something will come of it," Dougherty said. Dougherty said owners had argued that they could not sign black players because of the opposition of white players. Dougherty said it was a moot question whether players would approve of having a black teammate. If owners signed black players, white players would have to accept it. Dougherty also thought it was curious that McGraw objected to blacks in baseball. Dougherty acknowledged McGraw's interest in signing blacks. Given McGraw's recent answer to Powers, Dougherty questioned whether McGraw had ever really been interested in signing blacks. Lewis Dial of the *New York Age* also expressed his surprise that McGraw had answered as he had, "inasmuch as he is supposed to have tried to smuggle a Negro star into the [big] leagues some time ago, and at one time claimed that José Méndez . . . was one of the greatest pitchers of all time."[17]

Salem Tutt Whitney, a noted vaudevillian who had appeared in the Broadway run of *The Green Pastures*, wrote in the *Chicago Defender* that Major League Baseball would see an increase in attendance if it allowed black players. Whitney said he had written Joe Williams of the *New York World-Telegram* to suggest that the New York City teams — the Yankees, Giants, and Brooklyn Dodgers — would improve if they added at least one black player to their rosters. He appealed for Williams's support. Williams replied by telling him, "How can one little typewriter break down a hundred years of prejudice?" Whitney responded by asking, "How often have we asked ourselves that same question? Prejudice is as big as all humanity and one feels that one's puny efforts at resistance will prove futile. Yet, I have an idea, it is just an idea. I may be wrong." Whitney wondered if Williams had shown the letter to Broun, his colleague at the *World-Telegram*, who had then raised the issue at the baseball writers' dinner.[18]

The *Defender* asked Louis Comiskey if he would sign a black player for the White Sox. Comiskey responded as he did when asked by the *Courier*. Comiskey said he had never considered whether blacks should play in the big leagues. "Had some good player come along and my manager refused to sign him because he was a Negro I am sure I would have taken action or attempted to," Comiskey said. "I cannot say that I would have insisted on hiring the player over the protest of my manager, but at least I would have taken some steps — just what steps I cannot say for sure, for the simple reason that the question has never confronted me." When Comiskey was told that pitcher Willie Foster of the Chicago American Giants would improve the team and increase attendance, Comiskey's reply was short but hardly encouraging: "Yes, I expect so." A week later the *Defender* quoted Comiskey as saying, "I have never had the question put to me squarely. But without going into it fully I'd say let them in. It might add interest and color to the sport. Certainly, if they were admitted, the White Sox would be open to employing them. Nor for that matter would I vote against the proposal to admit them into the league."[19] Commissioner Landis and the other owners would never put Comiskey into the uncomfortable position of having to either accept or reject a proposal to allow blacks in baseball because the issue would never be raised.

The Comiskey family, which owned the White Sox for decades, was part of the cabal that had kept blacks out of organized baseball since the 1880s. Clark Griffith, who spent more than six decades as a player, manager, and then owner of the Washington Senators, endorsed segregation. So did Connie Mack, who spent more than sixty years in baseball, principally as the owner and manager of the Philadelphia Athletics. Tom Yawkey, the South Carolina plantation owner, had a particular aversion to blacks during the forty years he owned the Red Sox. The team was the last to become desegregated. Jacob Ruppert, who owned the mighty New York Yankees for a quarter century, and general manager Ed Barrow, the architect of the Yankees' dynasty, supported segregated baseball. So did Larry MacPhail, who succeeded Barrow with the Yankees and before that served as general manager of the Cincinnati Reds and Brooklyn Dodgers. Owners supported segregation for both personal and financial reasons. They leased their ballparks to Negro league teams, which could not afford to build their own, and therefore profited from segregation. Both white and black owners thought desegregation would hurt them economically. If the Major Leagues signed blacks, the Negro leagues would lose their best players, and fewer spectators would buy tickets. Black owners would lose money because revenues would decrease. White owners would lose money because there would be a decline in the revenues associated with exploiting black baseball. The New York Yankees, for instance, made one hundred thousand dollars a year from black baseball.[20] According to *New York Daily Mirror* columnist Dan Parker, whenever baseball publicized how it was helping black baseball by renting its stadiums for Negro league games, it merely demonstrated that talk was indeed cheap, though rent was not.[21]

Any owner who considered desegregating baseball knew he would make himself unpopular among Commissioner Landis and the other owners. When Landis was asked about the color line, he said any decision to sign blacks was left to team owners. This was, however, clearly dishonest. Landis ruled baseball with absolute control. If he wanted blacks in baseball, there would have been blacks in baseball. For twenty years Landis, whom the black press derisively called "the Great White Father," enforced baseball's color line with the complete authority of his office.[22] Landis did practically everything within his power to keep baseball segregated, but he could not have kept baseball segregated without the cooperation of league executives, team owners, and sportswriters. Baseball executives rarely had to defend the color line in the mainstream press because few white sportswriters raised the issue, allowing the color line to continue year after year without being challenged or even mentioned. For this reason white baseball fans did not know that blacks were prohibited from the game. They did not know that there were black ballplayers good enough to play in the Major Leagues or that blacks had once played in organized professional baseball. They did not know that many Major League managers and players supported desegregation. The color line could not have existed as long as it did without the participation of the nation's sportswriters, who, of course, had their own color line. There were no black journalists at the New York Baseball Writers' Association dinner at the Commodore Hotel in February 1933 because the association prohibited blacks.

Baseball could not have maintained the color line as long as it did without the aid and comfort of the country's white mainstream sportswriters, who participated in what black sportswriter Joe Bostic called a "conspiracy of silence."[23] When Broun confronted the color line, he violated the conspiracy of silence that protected the color line. White sportswriters may have grumbled to themselves and squirmed in their seats as they listened to Broun or read what he or Powers wrote, but they said nothing about the issue in their own columns and articles. But Broun and Powers sent a message to black sportswriters that they were not alone in their opposition to segregated baseball. Black journalists continued to raise the issue throughout 1933. In late August Bill Benswanger said he had seen a lot of Negro league games and said that a number of black players, including Oscar Charleston and Josh Gibson, had the ability to play in the Major Leagues. Ches Washington expressed optimism because the comment had come from one of the men who sat on "the highest council in baseball." In October the *Chicago Defender* told its readers to write Landis and team owners. The commissioner's office steadfastly refused to comment. A *Defender* writer tried to attend the annual meeting of big league executives in

December but was prohibited. "Yet despite the disappointments," Neil Lanctot wrote in his book *Negro League Baseball: The Rise and Ruin of a Black Institution*, "the effort during 1933 had successfully raised awareness of baseball's color line, forcing previously silent Organized Baseball officials to address the subject of integration, albeit gingerly, for the first time. Moreover, the black press had demonstrated a surprisingly assertive attitude toward integration."[24]

The *Pittsburgh Courier*, beginning in 1933, became ground zero in the campaign to desegregate baseball. The newspaper's interest in baseball was part of a larger crusade for racial equality in America. Not coincidentally, the newspaper also would be ground zero in the campaign for greater racial equality in America. Under editor Robert L. Vann, the newspaper achieved prominence by chronicling instances of discrimination and hate crimes against blacks, demanding antilynching legislation, protesting the racial caricatures of blacks in motion pictures and on radio programs, and advocating the integration of the armed forces. During World War II the *Courier* touted the "Double V" program — one *V* stood for victory in Europe and Asia, the other for victory over racial discrimination in America.[25] The *Courier's* criticism of racial discrimination resulted in the newspaper being investigated by the FBI and the U.S. Justice Department.[26] Vann distributed the *Courier* throughout the South, where the newspaper confronted racism where racism flowed from the drinking fountains and hung in the air. Southern cities prohibited the newspaper's distribution. Vann's formula, according to historian Roland Wolseley, was to confront racial discrimination whenever and wherever it appeared. "These campaigns were against Jim Crowism and discrimination against blacks in major league baseball," Wolseley wrote, "two of the classic targets of papers out to fight for black rights." Between 1933 and 1945 the newspaper's circulation increased from 46,000 to more than 260,000 — more than 100,000 over its nearest rival, the *Chicago Defender*.[27]

Between 1933 and 1945 the *Courier*, the *Defender*, and other black newspapers recognized a critical juncture in the crusade for racial equality in baseball and for racial equality in America and shared that story with their readers. While the issue of racial discrimination in baseball was perhaps too big for Joe Williams and other white sportswriters and journalists, it was small enough for black sportswriters and their readers to get their hands around. Black newspapers published stories that speculated about the end of the color line, and such stories dominated discussions in barbershops, diners, drugstores, and churches. When readers finished their newspapers, they passed them to others. Newspaper articles were read to those who could not read. To black America, if there could be racial equality in baseball, there could be racial equality elsewhere in U.S. society. The story of the campaign to end segregation in baseball was perhaps the most important story involving racial equality in the 1930s and 1940s.

When the Brooklyn Dodgers announced on October 23, 1945, that its president, Branch Rickey, had signed Jackie Robinson for the organization's top Minor League team, the Montreal Royals, black newspapers and their readers responded with rapture. For many black Americans, this was a moment they had dreamed about but wondered if it would ever come. To the black press and its readers, the announcement signaled the beginning of what was hoped to be a new day for fairness and equality. To black America the signing of Robinson transcended far beyond the white lines of baseball to the white lines of American society. "Coming at the end of a war that encouraged Americans to define themselves by a liberalism not found in Germany," historian William Simons wrote, "the announcement that Robinson would become the first black to participate in Organized Baseball since the late nineteenth century generated extensive public discussion about consensus, conflict, equality, liberty, opportunity, prejudice, democracy, and national character."[28]

The story of the campaign to desegregate baseball has never been given the context or content it deserves. This story is almost always framed around Rickey and Robinson. This version of history was Rickey's version of history. It is the version he dictated to sportswriters and biographers — and the one told and circulated in the days, weeks, years, and decades after the signing of Robinson. The Rickey version of this story is not a fabrication, but it is an oversimplification. Rickey deserves unqualified credit for confronting his fellow owners and their racist attitudes by signing Robinson and advancing the cause of civil rights in sport and in society. But the popular version exaggerates Rickey's role at the expense of all those who played a part in ending segregated baseball, which is an injustice not only to history but also to those who worked for years to end segregated baseball. The signing of Robinson was not an isolated act, restricted to two men. It was part of a far larger narrative that had been developing for years and would continue to develop. The story of the desegregation of baseball, therefore, does not begin with Rickey and Robinson — nor does it end with them. Giving this story the historical context it deserves does not detract from what Rickey accomplished. If anything, it heightens what Rickey accomplished because it puts Robinson and Rickey on a bigger stage. Their contributions should not be restricted to baseball, and the story of the desegregation of baseball should not be told separately from the overall story of the civil rights movement. The campaign to desegregate baseball cannot be understood if one looks only at the contributions of Rickey and Robinson. The color barrier collapsed when it did for reasons that had everything to do with Rickey and Robinson, and for reasons that had little to do with them.

The story of the desegregation of baseball is part of the larger narrative of the campaign for racial equality in the years preceding and immediately following World War II. One cannot truly appreciate the story of the desegregation of baseball without having an appreciation of what was happening in race relations in the United States. The campaign for racial equality in baseball was not just a baseball story to black journalists and their readers; it foreshadowed the campaign for racial equality in the United States. William Simons called the desegregation of baseball "the most commented on episode in American race relations of its time." Simons said these discussions addressed

America's unfulfilled promise that everyone was equal.[29] Discrimination in baseball — like discrimination in America — was institutionalized in the years and decades prior to the civil rights movement. For most Americans, segregation went unchallenged. Before civil rights could occur, attitudes had to change. The desegregation of baseball preceded desegregation in America because the processes necessary for change clicked into place earlier in baseball than in the rest of society.

The story of the desegregation of baseball "offers an opportunity to examine the ways in which the issues of race, segregation, and civil rights were covered by the black press, as well as how they were not covered, and compare them to coverage in the white mainstream press," Brian Carroll wrote in *When to Stop the Cheering? The Black Press, the Black Community, and the Integration of Professional Baseball.*[30] Black journalists took up the issue in their editorials and on their front pages. Black sportswriters — such as Wendell Smith, Sam Lacy, Joe Bostic, and Fay Young — chronicled the hopes and frustrations of the campaign in their columns. The campaign for racial equality in baseball, like the campaign for racial equality in America, included prominent black civil rights activists such as writer, lecturer, and baritone Paul Robeson; U.S. Representative Adam Clayton Powell Jr. of Harlem; New York City councilman Ben Davis Jr.; and attorney William Patterson, who chaired the Chicago Committee to End Jim Crow in Baseball.[31] White journalists, including Broun, Powers, Joe Cummiskey, Dave Egan, Dan Parker, Bob Considine, Shirley Povich, and Westbrook Pegler, also called for the end of segregated baseball. Their columns, though appearing infrequently, would be read by mainstream Americans who otherwise had little knowledge of baseball's color line. No white did as much to desegregate baseball as Rickey. But other whites who lent their support included U.S. Representative Vito Marcontonio, New York City mayor Fiorello La Guardia, Brooklyn city councilman Peter Cacchione, Brooklyn pastor Raymond Campion, and Chicago bishop Bernard Shiel. The New York City Citizens Committee to End Jim Crow in Baseball had scores of prominent members and received letters of endorsement from Eleanor Roosevelt, Paul Robeson, and

William O'Dwyer, who would succeed La Guardia as mayor of New York City. Poet and newspaper columnist Carl Sandburg called for the end of baseball's color line. Organized labor inundated Commissioner Landis's office with telegrams calling for blacks in baseball and picketed outside Major League ballparks to draw attention to the color line.

The desegregation of baseball was affected by seemingly unrelated political, social, and even international events. In early 1933 President Franklin Delano Roosevelt and German chancellor Adolf Hitler each took office. The policies and practices of these two men, though far different from one another, would each have an impact on racial discrimination in America. On January 30 Hitler became chancellor of Germany, signaling a rise in fascism in Europe and culminating with the beginning of World War II in September 1939. Hitler sought to dominate Europe with his ideology of an Aryan master race. He wanted to demonstrate German racial superiority at the 1936 Summer Olympics in Berlin. Americans put aside their own attitudes of racism and bigotry by cheering for black sprinter Jesse Owens at the Olympics and later for heavyweight fighter Joe Louis, "the Brown Bomber," who defeated German Max Schmeling in 1938. The United States fought World War II, in part, to confront Hitler's racist ideology. But World War II revealed America's own racial dilemma. The United States opposed a racist ideology while it practiced racial discrimination against black Americans. The war forced many white Americans — especially those soldiers who served with black soldiers — to reconsider their views on discrimination. When the army weekly *Yank* asked soldiers, "What changes would you like to see made in post-war America?" the most popular response was "the need for wiping out racial and religious discrimination."[32]

When FDR became president, the country was in the throes of the Great Depression. Black Americans, who had little before the financial markets collapsed, lost what little they had. The Depression caused many Americans — black and white — to lose their faith in the American way of life. The United States so many had known had broken down and appeared irreparable. The gloom and doom, the despair and hopelessness, and the fear of fascism made millions of Americans receptive to radical reform.[33] It was out of this climate of distrust in the established system that the U.S. Communist Party of America sought legitimacy.[34] The Communist Party, acting under orders from Moscow, tried to gain a foothold in U.S. society by recruiting those groups that had been either ostracized or ignored: labor unions and blacks. Nathan Glazer, author of *The Social Basis of American Communism*, wrote that the Communist Party devoted more effort to the recruitment of blacks than any other social group, except possibly industrial workers and trade unionists. Blacks, after all, were the most oppressed people in the country and were therefore the most susceptible to recruitment.[35]

By early 1933 Communists would become involved in two separate civil rights cases that would play out in the courts for years and would each ultimately make it to the U.S. Supreme Court. In one Angelo Herndon, a black Communist organizer, was arrested in Atlanta in 1932 while soliciting prospective party members. He was charged with insurrection. If guilty, he could be sentenced to death. On January 17 his attorney, Benjamin Davis Jr., himself a Communist, defended Herndon. "It is not Herndon who is the insurrectionist. It is the lynch mobs, the Ku Kluxers who are allowed to roam the land of this state burning innocent black people at the stake in defiance of every law of justice, humanity and right," Davis said in his summation. "Consider in your minds whether you want to see a Negro boy executed in the electric chair at a trial where Negro citizens have been denied their constitutional rights to sit on juries, a right which is guaranteed to every defendant and citizen by the Constitution of the United States." In 1931 nine young black men from Scottsboro, Alabama, were found guilty of raping two white women — even though one of the women recanted her story. The verdict was so egregious the U.S. Supreme Court ruled it violated the defendants' right of due process and ordered another trial. The guilty verdict in the second trial in early 1933 drew the scorn of both blacks and white social progressives, including Heywood Broun. "They say it was a quiet courtroom and a gentle day down in Morgan Creek when the jury filed in after 24 hours of deliberation," Broun wrote. "But could none of them hear the wind in the rigging of the slave ship, the creaking of her timbers, and the cries of the cargo?" Broun said that the prosecuting attorney would not look at the defendants because "he was afraid of the facts. He had reason to fear."[36]

The *Daily Worker*, which would vigorously defend Herndon and the so-called Scottsboro Boys, began its campaign to desegregate baseball following Jesse Owens's spectacular performance at the 1936 Olympics. Over the next decade no newspaper — black or white — would publish as many articles and columns calling for the end of segregated baseball. As early as 1933 the *Worker* commented on the injustice of racial segregation in Major League Baseball. Writer Ben Field described a scene at a Brooklyn Dodgers–New York Giants game at Ebbets Field on August 29. Field told his readers about watching the New York Black Yankees play at Yankee Stadium. During the game between the Dodgers and Giants, blacks worked at the stadium, but none took the field: "You spot a few Negro fans. Negro workers make good athletes. But where are the Negroes on the field? The Black Yankees are fine semi-pro players. But the big leagues will not admit Negro players. This is something else to chalk up against capitalist-controlled sports."[37]

Between 1933 and 1945 the *Daily Worker* and the black press confronted racial discrimination in baseball with hundreds of editorials, columns, and articles. Black and white social progressives took their campaign to Commissioner Landis and the baseball establishment. They met individually with a number of team owners who promised tryouts and then canceled them. Petitions with perhaps a million or more names were sent to Landis calling for the end of segregated baseball. Yet the story of the campaign to desegregate baseball remained unknown to most of America. The baseball establishment could ignore the campaign as long as the campaign was ignored by the mainstream press. Americans accepted baseball's policy of racial exclusion because the baseball establishment denied the existence of a color line, and the mainstream press conspired with their silence to protect the color line.

Americans accepted the national pastime's denials, in part, because of what Swedish sociologist Gunnar Myrdal, in his study of racism in America, called "the convenience of ignorance."[38] In the South racial discrimination was brutally enforced. Southerners practiced apartheid against blacks, while northerners ignored what was happening in the South and gave little mind to America's racial dilemma. "The Northerners want to hear as little as possible about the Negroes, both in the South and in the North. The result is an astonishing ignorance about the Negro on the part of the white public in the North," Myrdal wrote. "There are many educated Northerners who are well informed about poverty in foreign countries but almost absolutely ignorant about the Negro condition both in their own city and in the nation as a whole."[39] In the two Americas of the 1930s and 1940s, white Americans had little understanding of black America. White Americans may have known the names of a few black musicians, singers, and writers. But they knew nothing about most black musicians, singers, or writers, nor did they know anything about black doctors, lawyers, politicians, educators, journalists, and businessmen, because white newspapers ignored them. Most blacks went about their days, their weeks and months, invisible to whites. "I am invisible, understand, simply because people refuse to see me," Ralph Ellison wrote in his novel *Invisible Man*. "Like the bodiless heads you see sometimes in circus sideshows, it is as though I have been surrounded by mirrors of hard, distorting glass. When they approach me they see only my surroundings, themselves, or figments of their imagination — indeed, everything and anything except me."[40]

White sports fans, even casual fans, knew the names of black athletes who competed against whites in the Olympics or in sports such as boxing and college football because those athletes' names appeared regularly in the sports pages. White sportswriters wrote glowingly about Jesse Owens. They condemned Adolf Hitler for reportedly refusing to shake the sprinter's hand but said nothing of the white American coaches and athletes who would not shake Owens's hand. White sportswriters applauded Owens as a first-rate athlete and a shining example of how American democracy was superior to German fascism and racism but gave little mind to Owens's returning to the United States a third-class citizen. White sportswriters accepted Owens and Joe Louis as long as they remained silent and submissive and accepted their place in society. While blacks could be superior to the best of white athletes, they could never be equal to the least of whites in a restaurant or at a drinking fountain. Once back in the United States, Owens was no longer treated as an epic hero but as just another black person. Owens had found glory for a few days in Nazi Germany but returned to find his opportunities limited in the United States, never able to fulfill his tremendous potential as either an athlete or a man.

White sportswriters rarely wrote about racism in either sport or society. They did, however, frequently write about black athletes, and when they did so, they relied on racist stereotypes and characterizations. Westbrook Pegler, the influential columnist who got his start as a sportswriter, referred to black sprinters as "African savages" and called Joe Louis "the colored boy" and "a cotton-field Negro." Paul Gallico of the *New York Daily News* wrote that Louis "lives like an animal, fights like an animal, has all the cruelty and ferocity of a wild thing." Bill Corum of the *New York Journal American* wrote the following about Louis: "He's a big, superbly built Negro youth who was born to listen to jazz music, eat a lot of fried chicken, play ball with the gang on the corner, and never do a lick of heavy work he could escape." The southern-born Grantland Rice called boxer Jack Johnson "the Smoke" and "the Chocolate Champ," characterized Jesse Owens's performance at the Berlin Olympics as "a wild Zulu running amuck," and, in conversation, referred to Owens and later Jackie Robinson as "niggers." Furthermore, Rice, like other sportswriters, denigrated the success of black athletes by saying that their skill was "a matter of instinct" and not hard work, as was the case with white athletes. In his biography of Grantland Rice, Charles Fountain said Rice was a bigot by today's standards but was not unusual by the standards of his day and must be judged by them. "As such," Fountain concluded, "it can be served by no apologies or defenses, and deserves damnation less than it deserves understanding."[41]

Writers should be judged in the context of their times, but they should not be excused simply because they lived and worked when racial epithets and stereotypes were acceptable. Their actions deserve understanding, but they also deserve damnation. If sportswriters merely used racist stereotypes or if they were unaware of blacks with the ability to play in the Major Leagues, or even if they failed to report the existence of a color line, then maybe they could be forgiven. But this was not the case. Sportswriters did not merely ignore the color line; they defended it. They did not merely ignore racial discrimination; they practiced it. They knew that blacks had once played in organized professional baseball but did not report it. They knew Major League teams had given tryouts to blacks and promised tryouts to others and then canceled them without explanation. They neither reported it nor asked owners why there had been no tryouts. If sportswriters wrote about the color line, which was not often, they justified the absence of blacks in baseball with blatant dishonesty. They said segregation would cause race riots in the bleachers. They said that there were no blacks good enough for the big leagues. They said that neither black nor white players supported desegregation. Sportswriters bear culpability for prolonging baseball's "gentlemen's agreement" — just as baseball executives and team owners have been condemned for their role in keeping the national pastime segregated. Sportswriters reflected the views of baseball's management and served as its apologists and defenders. They served as participants in the greatest offense that baseball has exacted upon any group and left their fingerprints at the scene of the crime. They were willful conspirators in the perpetration of the color line.

During the early decades of the twentieth century, sportswriter Walter Camp regularly included blacks on his annual college football All-America team. Rice, his successor, ignored that precedent and virtually excluded blacks from his All-America team for the next three decades. White sportswriters all but ignored the Negro leagues. When sportswriters wrote about black baseball, their articles dripped with condescension. Ted Shane, writing in the *Saturday Evening Post*, said that black baseball was to white baseball what "the Harlem stomp is to ballroom dancing." Joe Williams, for instance, manipulated quotes and distorted facts to protect segregation. He wrote that Sam Lacy said that no blacks were ready for the big leagues. Lacy said he meant that black players would require socialization with whites in the Minor Leagues before playing in the big leagues. Williams, Larry MacPhail, and others used his quote "whenever it served their purpose," Lacy said. Williams responded to the signing of Robinson by saying that Rickey had signed him because of politics and not because of his ability. As a southerner, Williams said, he had seen blacks make progress, but their progress had been impeded by "pressure groups, social frauds and political demagogues." Peter Williams, the son of Joe Williams, said a number of authors had called his father, who was born in the South, a racist. Peter Williams said that his father's views were no different from those of other sportswriters of his time. If Joe Williams was a racist, Peter said, then so were most, if not all, of the other sportswriters of the day.[42]

J. G. Taylor Spink, editor of the *Sporting News* and the most influential sportswriter of his time, was no different from Landis and the other grand old men of baseball, including league executives and team owners. Like the grand old men of baseball, Spink defended segregated baseball with his silence. If need be, however, he did so with words. In August 1942 he wrote an editorial saying that baseball did not have a color line but that segregation was in the best interests of both blacks and whites because the mixing of races would create race riots in the ballparks. In his column Spink also said that black players opposed integration. He stated that white players and spectators objected to desegregation, but that big league executives and team owners did not. Spink's defense of segregated baseball was largely based not on fact but on fear and prejudice. Baseball did have a color line. Blacks did want to play in the big leagues. Blacks were prohibited from playing in white baseball because of league executives and team owners and not because of fans and players. There was no more influential sportswriter than Spink and no more influential sports publication than the *Sporting News*. Spink used that influence to perpetuate the color line. Spink and other white sportswriters said nothing about the millions of blacks and whites who wanted blacks in baseball. Spink and other white sportswriters said nothing about the sportswriters, managers, and ballplayers who had gone on record supporting blacks in baseball. Spink, instead, marginalized the campaign to desegregate baseball by blaming it on Communists and other "agitators." According to Mark Ribowsky, author of *A Complete History of the Negro Leagues, 1884–1955*, Spink "constructed the platform for the big league reactionaries . . . to rest their case, at least as long as they could get away with it."[43]

When Broun confronted baseball's color line in 1933, many sportswriters were present, but only Jimmy Powers reported what Broun had said. Over the next decade Powers criticized the color line more than any other mainstream sportswriter. Powers, it should be noted, also wrote for the daily newspaper with the highest circulation in the country. A relative few sportswriters raised the issue in their columns and articles. These columns did not appear particularly often, but they did appear, and as the campaign to desegregate baseball intensified, they appeared more often. Some were striking in both their poignancy and their bluntness. Yet most mainstream sportswriters said nothing. Some said nothing because they did not want to run the risk of offending their editors, readers, or advertisers. Others believed that segregation was in the best interests of both baseball and the country. Decades later Shirley Povich, who supported blacks in baseball, was asked why so few white sportswriters called for the end of the color line. "I'm afraid the sportswriters were like the club owners," he said. "They thought separate was better."[44]

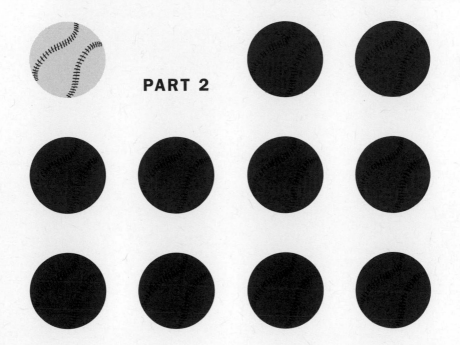

PART 2

CHAPTER 2

THE COLOR LINE

IS DRAWN

Alfred Henry Spink published the first issue of the *Sporting News* on March 17, 1886, in an office building at 11 North Eighth Street in St. Louis, Missouri. The entrepreneurial Spink saw the opportunity to capitalize on the growing popularity of baseball in the United States. Spink wanted to duplicate the success of the sports weekly the *Sporting Life*, which was published in Philadelphia. He had a vision of how to make the *Sporting News* the best sports publication in the country, and he had the ambition and the drive to accomplish it. Spink had once worked as a newsboy for iconic newspaper publisher Joseph Pulitzer's *St. Louis Post-Dispatch*. "When we were young boys, working for the St. Louis dailies for $5 a week," Spink later said, "Joe used to say, 'Given a good business manager and an editor who can really write, any newspaper should fast become a good paying institution.'" Spink became editor, and his brother Charles served as business manager. Within two months of his first issue, the eight-page *Sporting News* proclaimed it had "the largest circulation of any sporting paper published west of Philadelphia."[1] Within two years its circulation had increased from three thousand to sixty thousand subscribers.[2] By July 1889 the *Sporting News*'s circulation approached one hundred thousand.[3] In relatively little time, the *Sporting News* became the most circulated, best-read, and most important baseball publication in America. The *Sporting News* publishing anything and everything about the national game, including controversies, trades, box scores, and stories about players and managers and their teams, whether they were in the Major Leagues or in some distant outpost in the isolated West.

Al Spink saw himself as the chronicler, conscience, arbiter, and protector of baseball. From the first issue, Spink took seriously his self-professed role as the game's official scorekeeper and made the publication baseball's "paper of record." To those involved directly in the game or those who merely followed it, the *Sporting News* would be "the Baseball Bible." It is unlikely any publication approached the *Sporting News* in its coverage of baseball. Al Spink later sold his interest in the *Sporting News* to his brother Charles, whose son J. G. Taylor succeeded him in 1914 and remained publisher and editor for the next half century. The Spinks saw themselves as part of the baseball establishment, and their publication reflected the opinions and attitudes of the baseball establishment. J. G. Taylor Spink served as the official scorer during the World Series. During World War I J. G. Taylor Spink, in hopes of shoring up his publication's declining circulation, convinced American League president Ban Johnson to purchase 150,000 copies at a reduced rate to send to soldiers overseas. When the soldiers returned from the war, many subscribed to the publication. Commissioner Kenesaw Mountain Landis later awarded the *Sporting News* a lucrative contract to publish the *Official Baseball Record Book*.[4] When it came to matters relating to baseball, Landis and J. G. Taylor Spink, while their relationship was often strained because each considered himself "Mr. Baseball," were usually on the same page, especially regarding matters of race. Spink, like Landis and the baseball establishment, professed that every little boy could grow up to be president of America, or they could at least play in the American League — providing they had the requisite "ability," "character," and skin color.

Al Spink understood perhaps intuitively the symbiotic relationship between baseball and the press. Baseball needed sportswriters as much as sportswriters needed baseball. Spink's view was far from universal — among sportswriters or players, managers or owners. As sportswriting developed, sportswriters became baseball's greatest publicists and its greatest critics. "While often behaving like petty, carping critics, the reporters of this era helped to make public heroes out of good players and paying customers out of many urbanites," David Quentin Voigt wrote in his book *American Baseball: From Gentleman's Sport to the Commissioner System.* "By catering to public demand for news about baseball, the sportswriter became an important factor" in the rising popularity of baseball. Baseball players and managers liked it when articles praised them. They liked it far less when sportswriters criticized them. The *Sporting News* reported that the president of the International League had rebuked Syracuse Stars pitcher Doug Crothers, whom the publication called "our favorite pitcher," for saying he thought his team would finish near the bottom of the league in the next season. Crothers complained he had been misquoted.[5]

Baseball players and managers protested that sportswriters did not give them the praise they wanted. Sportswriters protested that baseball did not give them the credit they deserved.[6] Al Spink tried to broker peace. "No two professions are so allied together as that of the baseball writer and player, and yet, as a matter of fact, the bond of friendship between the two is of the frailest kind," the *Sporting News* said on May 10, 1886. "One is as much interested in the success of the game as the other, and when all come to learn this fact there will be better feeling all around and a more lasting bond of friendship than there is now." On January 22, 1887, the *Sporting News* again called for a better understanding between ballplayers and baseball writers. "Every player insists on the writer writing his way or not writing at all. Now this is all wrong," the editorial said. "Every time a professional's name is mentioned means additional notoriety, and notoriety means reputation and reputation money. So, after all, the best thing for the players and baseball writers to do is to shake hands over the bloody chasm and then to have at each other." The baseball establishment and the press eventually understood that if they put their differences aside and worked together, their mutual interests would be served. Ban Johnson, formerly the sports editor of the *Cincinnati Commercial-Gazette*, encouraged teams to cooperate with reporters and photographers. Sportswriters traveled with the teams they covered — usually at the teams' expense.[7] The result was mutually beneficial. Newspapers sold baseball and baseball sold newspapers, and both sold the idea that everyone was equal in baseball.

For a brief time after the Civil War there was reason to believe that baseball — like America — could achieve its promise of equality for all. During the 1870s and 1880s, dozens of blacks played in organized professional baseball. John W. "Bud" Fowler, long credited with being the first black professional ballplayer, learned how to play baseball on the sandlots of Cooperstown, New York, where Abner Doubleday, as myth had it, invented the national pastime.[8] Fowler and other blacks may have been tolerated for a time, but they were never accepted.[9] They were shunned by teammates, vilified by spectators, and brutalized by opponents. Historians credit both Fowler and Frank Grant, another black infielder, with inventing shin guards to protect themselves against base runners. "Fowler used to play second base with the lower part of his legs encased in wooden guards," one white ballplayer remembered. "He knew that about every player that came down to second base . . . had it in for him and would, if possible, throw spikes into him." One white player told the *Sporting News* that he "could not help pitying some of the poor black fellows that played in the International League." The player explained how Fowler and Grant knew that base runners would spike them every chance they had. In addition, the player said that "about half the pitchers try their best to hit these colored players when at the bat."[10] The *Sporting Life* said if Fowler had been white, he might be in the big leagues. "Those who know him say there is no better second baseman in the country," the article said.[11] As long as blacks were part of baseball, newspapers reported on and occasionally praised black ballplayers. But they were viewed as both different and inferior to their white counterparts. Black players were characterized not as minorities but as curiosities. "Columbus has a deaf mute and Cleveland a one-armed pitcher, Toledo a colored catcher and Providence a deaf centre-fielder," the *Sporting Life* reported in July 1883.[12]

The Toledo catcher was Moses Fleetwood Walker, son of mixed-race parents who had escaped from the South as fugitive slaves. In 1883 William Voltz, a former *Cleveland Plain Dealer* sportswriter, was managing Toledo in the Northwestern League and signed Walker. Toledo sportswriters praised Walker's talent.[13] The *Toledo Blade* wrote that "Walker has played more games and has been of greater value behind the plate than any catcher in the league." The *Sporting Life* also recognized Walker's talents. "Toledo's colored catcher," it said, "is looming up as a great man behind the plate."[14] But Walker, like Fowler, made enemies for no reason other than his skin color. During an exhibition game in 1883, Chicago White Stockings manager Adrian "Cap" Anson told Toledo manager Charlie Morton, who had replaced Voltz, that his team would not take the field if Fleet Walker did. When Morton told Anson that he would forfeit his gate receipts if the game was canceled, Anson backed off, reportedly saying, "We'll play this game, but won't play no more with niggers."[15]

In 1884 Toledo moved from the Northwestern League to the American Association, which was considered part of Major League Baseball, and Walker became the first black player to play in the Major Leagues. His brother Welday joined the team for several games at the end of the season. Toledo newspapers and the *Sporting Life* both provided sympathetic coverage of Walker, but they did not reflect the opinions of others in baseball. In April Anson's White Stockings were again scheduled to play an exhibition game with Toledo. The White Stockings sent a telegram to Morton that said, "No colored man shall play in your nine and if you . . . insist on playing him after we are there you forfeit the guarantee and we refuse to play." The game was not played. Anson's attitudes were not unusual for the day. When Toledo arrived in Richmond, Virginia, fans sent a letter to Morton that said if Walker took the field, a mob of seventy-five would attack him. Walker, who was injured, did not play.[16] After a game in Louisville, one of the city's newspapers attacked him for being of a lesser race.[17] If other players had a bad day, they might be criticized. But if Walker had a bad day, it was described as further indication of the inferiority of his race.

Walker, who was often injured, finished near the bottom of the league in fielding percentage. Injuries were an occupational hazard for any catcher — especially in a day when little protected him from foul tips, erratic pitches, or malevolent base runners. Walker's job was made more difficult because he often did not know what his pitcher was throwing. Toledo's star pitcher Tony Mullane, who pitched in sixty-eight games that season, most of them with Walker behind the plate, refused to take signals from his black catcher. Mullane, who finished his career with nearly three hundred victories, once admitted he had begrudging respect for his catcher. "He (Walker) was the best catcher I ever worked with," he said, "but I disliked a Negro and whenever I had to pitch to him I used to pitch anything I wanted without looking at signals." Walker's injuries — and his skin color — made him expendable when the season ended. Walker's play and conduct made him popular. "By his fine, gentlemanly deportment," the *Sporting Life* reported, Walker "had made a host of friends who will regret to learn he is no longer a member of the club."[18]

The *Sporting News*, though not as sympathetic on race as the *Sporting Life*, acknowledged the presence of racism. On December 18, 1886, the publication said that Newark of the International League would have a black battery: pitcher George Stovey and Walker. Stovey, the publication said, was good enough for the big leagues but was denied his opportunity because of his skin color. "Several of the League managers contemplated signing him last season. But the prejudice against his color prevented" that from happening, the article said. "Had he not been of African descent he would have pitched for the New York club last year." The *Sporting News* expressed sympathy for the plight of Stovey and other black ballplayers. "What fame they have won has been made in the face of very disheartening circumstances," it said. "Race prejudice exists in professional base ball ranks to a marked degree, and the unfortunate son of Africa who makes his living as a member of a team of white professionals has a rocky road to travel."[19] In May 1887 a white pitcher learned a lesson after insulting second baseman Frank Grant, who played for Buffalo in the International League. When Grant came to bat, the pitcher began whistling, "There's a New Coon in Town." Grant then hit the first pitch for a home run.[20]

By May 1887 the International League had so many black players the *Sporting Life* questioned whether it would soon change its name to the "Colored League."[21] In fact, there were only a handful of blacks, but they were all among the league's better players. More and more white players, reflecting either envy or the growing racism of the day, began complaining about having to share the field — or even a team photograph — with blacks. On June 11 the *Sporting News* said two white members of the Syracuse team, Doug Crothers, whom the publication once called one of its favorite players, and an outfielder, had refused to pose for a team picture with Higgins, whom the publication described as "a phenomenon." The team suspended the two players. When the team's manager confronted Crothers, the native Mississippian struck him. The *Sporting News* surmised that Crothers's behavior was related to jealousy. He had once been a good pitcher but had fallen on hard times, and now his talents were eclipsed by those of a black man. Crothers, who pitched briefly in the big leagues, often fought with his teammates and once was suspended for drinking. A week earlier, on June 4, the *Sporting News* reported that Syracuse had a clique of Ku Klux Klan members on the team who "ran things." When the team signed Higgins, the Klan members said they would not support him in the field. Nevertheless, the *Sporting News* reported that "the colored man Higgins has turned out well."

On July 14 Anson's White Stockings were scheduled to play an exhibition game against Newark, which had George Stovey and Fleet Walker. Again, Anson made his ultimatum that his team would not take the field if Newark had blacks in its lineup. Stovey was scratched from the lineup because of illness. The *Sporting Life* later reported that the Newark manager had benched Stovey because of Anson's threat.[22] According to one account, Anson once prevented John Montgomery Ward from acquiring Walker and Stovey for his New York Giants.[23] Years later a black newspaper in Cleveland said that Cleveland's American League team would have signed Walker had it not been for Anson's objections.[24] In his *History of Colored Base Ball*, Sol White wrote that Anson was the man most responsible for excluding "the black man from the white leagues." This is probably giving too much credit to Anson. While Anson was no doubt influential and no doubt a racist, who did everything within his power to exclude blacks, he could not have segregated baseball if baseball did not want to be segregated. Anson's prejudice was not uncommon for the day. When Walker needed a cane after spraining his ankle, one newspaper said, "Walker, the coon catcher of the Newarks, is laid off with a sore knee. It is insinuated by envious compeers that in early life he practiced on hen roosts until he got the art of foul catching down fine." The *Newark Daily Journal* reported that when it began to rain during a game between Newark and the black Cuban Giants, a black ballplayer ran from the field, screaming, "Scatter, men, de devil am splitting."[25]

In mid-July the directors of the International League met in secret and decided that no new contracts would be offered to black players. The six all-white teams voted for the establishment of a color line, and the four teams that had blacks on their rosters voted no. Newspapers in cities with teams with blacks on their rosters protested the color line. The *Newark Daily Journal* said that Fleet Walker was "mentally and morally the equal of any director who voted for the resolution." The *Syracuse Standard* called for the rule to be rescinded.[26] The appeals had no measurable effect. Binghamton immediately released Fowler, thus ending his career in white baseball. Banned from white baseball, Fowler played out the rest of his days with black teams. Fowler's career in organized professional baseball, Jules Tygiel said, "provides a microcosm of the black baseball odyssey in the nineteenth century—a composite of grudging acceptance, discrimination, physical abuse, and, ultimately, exclusion."[27]

The color line spread like a virus. On September 12, 1887, the *New York Times* reported the color line in Major League Baseball had been drawn for the first time by the St. Louis Browns. St. Louis president Chris Von der Ahe scheduled an exhibition game between the Browns and the black Cuban Giants at West Farms, near New York City. The *Times* reported that the game was expected to draw fifteen thousand spectators. While Von der Ahe was having supper the night before the game, one of the team's outfielders, "Tip" O'Neill, handed him a letter that said, "Dear Sir, the undersigned members of the St. Louis Baseball Club, do not agree to play against negroes tomorrow." Von der Ahe told the players that since this "seems to be a matter of principle with you, you need not play tomorrow." Charles Comiskey, the team's captain, told the *Times* he did not know anything about it. "I think that some of the boys wanted a day to themselves," Comiskey said. "They have played against colored clubs before without a murmur." The article said that the International League recently adopted a resolution prohibiting the employment of colored players by its clubs.[28]

The United States, like baseball, grew up and apart as segregation in baseball coincided with the implementation of segregation in America.[29] Baseball enforced the color line by disenfranchising leagues with black players as "outlaw leagues," thereby restricting blacks to independent leagues. After an Ohio league banned blacks, Welday Walker called the decision "a disgrace" in a letter to the *Sporting Life*. It "casts derision at the laws of Ohio—the voice of the people—that says all men are equal." In 1890 the teams in the Atlantic Association objected to admitting Harrisburg into the league because it had Frank Grant. "If the Harrisburg players themselves do not object to Grant and his colored associate," the *Washington Post* quoted one baseball fan as saying, "I see no reason why the other clubs should."[30] Within a relatively few years after the International League imposed its color line, blacks had virtually disappeared from organized professional baseball. "Probably in no other business in America is the color line so finely drawn as in base ball," the *Sporting Life* reported on April 11, 1891.

In 1896 the U.S. Supreme Court sanctioned the doctrine of "separate but equal" in *Plessy v. Ferguson.* Southern states amended their constitutions to disenfranchise blacks and create Jim Crow laws. Southern politicians appealed to their voters by bragging about how they had terrorized blacks. "We have scratched our heads to find out how we could eliminate the last one of them," U.S. Senator "Pitchfork Ben" Tillman said. "We stuffed ballot boxes. We shot them. We are not ashamed of it."[31] In 1900 the *Richmond Times* demanded rigid enforcement of segregation be "applied in every relation of Southern life" on the ground that "God Almighty drew the color line and it cannot be obliterated." Segregation was not enough for some whites. They wanted separation. The *Charleston (sc) News and Courier* called for blacks to be deported.[32] Many blacks did not disagree. In his 1908 book, *Our Home Colony: The Past Present, and Future,* an embittered Fleet Walker advocated that blacks leave the United States and emigrate to Africa. To return to Africa meant the opportunity for blacks to start over in a land where they were truly free. Walker never made it to Africa — nor did he realize his potential as a ballplayer or a human being. He died in 1924, "frustrated by both the American dream and the national pastime," biographer David Zang wrote. According to Zang, "Walker's life demonstrates both the devastation of racism and the role of baseball as a symbol of the nation."[33]

Once the color line was firmly in place, white sportswriters rarely made references to black ballplayers. If blacks were mentioned, they were referred to with contempt. Racial pejoratives were part of the country's vernacular, and even the relatively well meaning paid little mind to whom it might offend. American society was racist, and the men and women who lived then were simply products of their times. Why should baseball have been expected to be any different? "Today, apologists excuse such conduct on the grounds that men of the era were 'prisoners of their times,' for many Americans of the 1890's believed in the validity of racial inferiority theories and cast the Negro in roles depicted in the popular 'coon songs' and 'nigger jokes,'" David Quentin Voigt wrote. "This rationalization, however, persuades the more objective individual to view major league baseball as a reflector of the emotions and the values of a culture and to question the claim that the game builds character by its 'intrinsic' values of 'Americanism' or 'gentlemanly sportsmanship.'"[34]

As a result of *Plessy v. Ferguson*, southern states passed what C. Vann Woodward called "a mushroom cloud of discriminatory and segregation laws," restricting blacks from going where they wanted, how they wanted, and when they wanted. "Whites Only" or "Colored" signs were placed over entrances and exits of theaters, restaurants, hospitals, restrooms, telephone booths, and water fountains. Cities were partitioned. Whites lived in one part of a town and blacks in another. Southern cities passed vagrancy laws that restricted blacks during the day and curfew laws that forbade blacks from being outside at night. Birmingham, Alabama, prohibited blacks and whites from playing dominoes or checkers together. Segregation laws went beyond prohibiting blacks and whites from sharing the same ball field: Atlanta prohibited blacks and whites from playing ball within two blocks of one another.[35] On September 2, 1902, the *New York Times* reported that Mississippi Delta farmers were demanding that the state legislature prohibit the playing of baseball by blacks during the fall months of the year because the game took blacks off the cotton fields during harvest season. Three months later the University of Virginia told Harvard College it would cancel a game scheduled for the spring unless Harvard agreed to leave behind its black second baseman, William Clarence Matthews. Harvard refused and the game was canceled.[36]

Sol White reported that John McGraw, who managed Baltimore of the American League, was sitting outside the Eastman Hotel in Hot Springs, Arkansas, during spring training in 1901 when he was approached by a dark-skinned man, Charlie Grant, who asked for a try-out. The player impressed McGraw, but McGraw knew he could not sign him if he was black. He could, however, if he were an Indian. McGraw then signed Grant — who changed his name to Chief Tokohama. While Indians were allowed in organized professional baseball, they were still a novelty, and, therefore, the signing of Tokohama received more publicity than the signing of other prospects. The best-known Indian player was Louis Sockalexis, who had played for Cleveland between 1897 and 1899, until he fell victim to alcoholism. The *Baltimore Sun* reported that McGraw wanted to protect "Tokie" from the same fate as Sockalexis "until fire water and bad companions ruined him, and he eventually made him a vagrant and tramp." Newspapers reported that Tokohama would join McGraw and his team on the train north to begin the regular season. But Tokohama did not accompany the team. "It has been suggested," the *Sporting News* reported, "that the noble red man Tokohama got frightened at the railroad and ran away."[37]

Sportswriters began to express suspicion about whether Tokohama really was an Indian. The *Washington Post* reported that Tokohama was the "old-time colored player, Grant," who, the article said, was a mulatto. Charles Comiskey, the owner of the White Sox, objected to McGraw's trying to pass the black Grant off as an Indian. If McGraw persisted, Comiskey, according to the *Sporting Life*, said he would sign "a Chinese third baseman or whitewash a colored player." McGraw adamantly denied that Tokohama was Charlie Grant. McGraw insisted that Comiskey was merely trying to prevent the signing of Tokohama. Comiskey, McGraw added, "sent out the story that Tokohama is a Chicago negro, but it was only one of Commie's jokes, and people seem to have taken him seriously." Tokohama also denied Comiskey's assertion that he was black. He said his mother was a Cherokee and his father was white. If McGraw wanted proof of his ancestry, Tokohama could provide it.[38]

McGraw said that Tokohama was still in Hot Springs and would remain there until he could find a spot for him on the roster.[39] The *Chicago Tribune* said that Tokohama would join Baltimore as a second baseman. On April 24 Baltimore began its regular season without Tokohama. The *Sporting Life* reported that Tokohama would play that year for the black Columbia Giants.[40] In mid-May, however, newspaper accounts reported that McGraw had told Tokohama to join the Baltimore team in Boston.[41] If Tokohama did this, he did not play. On May 29 the *Washington Post* said that Baltimore was playing in Chicago and that Grant was in the city "but will not accompany the team." One newspaper reported that McGraw would have to exhibit Tokohama in all his war paint before the Chicago fans would believe that he had signed a genuine redman.[42] Grant never played in the Major Leagues. In 1902 McGraw left Baltimore to become manager of the New York Giants. While managing the Giants, McGraw considered signing José Méndez, the part black–part Cuban pitcher of the Negro leagues but, remembering the criticism he had received after trying to sign Grant, dropped the matter.[43] McGraw, nevertheless, signed a number of Indians, including catcher John "Chief" Meyers, who was rumored to be part black, and Olympic decathlete Jim Thorpe. He later confronted baseball's anti-Semitism by signing Andy Cohen.

The Tokohama story was perhaps not the only attempt to integrate baseball. Sol White said there was a rumor that a National League manager wanted to sign the former Harvard star William Clarence Matthews. White suggested that the manager was John McGraw. In recent years, however, Karl Lindhold identified the manager reportedly interested in signing Matthews as Fred Tenney of the Boston Nationals. Lindhold expressed skepticism about whether Tenney was indeed interested in Matthews — or whether the story was manufactured by a *Boston Traveler* sportswriter. After leaving Harvard in 1905, Matthews played for Burlington, Vermont, in the Northern League, an independent league, where he reportedly was the only black in professional baseball. The *Sporting Life* said rumors that Matthews might sign with the team threatened to "disrupt the league."[44] Two weeks after Matthews joined Burlington, the *Traveler* said that there was a rumor the Nationals would sign him. "I think it is an outrage that colored men are discriminated against in the big leagues," Matthews said. "What a shame it is that black men are barred forever from participating in the national game." The *Traveler* later quoted Matthews as saying, "A negro is just as good as a white man and has just as much right to play ball. . . . The negro question on the diamond might as well be settled now as any time." Despite Tenney's denial that he hoped to sign Matthews, the story was widely circulated. The *Traveler* said the *Atlanta Journal* reported that the presence of Matthews was destroying the Northern League, or, as the article put it, "The debut of the human chocolate drop is about to break up this league." Other Boston dailies either ignored the story or discounted it. Lindhold suggested the Matthews story was a creation of a *Traveler* sportswriter, who had a reputation for exaggeration. Lindhold wrote that Tenney, who attended Brown University, had progressive tendencies. He may have raised the issue among National League owners, where it was summarily rejected. The *Traveler* said that National League president Harry Pulliam, a southerner, would "resign in a minute" if Tenney signed Matthews. "His good Southern blood would never stand for it."[45]

Two years later, on September 8, 1907, the *Washington Post* reported that Tenney had signed a black pitcher with the name Joy from a Hawaiian team for the next season. The *Post*, which described Joy as "a cracking good pitcher," acknowledged the signing was "a powder keg." If Tenney followed through, the article said, he would have to face such issues as where Joy would eat or where he would stay where laws prevented blacks from sharing the same restaurants or hotels as whites. The article claimed racial discrimination had driven blacks out of baseball entirely. It reported that one black second baseman, presumably Grant, had found it so "uncongenial that he had to quit." It also said Matthews had played a month in a New England league before being forced out. Joy, the article made a point of clarifying, was not, strictly speaking, black but a Malay; however, "he is as dark as an Ethiopian." Joy's success ultimately would be determined by how well he did and how well he was welcomed by his teammates, the newspaper said. The article expressed doubt that Joy would ever play in the big leagues. Joy never played in the Major Leagues.

As the years passed, fewer and fewer white journalists questioned segregation or even mentioned that baseball had a color line. The *Washington Post* reported in 1909 that there were ballplayers in Cuba with the ability to play in the big leagues, but they were barred from playing in America because of the color line. "There is no color line in Cuba," the article said. During the off-season, Major League teams traveled to Cuba to play against teams that had black Americans. In 1910 Ban Johnson ordered big league teams to stop going to Cuba after the World Series champion Philadelphia Athletics had been embarrassed in a series of games. A year later John McGraw was sufficiently impressed after a series his New York Giants played in Cuba to remark, "Take me the next boat home! I didn't come down here to let a lot of coffee-colored Cubans show me up!" Major League Baseball did not approve of interracial games in the United States, but such games were regularly played. Both blacks and whites liked the extra money. For blacks there was the additional motivation that came with proving their superiority, and they reportedly won more games than they lost. Only rarely did the interracial games produce problems, either on the field or in the stands. In 1915 a temperamental Oscar Charleston punched a white umpire, which resulted in what was described as a "near race riot" when blacks and whites exchanged punches before police broke it up. In the history of interracial games, there were only three games with racial incidents, Timothy Gay wrote in *Satch, Dizzy, and Rapid Robert: The Wild Saga of Interracial Baseball before Jackie Robinson*, and all three involved Charleston. During a time when most blacks lived in fear of whites, Charleston was fearless. According to one account, Charleston once confronted a Klansman and ripped off his hood.[46]

No athlete in his time was more fearless and no black athlete more feared by white America than heavyweight champion Jack Johnson. Johnson was not simply better than other white heavyweights, and he knew it, and he believed himself equal to any white away from the ring. He drove expensive cars, wore expensive clothes, and dated white women. Johnson's possession of the heavyweight title infuriated whites who believed it was necessary to defeat him for the sake of white people everywhere. Former heavyweight champion James Jeffries, who became known as "the Great White Hope," challenged Johnson. When Johnson defeated Jeffries, the *Los Angeles Times* warned black America that they should not revel in Johnson's victory. "Do not point your nose too high. Do not swell your chest too much. Do not boast too loudly. Do not be puffed up. Let not your ambition be inordinate or take a wrong direction," the editorial said. "Remember you have done nothing at all. You are just the same member of society you were last week. . . . You are on no higher place, deserve no new consideration, and will get none."[47] Johnson would theretofore serve as an example of the "bad nigger." White sportswriters did not like him because he defeated whites and because he did not apologize for it. "A bad actor socially, Johnson was a poor representative for his race," Grantland Rice wrote. "He certainly didn't help the cause of the Negro." Rice had no such reservations about the flamboyant, womanizing, and hard-drinking "Babe" Ruth, whom Rice saw as a friend to everyone everywhere. Rice later praised nonthreatening Joe Louis as a good representative of his race.[48]

Baseball's color ban was racist, by definition, and absurd, by interpretation. Dark-skinned Latinos were prohibited, but light-skinned Latinos were allowed. Cincinnati Reds manager Clark Griffith, who would later own the Washington Senators, signed a number of Latin players who had to prove they were "genuine Caucasians" and not dark-skinned Cubans. Rumors, nevertheless, persisted that Griffith had

black players. Sportswriter Red Smith once wrote that "there was a Sen-
egambian somewhere in the Cuban batpile where Senatorial lumber was
seasoned."[49] Any ballplayer suspected of having black blood suffered
relentless abuse from teammates, beanballs and spikings from opponents, and relentless ridicule from spectators and sportswriters. George
Treadway, who played for Brooklyn in the late 1890s, was reportedly
driven from baseball because it was believed he might be part black.
Voigt said New York Giants catcher John "Chief" Meyers, an Indian,
was taunted with cries of "nigger."[50] When dark-skinned outfielder
Bing Miller played for St. Louis, his manager, Rogers Hornsby, called
him "Booker T." Miller. Throughout his career there were suspicions
that Babe Ruth was part black.[51] The Maryland-born Ruth said there
was no worse epithet for a white man raised in the South than being
called a "nigger."[52]

During the fourth inning of a game in May 1912, Ty Cobb, the
Georgia-born outfielder of the Detroit Tigers, raced into the left-field
bleachers and began attacking a crippled spectator who had called
the ballplayer "half nigger." When another spectator yelled that the
man had no hands, Cobb shot back, "I don't care if he has no feet."
Sportswriters, while critical of Cobb for the viciousness of his assault,
justified the ballplayer's response because of what he had been called.
The *New York Times* reported that a minister, after being told that the
man had no hands, said, "If he used the epithets ascribed to him it
were better if he had no tongue." Several years earlier Cobb attacked
a black groundskeeper during spring training at the Tigers' Augusta,
Georgia, training camp. When the man's wife tried to stop Cobb, the
ballplayer began punching her. "Cobb's Ben Tillmanism flashed quickly
and there was an instantaneous mix-up," the *Sporting News* reported.
"The darky's wife sailed in and Cobb's first swing set her to squeal-
ing." When Cobb punched a black construction worker on a Detroit
sidewalk, the *Washington Post* reported on the afternoon's game that
"Cobb hit three singles and a negro."[53]

Most sportswriters saw nothing wrong with using such language, and most saw nothing wrong with being publicists — rather than critics — of the game. A few sportswriters, including Heywood Broun, Ring Lardner, and Hugh Fullerton, however, tried to capture the game as it was and not as owners wanted it. In Ring Lardner's columns in the *Chicago Tribune*, one finds the unedited slang, boastfulness, and naïveté of real ballplayers that would ultimately define his fictional short stories. Lardner, too, was "a devotee of black baseball."[54] Like Lardner, Broun's irreverence put him at odds with other sportswriters. While working for the *New York Tribune*, Broun also broke ranks with most of his fellow sportswriters. In 1913 Frank Chance, then managing the New York Yankees, complained to Broun and Fred Lieb of the *New York Post* that the team's first baseman, Hal Chase, was throwing games. Lieb did not report Chance's criticism. Broun did. Yankees owner Frank Farrell criticized Broun but soon got rid of Chase, one of the most dishonest men to ever wear a Major League uniform. When Broun was promoted to sports editor, he told his writers he did not want "the usual stuff" about ballplayers starting their careers on sandlots. "But if my reporter finds out that a baseball player struck out with the bases loaded because he was out on a beer party the night before the game," he said, "that's the story I want."[55]

Few sports editors, however, believed as Broun did. Elsewhere in the newspaper, many journalists were less sentimental in their reporting. During the decade or two preceding World War I, muckraking journalists exposed individuals and corporations who manipulated society for their own good and violated the public trust. Their stories revealed deplorable conditions at meatpacking plants and the exploitation of factory workers, particularly children. These stories led to reforms, broke up trusts, and resulted in the arrest and sentencing of corrupt politicians. But, as Neil Henry recognized, muckrakers generally ignored the lynching of and the brutality toward blacks in the South. "The leading muckraking publications failed to fight lynching with anything near the zeal they employed against economic and political wrongdoing," historian Maurine Beasley wrote. "Part of the muckrakers' refusal to expose lynching for what it was — apparently stemmed from the philosophy of Progressivism, which revealed a blind spot regarding blacks."[56]

The Progressive Era has been characterized as a rebellion against the unfettered power of corporations and corrupt political machines. The popular impulse for reform, which appealed to workers, farmers, intellectuals, progressives, ethnic minorities, and radicals, provided the impetus for the growth of the American Socialist Party.[57] Starting with ten thousand members in 1901, membership in the Socialist Party increased dramatically, recruiting heavily from labor unions and the millions of immigrants from Germany and eastern Europe — many of whom were confined to slums and exploited by corporations and politicians.[58] Under "Big Bill" Haywood, himself a Socialist, membership in the Industrial Workers of the World — or the Wobblies — grew into the tens of thousands, including socialists, anarchists, and radical trade unionists. Because it confronted the status quo, the IWW was widely perceived as dangerous and remained an object of attention for law enforcement agencies and an object of considerable distrust from conservative America.

As World War I spread throughout Europe, rural and small-town America grew increasingly wary of socialism, progressivism, and immigration. Opportunistic politicians, businessmen, judges, and journalists capitalized on this suspicion by attacking German Americans, social progressives, and radical unions such as the IWW.[59] President Woodrow Wilson pointedly questioned the patriotism of German and east European immigrants — many of whom came from countries at war with U.S. allies. Once the United States entered the war, Wilson, with the enthusiastic support of Congress and conservative publishers, signed legislation such as the Sedition Act that made it a crime to question the government or even to belong to any organization that endorsed leftist ideologies such as socialism. Law enforcement agencies and extralegal mobs brutalized social progressives. Hundreds were arrested and either jailed or deported. Kenesaw Mountain Landis, then a grandstanding federal judge in Chicago, made headlines with his harsh sentences of socialists and members of the iww. "Few men have been as zealous in the suppression of minorities," author Henry Pringle observed about Landis, "and his charges to juries were dangerously close to patriotic addresses." President Theodore Roosevelt, who had appointed Landis, once said that Landis had "the face of a fanatic — honest, fearless, well meaning, but tense to a degree that makes me apprehensive lest it may presage a nervous breakdown."[60]

In the years during and after World War I, the United States returned to the nativism and bigotry that had defined the 1880s and 1890s. Whereas the Ku Klux Klan in the nineteenth century had existed primarily to intimidate and terrorize blacks, the Klan of the 1910s and 1920s expanded its hatred to Jews, Roman Catholics, immigrants, intellectuals, liberals, and anyone else who did not represent the values of God-fearing Protestant, small-town, narrow-minded America. Whereas the Klan in the years following the Civil War had been largely restricted to the South, the Klan of the 1910s and 1920s expanded beyond the South to the Midwest and beyond. In his book *Citizen Klansmen,* Leonard J. Moore called Indiana "the epicenter of the national Klan movement." Moore estimated that between one-quarter and one-third of all native-born men in the state belonged to the Klan.[61] Landis, who grew up in rural Indiana, did not belong to the Klan, but members of his family and close friends did. Landis opposed the Klan — though not as vocally as his brother Frederick, an Indiana congressman who was so outspoken in his criticism of the Klan that he carried a loaded gun with him as he traveled throughout the state.[62]

Baseball, because it drew so heavily upon the uneducated from the South and lower Midwest, included more than a few Klansmen among its players, managers, and team executives. Sportswriter Fred Lieb said stars like Rogers Hornsby and "Gabby" Street told him they belonged to the kkk.[63] John Drebinger of the *New York Times* told Hornsby that

Boston sportswriters said he was a Klansman. Drebinger told Hornsby he would confront and correct the Boston sportswriters in a column. An indignant Hornsby, however, told Drebinger that if the sportswriter said anything, he would never speak to him again.[64] In late November 1923 Philadelphia Athletics pitcher Robert Hasty, himself a Klansman, was arrested for his part in the flogging of a black man and woman in his hometown of Marietta, Georgia. Hasty was later exonerated by an all-white jury.[65] Hasty's arrest resulted in the disclosure of a rift on the Athletics team, which was owned and managed by Connie Mack, between those who belonged to the Klan and those who did not. The *Sporting News* expressed its dismay that something like the "hideous monster of racial or religious prejudice" could happen in baseball. "In Organized Baseball there has been no distinction raised except the tacit understanding that a player of Ethiopian descent is ineligible. The wisdom of which we will not discuss except to say that by such a rule some of the greatest players the game has ever known have been denied their opportunity," the editorial said. "No player of any other 'race' has been barred. We have had Indians, Chinese and Japanese playing ball; and if a Malay should appear who could field and hit he probably would be welcome. All shades from the lightest blonde to the darkest brunette have been admitted with the one exception of the wholly-haired race."[66]

In 1920 baseball owners appointed Landis commissioner to restore the game's integrity after eight members of the Chicago White Sox conspired to fix the 1919 World Series. Landis, at that point, according to his biographer David Pietrusza, had a reputation for being progressive on racial issues. Both black and white newspapers had praised him for his support of blacks. William Clarence Matthews, the former Harvard infielder who had become an assistant U.S. attorney, wrote Landis asking him to end the color line. "Why keep the Negro out if he can play the same grade of baseball demanded of the other groups? Are the big leagues more exclusive than the best colleges and athletic clubs in the land?" Matthews said. "If baseball leaders would adapt the open door policy toward the Negro player, don't you think it would be another guarantee on their part that baseball in the future is to be on the level?" David Pietrusza said there was no record that Landis responded to Matthews.[67] In his nearly quarter century as commissioner, Landis usually responded to the question of blacks in baseball with silence. According to a number of accounts, Landis ordered an end to off-season barnstorming exhibitions between Major League and black teams. In subsequent years Landis ignored letters and telegrams from black sportswriters and activists who wanted to discuss the issue.

The 1919 "Black Sox Scandal" may have damaged baseball's credibility. But Babe Ruth helped fans forget the scandal — and sportswriters transformed Ruth into a hero, a living example that only in the United States could a boy grow up in a reformatory school to become America's greatest ballplayer. If the United States was the land of opportunity, then baseball was the field of opportunity, where dreams came true to those who worked hard, obeyed their parents, went to bed early, and avoided liquor and loose women. While Broun and Lardner openly laughed at such rubbish, they had since left the sports pages for greater fame and glory. The profession would be left in the hands of men who not only did not report on ballplayers who were drinking the night before but were having drinks with the ballplayers and covering up their misdeeds. The sportswriters of the 1920s and 1930s — though some were gifted writers — believed they could get closer to the game by becoming closer to the athletes. They golfed, drank, and played cards with the ballplayers. Fred Lieb, whose career as a sportswriter lasted almost seventy years, believed that what a ballplayer did off the field did not belong in the newspaper. He had such a close relationship with Ruth that he mediated disputes between the player and the Yankees. When Bob Considine wrote his biography of Babe Ruth, it was Lieb — and not Ruth — who provided the background story.[68] Grantland Rice of the *New York Tribune* also saw nothing wrong with palling around with the ballplayers he wrote about. To Rice, this brought him closer to the athletes and gave him stories he otherwise would not have had. Rice was a fan of baseball and a friend to ballplayers and owners. He was interested in players as heroes and not in exposing their feet of clay. "He knew the athletes and he knew their failings," Charles Fountain wrote. "He knew that Babe Ruth was a sot and that Ty Cobb was a boorish churl. But he chose to celebrate their enormous gifts."[69]

Whereas sportswriters often called the 1920s "the golden age of sports," Westbrook Pegler of the *Chicago Tribune* called it "the era of wonderful nonsense." Decades later Robert Lipsyte of the *New York Times* condemned the style of what he called the "Rice-ites." Lipsyte said the writer who criticizes a ballplayer for making an error or striking out is "judging the athlete as a working professional." However, this was not so for the writer who compared the ballplayer to Greek gods and legends. To that sportswriter, Lipsyte said, the ballplayer is no longer an athlete but an object to be used to further the sportswriter's career. According to Lipsyte, Rice inspired "lesser talents who insisted, like the old master, that they were just sunny fellows who loved kids' games and the jolly apes who played them."[70] Paul Gallico of the *New York Daily News*, who would ultimately leave sportswriting to become a novelist, once reflected with some regret on his days covering sports in the 1920s. Sportswriters, he said, created "egotists out of normal young men and women by writing too much about them. . . . We create many (heroes) because it is our business to do so."[71] Ring Lardner Jr. once said his father was "a debunker of sports heroes" and that sportswriters like Rice glorified "heroes."[72] Pegler once criticized the state of sportswriting by referring to the "thousand flabby counterfeits" who imitated the "pantywaist stuff" created by Rice and other sportswriters.[73]

As sportswriters spread the name of Ruth and baseball, they also made names for themselves. Rice's column, "The Sport Light," for instance, was distributed to 250 newspapers, and young sportswriters imitated him.[74] These sportswriters, too, wrote about games as if they were epic battles and ballplayers as if they gods. They forgave athletes for their transgressions for the good of the athletes and the good of the game. Sportswriters became overly familiar with the ballplayers, witnessed their transgressions, and then kept those transgressions to themselves. Marshall Hunt, who wrote for the *New York Daily News*, was not merely assigned to cover baseball; his beat was Babe Ruth. During spring training Hunt accompanied Ruth as the slugger searched for signs for "chicken dinners." "What Babe really wanted was a good chicken dinner and daughter combination," Hunt remembered, "and it worked that way more often than you would think." When there were rumors of a paternity scandal, the *News*'s city editor ordered Hunt to ask Ruth directly. Hunt told the editor, "Listen, we've got along fine with the Babe and he's done a lot of things for us. You try to get somebody else to worm this thing out in New York, and not through 'the Babe.'"[75]

Sportswriters saw themselves as part of the game and were, therefore, reluctant to question it and far more likely to protect it. John Drebinger, who covered up Hornsby's membership in the Klan, said he did not feel comfortable criticizing the game.[76] John Kieran of the *New York Times* wanted to be one of the players, so he put on a big league uniform and worked out with them every spring. *New York Times* columnist Arthur Daley, according to one sportswriter, did not describe sports as they were but "as he wistfully would have them."[77] According to another writer, Daley "cultivated the image of an uncritical observer" who "was far more comfortable writing about a sport's genial, accommodating personalities rather than its controversies. Inevitably, he became identified as management's man on the sports beat, particularly the baseball diamonds." A lot of sportswriters earned extra money doing publicity work for Major League teams.[78] Whether sportswriters were on the team's payroll or not, too many acted more like publicists than reporters. Drebinger was McGraw's ghostwriter.[79] "Babe" Ruth's ghostwriter, Ford Frick, served as the first president of the New York chapter of the Baseball Writers' Association, where he put on blackface and became a part of the annual minstrel shows. Frick left the *New York American* to be a publicist for the National League and then succeeded John Heydler as the league's president. When Frick resigned as president of the New York Baseball Writers' Association, he was succeeded by Dan Daniel, of the *New York World-Telegram*, who wrote a weekly column for the *Sporting News*. Daniel said he was not interested in criticizing baseball. "I was eager to run baseball up," he said.[80]

To J. G. Taylor Spink, baseball represented the American dream, and nowhere was baseball's democratic myth more obvious that in the pages of the *Sporting News*. In 1925 the *Sporting News* called baseball "the truly national sport as much a part of American thought and life as the idea of democracy itself." In 1935 the *Sporting News* said, "Baseball yields to no enterprise in its democracy."[81] Spink was no different from most other sportswriters, who were conservative in their politics and evangelical in their belief that baseball represented the American dream because everyone was equal on the playing field.[82] Tommy Holmes of the *Brooklyn Eagle* wrote that baseball, like the United States, was a melting pot of different nationalities: English, Irish, German, Italian, Czech, and even Jewish. But opportunity was narrowly restricted to those eligible for the American dream. As author Richard Crepeau added, there was a catch: you had to be white, and it helped if you were not Jewish. According to one writer, most sportswriters "wrote fantasies about the great American pastime and were generally apathetic about baseball's color line" or other social issues.[83]

In 1931 Westbrook Pegler, however, wrote that the color line contradicted the sport's claim as the national pastime, and he chided owners for perpetrating discrimination and sportswriters for their silence. Why had not anyone, Pegler asked, "taken his pen in hand to wonder why white college boys can . . . compete against and associate with great colored athletes without embarrassment, whereas professional ball players must be protected by a regulation which the magnates haven't the gall to put on paper?"[84] The *Sporting News*, which published Pegler's column, ran a response from a fan demanding an apology from Pegler for his criticism of baseball.[85] While writing for the *Chicago Daily Tribune*, Pegler honed his scorched-earth style of writing that would later characterize his syndicated columns. In his sports columns, biographer

Finis Farr wrote, one found the genesis of what would later characterize his influential columns that appeared on editorial pages throughout the country. "Something was wrong," Farr said, "and needed correction."[86] In 1933 Pegler was hired to write columns for the *New York World-Telegram*. Pegler's conservative "Fair Enough" column appeared on the right side of the page to counter Heywood Broun's liberal views, which ran on the left side of the page. Pegler became famous as one of the most widely read newspaper columnists in America, eventually winning a Pulitzer Prize for his writing, which was known as much for its bite as its bile. Pegler was well paid for expressing his indignation — and neither he nor his typewriter ever seemed to run out of it. He used his column to rail against injustice and hypocrisy, whether in politics or in baseball.[87] In 1935 he condemned the "silly unwritten law that bars dark Babe Ruths and (Dizzy) Deans from the fame and money they deserve."[88] But as Pegler became more conservative in his politics, so did his views about integration in sports. Pegler opposed Joe Louis's fighting white opponents because it might provoke race riots and then condemned the campaign for racial equality in baseball and in America.[89]

Sportswriters could ignore the issue of race in baseball but found it nearly impossible to ignore it in their coverage of the 1936 Olympics in Berlin, Germany. Jesse Owens forced sportswriters and the American public to decide between their support of racism in the United States and their opposition to racism in Nazi Germany. "For the most part nationalism prevailed over racism," Fountain wrote. "Even those Americans who suffered from a less-virulent strain of (Hitler's) poisonous notion of Aryan superiority found themselves in the unlikely position of cheering for a black man." Rice, for instance, used language that was at best strained in his praise of Owens and other black athletes at the Olympics. "Brown is Germany's national color, and brown remains the official color of the Olympics games. The only change is from brown shirts to brown skins," Rice wrote in the first paragraph of his August 8 story. In the second paragraph he wrote, "You can call them all-browns or the sepia fusiliers. At any rate, they have turned Berlin's magnificent Olympic spectacle into darktown on parade." Rice also perpetuated stereotypes that black athletes were "genetically predisposed to excelling in sport due to their physical and emotional composition," Pamela Laucella wrote in her study of Rice's coverage of Owens at the 1936 Olympics, where he also wrote that "black individuals are lazier than other races." Rice also described the Ohio State University–educated Owens as a "noble savage," an "African" or "Ethiopian," or a "wild Zulu running amuck." Rice was not the exception. In spite of the success of athletes such as Owens and Louis, sportswriters used racial stereotypes that, according to Laucella, "reflected the times and reinforced prejudices."[90] Few Americans doubted the impressiveness of Owens's performance. But to sportswriters and their readers, once Owens stepped out of his track cleats, he had to return to his place at the back of the bus.

Jimmy Powers used Owens's success to revive his argument that blacks belonged in baseball. Powers had moved to the *New York Daily News* in 1928 after working for newspapers in Oklahoma, Wisconsin, and Ohio. His caustic style immediately won him readers, and when Paul Gallico quit the newspaper, Powers succeeded him and his column became required reading for many of the readers of the newspaper, which had a circulation of three million. "He had tremendous clout at the *Daily News*, which had a tremendous readership," a former *Daily News* sportswriter said. His brashness and often carelessness made him enemies. *New York Times Mirror* sports columnist Dan Parker charged him with such ethical transgressions as putting his byline on stories written by other members of the staff. Powers had to apologize after writing that Lou Gehrig, the stricken first baseman of the New York Yankees, had polio and that it had threatened to spread to his teammates.[91] Powers regularly criticized Branch Rickey, the president of the Brooklyn Dodgers, for his penuriousness by referring to the executive as "El Cheapo." No mainstream columnist wrote more columns calling for the end of segregated baseball. After Powers wrote that baseball should admit blacks after the 1936 Olympics, a reader challenged him by saying, "How would you like your sister being married to one?" Powers responded that he would not want his sister married to a lot of white ballplayers: "They're too grouchy," he snapped. "Are we discussing ballplayers — or brothers-in-law?"[92]

CHAPTER 3

INVISIBLE MEN

When Sam Lacy was two years old in 1905, his family moved from Mystic, Connecticut, to Washington DC. Lacy grew up near Griffith Stadium, home field of the Nationals, who would later change their name to the Senators.[1] The Lacys were affluent by the standards of the day. Band leader Duke Ellington lived in their neighborhood. Sam attended school with Charles Drew, who later created what became known as blood banks, and William Hastie, who would become a federal judge. Lacy said his father, Sam Sr., a researcher for a law firm, shared an interest in newspapers and baseball with his son. Sam Sr.'s salary made it possible for them to regularly attend games at Griffith Stadium. Lacy Sr. continued to attend games until he was almost eighty. The Senators walked in a parade to the ballpark before the first game of the season. Lacy Sr. was standing on the parade route cheering the team as it passed. "There he was, cheering, calling all the players by name, happy to be there," Sam Lacy Jr. later said. "And then this guy spits right in this nice old man's face." Sam Lacy Jr. said the guy who spit on his father was Nick Altrock, a Senators pitcher who, after retiring, coached the team for forty years. Sam Lacy Sr. "lived seven more years," his son said. "He never went to another game."[2]

When Sam Jr. was old enough, he began working at Griffith Stadium — shagging fly balls during batting practice before the games, and then either selling concessions or operating the scoreboard during games. He also ran errands for ballplayers, whether it was bringing them a cup of coffee or a cold drink or taking their suits to the cleaners. When the Nationals were on a road trip, the team's owner, Clark Griffith, leased the stadium to black teams. Lacy, therefore, saw both black and white teams. He said he saw many black players who were equal to or better than the whites who wore Major League uniforms.[3] This experience provided him with an unusual perspective and shaped his lifelong interests in both baseball and racial equality. Segregation, he said, deprived the best black ballplayers of playing in the big leagues, but it also deprived white spectators of watching those players.[4]

When Lacy was not working at the ballpark, he was playing baseball. He played whenever he could and became good enough to play against established stars like Dick Lundy and Pop Lloyd. "We didn't make a lot of money — ten, twenty, or thirty dollars a game, depending on the crowd and the take," he remembered. "We were furnished good equipment, but you had to buy your own gloves and shoes." As Lacy played on better teams, his teammates and he traveled in expensive automobiles lent to them by bootleggers. They also played in Major League ballparks. This, he said, was "a night and day difference" from playing on the makeshift fields he usually did.[5] But Lacy was never comfortable with the lifestyle that accompanied black baseball — what he called "the drinking, womanizing, and carousing." Lacy also knew that no matter how good he became, he would not be good enough "to play in the white man's game." After playing semiprofessionally for a few years, Lacy put aside his glove and cleats to take a more secure job as a journalist. How good a ballplayer was he? "I was as good as some of those big leaguers, who hit balls I chased during batting practice," he said.[6]

While Lacy was a teenager he also worked in a print shop, where he learned to set type and run a rotary press. By high school he was writing for one of the city's black weeklies, the *Tribune*. After attending Howard University, he worked for a radio station before the *Tribune* hired him as its sports editor in 1934. In one of his first columns, he asked why whites were paid more than blacks when they played one another. "Sometimes," he wrote, "me thinks I'll write about white athletes who come uptown to play our colored teams, snatch the long end of the purse, the game and everything else that matters and run back downtown to wait for another invitation to come up and get some more money." In August 1935 he wrote that integration would make baseball more exciting and therefore increase attendance at Major League ballparks. "Why not give baseball a little color?" he asked.[7] Lacy, having seen blacks and whites play on the same field, albeit in different games on different days, decided to ask Clark Griffith the same question. In 1937 Lacy walked two and a half blocks from his newspaper to Griffith's Georgia Avenue office — where he had a two-and-a-half-hour discussion with Griffith. Griffith listened but shook his head. He told Lacy that "the climate wasn't right." Lacy responded that "the climate would never be right if it wasn't tested." He told Griffith that Josh Gibson, Buck Leonard, and "Cool Papa" Bell belonged in the big leagues. Griffith disagreed. He said integration would destroy the Negro leagues. "But I said that the Negro leagues were a symbol of prejudice," Lacy said. But, Lacy added, "Griffith didn't budge. He didn't even entertain my thought."[8]

Over the next several years, Lacy would be joined by other black sportswriters — including Wendell Smith, Chester Washington, and Rollo Wilson of the *Pittsburgh Courier*; Frank "Fay" Young, Al Monroe, and Lucius Harper of the *Chicago Defender*; Joe Bostic of the *New York People's Voice*; Dan Burley of the *Amsterdam News*; Ed Harris of the *Philadelphia Tribune*; Art Carter of the *Baltimore Afro-American*;

Mabray "Doc" Kountze of the *Boston Chronicle*; and others — in calling
for the end of segregated baseball. Black sportswriters repeatedly challenged the white baseball establishment's claim that only "ability" and
"character" prevented a ballplayer from playing in the Major Leagues.
Lacy wrote that baseball's history demonstrated that character had
never been a requirement for wearing a Major League uniform. "A
man who is totally lacking in character has turned out to be acceptable," Lacy said. "But a man whose character may be of the highest
and whose ability may be Ruthian has been barred completely from
the sport because he is colored." Rollo Wilson wrote in the *Crisis* that
racism — not character or ability — precluded the possibility of blacks
playing in the Major Leagues. Wilson said many blacks had the ability to play in the big leagues. "Many of the men I have seen playing
the game in the years agone . . . might have been big league stars had
they been given the chance," Wilson wrote. He said the color line had
kept blacks out of the Major Leagues, leaving them to carve out their
own legacies on fields invisible to white America. "Denied their place
in the baseball sun because of racial prejudice," Wilson said, "Negro
players have gone along, playing for little or nothing and have made
reputations which have endured."[9]

Lacy, like the black players he observed at Griffith Stadium who
were denied the opportunity of playing in white baseball and being
cheered by white spectators, too, was denied the opportunity of working for white newspapers and having his columns and articles admired
by white readers. Lacy played sports with Bob Considine when they
growing up in Washington DC, and the two remained lifelong friends.
One day they were playing tennis, and Considine, who was white, told
Lacy, "Sam, you know it's a shame. When we grow up, I'm going to be
able to go a lot farther than you."[10] Considine later became a columnist
for the Hearst News Service and became one of the best-known and
most successful sportswriters in the United States.

The Baseball Writers' Association had its own color line. Black
sportswriters could not get press cards, which meant they were barred

from press boxes, dugouts, and locker rooms at big league ballparks. Blacks were barred from working on mainstream dailies, where they would have been paid more and their work would have been appreciated by more readers. Most of these sportswriters spent their careers telling stories not told in the white press, toiling for understaffed and underfunded weeklies that had a fraction of the circulation of metropolitan dailies. But their columns were as influential with their readers as the columns of Grantland Rice, "Red" Smith, and Arthur Daley were with their readers, wrote Jim Reisler, author of *Black Writers/Black Baseball*. Their greatest influence came in the campaign to end baseball's color line, and it took them beyond their words to the offices of baseball executives. "It was that same group who actively accompanied black players to tryouts with major league teams, making their case face to face with white owners," Reisler said. "Arguably, their campaign was what finally pushed big league owners to question and finally end the color ban."[11]

Sportswriters recognized that the campaign to desegregate baseball affected and reflected the campaign for greater racial equality in the United States in the 1930s and 1940s. The campaign for racial equality — whether in baseball or in the United States — was part of a long struggle that forced America to confront its enduring hypocrisy. Baseball was America's game because, like America, it stood for democracy, fairness, and equal opportunity. Racial discrimination contradicted those values. Black sportswriters knew that baseball could never really be the national game if it prohibited blacks. Black sportswriters could compare the talents of black players with those of whites because they watched blacks and whites play separately, and they watched them play against one another in barnstorming exhibitions. They chronicled the black game and provided a record that remained invisible to white America, Brian Carroll wrote in *When to Stop the Cheering?* "It is for this reason," Carroll said, "that black newspapers remain the most important source documents for histories of Negro league baseball, and, therefore, snapshots of a time, a place, and a people."[12]

Historian John Weaver wrote that no profession or organization carried a greater responsibility to inform and unify blacks in the campaign
for racial equality than the black press, adding, "The extent to which it
understood and met its responsibility can be observed in its handling
of the assault on professional baseball's 'color line.'" Black sportswriters repeatedly told their readers about the stars of black baseball who
had the right ability but not the right skin color to play in the Major
Leagues. They criticized the hypocrisy of the baseball establishment.
They knocked on the doors of Commissioner Landis, league executives, and team owners until their knuckles bled. Lacy said he knew
the desegregation of baseball would "shake up the social structure." If
there could be racial equality in baseball, then, perhaps, there could
be racial equality everywhere else in society. If baseball became desegregated, many of the best black players would leave black baseball
for the Major Leagues. But if the best players abandoned the Negro
leagues, black baseball would inevitably suffer, perhaps even collapse.
If blacks, therefore, whether in baseball or anything else, assimilated
into white America, they would have to sacrifice their distinctiveness.
W. E. B. DuBois referred to this as the "double consciousness" of being
both black and American. "It is a peculiar sensation, this double-con-
sciousness, this sense of always looking at one's self through the eyes
of others, of measuring one's soul by the tape of a world that looks in
amused contempt and pity," DuBois wrote.[13]

The campaign for racial equality in baseball serves as a microcosm of
the campaign for racial equality in American society. As black sportswriters fought for racial equality in baseball, black journalists fought
for racial equality in society. Whether calling for separation or integration, the black press was from its earliest days "a fighting press."[14]
America's first black newspaper, *Freedom's Journal*, which was published
in New York City in 1827, committed itself to the abolition of slavery.
The newspapers that followed *Freedom's Journal* also made the end of
slavery their primary objective. In 1847 Frederick Douglass wrote the
following in the first issue of the *North Star*: "The object of the *North*

Star will be to attack slavery in all of its forms and aspects, advocate Universal Emancipation; exact the standard of public morality; promote the moral and intellectual improvement of the colored people; and to harass the day of our freedom to our three million enslaved country-men." The *North Star* called for "free men, free soil, free speech, a free press, everywhere in the land."[15] Slavery split the country not into black and white but into proslavery and antislavery and finally into North and South. In 1863 President Abraham Lincoln signed the Emancipa-tion Proclamation. Two years later the North defeated the South in the Civil War, ostensibly freeing blacks from the shackles of slavery.

As hopes grew for a better day for blacks, so did the number of black newspapers. Between 1861 and 1877 more than a hundred black newspapers went into circulation. Editors used their newspapers to inform and to educate their readers. When freedom did not translate into equality, editors demanded that the government's promises for racial equality be fulfilled. Blacks secured a measure of success in the years following the Civil War. Racial progress, however, was met with resentment among whites, particularly those living in the defeated South. The Ku Klux Klan and other racist organizations terrorized emancipated blacks. Black schools were burned and teachers were attacked. Blacks who could be intimidated were intimidated. Those who could not often were either beaten into submission or murdered. Dur-ing Reconstruction perhaps thousands of blacks were killed by white southerners. Blacks learned—often violently—"that the Emancipation for which they had so deeply yearned exacted its own price and visited on them further indignities," Armistead S. Pride and Clint Wilson II wrote in their history of the black press. "While slavery had come to an official end, Reconstruction marked only the beginning of another tortuous journey filled with suffering, despair and deprivation."[16]

In 1877, following a compromise that ensured the election of Presi-dent Rutherford Hayes, federal troops were pulled out of the South. This began an erosion of racial progress, which would be replaced by racial extremism and then by racial exclusion. Black newspapers spoke to black America with a voice that alternated between hopefulness and hopelessness. Between 1877 and 1890 several hundred black newspapers went into circulation, although only a few would have the resources to last. Black editors lived a precarious existence, living issue to issue, often in fear of white retribution. Ida B. Wells, who became editor of the *Memphis Free Speech*, reported white atrocities, provoking racists to destroy the newspaper's printing press.[17] During the rise of Jim Crow, struggling black newspapers rarely confronted American apartheid, adopting a more conciliatory approach, believing, as much of white America did, that segregation was the way things were and how things would forever be, and therefore it was in the best interests of blacks to accept things as they were and make the most out of the circumstances. Booker T. Washington made this point in his famous "Atlanta Compromise" speech of 1895. "In all things that are purely social we (black and white) can be as separate as the fingers," he said, "yet one as the hand in all things essential to mutual progress." Washington's support for accommodation put him in conflict with other blacks such as W. E. B. DuBois, Ida B. Wells, and William Trotter, editor of the *Boston Guardian*, who advocated confrontation over accommodation.

Although their editorial philosophies may have differed, Washington, DuBois, Wells, and Trotter all understood the inherent power of the press. Washington owned the *New York Age*. In 1905 DuBois wrote of the need for a magazine for blacks that would "interpret the news of the world to them, and inspire them toward definite ideas." The magazine he had in mind would be the *Crisis*, which became the voice of the National Association for the Advancement of Colored People (NAACP). The conflict between the differing philosophies of Washington and DuBois divided the black press. "Such a confrontation between those two men at such a critical time," wrote Charles Simmons, "also divided the Negro press when survival of the race needed a united front." By the beginning of the twentieth century, Jim Crow had ravaged black America. "Black Americans," Pride wrote, "relied on their own press to chronicle the effects of segregation and racial discrimination and to provide leadership in the struggle to overcome them."[18] Between 1890 and 1915 a number of newspapers came into existence that would influence the fight for racial equality in the coming decades, including the *Pittsburgh Courier, Amsterdam News, Norfolk Journal and Guide, Boston Guardian, Philadelphia Tribune, New York Age, Indianapolis Freeman, Chicago Defender,* and *Baltimore Afro-American,* which would become the flagship newspaper in the *Afro-American* chain in the East.

In 1905 Robert Abbott edited the first issue of the *Chicago Defender* while sitting on a borrowed chair and working at a card table in a rented room on State Street. The *Defender,* which would become one of America's most important black newspapers, survived only because Abbott's landlady let him use her dining room as an office, provided him meals, mended his clothes, loaned him money, and took care of him when he had pneumonia. Unlike other black newspapers, however, the *Defender* avoided social activism for sensationalism. Instead of railing against lynching and discrimination, Abbott railed against prostitution and crime. Abbott published so many crime and scandal stories that the newspaper was criticized by black leaders. The *Defender* would not become a financial and critical success until it became involved in the cause of racial equality.[19] No newspaper — with the exception of the *Pittsburgh Courier* — would become more involved in either the overall cause of racial equality or the campaign to desegregate baseball. In 1920 Abbott wrote that he had stopped attending games at either of Chicago's big league ballparks because of the color line. "The day when any man regardless of race, creed, or color can play in the big leagues," he said, "is the day I shall be happy to watch such a game."[20]

Frank A. Young, credited with being America's first full-time black sportswriter, was born in 1884 and served as the *Defender*'s sports editor for nearly a half century. Young, who used his initials, "Fay," in his byline, began contributing articles to the *Defender* while working as a dining-car waiter on a train. By working on the train Young was privy to both news and gossip and shared both with the *Defender.* Because the *Defender* did not have the money to pay him, Young worked without a salary for several years. When Young began receiving a paycheck, he served as both the newspaper's sports editor and its managing editor.[21] Unlike white sportswriters, who were assigned to a particular team, black sportswriters had to write, edit, photograph, and, if need be, deliver their respective newspapers. Young, who served as the only staff member of the sports department, had a presence like no other sportswriter, alternatively serving as promoter, critic, and self-appointed conscience of black baseball. He was present at the creation of the Negro National League in 1920 and then served as the league's secretary and later as its director of publicity. In the 1930s and 1940s he repeatedly called for the reform of the Negro leagues and for the end of the color line. He acted as the patriarch of black sportswriters, condemning the haphazard structure of black baseball and scolding anyone who did not defer to his guidance.[22]

By 1907 two decades had passed since the International League drew the color line. Although there had been a few protests when the game evicted blacks, they faded as the next generation of black stars toiled in obscurity, completely overlooked by mainstream America and barely mentioned in the black press. White ballplayers had organized professional baseball, and black ballplayers had their own brand of baseball, disorganized and vaguely professional, separate but hardly equal. They played against other black teams or barnstormed against white big league and semipro teams, playing catch-as-catch-can, traveling long distances for little money and less recognition. According to Donn Rogosin, author of *Invisible Men: Life in the Negro Leagues*, the first generation of black ballplayers "passed their lives in obscurity, absent from the sports pages of the white newspapers, obliterated from American sports history."[23]

Black baseball's first era would have disappeared had it not been for Sol White, whose 1907 book, *Sol White's Official Guide: History of Colored Baseball*, rescued the early years of black baseball from oblivion, providing the only account of the beginnings of black professional baseball. Baseball historian Jerry Malloy called the book the "Dead Sea

Scrolls of black professional baseball's pioneering community."[24] In the preface of his book White wrote that black baseball began in 1885 at the Argyle Hotel in Babylon, Long Island, where Frank P. Thompson, the hotel's head waiter, organized a baseball team from among his waiters and played as an attraction for the hotel's guests.

White chronicled how different black teams found success by playing one another and by playing white teams, and how, for a relatively brief time in the 1870s and 1880s, blacks played with white teams in organized professional baseball. White identified "Cap" Anson as the architect of baseball's "gentlemen's agreement," which forced blacks out of organized baseball. "His repugnant feeling, shown at every opportunity, toward colored players," White wrote, "was a source of comment through every league in the country, and his position, with his great popularity and power in base ball circles, hastened the exclusion of the black man from the white games." Anson's hostility toward blacks, White said, was comparable to that of such southern white supremacists as "Pitchfork Ben" Tillman of South Carolina and James Vardaman of Mississippi, and the discrimination against blacks in baseball was comparable to the discrimination of blacks in the South. "The colored players are not only barred from playing on white clubs," White said, "but at times games are cancelled for no other reason than objections being raised by a Southern ball player, who refuses to play against a colored ball club."[25]

By the early 1890s blacks had all but vanished from organized professional baseball. In a relatively short time the color line had restricted black ballplayers where they played and whom they played, but it also restricted where they could stay and what they were paid. White documented that black ballplayers made a fraction of what white ballplayers did. At one point, White said, the Cuban Giants and other black teams stayed in first-class hotels, but that, too, had changed. Now when the Giants traveled, "all hotels are generally filled from the cellar to the garret when they strike a town," White said. White acknowledged that the discrimination found in baseball merely reflected the discrimination

of the day, and, given the racial climate of the United States, it would
be difficult to turn back the clock. White, nevertheless, reminded black
baseball players that they were professionals and needed to act accord-
ingly. He wrote in black newspapers for decades about the need for
ballplayers and fans to take the game seriously. As later sportswriters
did, White called on black baseball to organize itself better and standardize its rules to prevent players from jumping from team to team.
This, he hoped, might result in black baseball's becoming part of white
baseball. "An honest effort of his great ability will open the avenue in
the near future," he said, "wherein he may walk hand in hand with
the opposite race in the greatest of all American games — baseball."[26]

Black ballplayers were excluded from organized professional baseball, but this is not to say they were not vulnerable from the clutches
of white promoters like Nat Strong. Strong exploited black baseball by
monopolizing the booking of black games in white-owned ballparks.
Therefore, if a black team wanted to play ball, it had to pay Strong a
percentage of the gate. Strong booked games for the best black teams
and thus systematically monopolized black baseball. Any team that
challenged Strong found itself barred from future bookings. "There is
not a man in the country who has made as much money from colored
baseball as Nat Strong," Sol White said, "and yet he is the least interested
in its welfare."[27] Romeo Dougherty of the *Amsterdam News* said that
blacks should quit complaining about Strong's control over them and
organize their own league.[28] When Rube Foster founded the Negro
National League, he said he wanted to "keep Colored baseball from the
control of whites."[29] But because blacks did not own their own stadiums,
they remained under the thumb of agents, like Strong of New York
City and Eddie Gottlieb in Philadelphia, who charged 5 percent to 10
percent of the gate to book games.[30] In later years Abe Saperstein, also
of Philadelphia, booked Satchel Paige's appearances and other Negro
league games, including the annual East-West Classic all-star games.

The creation of the Negro National League in 1920 followed what
writer John Hope Franklin called "the greatest period of interracial

strife the nation has ever witnessed."[31] In May 1917 Abbott's *Defender* began "the Great Northern Drive" — or what would become known as "the Great Migration" — to urge southern blacks to shake themselves free of the shackles of southern bigotry, where they had no vote and little or no work, and where they lived at the mercy of white southerners who lynched and killed them with impunity.[32] The *Defender* told southern blacks they could find a better life in the North. The newspaper helped unskilled migrant workers find homes and jobs. It educated blacks on etiquette, conduct, and where to attend schools. "The *Defender*," Pride and Wilson wrote, became "advocate, defender, instructor, and an anchor in a strange world."[33]

The *Defender* saw its circulation — and subsequently its influence — increase by publishing a national edition. The newspaper's circulation reached nearly three hundred thousand, which was an unprecedented figure for a black newspaper. The *Defender*, which used black railroad porters to both report news and distribute newspapers throughout the South, worked surreptitiously to move tens of thousands of blacks by rail — many of whom slipped away from their homes in the middle of the night.[34] White southerners took action to stop the loss of their cheap labor. Blacks were taken from trains and arrested. Southern cities passed legislation to suppress the *Defender*. A Mississippi law declared that the newspaper was German propaganda and prohibited its circulation. When intimidation or legislation did not work, violence often did. A number of distributors were killed. Yet one black told the *Defender*, "In spite of all this, they are leaving every day and every night."[35] Neither intimidation, violence, nor legislation had the desired result. It became a status symbol among blacks to carry a *Defender*.[36]

Hundreds of thousands of blacks moved from the South to the North during "the Great Migration." Blacks sold everything they owned to pay for a ticket on the freedom train. They moved north with no jobs and little food or clothing for the industrial cities of the North.[37] "The fact that many Negroes who went North without sufficient funds and without clothing to keep them warm have suffered severely and have died in large numbers, has not checked the tide leaving the South," DuBois wrote in the *Crisis*.[38] The *Defender* observed, "To die from the bite of frost is far more glorious than at the hands of a mob."[39] Most blacks found better lives than what they had left behind but only marginally so; the promised land proved "illusory."[40] Like white southerners, white northerners were unprepared for the migration of so many blacks. Blacks ended up in crowded, segregated slums, where they learned that racism was not the province of the segregated South. White factory workers resented the hiring of so many blacks. Opportunistic politicians used prejudice to stir up white resentment. Whites tried to keep black neighborhoods from encroaching into their neighborhoods.[41] In cities like Chicago and Detroit, where tens of thousands of blacks had moved, it was only a matter of time before tensions would explode and there would be a race riot.

As America prepared for World War I, blacks believed that the war presented real possibilities for racial progress. The Wilson administration sold World War I as the "war to make the world safe for democracy." Blacks saw it as a war for their own democracy. If blacks could distinguish themselves in the war, then the United States, the greatest of all democracies, would surely reward them with equality. In his famous "Closed Ranks" editorial, DuBois appealed to blacks to "forget our special grievances and close our ranks shoulder to shoulder with our fellow citizens."[42] U.S. Senator James Vardaman and other segregationists opposed the conscription of blacks because they believed it would endorse racial equality.[43] President Woodrow Wilson, himself a southerner, agreed. He ordered segregation enforced where it already existed and created it where it had not existed. Of the 350,000 blacks who enlisted in the armed services, most were assigned to noncombat units and restricted to training bases, where they were prohibited from servicemen clubs. Black soldiers, who wanted to stand shoulder to shoulder with white soldiers, were assigned to the French army.[44] World War I may have preserved democracy in Europe, but it did little for the democracy of blacks in the United States. "This country of ours, despite all its better souls have done and reamed, is yet a shameful place," the *Crisis* said. "It lynches. . . . It disenfranchises its own citizens. . . . It encourages ignorances. . . . It steals from us. . . . It insults us. . . . We return. We return from fighting. We return fighting."[45]

When the war ended black soldiers returned from France, where they had been treated with respect, and believed that they had earned their right to be treated with respect in America. Having done their part to support their country during the war, blacks pressed for greater freedoms, and white America pushed back harder. If blacks "were determined to secure a larger share of democracy for themselves," John Hope Franklin wrote, "there were many white citizens who were as determined to see that there should be no wholesale distribution of the blessings of liberty."[46] Dozens of black war veterans were lynched in the South, many in their army uniforms.[47] This period coincided with an unprecedented rise in membership in the Ku Klux Klan, which saw its membership climb to five million, ensuring that blacks did not challenge white rule. "The Klan's grip in the South toward the inflaming of prejudice, the encouragement of racial violence, and the strengthening of the segregation code was powerful," C. Vann Woodward wrote.[48] Southern cities passed more and more ordinances prohibiting the mixing of races. Atlanta passed a law that white bus drivers would drive whites and black bus drivers would drive blacks. Other cities outlawed black newspapers or at least those that discussed racial equality. In 1919 Somerville, Tennessee, made it illegal for black newspapers to be circulated in that city. A year later the Mississippi legislature made it illegal for black newspapers to promote "social equality."[49] When newspapers in the state advertised that a black man would be burned alive, the state's governor, Theodore Bilbo, sanctioned the lynching. When there was disagreement over whether the man should be hanged or burned, the matter was settled by having him hanged, burned, and shot.[50]

Conditions for blacks were only marginally better in the North. Racial tensions in northern cities began with the Great Migration and then erupted during the bloody summer of 1919 in several cities, including Chicago, where thirty-eight died and more than five hundred were injured.[51] Chicago's tabloid dailies inflamed the tensions with headlines such as "Negro Brutally Murders Prominent Citizen," "Negro Bandits Terrorize Town," and "Rioters Burn 100 Homes — Negroes Suspected of Having Plotted Blaze." Walter White of the NAACP wrote in the *Crisis* that white officials told the press that blacks had been responsible for the fires, but it was later learned conclusively that whites had set them.[52] The U.S. Justice Department, nevertheless, blamed the black press, because its "constant protests against disenfranchisements and lynchings were incendiary." The government and white newspapers responded to what they saw as the increasing militancy of the black press by accusing it of being subversive or, in particular, "of being dominated by Communists."[53] Robert Vann, editor of the *Courier*, which had grown more influential as a voice for racial unity and equality, criticized the white press for stereotyping blacks as criminals, undesirables, and communists. According to Vann, the white press either ignored achievements by blacks or ridiculed them by using racist stereotypes and epithets.[54] As far as the charge that the black press was "dominated by Communists," Vann, a staunch anticommunist, responded, "As long as the Negro submits to lynchings, burnings, and oppressions — and says nothing, he is a loyal American citizen. But when he decides that lynchings and burnings shall cease even at the cost of some human bloodshed in America, then he is a Bolshevist."[55]

The *Courier*, *Defender*, and other black newspapers responded to the barbarism that followed World War I by confronting racial discrimination. They attacked southern politicians for lynching laws and northern politicians for doing nothing to address lynching laws. They called for an end to discrimination in residential segregation laws. After the *Amsterdam News* introduced the campaign "Don't Buy Where You Can't Work," blacks began boycotting white businesses.[56] Whether writing about baseball or society, black journalists wrote about the need for black pride, self-confidence, self-reliance, and self-esteem.[57]

If it was not possible to be accepted into white America, blacks would create their own identity apart from whites. If whites would not accept blacks into their businesses, schools, and sports, then blacks needed to become independent of whites and build up their own communities. If white dailies insisted on ignoring racial discrimination, then black newspapers would have to confront the problem themselves. "We cannot hope to have the daily newspapers give our viewpoint," N. D. Brascher of the Associated Negro Press wrote.[58] William White wrote in the *Chicago Defender* that blacks needed to reject inferior status and work toward racial solidarity and a greater sense of identity. To White, baseball could be a forum in which blacks could improve race relations and take more control of their lives. To do this, blacks would create a league of their own for black baseball.[59]

When Rube Foster, who owned and managed the Chicago American Giants, and five other team owners met in Kansas City to create the Negro National League in February 1920, they were joined by several sportswriters who drafted the league's constitution. The *Defender* reported that Foster let sportswriters decide league rules. Fay Young, who served as Foster's quasi publicist, defended Foster when he was criticized or provided the space so he could defend himself. Foster, like the white baseball establishment, understood the league needed the press and awarded season passes to black sportswriters. He encouraged teams to allow sportswriters to travel with them on road trips. But, unlike white newspapers, black newspapers did not have either the staff or the resources to do so. Newspapers had to rely on teams to contact them. Teams, therefore, often failed to notify newspapers about their games — especially when they lost — and therefore any attempt to accurately keep standings was problematic. To add to the confusion, because many of the games a team played were exhibitions against semipro teams, newspapers could not determine whether a game should or should not count in the league standings.[60]

Foster and other team owners hoped that if black baseball proved itself, the Major Leagues would open their doors to blacks.[61] This did

not happen. Neither the Negro National League nor the Eastern Colored League, which was founded in 1922, became either equal to organized professional baseball or truly organized, for that matter — only
a minority of a team's two hundred or so games counted in the league
standings. To make a living blacks hit the road, traveling from town
to town, playing catch-as-catch-can — playing wherever they could,
as often as they could, for whatever money they could, often depending on donations from poor fans.[62] While white ballplayers traveled
by train, blacks traveled by car. White players stayed in hotels; black
players sometimes had to sleep in fields. Whereas white players generally played one game a day, black players regularly played two or
even three and were generally paid far less than white players. The
indefatigable Foster was determined that the Negro National League
survive. He put that above everything else until his health, both physical and emotional, wore out. After Foster's death the Negro National
League and then the Eastern Colored League fell into disrepair and then
discontinued. Foster's league did not achieve equality with the Major
Leagues, however, Robert Peterson wrote. "It did provide a measure
of stability and permanence to many black teams, which, before him,
had been little more than loosely organized groups of barnstormers."[63]

Black newspapers — at least initially — committed their energies
toward building up black baseball rather than desegregating white
baseball. Brian Carroll wrote that there was little discussion of white
baseball's color line in either the black or the white press. "It was not
an issue for blacks or whites, at least not as it related to professional
baseball, not yet," Carroll wrote. "The pendulum of race had swung so
dramatically toward separation," black newspaper and baseball owners
tried to build up the game and did not directly challenge, in historian
Donn Rogosin's words, "the inherent irrationality of American segregation." Black newspapers also — at least initially — gave their unequivocal
support to the black baseball establishment, in part, of course, because
journalists were part of the black baseball establishment. Ira Lewis,
the managing editor of the *Pittsburgh Courier*, was also the league's

secretary. Lewis officiated over league meetings and then reported on them for his newspaper. Sportswriters often wrote the rules, acted as publicists for teams, publicized the games and the players, criticized ballplayers who acted unprofessionally, and kept standings and statistics, such as they were. As black baseball struggled financially, Sol White called on the press to revive black baseball. "The colored press has played a big part in shaping the course of the game in late years," White said. "If baseball has veered towards the shoals of business inactiveness and sloth, let the press put it on the right course and bring it up to where it belongs — one of the greatest institutions of the race."[64]

In the 1920s black baseball executives, like white baseball executives, perceived sportswriters to be an implicit part of their teams rather than independent of their teams. This left black baseball with the impression that the press served their interests. The cozy relationship between sportswriters and black baseball did not last. Carroll said the relationship between black baseball and the black press went through three phases: initially, they worked together; then came increasing skepticism in the black press; and finally, outright enmity.[65] Shortly after the Negro National League was revived in 1933, sportswriters asserted their independence by criticizing black baseball for its haphazard organization.[66] Owners responded by banning sportswriters from league meetings, which, of course, only brought more criticism. Fay Young openly chided black baseball for its poor structure and lack of professionalism. So, too, did Sam Lacy. "What with petty jealousies, cut-throat aspirations and willful disregard for rules and agreements on the parts of promoters and club owners," he said, "and team-jumping and general wrangling on the parts of players keeping so-called organized Negro baseball in perpetual chaos, it makes one ponder the advisability of entering the breach to submit recommendations."[67]

Gus Greenlee, who made his fortune in the numbers racket, used his money to buy up the best players for his Pittsburgh Crawfords. His wealth also afforded him independence from the clutches of white Major League owners. Instead of having to pay the exorbitant costs to rent a big league stadium, Greenlee built his own park, Greenlee Field. Not only did he own the best team in the Negro National League, but he also served as the league's first president. During the 1930s and early 1940s the Great Depression paralyzed much of white America. Black America, which did not have much to begin the decade, lost what little it had. But behind Greenlee's money and acumen, black baseball, which included the Negro National League and the Negro American League, would not merely survive but become one of the most important black businesses in America — a "three million dollar business," according to the black press. Baseball became a source of income for black athletes and a source of pride for black fans. "With twelve to fifteen teams, each league playing across the entire nation and employing hundreds of people," Rogosin wrote, black baseball "may rank among the highest achievements of black enterprise during segregation." Rogosin called black baseball "a sorry comment on segregation, but a tribute to the world that Negro Baseball made." Art Rust called the Negro leagues an "empire built on poverty."[68]

On September 8, 1933, Greenlee, in cooperation with black newspapers, organized the first East-West Classic all-star game at Comiskey Park in Chicago. The black press relentlessly promoted the game, which would become what Rogosin called "the single most important black sports event in America."[69] Roy Sparrow of the *Pittsburgh Sun-Telegraph* sent press releases to both black weeklies and white dailies throughout the country. More than twenty thousand fans attended the inaugural game, which coincided with Chicago's annual pageant of music, "O Sing a New Song," at Soldier Field. The *Defender* described the August weekend as "the biggest event in the history of the Race."[70] William Nunn of the *Courier* observed the following after watching the game: "They made me proud that I'm a Negro, and tonight I'm singing a new song."[71] Future East-West Classics would draw crowds of fifty thousand and would become a source and symbol of racial pride for blacks — whether they attended the game or not. Blacks scheduled their vacations around the game and came from all over the country.

The Illinois Central and Union Pacific railroads added extra trains to accommodate the crowds. "It was a holiday for at least 48 hours. People would just about come from everywhere, mainly because it was such a spectacle," Sam Lacy remembered decades later. "I would go on my vacation during all-star week so that I could be there the entire week. I didn't want to miss anything."[72] Each East-West game put the talents of the best black players on display in front of crowds, which increasingly included white spectators. Black sportswriters used the game to question the color line. "You read about the 50,000 persons who saw the East-West game and the thousands who were turned away from the classic," Ed Harris wrote, "and you get to wondering what the magnates of the American and National leagues thought about it when they read the figures."[73]

White America may not have read black newspapers, but black America read white newspapers. Whenever a white sportswriter wrote about the color line, black baseball, or even individual black ballplayers, black newspapers reported it. When Westbrook Pegler criticized the color line in baseball, the *Baltimore Afro-American* praised him. In March 1936 Washington quoted a white sportswriter as saying that current big leaguers lacked the excitement and personality of those who played in the past. This was not the case in black baseball, Washington wrote. "Not only in the shading of their skin, but in the brilliant and dazzling brand of baseball they play, they are more 'colorful than the leaves of autumn,'" he said. In the column Washington included a list of about twenty black ballplayers good enough to play in the Major Leagues. "One of these days," Washington wrote, "some courageous big-league owner will be broad-minded, resourceful and far sighted enough to realize that the infection of some stellar Negro players will add the color that the majors need, and our boys will be give the chance they deserve."[74]

Later that year Jimmy Powers used Jesse Owens's performance in the Berlin Olympics to argue that blacks belonged in baseball. After Powers wrote that baseball should admit blacks, a reader challenged him by saying, "How would you like your sister being married to one?" Ed Harris, with sarcasm dripping, chafed at the question in his column in the *Philadelphia Tribune*. "Now that, my friends, is a product of deep thinking, of a careful association of all the factors involved in the case and the resultant conclusion," he wrote. "Nothing but a brilliant man could have reached a decision whereby he felt that marriage and ball players were related." According to Harris, such arguments were so fraudulent they defeated themselves. Harris also questioned the belief held by the white baseball establishment and white sportswriters that the mixing of races would be so toxic that racial incidents were inevitable. Harris said that even in the more southern baseball towns such as Cincinnati, St. Louis, and Washington DC, white spectators regularly attended interracial college football games without incident. "I have yet to hear of any mob violence," Harris said, "because some prejudiced white became infuriated at seeing a colored star play with white boys.[75]

Harris also questioned the argument that blacks lacked the character to be big league ballplayers. From what he knew about big leaguers, black ballplayers would improve and not detract from the caliber of ballplayer in the big leagues. White big leaguers did not, after all, come from eastern boarding schools. "It is my conclusion that very few of them spring from what might be termed 'the best homes,'" Harris said. Major League officials said that baseball did not prohibit blacks. But the reality, Harris said, was there were no blacks in baseball, and this would continue until a manager put a black player on his lineup card. "Some manager with guts and vision might precipitate things by signing up a colored player and seeing what would happen. It would clarify things a great deal. We would get some sort of decision, pro or con, instead of a lot of theories," he wrote. If blacks were allowed, teams would see an increase in attendance. But all that was theoretical. "But, like all men, I live in hope," Harris said. "Some day, someone will surprise the baseball world and sign a couple of good colored players. And the baseball world will be surprised to find out that after the initial interest and excitement that the Negro will be accepted as part of the club and the world will go its own way."[76]

Wendell Smith, Sam Lacy, Fay Young, Joe Bostic, Dan Burley, and other sportswriters came to believe that this day would not happen without pressuring the baseball establishment. Lacy often reminded his readers about his meeting with Griffith, as if to characterize the meeting as a breakthrough in the campaign to end segregated baseball. Lacy said he was the first black sportswriter "to quote a big league owner on the issue." Lacy later praised Griffith for being open-minded on the issue because "he allowed me to interview him."[77] Such columns exaggerated both the importance of such meetings and the sympathies of men like Griffith. Baseball executives such as Griffith, Philip Wrigley of the Cubs, Larry MacPhail of the Dodgers, Jacob Ruppert of the Yankees, and others met purely as a courtesy so as not to offend blacks who patronized their ballparks. They would appear interested in the cause, smile condescendingly, tell black journalists they would like to sign blacks but could not because of Commissioner Landis, or because of the attitudes of white players, white fans, or white society for that matter, and then shut the door, and with it any interest in integration. Owners were not interested in signing blacks, regardless of the seemingly apparent contradiction between preaching racial equality and practicing racial discrimination.

Only one man in organized professional baseball had the influence to end the color line, and that was Kenesaw Mountain Landis. Lacy contacted Landis from Washington DC, when he worked for the *Washington Tribune* and then when he worked for the *Washington Afro-American*. In 1943 Lacy quit the *Afro-American* and then moved to Chicago to become national editor of the *Defender*.[78] Landis's office also was in Chicago. Lacy tried to schedule a meeting with Landis. Landis, according to Lacy, had no interest in discussing the possibility of ending segregation. "Judge Landis did everything possible to avoid meeting with me or anyone to talk about the segregation issue," Lacy said, adding, "I sent him a note that said I would meet with him any

hour of any day, any day of any week, any week of any year, any time
of time," Lacy said. "I got no response."[79] Finally, in late 1943, Landis
agreed to allow a delegation of black activists to make their argument
for integration at the owners' annual meeting. Lacy thought he would
have a seat at the table. But when the time came, he was replaced by
former Rutgers football star–turned–opera singer Paul Robeson. Lacy
knew that Landis, by inviting Robeson, a staunch and outspoken Communist, had played into the anticommunist feelings of the owners.

The involvement of the Communists in the struggle for greater civil
rights — whether in baseball or elsewhere in U.S. society — made a lot
of blacks uncomfortable. Although a lot of prominent blacks rejected
the Communists, others were card-carrying members of the Communist Party. Abbott, DuBois, and Adam Clayton Powell Jr., who would
become a congressman, may not have supported communism, but
they acknowledged — at least at some point — that progress was not
possible without sympathetic whites, and if those sympathetic whites
happened to be Communists, then blacks were hardly in a position
to reject them. In 1932 DuBois wrote newspaper editors asking them
to express "their opinion of Communism." Carl Murphy, editor of the
Baltimore Afro-American, responded that "Communists appear to be
the only party going our way. They're as radical as the NAACP was
twenty years ago." Robert Vann of the *Courier*, however, said that "few
intelligent Negroes are to be found in the Communist movement."[80]
Vann's view obviously was not universally held. Paul Robeson; A. Philip
Randolph, president of the Brotherhood of Sleeping Car Porters and
onetime president of the National Negro Congress; Max Yergan, who
also served as president of the National Negro Congress; William Patterson, president of the Civil Rights Congress; Benjamin O. Davis Jr.,
who served on the New York City Council; and other prominent blacks
were — at least for a time — Communists. Many black Communists
supported the desegregation of Major League Baseball. Patterson, who
represented Sacco and Vanzetti and then assisted the counsel defending
the Scottsboro Boys, was influenced by Randolph's *Messenger* and later

wrote for the *Daily Worker*. Patterson also chaired the Chicago-based Committee to End Jim Crow in Baseball, which confronted Landis and Cubs owner Philip Wrigley about the color line.[81]

Black sportswriters, like their editors, were divided on communism. A few black newspapers, including the *Defender*, praised Lester Rodney and the *Daily Worker*. Wendell Smith of the *Pittsburgh Courier* was initially friendly toward Communists, but then distanced himself. Although Smith once wrote a letter of appreciation to Rodney, he rejected the Communists' methods as too confrontational. "I always tried to keep it from becoming a flamboyant, highly militant thing," Smith said much later in his career. "I think that's why it succeeded. If there had been picketing . . . this thing wouldn't have developed the way it did." Sam Lacy, too, believed in being persistent but not confrontational. Lacy disliked communism, wanted no part of the Communists, and criticized them when they picketed outside ballparks. "Members of this organization apparently believe that quicker and better results will be obtained through intimidation than through impression," he wrote in 1939. "I regret that I am unable to see the wisdom in such a program."[82]

Because Landis refused to use the authority of his office to end the color line, black sportswriters made their case to individual owners. They knew they did not have to convince a majority of owners. They only had to convince one. For years it appeared that owner might be Bill Benswanger, president of the Pittsburgh Pirates. Benswanger, who inherited the position after the death of his father-in-law, Barney Dreyfuss, expressed his openness on the issue shortly after he took over the team in 1933. As a Jew, Benswanger certainly understood discrimination. Unlike other team executives, Benswanger did not exhibit any outward racism and, more than once, appeared open to signing black players, meeting with black sportswriters, and expressing publicly his interest in signing blacks. Clearly, if any baseball executive understood either discrimination or the talent that lay hidden in the Negro leagues, it was Benswanger. The Pittsburgh Crawfords and the

Homestead Grays, two of the dominant teams in black baseball, shared a city with the Pirates, which did not win any pennants in the 1930s and 1940s and rarely found themselves rising above mediocrity. The Pirates rented Forbes Field to black teams. Benswanger knew — or at least should have known — he could have made his team a pennant contender by signing a few of the black players who played in the city. Benswanger had both the motive and the opportunity to sign blacks.

Courier sportswriters told Benswanger he could turn his team into an immediate pennant contender if he signed players from either the Crawfords or the Grays. On February 12, 1938, Ches Washington reported that Benswanger had told the columnist Cum Posey, owner of the Grays, "If the question of admitting colored ball players into organized baseball becomes an issue, I would be heartily in favor of it." After baseball became desegregated, Benswanger claimed he attempted to sign Josh Gibson and "Buck" Leonard but that Posey refused to cooperate. "I tried to buy Gibson more than once," Benswanger said in 1950, but Posey always replied, "Lay off, will you. If I did it would start a movement that would eventually break up the Negro Leagues." Wendell Smith rejected Benswanger's version as "unmitigated" storytelling.[83] Smith once reported that Posey had agreed to sell Josh Gibson and Buck Leonard, but Benswanger rejected the offer.[84] In 1942 Benswanger told Smith that he would give a tryout to black players. But no tryout was ever held. Benswanger was no doubt tempted, but, either lacking the resolve or the courage to face the wrath of other owners, he did not follow through.

Wendell Smith, who was born in Detroit in 1914, used a boyhood experience with racial discrimination to become what Jules Tygiel called "the most talented and influential of the black journalists of the era." From childhood Smith learned that blacks could live and succeed with whites, or they could live and succeed apart from whites. Unlike most other blacks, Smith had had experience in both worlds. His father, John, was a Canadian who moved to Detroit as a young man, where he began working as a dishwasher and then a cook, eventually becoming

Detroit automaker Henry Ford's chef. When Wendell Smith was ten years old, his father began taking him to the Ford mansion with him. "It was like a castle," Smith remembered. "In the summers I was there once a year. I knew the Ford kids, Edsel, Benson and Henry. We played ball together. The first time I met Mr. Ford, my father said, 'Mr. Ford, this is my son, Wendell.' Mr. Ford shook my hand, patted me on the back and said, 'He's a fine looking boy, John. What does he want to be when he grows up?'" At that age Smith knew he wanted to be a ballplayer and played whenever he could, almost always with and against whites. He grew up in a white neighborhood and attended Southeastern High School, where, he remembered, he was the only black. He encountered few problems. He said his first distinct experience with prejudice came on a baseball field when he was in high school. During the summer of 1933 Smith pitched his American Legion team to a 1–0 playoff victory. After the game Wish Egan, a scout with the Detroit Tigers who had signed Hall of Fame second baseman Charlie Gehringer and other big league players, signed both the losing pitcher and Smith's catcher, Mike Tresh. "I wish I could sign you, too, but I can't," Egan told Smith. The scout's words made a searing impression on Smith. "That broke me up," he remembered. "It was then I made a vow that I would dedicate myself and do something on behalf of the Negro ballplayers. That was one of the reasons I became a sportswriter." Smith could not help but wonder what might have been. Tresh, after all, played twelve years in the Major Leagues.[85]

After attending West Virginia State College, he went to work for the *Pittsburgh Courier* in 1937. Smith found the right newspaper for someone interested in racial equality. "The *Courier* always had some kind of program going on, a crusade for something of consequence," Smith remembered. He got hired at seventeen dollars a week and, as he later said, "learned the mechanics of the business." A year after he began working for the *Courier*, Smith was promoted to assistant sports editor. Shortly after he became assistant sports editor in 1938, he asked why blacks should continue to patronize Major League Baseball games, though they were prohibited from the game. "We keep on crawling, begging and pleading for recognition just the same," he wrote. "We know they don't want us, but we still keep giving them our money. Keep on going to their ball games and shouting till we are blue in the face — we pitiful black folk. Yes, sir — we black folk are a strange tribe."[86] Smith's activism would go far beyond shaming black baseball fans and pleading with white baseball. His column, "Wendell Smith's Sports Beat," became his pulpit, and from it he preached integration. David Wiggins wrote that "Smith believed the desegregation of baseball would give Blacks a new dignity and self-esteem, ingredients that were not only inspiring in and of themselves, but necessary components of the ultimate destruction of discrimination in this country."[87]

In January 1939 he proposed that something similar to the National Association for the Advancement of Colored People be organized to attack the color line "until we drop from exhaustion."[88] A month later Smith suggested to the newspaper's editors that the newspaper become more active in pressuring baseball to sign blacks. "I suggested a campaign for the admittance, the inclusion of Negro ballplayers in the big leagues. The paper picked up on it," he said. "Everyone seemed to think it was a very good idea." Soon after, Smith interviewed National League president Ford Frick, who, like others in the baseball establishment and the white press, said that the color line was in the best interests of baseball. Frick said that owners and league executives did not oppose blacks in the big leagues. He blamed segregation on Major League ballplayers, who, he said, objected to playing with or against blacks. Smith then interviewed dozens of players and managers and found that few players and managers objected to playing with or against blacks. "My stories were a revelation," Smith later said, "because the baseball owners had been constantly saying that the major league ballplayers would not play with Negro ballplayers."[89]

CHAPTER 4

"AGITATORS" AND "SOCIAL-MINDED DRUM BEATERS"

Written with Kelly Rusinack

On August 13, 1936, the *Daily Worker* announced the following:

The Crime of the Big Leagues!

The newspapers have carefully hushed it up!

One of the most sordid stories in American sports!

Though they win laurels for America in the Olympics — though they have proven themselves outstanding baseball stars — Negroes have been placed beyond the pale of the American and National Leagues.

Read the truth about this carefully laid conspiracy.

Beginning next Sunday, the Sunday Worker will rip the veil from the "Crime of the Big Leagues" — mentioning names, giving facts, sparing none of the most sacred figures in baseball officialdom.[1]

Three days later the *Sunday Daily Worker* published a banner headline that read: "Fans Ask End of Jim Crow Baseball." The unsigned editorial, written by Lester Rodney, began with the following pronouncement: "Jim Crow baseball must end." Thus began the communist newspaper's campaign to end discrimination in the national pastime. Rodney said that black ballplayers would improve the quality of play in the Major Leagues. He appealed to readers to demand that team owners, or "magnates," as they were referred to, admit black ballplayers: "Fans, it's up to you! Tell the big league magnates that you're sick of the poor pitching in the American League. . . . You're tired of a flop team in Boston, of the silly Brooklyn Dodgers, of the inept Phillies and the semi-inept Athletics," the story said. "Big league ball is on the downgrade. You pay the high prices. Demand better ball. Demand Americanism in baseball, equal opportunities for Negro and white stars."

Over the next decade, the *Daily Worker* and its Sunday edition, the *Sunday Worker*, published hundreds of articles on the issue of segregated baseball. The newspaper did not just publish more articles on the issue than any other daily newspaper; it published more articles than all other daily newspapers combined. The newspaper was not merely the most vocal critic of segregated baseball among the country's newspapers but the only daily that gave the color line any sustained coverage. "We were the only non-black newspaper writing about it for a long time," Rodney said.[2] The newspaper's sportswriters, including Rodney, Nat Low, Bill Mardo, Dave Farrell, Ted Benson, Phil Gordon, Mike Kantor, and others, challenged baseball's establishment to permit black players, condemned white owners and managers for perpetuating the color ban, criticized mainstream sportswriters for their silence, organized picket lines and petition drives, distributed antidiscrimination pamphlets outside and inside Major League ballparks, publicized the exploits of Negro league stars, informed readers of the successes in the campaign to end segregated baseball, and pressured Major League team owners to give tryouts to black ballplayers.

The *Worker* pounded away at the injustice, denial, and apathy that surrounded baseball; shamed the sport into defending itself against racism; and educated — and even convinced — many about the need for integration in the national pastime. The newspaper's sportswriters made their enemies and were criticized by the baseball establishment as "agitators" and "social-minded drum beaters." To this *Worker* sportswriters unapologetically agreed: they were indeed social-minded drum beaters — and they understood that the more noise they made, the more they disrupted the wall of silence that protected segregated baseball. The *Worker's* sarcastic and even belligerent articles offended baseball's establishment, such as Kenesaw Mountain Landis, Ford Frick, Branch Rickey, Larry MacPhail, and *Sporting News* editor J. G. Taylor Spink. Segregationists could not defend the color line from a moral high ground. They could, however, with the aid and comfort of mainstream sportswriters, characterize the campaign to integrate baseball as a communist front, thus making it less acceptable to mainstream America. In Jules Tygiel's groundbreaking *Baseball's Great Experiment*, he wrote that "the success of the Communists in forcing the issue before the American public far outweighed the negative ramifications" connected with their involvement.[3]

While Rickey and, to a lesser account, the black press have been duly recognized for their role in the desegregation of the national pastime, the role of the *Daily Worker* has received only marginal attention. But one cannot tell the story of the desegregation of baseball without including the Communists. Brian Carroll noted that scholarship on the desegregation of baseball had failed to give credit to the sportswriters working for the *Daily Worker*, who, he said, were responsible for petition drives that generated more than one million signatures and for prodding Landis to break his silence on the color line. Arnold Rampersad, author of the most exhaustive biography of Jackie Robinson, wrote, "The most vigorous efforts came from the Communist press, including picketing, petitions and unrelenting pressure for about ten years in the *Daily Worker*." In his autobiography William L. Patterson, himself a prominent black Communist, said that Rodney and the *Worker* "were second to no other voices in the United States in the fight to get Negroes on the rosters of Big League baseball clubs."[4]

The *Worker*, though it was prone to hyperbole and occasional errors in its coverage, may very well have created the truest story of the desegregation of baseball. *Worker* sportswriters refused to be a part of baseball's conspiracy of silence that allowed the color ban to continue as long as it did. For a decade the *Worker* was, as Mardo put it, "actively dedicated to ending Jim Crow in baseball." When asked to assess the impact that the newspaper had on ending baseball's color ban, Mardo answered, "I think it had a major effect." Rodney said that the desegregation of baseball was inevitable but that because of the *Worker*, it happened sooner than it would have otherwise. "I'm not silly enough to think that it wasn't going to happen," he said. "I think we probably speeded up the process by a few years." It is difficult, probably impossible, to quantify the newspaper's contribution in terms of years, months, or weeks. But this much is clear: No newspaper was more insistent in demanding that baseball live up to its democratic ideals. No newspaper called more often for baseball to admit blacks. And no newspaper recruited more people to protest against the color line. "We were the conscience of journalism," Rodney observed.[5]

America's baseball establishment, like its political establishment, preached equality as one of the country's inalienable rights. But these promises rang hollow as one generation after another saw the American dream deferred. The baseball establishment could, for the most part, simply ignore this contradiction because so few mainstream journalists acknowledged it. Because of this the issue failed to gain traction in mainstream America. "Racism was culturally acceptable," Rodney said. "People felt comfortable in a racist society. The sheer ignorance of the details of racism kept people from understanding it." The *Worker* confronted the myth that baseball was a field of equality to any ballplayer with the requisite skills and character. The *Worker* understood and exposed the hypocrisy of baseball's color line. *Worker* sportswriters pointed out that discrimination in either baseball or society was incompatible with democratic values.[6]

Today, it is difficult to understand either the vastness of racism, the popularity of communism, or even the influence of organized labor in the 1930s. These three things would converge in the *Worker*'s campaign to integrate baseball. Published in New York City, the newspaper did not have the circulation of other New York newspapers. Its circulation, which included foreign-language editions, may have been as high as a hundred thousand in the 1930s and then after World War II.[7] But as was the case with black newspapers, when one reader was done with the *Worker*, it was passed to another reader and then another. There were no other dailies like the *Worker* in America. The newspaper, which was supported largely by membership dues, presented white social progressives and Communist sympathizers an opportunity to condemn racial injustices. The *Worker*'s campaign to integrate baseball was a crusade of self-righteous indignation against what it perceived as a morally objectionable idea: racism.

Communists and blacks both wanted to end baseball's discriminatory practice of barring black ballplayers. They may have shared a common message, but they had a distinctly different readership. Black journalists preached to readers who were already aware of the injustices of racism and the need to end segregation. But few, if any, black journalists had political clout in white America. The *Worker*'s readers included prominent white liberals and social progressives, including congressmen, state legislators, and city council members, who could change the discriminatory laws that restricted blacks. In addition, black newspapers were read by blacks, whom the rest of society treated as second-class citizens; even strong black political leaders of the day had little influence in mainstream society. *Worker* readers included social activists who had a political base in New York politics. "The difference between the stories in the black press and the *Daily Worker* was that one paper was an activist newspaper," Bill Mardo said. "It could spur political activity in many organizations. The black press talked to black readers."[8]

The growth of the radical Left began during the Progressive Era as a response to robber-baron excesses, corporate greed, and the exploitation of workers, including children. American socialism, which also grew rapidly in the first decade and a half of the twentieth century, was inseparable from the Progressive Era. The popular impulse for reform, which appealed to workers, farmers, intellectuals, progressives, ethnic minorities, and radicals, became the impetus for the growth of the American Socialist Party.[9] Starting with 10,000 members in 1901, the Socialist Party grew to 118,000, recruiting heavily from the millions of immigrants from Germany and eastern Europe. By 1912 more than 1,000 socialists held office in the United States, including a congressman, Victor Berger of Wisconsin, and seventy-nine mayors.[10] No group was better represented in the radical Left than organized labor, particularly the Industrial Workers of the World (or Wobblies), which was founded in Chicago in 1905. If the IWW could not make its argument with words, it did so with violence. The American business and political establishment responded by crushing radical labor unions. When World War I erupted, the United States, while neutral, supported Britain, which was at war with Germany. As the war bogged down in Europe, America became increasingly anti-German. Public opinion was divided on whether to go to war. Wilson warned his critics, "Woe be to the man or group of men who stands in our way." U.S. entry into World War I intensified suspicion of German Americans, radical politics, and labor unions, resulting in the arrest, assault, and harassment of those with German or radical sympathies. "The fear that raged through the land during the 20 months of America's formal participation in the 'war to end all war,'" John Stevens wrote in *Shaping the First Amendment*, "left an ugly scar, both on our traditions and in our statute books and court opinions."[11]

On June 15, 1917, Congress, at the urging of the Wilson administration, passed the Espionage Act, which provided for fines of ten thousand dollars and imprisonment of up to twenty years for anyone obstructing military operations. With Wilson's support, law enforcement agencies and vigilante groups attacked their enemies on the Left. This would be the beginning of the end for the socialist movement, the radical press, and dissent in general. Nearly all the Socialist Party leaders were jailed or deported, including Emma Goldman, Victor Berger, Bill Haywood (president of the IWW), and presidential candidate Eugene Debs, whose conviction would later be upheld by the U.S. Supreme Court.[12] Joseph Conlin wrote that the Department of Justice raided the headquarters of the Industrial Workers of the World in more than thirty cities, displaying "a cheerful disregard" for such constitutional protections as search warrants. In April 1918 Kenesaw Mountain Landis, then a federal judge, presided over the trial of 113 defendants, including Haywood, who were charged as a result of raids on IWW halls. Haywood and other IWW leaders were sentenced to twenty years apiece. The *New York Times* and other newspapers praised Landis's handling of the case. Not everyone agreed. A few days after Landis announced his verdict, a bomb exploded near the entrance of the federal building where the trial was held. The government suspected the IWW.[13]

After World War I the more radical wing of the Socialist Party split and created the Communist Party. Given what had happened in the Soviet Union, there was considerable fear in the United States that the Communists would attempt to overthrow the U.S. government. U.S. Attorney General Mitchell Palmer conducted raids to stop any Communist insurrection before it took root. In January 1920 hundreds of federal law enforcement agents and untold other local police raided meetinghouses, restaurants, bowling alleys, and pool parlors in cities throughout the country and arrested ten thousand suspected Communists.[14] U.S. Communists went underground, hid from law enforcement officers, and fought among themselves for control of American communism. The Workers Party of America sought legitimacy, eventually taking the name of the Communist Party, USA.[15] The CPUSA tried to separate itself from its bomb-throwing brethren. To do this it sought credibility through more acceptable channels. To accomplish this goal the CPUSA created the *Daily Worker*.

The *Daily Worker* began in January 1924 as what its editors called "the only basically truthful daily paper in our country." It was an alternative newspaper — representing the workers and not the corporations. Whereas mainstream editors, reporters, and columnists could not question the sacred cows that influenced content, the *Worker* had no such restrictions. The newspaper was supported not by advertising but by, in its own words, "the nickels, dimes and dollars of the men and women of labor." The *Worker* was unrestricted by the journalistic constraint of objectivity, the economic constraints of commercialism, or even the constraint of public opinion itself. The newspaper supported Sacco and Vanzetti, the Scottsboro Boys, Angelo Herndon, and later the Hollywood Ten. It reminded its readers that "the daily press of our country rests on the big lie that capitalism is good for the American people. . . . It will always make sure that its readers stay loyal to the social system of Stock Exchanges and private, capitalist ownership."[16] The *Worker* espoused the beliefs and philosophies of the Communist Party. The CPUSA found it propitious to champion the cause of ending segregation as part of an overall campaign to end discrimination against blacks in all phases of American life. The CPUSA realized the possibilities of increasing its popularity by appealing to blacks and sympathetic whites. The party seized the issue of segregation in baseball because it represented one of the more obvious evidences of discrimination. The newspaper's journalists understood that ending discrimination in baseball could make a truly revolutionary change in American society.

The CPUSA found it difficult to achieve acceptability during the 1920s. It entered the 1930s, according to Earl Browder, the CPUSA's general secretary, with "a tattered remnant of seven thousand embittered members, a bad reputation as splitters, an unfavorable 'public image,' and an unknown, untried leadership."[17] During the decade the devastation caused by the Depression made people more receptive to radical politics and progressive social reform.[18] The CPUSA sought to establish itself.[19] In 1935 the international Communist Party, or Comintern, was aware that blacks were vital to the success of the

CPUSA. The Seventh World Congress of the Communist International called upon U.S. Communists to work with socialists to stop fascism and to defend democratic traditions. Communists were told to associate their movement with egalitarian principles, regardless of whether they embodied class struggle or explicitly advocated Marxist ideals or objectives. Soviet premier Vladimir Lenin had a keen sense of focusing the party's recruiting efforts on the people where resentment and hatred were greatest. Lenin's successor, Joseph Stalin, was interested in the discrimination of blacks in the United States.[20] Nathan Glazer, author of *The Social Basis of American Communism*, wrote that the Communist Party devoted more effort to the recruitment of blacks than any other social group, except possibly industrial workers and trade unionists. Blacks, after all, were the most oppressed people in the country.[21] This would, in turn, have an impact on baseball.

Worker sportswriters superimposed the capitalist hierarchy upon the U.S. professional sports establishment, declaring that professional athletes were workers, too, who labored but did not receive a fair share of the fruits of their labor, the same as any factory worker. Neither the athlete nor the worker had unions to protect his interests. In both cases their employers became wealthy off the profits of their work. By characterizing athletes in such a way, the Communists could provide sports coverage and commentary without appearing to approve of capitalist values. Other Communists were not convinced that the newspaper should have a sports page. "This is ridiculous," Rodney remembered another Communist Party member telling him. "It's kid stuff. Does it make sense for a hard-pressed, radical paper to give one-eighth of its space to games?"[22] When one reader admonished the *Worker* for inserting "radical propaganda in a sports column," Simon Gerson replied that the newspaper had an obligation to report sports different from the capitalist press. Gerson wrote that he did not think that New York Giants infielder Blondy Ryan, for example, was "a conscious agent of the capitalist class seeking to dope the workers with his swell infielding. That would be the sheerest nonsense." However, Gerson continued, when hundreds of ballplayers, "with the aid of hundreds of sportswriters, rivet the attention of millions of workers upon themselves rather than upon unemployment, wage cuts and wars, then we can draw the conclusion that Ryan, et al., unconsciously serve the purposes of the ruling class."[23]

Heywood Broun acknowledged that you could find the struggle between the owners and the working class in baseball. During the middle of the 1938 season, Rodney used Marxist ideology in a column condemning Detroit Tigers owner Walter O. Briggs for dismissing manager Mickey Cochrane, who, as player-manager, had led the team to pennants in 1934 and 1935 and second-place finishes to the Yankees in 1936 and 1937. To Rodney, the firing of Cochrane, whose playing career had ended when he was beaned — and nearly killed — by a pitched ball in 1937 demonstrated that workers were nothing but property to the ruling class. Broun quoted Rodney's column and then added in his own words: "Now he (Cochrane) is tossed out without notice. Mr. Briggs builds bodies, and maybe finds it hard to distinguish between a dented fender and a ball player with a fractured skull. Scrap iron is scrap iron in men or materials." Broun then quoted John Kieran of the *New York Times*, who said that Briggs had hired Cochrane and could fire him, and anybody who did not agree did not understand America. Broun then concluded by facetiously writing that Cochrane should be grateful for the Tigers for all they had given him. "Where's his gratitude? When he lay at the door of death after his skull was fractured in a ball game, Mr. Briggs paid all his hospital bills."[24] Rodney later praised Broun for his support of the Far Left, in general, and the *Daily Worker*, in particular. "A real sports fan, he was genuinely intrigued by the sight of a completely honest sports page," Rodney said.[25]

Rodney was born in 1911 in New York City. As the family's silk factory prospered, it moved to a bigger house in Brooklyn. Rodney became an avid Dodgers fan. But the Rodney family's affluence ended when the stock market crashed in 1929. Rodney said his politics were shaped in part by watching his family lose everything. My father "became an old man overnight," and his mother ended up running a boardinghouse. After high school Rodney worked a series of odd jobs during the day: he was a lifeguard at a resort, a gas station attendant, a shipping clerk, and a chauffeur.[26] At night he attended night school at New York University, where he picked up his first *Daily Worker*. "In the 1930s on any college campus in New York, if somebody wasn't a Communist, a socialist or a Trotskyist or some variation of radical," Rodney said, "they were pretty much brain dead."[27] Rodney began reading the newspaper but found the sports section too ideological. The newspaper did not cover sports, he said; it criticized them as the "opiate of the masses."[28]

At one point Rodney wrote to the editor suggesting how the newspaper could improve its sports coverage. The editor called Rodney for an interview and asked him to contribute articles to the newspaper — "gratis of course," Rodney remembered. "So I said, 'sure.'" He stayed with the paper until 1956 — except for a stint in the U.S. Army during World War II.[29] With Rodney as sports editor, the newspaper shifted from emphasizing amateur industrial and union league play to professional mainstream sports. As sports editor Rodney, a Jewish American, had a forum to advance his ideals of racial equality. Rodney later acknowledged that Hitler's rise to power prompted within him a "kind of Jewish consciousness."[30] These feelings, in turn, merged with his love of baseball. Rodney understood the significance of baseball to the American psyche. Baseball was, in more than name, the national pastime. To Rodney, separate leagues for white and black ballplayers was not just unfair or unsportsmanlike but un-American. Rodney also realized that if the newspaper wanted to write about the color line, it was theirs and theirs alone. "No one was covering it," he said.[31]

A lot of mainstream sportswriters acknowledged Jesse Owens's accomplishments in the 1936 Summer Olympics. Some, like Jimmy Powers, even recognized that American sports should no longer discriminate against blacks in baseball. For Rodney and the *Worker*, however, Owens's performance in Berlin was an awakening. Adolf Hitler's apparent snubbing of Owens provided U.S. Communists a bugle call for their campaign against discrimination in the United States, including Major League Baseball. On August 13, 1936, the *Worker* promoted the beginning of its campaign to desegregate baseball. Three days later Rodney wrote his page 1 editorial "Jim Crow Baseball Must End." The newspaper's campaign posited three arguments. First, it said blacks had proved their worthiness to participate in American professional sports through their success in the recently completed Summer Olympics. Second, Communists felt that racism was racism, regardless of whether it was perpetuated by Nazi Germany or by a democracy such as the United States. "There is not much difference between the Hitler who, like the coward he is, runs away before he will shake Jesse Owens' hand and the American coward, who won't give the same Negro equal rights, equal pay, and equal opportunities," Rodney wrote. And third, the newspaper's sportswriters argued that the addition of blacks would improve the level of competition in the big leagues. In short, as Rodney put it, baseball's color line not only was discriminatory because it prohibited blacks from organized baseball but also cheated fans because it detracted from the game's overall quality of play. Rodney agreed with Sam Lacy. Black players were denied the opportunity to play, and white spectators were denied the opportunity of watching them.

In his autobiography, *Press Box Red*, Rodney summarized the *Worker*'s strategies as follows: First, the newspaper wanted to "raise hell about the color ban and get it into the public consciousness," Rodney said. The issue was thus far restricted to the black press, he said, which had limited impact. Second, the newspaper publicized the talented stars of the Negro league. Third, the newspaper interviewed white Major League ballplayers and managers to see if they opposed integration; most of those they interviewed did not. Fourth, the newspaper confronted the commissioner and league presidents, asking them whether there was a rule or "gentlemen's agreement" that prohibited blacks. The newspapers quoted the baseball establishment as denying the existence of a rule forbidding teams from signing blacks. Fifth, Rodney said, the newspaper wanted to generate public interest in the campaign to integrate baseball.[32] To Major League Baseball, the *Worker* would be a persistent and unwanted intruder. Once the newspaper took on the issue of discrimination in Major League Baseball, it did not let up. It demonstrated an ability to pick through Jim Crow rhetoric to expose the unfounded fears of integration. The *Worker's* sportswriters gained early rhetorical victories of their own in their quest to overturn baseball's color ban.

The first victory, of sorts, came on August 23, 1936 — a week after the newspaper declared that "Jim Crow baseball must end." The newspaper quoted National League president Ford Frick, who said there was no ban that prohibited Major League teams from signing black ballplayers. "Beyond the fundamental requirement that a Major League player must have unique ability and good character and habits," Frick said, "I do not recall one instance where baseball has allowed either race, creed or color to enter into the question of the selection of its players." Frick said that the responsibility for signing blacks was with team owners and not with league executives. Ted Benson said Frick was merely passing the buck and urged readers to put pressure on baseball to admit blacks. "Let's hear from you fans. Tell the big league magnates what you want them to do about the Negro," he wrote. "Make baseball a truly national game."[33] If there was no rule prohibiting blacks, according to the *Worker*, then there were no blacks in baseball because there were none good enough. *Worker* sportswriters repeatedly told their readers of the talented stars of the Negro leagues who were indeed good enough for the Major Leagues. Columns and articles urged readers to attend Negro league games and see for themselves what was missing from the Major Leagues. The *Worker* also informed its readers of the history of the Negro leagues. From these stories, readers learned about the undiscovered world of black baseball.

In hopes of broadening the *Worker's* appeal, Rodney asked the New York Yankees' Dartmouth-educated third baseman, "Red" Rolfe, if he would write a column for the newspaper. Rolfe, who got his nickname because of his hair color and not his politics, agreed and began contributing to the newspaper during the 1937 World Series. Rolfe, Rodney said, knew the *Worker* was a Communist newspaper but did not inject politics into his writing. During the 1938 World Series, Rolfe wrote from the Yankees' perspective, and "Rip" Collins, whom Rodney described as a card-carrying member of the United Mine Workers, wrote from the perspective of the Chicago Cubs, the Yankees' opponent. Rolfe quit writing for the *Worker* in early 1939 under orders from his manager, Joe McCarthy, who complained that the column was taking up too much of his time. Rodney said that Rolfe never raised the color line and that the *Worker* sports editor never pressured the third baseman. "If I said to Rolfe, 'What do you think about Negro players? Shouldn't the Yankees have a Negro player?'" Rodney said, "Somebody probably would have said, 'See. They only wanted you to get the nigger question in.'"[34]

The *Worker*'s campaign, according to Rodney, was equal parts confrontation and education. "When the Negro Leagues played in New York, we'd cover them and highlight players we thought were good enough for the Big Leagues," Rodney said. The *Worker* was not the only New York City newspaper that covered the Negro leagues, Rodney said, but it was the only one that regularly raised the issue of baseball's color ban. "The other papers, like the *Times* and the *Post*, might have briefly reported a Negro league game," Rodney said. "But if Satchel Paige pitched a shutout or even if Josh Gibson hit the longest home run ever at Yankee Stadium, they'd never say, 'Why isn't that guy playing for a major-league team.'"[35]

Worker sportswriters also emphasized they were not alone in their belief that blacks should play in the Major Leagues. Whenever possible, the newspaper printed supporting opinions from white fans, players, managers, and other sportswriters. On August 30, 1936, the newspaper printed a letter from a reader in Philadelphia, who said there were twenty blacks who could play better than many of the players on the roster of that city's teams, the Phillies and Athletics. "I, for one, have always wondered why in a supposedly free and equal country such stupid discrimination must be shown," the letter said.[36] Whether to contradict Frick or merely educate its readers, the newspaper frequently quoted Major League ballplayers, including New York Yankees outfielder Joe DiMaggio, St. Louis Cardinals pitcher Dizzy Dean, retired Washington Senators pitcher Walter Johnson, and managers Leo Durocher and Bill McKechnie, who praised black players and expressed their support for desegregation. Other players and managers, however, would not. Rodney remembers an interview with Burleigh Grimes, who was then managing the Brooklyn Dodgers. Grimes, a former pitcher who had won 270 games in his Major League career, acknowledged that he had been impressed by black players during off-season exhibition games. "How would you feel about putting a Dodger uniform on Satchel Paige and Josh Gibson?" Rodney asked Grimes. The question made Grimes uncomfortable. "You're wasting your time," Grimes answered. "That'll never happen as long as there are segregated trains and restaurants." Rodney then said, "Can I say how good you think these players are?" "No, no," Grimes answered. "He didn't want to stick his head out," Rodney said.[37]

In January 1937 Mike Kantor quoted Dodgers president Judge Steven McKeever as saying that he would sign black players but did not have the authority to do so. He said that such a decision would have to come from Grimes — even though McKeever, as president, ranked higher on the team's hierarchy than the manager. But Grimes told Kantor that any decision to sign black players would ultimately come from Frick, the league's president. To the *Worker*, if there was not a gentlemen's agreement prohibiting blacks, there was certainly a conspiracy whereby no one — not the commissioner, league presidents, or team executives — would take responsibility for the color ban. *Worker* sportswriters continued to tell their readers that struggling teams like the Dodgers, Athletics, and Phillies could improve their lineups by signing Negro league stars. The newspaper reported that there was a rumor that Brooklyn would sign Satchel Paige but then dismissed it because it would require the approval of Grimes. "You see, Burleigh Grimes is a Southerner," Ted Benson wrote, "and Satchel Paige . . . is a negro."[38]

During the 1937 season reporters were interviewing Joe DiMaggio, then in his second year in the Major Leagues. When DiMaggio was asked to name the best pitcher he had ever faced, the Yankee center fielder replied, "Satchel Paige." DiMaggio had faced Paige during a series of postseason exhibition games. When Rodney heard DiMaggio's comment, he knew the *Worker* had a headline for the next day.[39] Other white sportswriters heard DiMaggio's comment but did not print it. "I wasn't the only one he mentioned it to. I was the only one who printed it," Rodney said.[40] Rodney then sought out Paige. In the course of their conversation, Paige issued a challenge to the Major Leagues: "Let the winners of the World Series play an all-star Negro team just one game at Yankee Stadium — and if we don't beat them before a packed house they don't have to pay." When Rodney asked Paige why he appeared so confident that a team of black all-stars could beat the World Series champions, Paige told him that no team with white big leaguers had ever beaten the black all-stars in postseason games in California. Paige then added that blacks were not excluded from the big leagues because of either the players or the fans. "Must be just a few men who don't want us to play Big League ball. The players are okay and the crowds are with us," Paige said in a September 16, 1937, story, adding that baseball fans wanted a game between black and white all-stars at Yankee Stadium. "Just let them take a vote of the fans whether they want us in the game. I've been all over the country and I know it would be one hundred to one in favor of such a game. Yankee Stadium couldn't hold the fans who'd come out for that game." Paige, according to Rodney, wanted his challenge in the white newspapers, but mainstream sportswriters would not report it — just as they did not report DiMaggio's comment about Paige. "The challenge was never accepted, of course," Rodney said. "And none of the other papers carried it. That doesn't mean the other sportswriters and the baseball establishment didn't know about it."[41]

Whenever possible, the *Worker* quoted from mainstream sportswriters who expressed support of desegregation from other newspapers. In 1937 it quoted Pat Gannon of the *Milwaukee Journal*, who wrote there were at least ten black ballplayers in Cuba who could play in the Major Leagues if given the opportunity. They could not play — not because there was a color line, he added sarcastically, but because Major League Baseball insisted that no blacks were good enough. On May 2, 1937, "Doc" Daugherty wrote that an informal poll of New York City sportswriters had concluded that five of the eight surveyed supported allowing blacks in baseball. Daugherty praised Hugh Bradley of the *New York Post* and Dan Parker of the *New York Daily Mirror*, who, he said, "lifts the lid from the unsavory professional sports pot every now and again and reveals that the stew meat is putrid." In 1938 the *Worker* quoted Bradley as saying that there were at least twenty black ballplayers good enough for the Major Leagues. Later that year Rodney praised Jimmy Powers for his repeated attacks against baseball's color ban. He called Powers "the most articulate and consistent supporter of the Negro stars since the campaign to end Jim Crow baseball began to catch hold."[42]

The *Worker* often miscalculated both the severity of racism and the opposition to it. Sportswriters often wrote that integration was just around the corner when in reality it was years away. The newspaper's inflated optimism could have been part of a strategy to draw others into the campaign, or it was an example of its sportswriters' naïveté, or perhaps it was both. Too often the newspaper was guilty of misreading the writing on the wall, of being caught up in a crusade without an understanding or an appreciation of the context of what was happening elsewhere, or the newspaper simply underestimated the depth and breadth of racism in America. On September 17, 1937, a day after publishing the interview with DiMaggio, a *Worker* headline said, "Jim Crow in Baseball Nearing End." On September 26 the newspaper stated, "Jim Crow in Major League Baseball Is on Its Last Legs." On December 27 the newspaper said it had struck a blow against Jim Crow baseball and that "for the first time the whole country was acutely aware" of discrimination in the national pastime and that progress had been made to end it.

Although one could doubt the veracity of some of the *Worker*'s claims, no one could doubt its persistence. In 1937 the newspaper published more than fifty articles that mentioned the campaign to end baseball's color ban. In 1938 it published nearly a hundred articles. The *Worker* directed the brunt of its criticism at the owners but also acknowledged the culpability of the nation's sportswriters. In February Bill Mills wrote that sportswriters had characterized the success of Jesse Owens and Joe Louis as atypical for black athletes. Those writers, Mills said, wanted to reassure their readers that most blacks were inferior to white athletes. Owens's and Louis's success was not because of "structural peculiarities," as a Hearst newspaper columnist had written, but because of the same things that made a white athlete great. "All in all," Mills wrote, "I think it much fairer to give credit to the things that make a champion in any sport and not to some phony 'structural peculiarity.' These things are sound coaching, rigid training, constant practice, and competitive spirit. It is impossible to confine these qualities to one race."[43] On April 20, 1938, Mills blamed baseball owners for the color ban but also criticized sportswriters and fans for not putting more pressure on the baseball establishment. "The blame for the absence of Negro players rests squarely on the shoulders of . . . hypocritical owners." If mainstream newspapers would not pressure owners, then others needed to do so. "Therefore," Mills said, "it only remains for some public spirited citizens to form such an organization and get to work." On April 26, 1938, a few days before May Day, the International Workers Day, the *Worker* published an editorial cartoon showing a baseball player holding a bat that said, "May Day Unity," looking off into the distance as if he had just hit a home run. The cartoon's caption said, "Over the Fence!"

Black sportswriters agreed with the Communists on the need to end baseball's color line. Black sportswriters also knew they needed the cooperation of whites to end the color line. But this did not mean they needed the Communists. Influential black sportswriters — like Sam Lacy and Wendell Smith — may have shared the same objective with the Communists but distanced themselves from the Communists for reasons that were more ideological than editorial. Smith understood that the blacks and Communists were on the same side — and he was willing to work with Rodney if it might lead to desegregation. His relationship with the Communists, therefore, was one of convenience. According to Rodney, he and Smith had an arrangement whereby the *Worker* and *Courier* would print one another's articles — though, as Rodney noted, the *Courier* rarely mentioned the Communists in print.[44] During the summer of 1939 the *Courier* ran a series of articles quoting a number of managers and players who supported signing black players. The *Worker* reprinted part of the series. *Courier* sports editor Wendell Smith responded with a letter that thanked Rodney and the *Worker* for its contribution to the campaign. By publishing the letter, Rodney could tell his readers that the newspaper's effort was being recognized, but it also represented a success in the Communist Party's bid for acceptance in the black community.[45]

Lacy, however, agreed with neither the *Worker*'s politics nor its methods. Lacy preferred to work within the existing system with sympathetic Major League executives. He feared that both he and his work were tainted by the involvement of Communists. In an interview Lacy said, "It upset me that I might be considered a Communist." Those fears were justified. Both the baseball establishment and right-wing columnists like Westbrook Pegler charged black social activists with being Communists. Lacy never wanted — or, for that matter, had — anything to do with the Communists or any part of communism. "From the beginning he would have nothing to do with the *Daily Worker*," Rodney said. "'I don't want to get mixed up with that,'" he said.[46] Rodney said Lacy objected to being criticized in print. Lacy once quoted Clark Griffith, who said black players did not have the skills for the big leagues, and even if they did, they would be treated so poorly by white players and fans that desegregation would be neither in the best interests of blacks nor in the best interests of the big leagues. The owner suggested it might be possible for the Major Leagues to add a separate minor league of black players. Rodney questioned Lacy for not putting more pressure on Griffith. He also said separate leagues were unnecessary because that notion perpetuated Jim Crow and there were blacks already capable of playing in the big leagues. Rodney told Griffith that adding blacks to the Senators would strengthen the team and increase crowds at Griffith Stadium.[47]

Communist sportswriters had doors open to them that were closed to black sportswriters. *Worker* sportswriters were permitted to join the Baseball Writers' Association. Rodney initially had trouble receiving a membership because the *Worker* had only recently added a sports section. "It took a year before I was admitted as a working profes-sional for a regular sports section," Rodney said. "They wanted to see that we were really covering sports and not just writing 'Communist propaganda.'"[48] Once he was admitted he received his membership, which he called "a magic pass onto the field."[49] His membership card gave him access to locker rooms, dugouts, press boxes, and the play-ing fields. Other sportswriters, however, did not approve of Rodney's membership. Dan Daniel, Rodney said, "hated the idea of a Communist in the press box. . . . He had a special venom about it, as though his father had suffered because of Communists or something."[50] Jimmy Cannon of the *New York Post* once called Rodney a "young snotnose" in a column because Rodney had included a "class angle" in a piece he had written. Rodney said that some sportswriters had nothing to do with him because of his politics. He said Milton Gross of the *Post* never spoke to him. *New York Times* sportswriters John Drebinger and Lloyd McGowan would say hello to him but would otherwise have nothing to say to him. They were exceptions, Rodney said. He said he ate and drank with other sportswriters. Others — like Dick Young of the *New York Daily News* — sought him out with certain stories because they were forbidden from writing anything about the color line. "I can't tell you how many times they would say, 'Here's a little something. I can't use it, but I'd love to see it in print,'" he said.[51] It was as if, Rodney observed, "we were the conscience of the trade."[52]

In addition, in the late 1930s and 1940s, the radical Left also had friends in New York politics. Communists Benjamin Davis Jr. and Peter Cacchione served on the New York City Council. During the spring of 1939 New York state senator Charles Perry introduced a resolution that condemned baseball for discriminating against black ballplayers by preventing them from the game. "There are in the United States many baseball players whose skill is equal to or surpass that of many now playing in the many leagues of organized baseball," according to the resolution, which the *Worker* published on May 21. The resolution was then forwarded to Landis and the presidents of the American and National leagues, William Harridge and Ford Frick. According to Rodney, the resolution was written by Mike Singer, the *Worker*'s Albany correspondent.[53] In 1943 Perry introduced another resolution criticizing organized professional baseball for its unwritten law barring "certain people because of their race."[54] In 1945 Representative Vito Marcantonio of Brooklyn introduced a resolution in the U.S. House of Representatives authorizing the U.S. Commerce Department to investigate racial discrimination in Major League Baseball.

The *Worker* would be successful in creating, organizing, and publicizing cooperation between itself and other socially progressive organizations such as labor unions. The *Worker* reported that the Communist-run National Negro Congress's Brooklyn branch sent a petition to the Dodgers to sign Paige.[55] The Young Communist League (YCL) also was heavily involved in promoting the desegregation of baseball. In September 1939 the *Young Communist Review* quoted Randy Dixon of the *Pittsburgh Courier* as saying that the Communists were distributing a petition calling for the entry of blacks into organized baseball. The *Worker* let its readers know that the newspaper was getting into the right hands. During one Negro league game, Young Communist League members were circulating petitions. On July 24, 1939,

Rodney reported that a petition was given to A. Philip Randolph, the influential black labor leader, who, after signing it, reportedly told the sportswriter, "That's a wonderful campaign your paper is carrying on, and it's getting results." YCL members collected signatures outside Major League ballparks, calling for the inclusion of blacks into the national pastime.[56] The *Worker* said petitions with the signatures of more than a million names were sent to Landis, Frick, and Harridge. The petitions read, in part, "Our country guarantees the rights of life, liberty, and the pursuit of happiness to all, regardless of race, creed, or color. Yet in our national sport we find discrimination against outstanding negro baseball players who are equal to or surpass in skill many of the present players in the National and American Leagues."

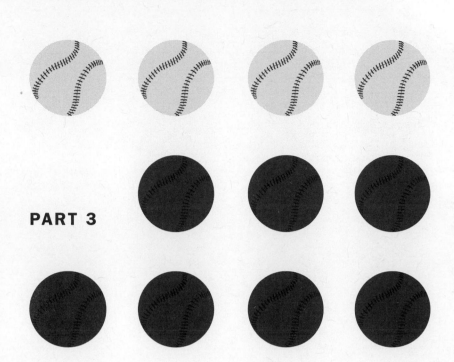

PART 3

CHAPTER 5

"*L'AFFAIRE* JAKE POWELL"

During a pregame interview at Comiskey Park in Chicago on July 29, 1938, WGN radio announcer Bob Elson asked New York Yankees outfielder Jake Powell what he did during the off-season. Powell said that he was a policeman in Dayton, Ohio, where he kept in shape by cracking "niggers" over the head with his nightstick. Before the next day's game, a delegation of blacks presented a petition to umpires demanding that Powell be banned from baseball for life. Commissioner Kenesaw Mountain Landis suspended the ballplayer for ten days. The *Sporting News* reported that it was the first time that a Major League ballplayer was suspended for a racist remark. While baseball had thus far turned a deaf ear to criticism of its color ban in the black press, it could neither dismiss nor deny the outcry over Powell's remark, made live on radio and heard by thousands, perhaps tens of thousands, of listeners. Author Donn Rogosin suggested that not only did the incident solidify the sense of outrage against baseball's color line, but it illustrated the instability of segregated baseball, where a single intemperate remark embroiled the sport in controversy.[1] Both Commissioner Landis and the Yankees were forced to respond. It is doubtful whether Landis, given his position on segregation, would have suspended Powell without outside pressure.[2] The Yankees' management, responding to the threat of a boycott of their games, met with black journalists and activists, asking what could be done to improve relations. The team ordered Powell on an apology tour of black newspapers and black-owned bars in Harlem.

"*L'affaire* Jake Powell," as the *Nation* called it, was important because it united those who had begun campaigning for integrated baseball — blacks, Communists, and social progressives. The *Nation* said the Powell incident captured the hypocrisy of segregated baseball, noting that the baseball owners — "none of whom allowed Negroes on their team — were quick to denounce Powell's uncouth chauvinism."[3] The publicity surrounding the Powell story made it harder — though obviously not impossible — for baseball to ignore the issue of race. If Powell contributed to desegregating the sport, this was not the story's only irony. For instance, Powell was suspended by Landis, who enforced baseball's discrimination against blacks for twenty years. In addition, in 1936 the Washington Senators traded Powell to the Yankees for the virulent racist Ben Chapman of Alabama. Finally, Powell never worked as a police officer in Dayton — though a decade later he died as a petty criminal in a police station in Washington DC. Powell's claim of being a police officer went unchallenged in the mainstream press.

Alvin Jacob Powell was born in Silver Spring, Maryland, in 1908, and grew up in the shadows of Washington DC. Garret Waters, who managed a local semipro team, said Powell was one of the best ballplayers to come out of the Washington DC area. When Powell learned that Senators owner Clark Griffith would be at a game to scout a pitching prospect, Powell said, "Pitcher? I'll make him look at me today." He had four hits in four at-bats and made a number of good defensive plays in the game. Griffith signed Powell.[4] Before being promoted to the Major Leagues, Powell played for several Minor League teams, including the Dayton, Ohio, Ducks. He was known as a hustler — on and off the field. During a road trip to Zanesville, Ohio, he tried to leave his hotel room with a circular fan, the drapes, and the bedspread, but was caught. No charges were filed after he returned everything. "He probably would have taken the mattress if he could have got it in his suitcase," his Dayton manager remembered. Powell and his wife made their home in Dayton. Newspaper clippings portray him as "irresponsible" and "fun-loving," someone who took baseball seriously but not much else. He talked frequently with friends of joining the city's police department. According to one account, he applied once but was rejected; according to another, he was offered a job but rejected it, thinking he could become a police officer when he retired from baseball. If he were a cop, he would use his nightstick on blacks, he used to joke to friends.[5] Powell played three games in the Majors in 1930 before being sent back to the Minors. After hitting .361 with Albany in the triple-A International League, he returned to the Major Leagues with Washington for nine games in 1934. In his first full season in 1935, he hit .312 with ninety-eight runs batted in. Powell's behavioral problems surfaced with Washington, when he was fined two hundred dollars for missing the team's train out of Florida to go north to begin the season.[6] The Senators wanted to unload the uncontrollable Powell when his creditors in Dayton threatened to sue the team to settle the ballplayer's debts.[7]

In mid-June 1936 Washington traded Powell to New York for Ben Chapman. The Yankees, in turn, wanted to get rid of Chapman, who had seen his playing time decrease with the addition of Joe DiMaggio to the team's outfield. Chapman had also held out during spring training, demanding to be traded. The Powell-Chapman trade, as it turned out, was a racist-for-racist, straight up. While playing for New York in a game against Washington in 1933, Chapman provoked a fistfight with Washington second baseman Buddy Myer, a Jew. Benches emptied, and spectators also came onto the field. Chapman was joined by his teammate "Dixie" Walker, a fellow Alabaman who also did little to conceal his racist attitudes. After the fight had been broken up, Chapman was being escorted off the field when he sucker punched Washington pitcher Earl Whitehall. Chapman, Walker, and Myer were ejected from the game.[8] In addition, Chapman had long feuded with Yankees manager Joe McCarthy.[9] Chapman had also become unpopular with the team's management after making anti-Semitic slurs at Jewish fans at Yankee Stadium.[10]

Powell, too, was a fierce athletic competitor who often provoked fights and confrontations with opponents. During a game against Detroit in May 1936, Powell ran over the Tigers' Jewish first baseman, Hank Greenberg, on a routine play. The collision broke Greenberg's wrist and ended his season. Because of the deliberate nature of the collision, Powell was heavily criticized. A few days before Powell was traded, Powell ran over Chicago White Sox second baseman Jackie Hayes and then two innings later first baseman Zeke Bonura. When Powell came to bat the next time, Chicago pitcher Ted Lyon hit him with a pitch.[11] After being traded to New York, Powell collided with Washington first baseman Joe Kuhel, resulting in a fistfight between the two ballplayers. Several Senators came off the bench and jumped on Powell before umpires broke it up. When Powell took his position in left field, Washington fans began throwing bottles at Powell. Powell waved the groundskeepers away and began picking up the bottles and throwing them back at the fans.[12] Powell inspired such ill feelings that he was frequently thrown at by pitchers. In May 1938 Boston Red Sox pitcher Archie McCain threw at him twice before finally hitting him, prompting a fight between Powell and Boston manager Joe Cronin. Powell was fined and suspended for three games.[13] During the off-season Powell earned extra money barnstorming against black teams.[14]

Powell hit .302 in 80 games after joining the Yankees, who won the

American League pennant in 1936. He led the team in hitting and runs scored during the World Series — the first of four straight series championships for the Yankees, who had a lineup that included Joe DiMaggio, Lou Gehrig, Tony Lazzeri, Bill Dickey, and pitchers Red Ruffing and Lefty Gomez, all members of baseball's Hall of Fame. Within a few hours after receiving his World Series check of five thousand dollars, Powell gambled it away. Columnist Vincent X. Flaherty wrote that Powell once drove home, got up later, and discovered his car was stolen. Police later found the car in his garage, where he had left it.[15] In 1937 Powell played in 97 of the team's 154 games and hit .263. In 1938 his playing time was further reduced — particularly after his "nightstick" comment. By late July 1938 Powell had played in only 30 games and had 134 plate appearances. He was batting .254. After Powell finished batting practice on July 29, WGN broadcaster Bob Elson asked him for a dugout interview, and the ballplayer obliged. As soon as Powell made his derogatory remark, the station cut off the interview. Unaware he had said anything offensive, Powell went to the team's dressing room to change into his uniform.[16]

WGN immediately heard from offended listeners. Hundreds called the radio station and Landis's office, which was located in Chicago. Others called the Yankees' hotel in Chicago. After Elson cut off Powell, the station broadcast several apologies and pointed out that it could not control the remark "because of the spontaneous nature of the interview."[17] Elson also apologized.[18] Powell initially denied making the remark. "To the best of my knowledge," he told reporters, "I said I was a member of the police force in Dayton during the winter months, and simply explained my beat was in the colored section of town."[19] There was some question over the precise language used by Powell. The station did not tape the broadcast. This left Powell's words open to interpretation. Newspapers had different accounts of what was said. To white sportswriters what Powell said was "careless" or "uncomplimentary." For instance, the *New York Times* characterized the comment as "a flippant remark that was taken to be offensive" by Chicago's black population. The *Chicago Tribune* said that the comment had been made "in the jocular vein," adding that the ballplayer had "used a colloquialism resented by" blacks. The *Washington Post* said that Powell had made an "uncomplimentary remark about a portion of the population." *Post* columnist Shirley Povich quipped that blacks in Dayton had little to worry about if Powell "is no more effective with a police club that he is with his bat." The Associated Press (AP) characterized the comments as "slighting remarks" against blacks. This description was repeated in the *Daily News* in Dayton, where Powell lived in the off-season. The *Journal*, the other daily in that city, said nothing about the incident. The *Sporting News* described what Powell had said in the interview as "remarks considered derogatory by the colored race."[20]

Whereas the story received relatively little attention in mainstream dailies, black weeklies put it on page 1 and included more details and more commentary. Floyd Calvin of the *New York Age* wrote that whereas the white press did not take up the issue, black newspapers did. In a page 1 story on August 6, the *Chicago Defender* reported that Elson asked, "How do you keep in trim during the winter months in order to keep up your batting average?" Powell then replied, "Oh, that's easy, I'm a policeman, and I beat niggers over the head with my blackjack." The same language appeared in the *Dayton Forum*. Leon Hardwick of the *Baltimore Afro-American* quoted Powell as saying he worked the winter months as a cop in Dayton "cracking N——— ———s over the head." The *New York Age* quoted the ballplayer as saying he spent most of his time as a policeman "whipping the heads of niggers." The *Pittsburgh Courier* reported that Powell's "chief hobby was 'hitting niggers over the head.'" The *Philadelphia Afro-American* editorialized that Powell merely reflected the opinions of the baseball establishment, which had kept the game segregated. Ed Harris of the *Philadelphia Tribune* said the story had received little attention in the daily press by writing that "it was astonishing the ease with which our so-called 'fair' sportswriters found it convenient not to say anything about the case of that half-wit Jake Powell." Fay Young, however, mentioned that the *Daily Worker*, Jimmy Powers, and Westbrook Pegler had criticized baseball's handling of the Powell incident.[21]

Powell did not accompany the Yankees for the next day's game at Comiskey Park. In the morning Louis Comiskey, owner of the White Sox, heard the protests of a delegation that included the executive secretary of the Chicago Urban League and executives of the *Chicago Defender*, including Fay Young.[22] When umpire-in-chief Harry Geisel and the other umpires came onto the field before the game, they were met by a second delegation of representatives of Chicago's black community that presented a resolution demanding that Powell apologize and be suspended from baseball for life. A formal petition would be sent to Landis.[23] Other organizations that called for suspending Powell included the NAACP, the National Negro Congress, the International Workers Order (IWO), and the Packing House Workers Organizing Committee.[24] In his official statement announcing the suspension of Powell, Landis said, "In a dugout interview before Friday's game by a sports announcer, player Jake Powell of the New York Yankees made an uncomplimentary reference to a portion of the population. Although the commissioner believes the remark was due more to carelessness than intent, player Powell is suspended for 10 days." David Pietrusza, Landis's biographer, said the commissioner's prompt action was uncustomary because of his "less-than-progressive reputation on social issues," but also because he typically let league officials handle their own affairs. "Yet in the Powell case Landis — with little prodding from the white press (who virtually ignored the incident) — jumped in feet first," Pietrusza said. Powell's reaction was brief: "I'm suspended. That's all there is to it."[25]

The Yankees did not question the suspension but also did not criticize Powell. General manager Ed Barrow said the ballplayer's comments did not reflect the attitudes of the team's management. In an interview with the *Pittsburgh Courier*, Barrow apologized for Powell's remark, calling it a "slip of the tongue." Barrow said blacks were "justified" in reacting angrily. "The entire Yankee management, from Mr. Ruppert, the owner, on down, regret the incident very much," Barrow told the *Courier.* "We have talked to Jake and he feels very badly about it because he says it just popped out and he didn't intend it as an insult to the Negro race."[26] Barrow added there was nothing more the team could do. Barrow said he had spoken with his two "colored servants," who told him they thought it was just an unfortunate mistake and would not happen again.[27] In addition, manager Joe McCarthy said Powell meant no harm and blamed the radio station for the incident. "Perhaps he just meant to get off a wisecrack. So the radio people ran off cold with apologies and I'm out a ballplayer for 10 days in the thick of a pennant race," said McCarthy, adding there would be no more radio interviews with any of his ballplayers without a prepared script.[28]

An editorial in the *Sporting News,* presumably written by J. G. Taylor Spink, used practically the same language as Landis by characterizing Powell's comment as "careless" and not intentional. According to the editorial, the remedy against such remarks was restricting radio interviews. The editorial agreed with McCarthy. "Powell was on the spot and was the victim of circumstances, which should not be held against him by the fans," it said. "Other players, in other instances, might offend other groups." In his column in the *Sporting News,* Dan Daniel reported that the controversy would lead to a ban on broadcast interviews of ballplayers. Daniel called Powell the first player in baseball to be suspended for using derogatory language, adding that he thought the controversy would quickly fade away with no impact on the ballplayer or his career. Daniel was sympathetic to the ballplayer. "Powell could have been more careful," Daniel said. "But he is a hustling player, aggressive, and always getting into a jam."[29] To Daniel, talking of cracking blacks over the head with a nightstick was equivalent to taking an extra base on a hit. To both Spink and Daniel, Powell was the victim of circumstances.

Los Angeles Times sportswriter Jack Gallagher wrote that Powell had been baited by Bob Elson. Gallagher also blamed Powell's troubles not on the ballplayer but on "impromptu interviews on the radio." He said Landis should forbid any ballplayer from any interviews unless there was a written script that had been prepared in advance and approved by the ballplayer's team. Gallagher asserted that ballplayers had long complained that Chicago ballparks — Wrigley Field and Comiskey Park — were "infested with radio announcers" who "stick mikes under the players' noses and boldly start interviews." Gallagher said what had happened to Powell could have happened to other ballplayers. Gallagher said that Powell was receiving a lot of support throughout the Major Leagues. "They might even make a purse to reimburse him for the ten day suspension inflicted by Judge Landis," Gallagher said.[30]

Pegler, on the contrary, wrote one of the most scathing indictments of the color line by any mainstream journalist during the decades of segregated baseball. He used specific rather than vague language when quoting Powell, telling readers that the ballplayer had said he hit "niggers" over the head with his club while working as a police officer. Pegler recognized that Landis and the baseball establishment had enforced baseball's racist color line and then suspended Powell for making a racist statement. Baseball, Pegler said, "has always treated the Negroes as Adolf Hitler treats the Jews." Pegler, a former sports columnist, had both the knowledge and the conservative politics to challenge baseball on its own ground and not be dismissed as a communist sympathizer. Pegler directed his outrage at Landis and the baseball establishment for perpetuating a racist policy and informed readers of the injustice of segregation. If Babe Ruth had been black, Pegler wrote, he would "not have risen above the rank and pay of the leaky-roof leagues in which dark men operate as semi-pros."[31]

In addition, Pegler challenged baseball's argument that there were no blacks in the big leagues because none had the ability or because black and white ballplayers could not share a ball field. For decades, he said, white ballplayers had competed against blacks during the off-season. He wrote that Major League teams avoided exhibitions against black teams for fear of losing. He admitted that southern laws and customs would put restrictions on blacks; however, there were no such restrictions in the North. If a big league team were to experiment with a black player, it would soon learn that "customers would suffer no shock, and the Southern white boys would find after a few games that it didn't hurt them much after all." Remarks by Jake Powell, he said, were a natural and unavoidable reaction as long as there was a color line. "Powell can argue plausibly that he got his cue from the very men whose hired disciplinarian has benched him for an idle remark," Pegler said.[32]

Los Angeles Times columnist E. V. Durling praised Pegler. Durling criticized the color line in baseball for prohibiting blacks from organized baseball. "A Negro boxer, jockey, actor, singer or dancer can realize his talents to the full extent," he said, "but a Negro baseball player, of which there have been very great ones, must pick up what he can around the sandlots and in his semi pro ranks." *New York Post* columnist Hugh Bradley accused Landis and baseball of "smug hypocrisy." Baseball executives suspended Powell, and then, he said, "they calmly proceed with their own economic boycott against this minority people." The *Nation* wrote that baseball was quick to denounce Powell — even though no team had any blacks on its roster. *Daily Worker* sports editor Lester Rodney also recognized the irony of the suspension coming from Landis, the commissioner of a sport "that continues the un-American practice of discrimination against the race that has given so much to the sports world." Rodney called on baseball executives to suspend themselves. He acknowledged Powell's reputation as a dirty player, noting that he had run over Hank Greenberg and been involved in a fight with Joe Cronin. Although the *Sporting News* published this information, the *Worker* used far stronger language, characterizing the ballplayer as "a contemptible rat." The *Daily Worker* said that many people wanted Powell expelled from baseball and fired from the Dayton Police Department.[33]

The contrast in coverage between white and black newspapers was apparent in Powell's hometown of Dayton. The *Daily News* reported in a three-paragraph story on its front page that Powell had been suspended. In its sports section, it published a separate story with more details, including the ballplayer's denial that he had made the racist remark. In addition, it said that Powell had once played for the Dayton Ducks and been offered a job by the police department but had rejected it to play baseball. The *Journal* did not mention the incident until Powell returned to the field after serving his suspension. By contrast, the story received two front-page stories in the *Dayton Forum*, the city's black weekly. One story said that Powell had told a radio interviewer that he was a policeman in Dayton, where he "beat niggers over the head with a blackjack." A sidebar quoted the city's director of public safety, who said the ballplayer had never been an employee of the police department. "In so many words," the article added, the city official "branded as lies the alleged statement made over the air of the big-mouthed, cocky professional baseball player." The *Chicago Defender* also published a statement by the mayor of Dayton denying that Powell was a police officer. It told its readers that Ruppert had asked the Dayton Police Department to "overlook Mr. Powell's thoughtless blunder and give him a second chance."[34] But the Dayton Police Department could not have fired Powell if it wanted. Powell did not work as a police officer in Dayton or in any other city. Newspapers — with the exception of the *Dayton Forum* and *Chicago Defender* — made no attempt to verify whether Powell was a police officer.

To black weeklies the Powell incident provided an opportunity to channel their long-standing indignation toward collective action. *Baltimore Afro-American* columnist Leon H. Hardwick wrote that athletes like Powell "poison the minds of fair-minded" sports fans. He said Powell's defenders had called the comments inadvertent and not deliberate. "It's the unguarded moments that show a man for what he is," Hardwick said. Hardwick praised Landis for suspending Powell but added that baseball had underestimated the problem, which the columnist suggested might "yet develop into something even more serious." *Norfolk Journal and Guide* columnist E. B. Rea said if the Yankees did not do

something about Powell, not only would thousands of fans stay away
from their ballpark, but others might seek revenge against Powell. Ed
Harris predicted that Powell's remark could cost the Yankees economically. "The Yankees and the players on other teams have got a good
lesson in just what decency and a sense of non-prejudice is worth," he
said, "by the hard way — the cash box."[35]

The *Defender* reported the black community was incensed over
the remark, adding that the city's racial climate was the worst since its
race riot in 1919. An editorial called Landis's suspension insufficient.
It called Powell "a skunk," "a riot breeder," "a professional bully," and
a "'riot breeder' clothed in the uniform of law and order." It added,
"For the good of all, Jake Powell should be banned from organized
baseball and discharged from the Dayton, Ohio, police force." Fay
Young used equally strong language. "Jake Powell is the type that causes
race riots," he said. "It is easier to get rid of a skunk like him than to
spend hundreds of thousands of dollars to put an end to the trouble he
will stir." The newspaper included a brief, albeit possibly apocryphal,
item that Powell had been a spectator during a game with the Tigers
in Detroit when someone yelled, "Say again what you said over the
radio." When he turned around he saw black heavyweight champion
Joe Louis glaring at him.[36]

The *Defender* used the threat of an economic boycott to make certain
they were not only heard but listened to. The newspaper, in an open
letter to brewer Jacob Ruppert, Old Gold cigarettes (the tobacco company that sponsored the broadcast of the interview), and the citizens
of Dayton, demanded that Powell be banned from baseball and fired
from the Dayton Police Department and insisted that Ruppert and Old
Gold cigarettes apologize to black America.[37] The Yankees defended
their record of fair treatment toward blacks in an interview with an
American Negro Press reporter. Ed Barrow said that the team distributed hundreds of complimentary tickets every year to black spectators,
donated regularly to the Harlem branch of the YMCA, and hired blacks
as plainclothes security officers to patrol the stands where blacks sat.

Barrow also said the Yankees traded Ben Chapman after he made anti-Semitic comments to spectators. But the team had no immediate plans to trade Powell. It considered Powell a good player, adding, however, that if the fans did not want him, "we will have to release him." Barrow said he did not think the team owned any responsibility for the slur. He blamed the radio station for airing the interview. The story concluded by quoting Barrow as saying that the team would not permit any more radio broadcasts in Chicago.[38] The Yankees had indeed traded Chapman to Washington for a lesser player in Powell. Chapman had been a solid hitter for the Yankees since 1930, hitting .299 or better five years and hitting .289 during his other full season. He had dropped to .266 in 1936 when he was traded. In return, the team got Powell, a lesser talent who had been relegated to a part-time player.

Defender columnist Al Monroe reported that Yankees manager Joe McCarthy wanted to get rid of Powell because he "does not particularly care for Southerners." Monroe said Chapman became expendable because he was "a southerner with southern ideas."[39] Why then did the Yankees not get rid of Powell? Perhaps they tried to trade him but could not find another team who wanted him. Why then did they not release him? The Yankees asked the editor of the *Amsterdam News* what the team could do to improve relations with the black community. When they were told they should trade or release Powell, they responded that it would be unfair to the ballplayer who had contributed to the team's success.[40] But Powell was no Joe DiMaggio or Bill Dickey or Lefty Gomez. The Yankees could have released Powell and gone on winning. One can only speculate why the team kept Powell. Perhaps the team's management did not want anyone else dictating personnel decisions. Yet the team had traded Chapman. Or perhaps the Yankees management simply did not understand what the fuss was about. Instead of releasing the ballplayer, they kept him on the team's roster but did not play him.

The *New York Age* and *Amsterdam News* reported that blacks were calling for Powell's expulsion from baseball and that the number of names on a petition to ban Powell was increasing every day.[41] The news-paper's sports editor, St. Clair Bourne, sent a telegram to the Yankees demanding a stronger punishment for the ballplayer. As long as Powell continued to wear a Yankees uniform, he said, the team would be "just a bunch of mugs named 'Cracker,' regardless of how many pennants the team had won."[42] The *Age* reported that hundreds of letters had poured into the Yankees' office. The newspaper printed a letter by Dr. Channing Tobias, who served on the national board of the YMCA, to Joe McCarthy. Tobias said it was disturbing to read that Powell said he spent his winters "cracking niggers over the head" while working as a police officer in Dayton. But he was more disturbed by the explanation of McCarthy, who said Powell was just trying to "get off a wisecrack." If a player had said he spent the winters "cracking dogs over the head," he probably would have been suspended or released, Tobias said. Even if Powell had been joking, as McCarthy suggested, Tobias wondered about the timing of such a wisecrack, given the racism in both Europe and America. As a Catholic, which had been discriminated against in the recent past, Tobias said McCarthy should have been more sensi-tive to bigotry.[43]

Whether it was the threat of a boycott, the petition drive, or some-thing else, the Yankees ordered Powell on an apology tour of black newspapers, businesses, and bars. Powell began at the New York office of the *Chicago Defender*. The *Defender* published a photo of Powell with the headline: "Jake Powell 'Begs Pardon.'" The newspaper published Powell's letter of apology. In it he said he regretted his slur and asked to be forgiven by those he had insulted. He probably should have quit there; instead, he added, "I have two members of your race taking care of my home while myself and wife are away and I think they are two of the finest people in the world. I do hundreds of favors for them daily." Al Monroe wrote that Powell begged for forgiveness. "Can't you please tell them I am sorry," he said. "I wouldn't harm anyone. I beg their forgiveness. Tell them through your paper that I shall do anything to atone for my admitted wrong doings."[44]

In the days following the team's return to New York, Powell visited
a number of Harlem bars, including the Mimo Club, where a local
mover and shaker named Hubert Julian introduced himself. Julian told
Powell he could "fix" the ballplayer's problem and then accompanied
the ballplayer to the rest of the bars. Powell said he had not intended
to hurt anyone's feelings. He bought drinks for the patrons and offered
to appear at a benefit game for a black charity.[45] Having apologized
in the office of the *Defender*, Powell then denied making the remark
in a written statement. During the interview Powell said Elson asked
him why he lived in Dayton during the off-season, and he replied
that he worked as a police officer in the black section of town. Powell
was then asked how he kept in shape working as a police officer. "I
answered that if a fellow worked hard enough at whatever he did, he
could find it easy enough to keep in shape," Powell said in his statement. Powell then said he heard the team's trainer yelling at him so
he left the microphone. Then, according to Powell, Elson said, "Say,
Jake, how about a few questions about your work among the Niggers?"
Powell said he then yelled back, "I am sorry I have to leave. You can
say anything you wish," he said, adding, "When I gave the interviewer
this blanket authority to quote me, I did not realize the damage that
could be done, and I did not foresee that an unfair advantage would
be taken of this." When he read how Elson had quoted him, he said,
"Needless to say I was angry and horrified when I saw the remark the
interviewer attributed to me."[46]

Powell's statement ignored the fact that radio listeners heard his voice
make the offending quote, that he had already admitted to making the
offending quote, and that Commissioner Landis had suspended him
for the comment. "For Powell to deny that he made them is to state
a falsehood," *New York Age* columnist William E. Clark wrote. Clark
said that Powell should make his apology on the radio. "Because the
remarks were made over the ether waves and not in Harlem," he said,
"we believe that Powell owes an apology to the country and that apology
should also be broadcast in the same manner the original statement

was made." In an editorial, the *Age* said neither Ruppert, Barrow, nor McCarthy needed to apologize for the slur, but the team needed to get rid of the ballplayer. The editorial acknowledged that Powell's slur had angered a lot of blacks, who, it hoped, would not turn to violence to satisfy their sense of vengeance. The editorial warned against "loose talk" and the "lynch spirit" directed at Powell. "We, as a group can ill afford to do the very things that we protest so loudly and condemn so long whenever we are the victims."[47]

When Powell returned to the field in Washington against the Senators on August 16, fans reacted angrily, loudly booing and cursing him — and some threw bottles at him. The *New York Times* reported that there were several delays during the game as black groundskeepers came onto the field to pick up bottles thrown by black spectators at a white ballplayer.[48] American League president Will Harridge told Clark Griffith that his team would have to furnish protection for Powell during the rest of the series.[49] Writing in the *Washington Post*, Shirley Povich questioned the judgment of playing Powell in a city where blacks sat together and fed off one another's anger. The *Sporting News* reported that Powell would have to "face the music." The *Worker* reported that fans in Washington had thrown bottles at Powell. The *Worker* said the Yankees were trying to trade Powell but found no teams interested. "Washington, from whom he came, wouldn't take him back as a gift," the newspaper said. "He was showered by pop bottles upon his last appearance." New York's next road game would be in Philadelphia. Ed Harris wrote in the *Philadelphia Tribune* that fans were preparing for Powell by warming up their throwing arms.[50]

In a front-page editorial, the *Defender* reported that blacks in Harlem had protested outside Yankee Stadium. The newspaper called on all blacks to boycott Ruppert's beer and Old Gold cigarettes until they apologized. An editorial called the Powell story a metaphor for "fair play" in society. Within an hour after Powell's remark, hundreds of protests had been sent to the newspaper's office and WGN radio from people who recognized the comment violated American ideals of decency and fairness.[51] In an editorial the newspaper said that segregation made acceptable comments like Powell's. "If black players had been in baseball," it said, "the Jake Powell incident would never have occurred, for as in Congress, legislatures and city councils, where we have elected officials, the presence of our men reminds — and demands — respect."[52] Fay Young warned Landis and the Yankees that playing Powell might incite black spectators throughout the American League. Black people were not satisfied with just a ten-day suspension, he wrote. He told readers to continue to put pressure on Landis and the Yankees.[53] In his column the following week, Young wrote that the upcoming East-West Classic in Chicago could be a turning point for black baseball. There would be white sportswriters, baseball executives, and spectators at the game.

In its coverage of the game, the *Defender* gave its readers an extensive account of the all-star game, which drew a crowd of about fifty thousand, including Lloyd Lewis of the *Chicago Daily News*. Young quoted Lewis as saying it was "inevitable" that blacks would one day play in the Major Leagues. He said there was no written rule prohibiting blacks, but integration would require approval by a majority of the owners, and none was willing to make such a motion. "It is inevitable," Lewis said. "Just how soon no one can tell, but it is sure to come." The *Defender* reprinted Lewis's column, in which he said that Willie Wells, in particular, could play shortstop in the Major Leagues and that there were a number of black pitchers with Major League ability. Lewis praised the speed of the black game, writing, "The bases were run with swiftness and daring absent from the white man's game for 20 years." He also observed that the arms were as good as any in the Major Leagues. "A welcome sight in a big-league ballpark was the willingness of Negro outfielders to throw out base runners and or pitchers to whip bunts to second for force plays," he said. "Such risks are almost things of the past in the white man's circuits."[54]

Black newspapers continued to keep Powell's name in the news. In September several black newspapers reported that Powell was on the trading block but that the team could not unload him because of his baggage.[55] The *Chicago Defender* described him as "*persona non grata* to nearly every big league town.*" The *Defender* said that Joe McCarthy would not dare use him in a ballpark in a city with a large black population such as Washington, Philadelphia, St. Louis, or Chicago. "That definitely narrows the field to a small number of clubs," the article said.[56] The Yankees would not trade Powell until 1943, but he would see little playing time after his radio interview. He batted just thirty times in the last two months of the 1938 season and only once in the World Series. During the off-season the death of Jacob Ruppert gave Ed Barrow more control of the team. The *Defender* observed that Barrow was less supportive of Powell and would likely release him.[57] Barrow, however, told the *Baltimore Afro-American* that he considered the matter closed. "Powell has done everything he could do to prove he meant no harm in that broadcast," he said.[58]

Afro-American reporter Harry Webber said that anger toward Powell had subsided, but it might flare up again with the beginning of a new baseball season. As the season approached it became clear that blacks had neither forgotten nor forgiven Powell. A number of organizations demanded that the Yankees get rid of Powell. Civil rights organizations said it would carry signs outside Yankee Stadium that said "Park Powell Elsewhere." The newspaper quoted a spokesman with one of the organizations as saying there were plans to send a committee to Barrow's office. "We do not intend allowing that fellow to continue to play baseball in New York," he said. The article said that the Yankees had tried to trade Powell back to the Senators, but Clark Griffith was not interested.[59] On April 22 Al Monroe of the *Defender* wrote that blacks in Harlem were angry over comments by Joe McCarthy that Powell would figure prominently in the team's plans for the upcoming season. "Harlem is definitely opposed to Jake Powell remaining on the Yankee squad," he said. Monroe ended his column by directly addressing Powell: "Yes, Jake, you are in for a tough time. We've seen the banners; talked with the fans of Harlem and for that reason can speak with authority. Maybe it wouldn't be a bad idea to start figuring on that police job back in Dayton." On May 6 the *Defender* reported that New York City daily newspapers were involved in a public relations campaign on Powell's behalf to convince blacks that the ballplayer was a changed man. The stories were published under headlines that said Powell was no longer the team's "bad boy." The *Defender* called the articles a "whitewashing." It said that the Yankees had ignored protests to either release or trade Powell. The articles on Powell tried to portray him positively, but they would have little effect on the attitudes of blacks. "Harlemites," the *Defender* said, "declare they do not intend letting up but will continue to try to drive the outfielder from major league circles."

On May 27 the *Defender* said the Yankees had initially planned to platoon Powell in right field but that Charlie Keller had become the team's regular right fielder. Al Monroe defended Barrow's decision to keep Powell on the team. "A man who is drawing Powell's salary cannot be cut adrift without getting something for him," Monroe said. "And it is doubtful if the player can be sent to the minors. He would perhaps have to be made a free agent which would mean the Yanks would get nothing for him." Powell played thirty-one games in 1939, batting eighty-six times and hitting .244. Powell then cracked his skull running into an outfield wall during a spring training game in 1940. He played twelve games for the Yankees that season. At one point, according to Shirley Povich, the temperamental Powell had played two games but been ejected from three. In December the Yankees sold him to the San Francisco Seals of the Minor Leagues. On December 11 columnist Bob Considine wrote a sympathetic column about Powell, wondering why no big league teams had signed him; when he had last been healthy, Powell had led the Yankees to the World Series title, in 1936. This was not the case. Powell had not been injured until 1940. Considine said that if the "energetic" Powell did not have the ability to play in the big leagues anymore, "that's a terrible thing."[60]

After two years in the Minor Leagues, Powell was sent back to Washington. He retired at the end of the 1944 season to become an officer with the Montgomery County police force in Rockville, Maryland. Walter Johnson, the once-great pitcher of the Senators who now worked for Montgomery County, voted against Powell's appointment. Powell then resigned from the police department in April 1945 to resume playing for the Senators.[61] About halfway through the 1945 season, he was then dealt to the Phillies, where his manager was Ben Chapman. Powell's career ended after the 1945 season. A month after the end of the season, the Montreal Royals announced it had signed Jackie Robinson. After Powell's career was over, he returned to Dayton. A few of his friends, including a retired Dayton police officer, Frank McNew, found him a job as a security guard at the Monsanto Chemical Company.[62] Powell left Dayton to make a comeback in baseball with a team in the Florida State League in 1947. After hitting under .200, he was released by a team in Leesburg.[63]

While in Florida he met and began dating Josephine Amber. When he learned that he was wanted for passing bad checks, Powell fled Florida with Amber. While heading north he contacted McNew. McNew later said that Powell told him he was on the lam and said, "They'll never get me. I'll die first."[64] On November 4, 1948, Washington DC police, acting on a complaint from a hotel that Powell had written three hundred dollars worth of bad checks, arrested the former ballplayer and Amber outside Union Station. While being questioned by detectives at a police station, Powell asked if he could speak to Amber. During the conversation Amber told Powell that she had decided against their plans to go to New York and get married and would return to Deland, Florida. Powell, according to Amber, then told her that he would kill himself. When Amber told detectives they had better frisk Powell, the ballplayer suddenly said, "Hell, I'm going to end it all," and pulled a .25-caliber revolver out of the pocket of his sport coat and shot himself twice — once in the chest and once in the right temple. He was pronounced dead shortly thereafter. Powell's companion told police the two were going to get married the next day; however, Powell was still legally married to his wife, Elizabeth, in Dayton.[65] Powell's obituary in the *Dayton Daily News* said, "He died in Washington DC, not as a cop as he often dreamed of being, but as a man arrested on a bad check charge, the last of a series of his madcap adventures."[66]

The *New York Times* gave him more attention in death than it had during the summer of 1938. Most of the eleven-paragraph article chronicled the developments that led up to his suicide. The article then summarized his playing career before ending with a paragraph that mentioned that he had been suspended after making a comment on the radio that was "interpreted widely as offensive to Chicago's negro population." In the next — and last — sentence of the story, it said that Powell had once worked as a policeman in Dayton, Ohio. But Powell never worked as a police officer in Dayton. This error has been repeated in subsequent articles about Powell. Sgt. Jim Wheeler of the Dayton Police Department checked employment records and found no mention of Powell. "History has confused a crucial component of this story, and its retelling continues to blacken the eye of the city of Dayton and its police department," he wrote in a letter to the *Dayton Daily News*.[67]

Fay Young was unforgiving of Powell in his column about the ballplayer's death. "We have no sympathy for any of the Jake Powells who remain on this planet," he said. When asked to remember Powell a half century after his death, Sam Lacy called him a "bigot. . . . Baseball took care of him." Shirley Povich described the ballplayer as "a bigot, a drunken bigot. It was a big story." The Powell incident was indeed a big story in the black press. But whether in life or in death, Powell made little impression in the mainstream press. The mainstream press failed to recognize the cruelty of the ballplayer's remark. To make matters worse, Powell was viewed sympathetically, especially in death. When Powell died, the *Sporting News* provided a lengthy obituary for him but said nothing about his racist remark in 1938.[68] In addition, a week after the obituary, the *Sporting News* published sympathetic columns of

Powell by three of the country's most respected sportswriters: Povich, Vincent X. Flaherty of the *Los Angeles Examiner,* and Red Smith of the *New York Herald Tribune.*

Povich chronicled Powell's many fights but mentioned the ballplayer's racist remark only in passing. After reporting that Powell had said he spent his off-season in Dayton "clubbing citizens over the head," Povich added the following cryptic comment, "He was only being sincere." Flaherty said he knew Powell from his days playing for the Takoma Park Tigers. "Jake was never a bad kid. I'll *never* believe he was a bad man," Flaherty said. "If anything was wrong with Powell, it was baseball's fault — not because baseball breeds wrongdoing, but because Powell was led astray by the easy money that came to him from a game he would have happily played for nothing." Flaherty quibbled with Povich's interpretation of the Hank Greenberg incident. Povich said that Greenberg was taking a routine throw when Powell barreled into him. Flaherty said the throw brought Greenberg into the baseline. When Powell's talents faded, his drinking and fighting became worse. Things would have worked out differently if Powell had just been a little luckier or a little more talented. "If only for a little more ability, which would have made him great," Flaherty said. "Disappointment and failing confidence do things to a man — bigger and tougher men than Jake ever dreamed of being."[69]

Of the three, only Smith referred to Powell's infamous comment in any detail. When Powell was interviewed before a game in 1938, he made, according to Smith, "a thoughtless remark that offended thousands of Negroes." Smith did not mention the suspension but said that there was talk about boycotting Yankees games. "Jake had been as wrong as wrong could be," Smith said. But Powell was determined to make things right again. When the team returned to New York, Powell visited every bar in Harlem. "In each he introduced himself. He said he was Jake Powell and he said he made a foolish mistake and that he was sorry. Then he ordered drinks for the crowd and moved on to the next joint," Smith said. "He did that by himself, on his own initiative, after dark, in a section where he had reason to believe feeling ran high against him. That's one story about Jake Powell."[70]

Richard Crepeau wrote that the coverage of the Powell story reflected generalizations about coverage of black issues in the mainstream press. One was that nothing important happened in black communities. The other was that the white press was subservient to Landis and the baseball establishment.[71] Crepeau said the story reflected differences between white and black America and how issues in the black community were ignored by the white press. It taught black journalists that while the white press could ignore protests in the black community, the baseball establishment could not. It also demonstrated the ability of the black press to mobilize public opinion and to organize a protest to challenge racial injustices, something that would become more apparent during the civil rights movement. "America," the *Dayton Forum* said two weeks after Powell's remark, "is beginning to take notice when the Negro protests en masse."[72]

CHAPTER 6

MAJOR LEAGUE MANAGERS
AND BALLPLAYERS CALL
FOR END OF COLOR LINE

On the morning of Sunday, February 19, 1939, Wendell Smith, the assistant sports editor of the *Pittsburgh Courier*, sat down with National League president Ford Frick in the lobby of the William Penn Hotel in Pittsburgh. If there was indeed a formal policy prohibiting blacks, Smith wanted to get that in the record. If there was not a policy prohibiting blacks from baseball, he wanted to hear that directly from Frick. When Smith asked Frick why there were no blacks in the big leagues, Frick replied that there was a misunderstanding there were no blacks because baseball did not want them. He insisted that the big leagues wanted blacks but could not add them until society became more tolerant. "Many baseball fans are of the opinion that major league baseball does not want Negro players," Frick explained, "but that is not true." Frick said there were no blacks in baseball, because "the general public has not been educated to the point where they will accept them on the same standard as they do the white player."[1]

Until society became more racially progressive, Frick suggested, segregation was in the best interests of baseball — especially, he said, during spring training in the South, where laws prohibited blacks and whites from sharing the same hotels, restaurants, or ball fields. "A ball club spends six weeks in the Deep South and half the season on the road," Frick said, "and there were many places where we could not take a Negro because of social problems. Such situations bring about embarrassment and dissatisfaction for all concerned." Frick did not explain what he meant by this, or else Smith did not ask. Smith, however, asked if it would be possible to separate the black players from the whites where segregation laws existed. Frick answered that separating blacks and whites would not be in a team's best interests. "A ball club is a unit," Frick answered. "The only way a manager can develop team spirit is to keep his men together as much as possible, especially on the road. It would also mean that ball players who were not broadminded would take advantage of the situation and use it to further their own cause." Frick did not explain what he meant by saying that there were ballplayers who would "take advantage of the situation and use it to further their own cause."[2]

When Smith asked Frick if there was a formal policy barring blacks, Frick said there was not. He said that segregation represented the attitudes of fans and players and not the attitudes of managers, team owners, and other baseball executives. "I am sure that any of the major league managers would use a colored player if he thought the fans in his particular city would stand for it," Frick said, adding that there was a time when Jews were not accepted but that was not the case anymore. Eventually, the time would come when blacks, too, would be accepted. "I think that in the near future people will be more willing to accept the Negro ball players just as they have the Negro boxer and college athletes," Frick said. "Times are changing." Smith pressed Frick on how long it would take before there were blacks in organized baseball. Frick was noncommittal. "I can not name any particular day or year, but assure you that when the people ask for the inclusion of your players we will use them. I do not think the time is far off and with constant crusading by the press of both races it is bound to come. However, you must keep fighting," Frick said. "Never let the issue die, because there is no way to measure public opinion. It may change tomorrow."[3]

Frick said the responsibility for ending the color line belonged to fans and society, in general, and, according to Frick, it was the responsibility of the press to change the attitudes of fans and society. There simply was nothing the baseball establishment could do about the color line until public opinion supported integration. The baseball establishment had the authority to put black ballplayers in big league uniforms. It set the rules of the game. It simply did not exercise that authority. There were no blacks in baseball for reasons that had everything to do with the attitudes of league executives and team owners and little to do with the attitudes of ballplayers and fans. When Smith asked Frick if black baseball would be included in the year's centennial celebration of baseball, the league president said that plans had not yet been finalized. However, he added, he could not think why black baseball would be omitted from the celebration. "After all," he said, "this is not our game, baseball is everybody's game."[4] But if baseball was everyone's game, why were blacks not allowed to compete in organized professional baseball? As it turned out, blacks were not included in baseball's centennial celebration.

The *Courier* published Smith's interview with Frick on February 25 on page 1. The newspaper's front page also had stories on singer Marian Anderson, whose concert in Constitution Hall in Washington DC had been canceled when the Daughters of the American Revolution (DAR), owners of the hall, learned the singer was black. The Howard University School of Music then requested the use of the Central High School auditorium for the Anderson concert. The city's board of education rejected the request. The *Courier* reported that the Marian Anderson Protest Committee had begun picketing the board of education, which, it noted, had not been done in more than a decade.[5] Thirteen years earlier, when tenor Roland Hayes had been denied the use of Constitution Hall, there had been a mild protest. The banning of Anderson — first from Constitution Hall and then from the Central High School auditorium — resulted in louder protests. Blacks expressed their anger in letters to their newspapers and to their congressmen. Hundreds of Washington DC schoolteachers signed a petition asking the board of education to reverse itself. The Marian Anderson Citizens Committee pressured the White House. First Lady Eleanor Roosevelt canceled her membership in the DAR in protest. This put the issue on the front page of daily newspapers.

Interior Secretary Harold Ickes granted permission for Anderson to sing at the Lincoln Memorial on Easter Sunday. Tens of thousands attended her concert. "The 600 newspaper clippings from Singapore to London would never have been possible," John Lovell Jr. wrote in the *Crisis,* "if the Marian Anderson Citizen Committee had not set off the explosion." Lovell suggested that the Anderson issue had served as a wake-up call for blacks far beyond the nation's capital. Black America read what had happened and acknowledged that it did not have to accept what it previously had. Lovell said that tens of thousands who heard Anderson clearly demonstrated that blacks were committed to achieving racial equality. He said that columnists in the white press had warned that the black man could not achieve what he wanted through confrontation.[6]

In his book *1939 — Baseball's Tipping Point,* Talmage Boston called 1939 the most significant year in baseball history. Baseball first began being broadcast on radio, taking the game from ballparks to living rooms; Little League Baseball began in Williamsport, Pennsylvania, taking youngsters from the sandlots to organized amateur ball; Lou Gehrig's consecutive-game streak ended, which was then followed by the diagnosis of the disease that would take his life; and Ted Williams began a career in Boston that would culminate with his being perhaps the greatest hitter in Major League history. The National Baseball Hall of Fame and Museum opened in Cooperstown, New York, on the centennial anniversary of Abner Doubleday's supposed invention of the game. Baseball's creation myth was every bit as illusory though far less benign than its democratic myth, which claimed that everyone was equal. The title of Boston's book referenced Malcolm Gladwell's best-selling book, *The Tipping Point*, which said that "social epidemics are driven by the efforts of exceptional people," and "what must underlie successful epidemics, in the end, is a bedrock belief that change is possible, that people can radically transform their behavior or beliefs in the face of the right kind of impetus." In 1939, according to Boston, baseball and society transformed one another. "White America could no longer ignore the black game," Boston said. In April retired Washington Senators pitcher Walter Johnson told Shirley Povich of the *Washington Post* that Josh Gibson was better than Yankees catcher Bill Dickey, who was then considered the best catcher in the Major Leagues. Gibson, Johnson said, was worth two hundred thousand dollars to any Major League team. "Too bad that Gibson is a colored fellow," Johnson said. Povich then added, "There's a couple million dollars worth of baseball talent on the loose ready for the big leagues, yet unsigned by any major leagues. Only one thing is keeping them out of the big leagues — the color of their skin."[7]

Two weeks after his front-page story on his interview with Frick, Smith criticized the National League president in a column. Unlike Ches Washington, who praised the candor of the baseball executives he interviewed in 1933, Smith was blunt in his criticism. "According to Mr. Frick's theory, the American public doesn't mind seeing a Cuban third baseman throw out a Greek base runner, or a Russian outfielder catch a high fly by a Japanese batter," Smith said. "But this land of the 'free' will not stand to see a black man do anything on a major league club, but sweep out the locker room." Smith said that Frick could not explain why white Americans would pay one hundred dollars to see Joe Louis knock out a white man but would not pay to see a black pitcher strike out a white batter. Frick also could not explain why blacks played with and against whites in college or why integrated teams traveled into segregated states without, as Frick put it, "embarrassment and dissatisfaction for all concerned." Smith told his readers that the color line was un-American. "A real American doesn't give a hoot if a man is black, blue or pink, if he can whale a horsehide pellet," he said. "They call organized baseball our national pastime, the game of the American people. But they really don't believe that. How can they?" The national pastime, he said, did not include blacks on big league rosters, nor were there any blacks currently in any of the spring training camps. Baseball continued to say that it represented the ideals of America, Smith said, but segregation misrepresented those very ideals.[8]

Smith decided to investigate Frick's argument that it was the players — and not baseball executives — who opposed the integration of races in the national pastime. Over the next few months Smith interviewed forty players and all eight managers in the National League to see if they objected to having blacks play in the big leagues. Smith, who was denied a press card because of his race, was restricted from dugouts, locker rooms, and press boxes. He could enter only if given permission. Most of Smith's interviews came in the lobby of the Schenley Hotel, where opposing teams stayed when they came to Pittsburgh. "The ballplayers were sitting around, you know how ballplayers sit around in the lobby," Smith said. "That's where I did most of my interviewing." Smith said he would start off by asking, "Have you see any Negro baseball players who you think could play in the major leagues?" Most of the ballplayers and managers he interviewed had played against blacks in off-season exhibition games. Smith's interviews revealed that just about everyone he interviewed could name at least one black ballplayer, and maybe even several, with big league ability.[9]

Five months after Smith interviewed Frick, the sportswriter wrote the first of his articles that confronted the baseball establishment's justifications for keeping baseball segregated. When Major League executives and team owners were asked about black baseball, they sneered at the Negro leagues and the quality of its players. They said that the Negro leagues were leagues in name only, held together by Scotch tape and string. Major League executives and owners also dodged responsibility for the color line by saying that the decision of whether a team signed a black was left to the managers. Major League Baseball's establishment also said that white players objected to playing with or against black players. The perception was that there were no blacks in baseball because managers and players did not want them. "It was this biased theory," Smith wrote, "that inspired us to dig down deeper to rip open the seams of big league baseball and get the testimonials and opinions of the cream of the National League players." On July 15 Smith wrote that the world found itself on the verge of war. America, if need be, stood prepared to defend its democracy. But blacks were being denied equality. Organized baseball refused to let blacks take their place with other players of all other nationalities. "Despite the fact that he is qualified and willing, strong and able, he is shunned and ignored," Smith said, calling the color line in baseball "the great American tragedy." Smith opened the series with an interview with Cincinnati Reds manager Bill McKechnie. Smith asked McKechnie if he had seen any blacks who he thought were good enough for the big leagues. "I have seen at least 25 colored players who could have made the grade," answered McKechnie, who included the names of Satchel Paige, Oscar Charleston, Josh Gibson, Joe Rogan, and others. "Some of the greatest ball players I have ever seen were Negroes," he continued. "And those whom I have named would have been stars on any major league team in the country." Smith then asked McKechnie if he would be willing to have a black on his roster. "Yes, if given permission, I would use a Negro on my team," McKechnie said, adding, "I would use some of them if given permission by those above me. However, it is not up to me to decide upon that question. It is the duty of the league officials and owners to pass on that."

In addition to his interview with McKechnie, Smith quoted several Cincinnati players, including shortstop and team captain Billy Myers, first baseman Frank McCormick, catcher Ernie Lombardi, and star pitchers Bucky Walters and Johnny Vander Meer. All knew the names of current black players, and none opposed either playing with or against blacks. "I certainly wouldn't object to a good Negro ball player on our team," Vander Meer, who was from New Jersey, said. "I don't see why they are barred." Myers remembered playing against blacks during the off-season in Puerto Rico in 1936. "I saw any number of Negroes there who played good enough to make the majors," Myers said. Lombardi, who had led the National League in batting average the year before, said he faced Paige during an exhibition game in Oakland and Paige struck him out.[10]

In his column Ches Washington responded to McKechnie's quote that managers had long been interested in signing black players. John McGraw, McKechnie said, had tried to sign Charlie Grant. Washington wrote that after McGraw saw Oscar Charleston play, he remarked, "I could use that fellow . . . if I could put a coat of white paint on him." A number of today's managers might say the same thing, Washington said. Managers, he added, wanted to win games and knew that they could probably win more games if they could sign blacks. Washington said that the *Courier*'s series contradicted the owners' argument that players were responsible for the color ban. Washington wrote that the newspaper would be mailing copies of each article in the series to Frick and to National League team owners. "After reading them," Washington said, "we're convinced that they won't be using the big league players again as an alibi in trying to explain why the sepia stars aren't given a chance to ply their parts in baseball's big-time show."[11]

On July 22 Smith said he called New York Giants manager Bill Terry of Memphis, Tennessee, from the hotel lobby, identified himself, and asked if he could speak to him. Terry replied, "No, absolutely, no!" and hung up. Smith then waited for him outside Forbes Field, the Pirates' ballpark. When Smith was admitted into the clubhouse, he was told to wait until Terry was through talking with Pittsburgh manager "Pie" Traynor. After an hour of waiting, Smith asked Terry if he knew of any blacks with the ability for the big leagues. "I know, as well as everybody else does, that there are a number of Negroes who have the ability to play in the major leagues," Terry said. Smith then asked if blacks would ever be admitted to the Majors. "No, I do not think Negro players will ever be admitted to the majors," Terry said. Smith said he was not surprised by Terry's response. Terry, according to Smith, was a "dyed-in-the-wool conservative. He is neither liberal nor sympathetic." Terry explained that it would not be possible to allow blacks in the Major Leagues because it would require blacks and whites to travel together, sharing trains and hotels. Smith then told Terry that blacks and whites traveled together in show business without incident. "Nevertheless," Terry replied, "I think they can be more successful with a league of their own." Smith pressed the issue but understood that Terry would not budge.[12]

Smith said he followed Terry onto the field, where he interviewed Giants slugger Mel Ott, whom Smith described as the "Louisiana Lasher." Ott said that he, too, had seen black players who were good enough for the Major Leagues but could not remember their names. Smith received the same answer from first baseman Zeke Bonura and Minor League manager Tony Lazzeri, who had once been a star second baseman with the New York Yankees. Smith then sought out Carl Hubbell, one of the best pitchers in big league history. Terry had told Smith that the quiet Hubbell would have nothing to say. Hubbell, however, began talking about Josh Gibson, whom he called one of the greatest catchers "in the history of baseball." Hubbell also talked about Paige, Rogan, and other black stars. "I'll say this," Hubbell continued, "that the players I've named, and some of those whose names I can't remember at the present time, would have been in the majors had their skins been white. Only their color kept them out of big-league baseball."[13]

On July 29 Smith interviewed Philadelphia Phillies manager James "Doc" Prothro, who worked as a dentist in the off-season in Memphis, Tennessee. Prothro said he once played in a series of exhibition games in California where he had seen at least six blacks with the ability to play in the big leagues. He described Paige, in particular, as "one of the greatest pitchers in baseball." If given permission, Smith asked, would Prothro sign black players? "I certainly would," he answered. "If given permission, I would jump at the opportunity to sign up a good Negro ball player. I need good players and if I ran across a colored player who could make the grade, I wouldn't hesitate signing him up." When Prothro was asked if he thought teams would sign black players, Prothro said he did not know. "That is up to the owners and league officials, not the managers. I can't say just when that will happen," he said. "Maybe sometime soon, maybe never."

Smith also interviewed Philadelphia Phillies players like Morrie Arnovich, a Jew, who Smith said was sympathetic to blacks because Jews, too, had once been barred from baseball. Pitcher Hugh Mulcahy said he had not seen some of the better black ballplayers but had heard from a lot of white players that Paige and Gibson were the equal of any big leaguer. Smith then interviewed the team's catcher, Virgil "Spud" Davis, of Birmingham, Alabama. Davis said that there were people of most nationalities in the Majors and that he did not object to blacks. He was then asked if other players would object. "Well, I suppose some of them would. Some of the players from the South might kick, but I wouldn't say for sure," he said. "If a good Negro player was signed by a club that was having a difficult time and the fans took to him, I don't suppose it would make much difference who kicked."[14]

On August 5 Brooklyn Dodgers manager Leo Durocher told Smith he owed his baseball career to a black man he had known in Massachusetts. When the New York Yankees signed Durocher in 1925, he was told to report to the organization's Minor League team in Hartford. Durocher, however, did not think he was good enough for Hartford and ignored the letter. David Redd, a black who worked with Durocher in the same factory, told Durocher that he secretly yearned for the opportunity of playing for Hartford with the hope of one day playing for fame and glory in a Yankees uniform. When Durocher told Redd he had decided to pass on the opportunity, the man exploded, "Why, you bonehead, you're missing the opportunity of a lifetime! If you don't go to Hartford and try out for that team, I'll never speak to you again! You little fool. I know hundreds of men who would give up everything for such an opportunity! I know men who are dying for such a chance and here you are laughing it off like it is nothing!" Redd said, adding, "You're going to Hartford, and you're going to stay there! You're going to stay there — and make good. Some day, you're gonna be on the New York Yankees!" Durocher made good on his tryout with Hartford and then broke into the Majors with the Yankees in 1925 and played for seventeen years — much of that time as a player-manager. Smith noted that Redd, however, was denied his chance for fame and glory because of racial discrimination. "David realized the futility of his dream," Durocher said. "He realized there were hundreds of young Negroes, better ball players than he, having similar dreams in every section of the country." Smith wondered if maybe Redd's sense of righteous indignation could have transferred to Durocher, who would go from being unsure of his own ability to being one of the fiercest competitors in baseball. "Perhaps from his association with David Redd," Smith said, "the Brooklyn manager knew of the yearning that lies within the heart of every Negro ball player."[15]

When Smith asked Durocher if he knew of any blacks who were good enough for the big leagues, Durocher did not disappoint him. "I've seen plenty of colored boys who could make the grade in the majors. Hell, I've seen a million. I've played against some colored boys out on the coast who could play in any big league that ever existed," Durocher said. Durocher said Josh Gibson was good enough for the Majors. Durocher recalled a game he played against Gibson. "Josh hit one of the longest balls I've ever seen. There are plenty of colored players around the country who should be in the big leagues right now. However, that decision is not up to the managers," Durocher said. "Personally, I have a liberal attitude toward the Negro ball player. I cannot say just when they will be admitted, because I do not know how the owners look upon the situation. I certainly would use a negro ball player if the bosses said it was all right." Smith found that other Brooklyn players were of the same mind as their manager. Michigan-born pitcher Luke Hamlin said that Paige could make the big leagues "any day in the week," adding, "I swear I don't see how in the world he can throw a ball so fast. They say you can't hit 'em if you can't see 'em. Which means that Paige doesn't have a worry in the world." Pitcher Forest Pressnell, catcher Babe Phelps, first baseman Dolph Camilli, outfielders Cookie Lavagetto and Tuck Stainback, and coach Charlie Dressen also said there were a number of black players who could play in the big leagues.[16]

In a separate article in the same issue, the *Courier* reported that there had been protests against the color line in the Connecticut State Baseball League. The New Britain Cremos had signed Johnny Taylor, who had once played for the New York Black Yankees and the Pittsburgh Crawfords and was now pitching in Mexico. The New London team protested a game against New Britain because it said New Britain had violated a verbal agreement between the league's owners that barred black players. The New Britain and Hartford teams voted against the ban. New Britain called the vote "un-Christian," saying it promoted discrimination. The story concluded by saying that protests against the discriminatory practices in the Connecticut league were representative of other protests against racial discrimination elsewhere in the country.[17]

On August 12 Chicago Cubs manager "Gabby" Hartnett also endorsed blacks in the big leagues. As a boy growing up in Rhode Island, Hartnett said he saw "Smokey Joe" Williams and Rube Foster pitch. "Although I was just a kid, I was convinced that they were certainly good enough for the majors," Hartnett said. "'Smokey Joe' was as fast as any pitcher I've ever seen. . . . He would have been worth plenty to some big league manager when he was in his prime." Hartnett said he had not seen many Negro league games over the past several years, but he had heard a lot from other players and managers. The day before Smith interviewed Hartnett, the New York Black Yankees and Homestead Grays, with Josh Gibson, played a game at Forbes Field. Hartnett said that a number of his players had gone to the game. "My players came back and told me about it. They were impressed with Gibson and two or three of the other players," he said. When asked if he would sign blacks if he were allowed, Hartnett said, "If given permission, I wouldn't hesitate one minute." Hartnett said the race issue could not be solved by the managers or the players but would have to be resolved by baseball owners and executives. Smith interjected that Hartnett's answer contradicted that of Frick, who said that the color line was necessary because of the attitudes of managers and players. "There are any number of good Negro ball players around the country," Hartnett added, "and I am sure that if we were given permission to use them, there would be a mad scramble between managers to sign them up."[18]

Arkansas-born pitcher Dizzy Dean, who was then at the end of his Hall of Fame career, had pitched in a number of games against Negro leaguers during off-season exhibition games. His quotes about the talents of black players were well circulated in the black press. Dean told Smith that he had faced Paige six times and that Paige had won four or five of the games. Dean said that Paige belonged in the big leagues. "Only his color holds him back," he said. He added that he had seen Paige strike out big leaguers as if the big leaguers were kids playing on sandlots. When Dean was told that the great white pitcher Walter Johnson had said that Gibson was worth two hundred thousand dollars to any big league team, Dean agreed. Dean then added that black teams were often superior to the white teams they played. "I have played against a Negro all-star team that was so good we didn't think we had a chance," he said. "We had a team of big leaguers, too. When we beat them we thought we had accomplished something." Other Cubs players, including outfielder Augie Galan, Clay Bryant, and Earl Whitehill, also praised Negro leaguers like Paige, Gibson, and Earl "Mule" Suttles. After facing Paige, Bryant said, he said could not understand why Paige was not in the big leagues.[19]

On August 19 Smith included his responses from the St. Louis Cardinals, which, he said, were based in a city in a former slave state. Manager Ray Blades, however, confirmed what other managers and players had already said. Blacks were being kept out of baseball because of team owners and league executives. "It is not up to the managers and play-ers," the Illinois-born Blades said, "but up to the men who pay out the salaries." "Pepper" Martin, the team's captain, said that black athletes had already won over fans in other sports. He said that boxers such as Joe Louis and Henry Armstrong had demonstrated that white fans were more interested in the ability of the athlete than in the color of his skin. "Joe Louis has done a great deal toward easing the Negro athlete's burden," Martin said, "and has won the admiration of millions of white people." Martin believed that blacks would eventually be admitted into organized baseball. When that day came, he said, there would be protests. "Some of the big league players would object," Martin stated, "but on the whole I think they would be accepted right along with the others. After all, we're playing this game to make a living and just as long as the money keeps rolling in twice a month, that's all that matters." After interviewing Blades and Martin, Smith approached Paul "Daffy" Dean, Dizzy Dean's younger brother, introduced himself, reached out his hand, and asked Dean if he would answer a few questions, Dean refused Smith's hand and snapped, "Naw, I don't wanna talk to ya." Martin then approached Dean, spoke to him, and said to Smith, "He'll talk to you now." Dean then sat down with Smith. "Would you object if a colored player was signed by the Cardinals?" Smith asked. "No, I would not care," Dean said. "All I want is my money."

In his column Ches Washington wrote that forty thousand spectators had attended the Negro league's recent East-West game in Chicago. He said that he heard from a number of spectators that such crowds might convince baseball to open the game to blacks. Washington said he sat in the press box with *Chicago Daily News* sports editor Lloyd Lewis and several other white sportswriters. Washington quoted Lewis's article on the East-West game that said that black baseball players had more speed and grace than white ballplayers but that whites had better training and coaching. In the same issue the *Courier* quoted Charlie Grimm, a former player and manager who was now working as a broadcaster, as saying that the National League "is generally weaker than at any time in my 22 years with the majors." He said that baseball needed to go out and develop better prospects. The newspaper included an editor's note that said, "The major league could acquire some much needed material by giving Negro ball players an opportunity."[20]

On August 26 Smith quoted Casey Stengel, the Missouri-raised Boston Braves manager, as saying that blacks were natural athletes. "Most Negro players are what we call naturals. They can hit, run and throw exceptionally well. They seem to take to the game naturally, and play it with all their heart and soul," said Stengel, the former New York Giants ballplayer who would later manage the Yankees. Stengel praised a number of blacks, including "Biz" Mackay, Gibson, Méndez, and Paige, who, he said, were not "given the opportunity to show exactly how good they are." Smith then asked Stengel if the time was near when blacks would be given the opportunity to play in the Majors. "I can't say anything about that," Stengel answered. "That is solely up to the owners." Stengel, however, expressed doubts whether integration would be in the best interests of either the Major Leagues or the Negro leagues. Black spectators did not support their teams, he said; therefore, there was no reason to think they would attend big league ballparks to watch blacks playing for big league teams. "I wonder if it would be profitable to admit Negroes in the majors. I wonder if the Negro fans would follow them to the extent where their presence on a big league team would be justified," Stengel said. Smith explained that black teams had to travel a lot and therefore returned home for a proportionately few games during the season. Stengel also expressed concern over the rowdy behavior of black spectators during Negro league games.

Major League owners were concerned that if they brought blacks into baseball, black fans would bring their behavior to the big league ballparks. Such thinking was shortsighted, as Smith and other integration advocates argued. They said that owners were wrong if they believed that white fans would quit attending games if blacks began playing in the big leagues. There was little or no evidence of this happening in other sports. In fact, Smith said, the reverse would happen: attendance would increase. "Club owners could put a few black players in their lineups and pack their parks," Smith said. "Can you imagine Satchel Paige pitching against Lefty Grove in an empty stadium? No! Neither can the club owners. They know Paige would pack their parks, but they would rather lose money than give black boys a chance. Yet they make every appeal to the black fans to attend their lily-white shows."[21]

Sportswriters began questioning why black baseball was allowing white owners to make so much money from the black game. Writing after the 1939 East-West game in Chicago, *Chicago Defender* columnist Lucius Harper said that black baseball had paid eight thousand dollars to rent Comiskey Park for the game and received none of the money from concessions. Harper scolded Negro league executives for accepting an agreement that benefited white baseball at the expense of black baseball. This, he wrote, "is too much money to go out of the poverty-stricken black baseball into the hands of already white wealthy white baseball." Harper wrote that some of the money from the game should go toward building a ballpark "with the idea that someday we may play the game there and not forever in the other fellow's yard at unreasonable rentals."[22]

Segregation, contrary to Ford Frick's opinion, did not reflect public opinion as much as it reflected the attitudes and greed of Major League owners. Owners leased their ballparks at great expense to black teams because black teams did not have their own ballparks. If the Major Leagues signed blacks from Negro league teams, its stars would leave their teams, black baseball would fail, and big league owners would lose the revenue associated with exploiting black baseball.

Neither white nor black owners wanted the Negro leagues to be absorbed into the Major Leagues. Black ballplayers were divided on the issue, according to Sam Lacy. He quoted Vic Harris, captain of the Homestead Grays, who expressed concern that as the better players joined big league teams, the quality of ball would suffer in black baseball. Jud Wilson of the Philadelphia Stars did not think organized baseball would be integrated because of the strong southern influence of ballplayers and the segregation laws in southern states. Felton Snow, manager of the Baltimore Elite Giants, feared that an owner might sign "the wrong player" to break the color line. If this happened, Snow said, it would give weight to the segregationists who said that blacks lacked the talent and temperament for the big leagues. Dick Lundy, shortstop of the Newark Eagles, said that there would not be such an interest in blacks playing in the big leagues if black baseball were not run so poorly.[23] Lacy later said that black players gave little thought to playing in the big leagues because it seemed so improbable. They simply accepted segregation. "It was like saying, 'How would you like to be a millionaire?'"[24]

Smith responded to a letter from a reader who asked the sportswriter if integration would destroy the Negro leagues or if it was possible for black baseball to join organized baseball as a minor league. Smith replied that the big leagues would have to sanction the Negro leagues as a minor league, which would require that big league teams buy players from Negro league teams. This, Smith said, would give black teams the capital to invest in players to replace those who went to the big leagues. "That way," Smith said, "we would have idols in the big leagues, and idols with a definite future still playing in the Negro leagues, under major league supervision. Maybe we're wrong, but that seems to be the most logical solution."[25] Al Monroe of the *Chicago Defender* agreed. "I think the better thing to do would be to have the majors recognize our league," Monroe said, adding that this would give credibility to black baseball.[26] This would require black baseball, as a number of sportswriters had advised, to adopt uniform rules and standards consistent with white baseball. Even if Negro league executives were willing to do this, and they had demonstrated no willingness, they would have to surrender their control to Commissioner Landis and the white baseball establishment. Such an arrangement also would require the approval of Major League owners. Given their particular attitudes on race relations, this would be even more unlikely.

Smith's series concluded on September 2 with the Pittsburgh Pirates. Pittsburgh manager Pie Traynor, once a star third baseman with the team, named several blacks who could have been stars in the big leagues, if given the opportunity. Traynor, a Massachusetts native, remembered an off-season exhibition game in California when his team was scheduled to play against Paige. Traynor knew that Paige was in top form and his players were not, so he asked that Paige not pitch. "We would have been on the spot had we let him pitch. He was too good right then. I'd be willing to bet that he would have fanned 16 or 17 of the boys that day," Traynor said. When Traynor was asked if he would sign blacks if allowed, he said he would. "If given permission, I would certainly use a Negro player who had the ability," he said. "Personally, I don't see why the ban against Negro players exists at all. It is a known fact that there are plenty of Negroes capable of playing the big leagues." Traynor then added that other managers and players believed as he did. "I have heard managers and players in the big leagues state that they would like to have Satchel Paige, Josh Gibson or some other outstanding Negro player along to help them out of a tight spot," he said.[27]

Pirate infielder Bill Brubaker, who grew up in Ohio and graduated from the University of Southern California, told Smith he often played against blacks while he was living on the West Coast. He said he "had seen scores" of blacks who could have played in the big leagues. Brubaker remembered when Mule Suttles hit a game-winning home run over a fence 470 feet from home plate. He called Cool Papa Bell the "the fastest man I have ever seen in baseball." Brothers Paul and Lloyd Waner, who were nearing the end of their Hall of Fame careers, also said they had seen a number of blacks good enough for the big leagues. So did Pittsburgh coach Jewel Ens. Another coach, Honus Wagner, one of the greatest big leaguers in history, called Rube Foster "one of the smartest pitchers I have ever seen in my years in baseball." Wagner, who was then sixty-five, told Smith about the great black shortstop John Henry Lloyd, who had been called the "black Wagner." Wagner said that after he had heard the comparison, he wanted to see Lloyd play. "After I saw him," he said, "I felt honored that they should name such a great player after me."[28]

Ches Washington reported that American League president William Harridge said he had been closely following the series.[29] In addition, Jimmy Long, a publicist for the Pittsburgh Pirates, told the *Courier* that the team's front office, including team president Bill Benswanger, was reading the series "with great interest." Benswanger again said that he supported the addition of black players in the big leagues. Washington wrote that *New York Daily News* columnist Jimmy Powers had written that Josh Gibson would be worth twenty-five thousand dollars a year to any big league team. In his column Powers told readers to attend Negro league games at Yankee Stadium. "I have seen personally at least ten colored ball players I know are big leaguers but are barred from play by the Jim Crow law that Frick of the National League insists does not exist," Powers said, adding that Gibson could immediately transform a struggling team like the Brooklyn Dodgers. "Some day some owner will come along with enough courage to sign a fine young catcher like Josh Gibson. Then baseball will become a truly national sport," Powers said. Washington quoted Lester Bromberg of the *New York Herald Tribune* and Frank White of the *New York Post* who also praised black players. According to Bromberg, blacks would play in the big leagues as soon as team owners gave their approval.[30]

On August 19 Al Monroe praised Powers for his frequent columns criticizing baseball for practicing discrimination. "Last week he asked the question, 'Wonder how Leo Durocher and Bill Terry would feel if they awakened one morning and found a hitter of the Josh Gibson type and a pitcher like Satchel Paige on their roster?'" Fay Young praised Powers for a late-August column that told his readers to attend the black all-star game at Yankee Stadium.[31] The *Defender* praised Powers for quoting Durocher, but the newspaper did not credit the *Courier*. The *Defender*, the *Courier*'s primary rival among black newspapers, certainly knew about the series. The newspaper certainly believed in the desegregation of baseball. Yet it did not report that ballplayers and managers had gone on the record in the *Courier* supporting blacks in baseball.

The *Daily Worker* reprinted much of Smith's interview with Frick. Lester Rodney called Frick's openness a hopeful sign that baseball would end its prohibition against blacks.[32] When Smith began his series in July, the *Worker* liberally quoted from it in its newspaper, telling its readers that managers and ballplayers supported integration. Rodney objected to Bill Terry's argument that blacks should have their own league but that it would be a mistake to mix blacks and whites, again telling readers that blacks and whites already competed against one another without racial incident.[33] The *Worker* quoted Leo Durocher, Pepper Martin, and Bill Benswanger as supporting desegregation.[34] Wendell Smith wrote Rodney, commending him for his contribution to the campaign to end segregated baseball. "I take this opportunity to congratulate you and the *Daily Worker* for the fine way you have joined with us on the current series concerning Negro players in the major leagues, as well as all your past efforts in this respect," Smith said. "Incidentally, in the future, perhaps we can work out something similar to the present series together too. In the meantime, I wish you the best of luck and admire you for your liberal attitude."[35]

Never before had so many managers and ballplayers expressed support for allowing blacks in the Major Leagues as they did in 1939. This provided a written record that there were a lot of ballplayers and managers who supported desegregation, contrary to what Commissioner Landis and other executives claimed. But simply because Smith found that most of the players and managers he interviewed had no objections to blacks in organized baseball should not necessarily presume that support among players and managers was so widespread. There is no way of knowing whether Smith quoted everyone he interviewed or whether he avoided those players who were likely to object to blacks in baseball. It is logical to assume that there were ballplayers who expressed themselves one way to Smith but held different beliefs privately, or would have answered differently if it appeared baseball was about to become desegregated. For instance, Spud Davis was ambivalent in his answer to Smith in 1939. When Robinson was signed in 1945, however,

Davis, then coaching the Pittsburgh Pirates, said that integration was "all right as long as they are with some other team."[36]

A lot of baseball players, like the owners who paid them and the spectators who paid to watch them, held racist views or were outright racists. When Jackie Robinson was promoted to the Brooklyn Dodgers in the spring of 1947, a number of players — Dixie Walker and Bobby Bragan of Alabama, Kirby Higbe of South Carolina, Hugh Casey of Georgia, and Carl Furillo of Pennsylvania — told Branch Rickey they would not play with a black teammate.[37] Neither Casey, Walker, Bragan, nor Higbe — who were all playing in the big leagues in 1939 — was quoted in Smith's survey. Walker was traded during the season from the Detroit Tigers of the American League to the Brooklyn Dodgers. He may or may not have been on the Dodgers when Smith did his interviews. It is unlikely Walker would have endorsed the addition of blacks to big league rosters. Walker's teammate with the Tigers was George "Pinky" Higgins of Texas, who did not conceal his racial prejudice. Years later when Higgins was manager of the Boston Red Sox, a sportswriter praised a black player on an opposing team, and Higgins called the sportswriter "a nigger lover." Higgins also famously said the Red Sox would have "no niggers on this club if I have anything to say about it."[38]

In 1939 Art Rust Jr., who grew up near the Polo Grounds in New York City, remembered in his book *Get That Nigger Off the Field*, that a police officer told his father that New York Giants manager Bill Terry did not want "nigger cops" working at the Polo Grounds. Rust and his friends used to try to get players' autographs before games at the Polo Grounds and Yankee Stadium. When he asked Washington Senators outfielder Taft Wright of North Carolina to sign his program before a game at Yankee Stadium, Wright called him a "black son of a bitch." St. Louis Cardinals pitcher Clyde Shoun of Tennessee rubbed Rust's hair for luck as he walked out of the team's dressing room. Rust, who had a collection of photographs of Major League players, waited outside the Polo Grounds and asked players to sign their respective photos. After

Enos Slaughter signed his autograph, the ballplayer muttered, "How did that little nigger get all those photographs?" Rust remembered thinking, "With all those crackers, ain't no way a black guy's gonna play ball in the majors." Rust remembered Branch Rickey, then an executive with the St. Louis Cardinals, putting his arm around him and telling him that blacks would one day play in the big leagues.[39]

While many Major Leaguer players and managers opposed having blacks in baseball, many others, as Smith's series demonstrated, had no objections. Smith later wrote that the series received a lot of publicity in the mainstream press. He said his stories were reported in the Pittsburgh dailies and in the *Sporting News* — though neither said anything substantial about it.[40] In a brief article buried deep in its July 20 issue, the *Sporting News* reported that the *Courier* was running a series "purporting" that a number of blacks were good enough to play in the big leagues. Smith's series, the article said, "claims officials of the game were merely passing the buck when they stated that that players 'would not stand for' the introductions of colored stars." The Associated Press reported that ballplayers and managers were not opposed to the possibility of putting blacks in big league uniforms. A lot of daily newspapers probably mentioned Smith's articles, but it is doubtful that they gave the series any more than a passing nod, and therefore it got swept away in the tide of other sports stories. For the series to have made a substantial difference required that white sportswriters, particularly prominent white sportswriters, write about it in their columns.

Smith's series established him as one of the leading voices in the campaign to desegregate baseball. "It really got me on my way," Smith said, and "gave me a name in the sportswriting business because these stories were a revelation because the baseball owners had been constantly saying that the major league ballplayers would not play with Negro ballplayers."[41] The series demonstrated that many big leaguers had played against blacks and had highly respected their talent. Finally, the series demonstrated that players and managers could name several blacks with the ability to play in the big leagues. White players and managers knew that blacks and whites could compete against and with one another without a race riot because they had played so many games against one another. The baseball establishment knew this. They, too, had watched games or surely heard about them. They had even profited from such games. White sportswriters also saw or heard about these games but said nothing about the color line that kept blacks out of organized baseball. Sportswriters read or heard about Smith's series, but most said nothing about it, and if the issue was raised, they continued to defer to the opinions of Landis, the owners, and the rest of the baseball establishment.

In 1940 Smith succeeded Ches Washington as the *Courier*'s sports editor. Unlike Washington and his generation, Smith did not accept segregation. Unlike those who merely called for the end of segregated baseball, Smith injected himself directly into the issue. Smith was relentless in his columns in calling for the end of segregation in baseball. Black activists could indeed argue until they "dropped dead from exhaustion," as Smith put it, but baseball would not become desegregated until at least one Major League owner challenged the baseball establishment.[42] During the coming years black and sympathetic white sportswriters quoted Smith's survey to demonstrate that many, if not most, Major Leaguers did not oppose integration. During the summer of 1942 Landis responded angrily when Leo Durocher's quote was reprinted in the *Worker*. Landis summoned Durocher to his office, and then the commissioner told reporters he had no objections to blacks in baseball. Landis's statement disrupted the silence that protected segregated baseball. In response, a number of owners in organized professional baseball told reporters they were interested in trying out black players. If Heywood Broun's speech at the Baseball Writers' Association in 1933 could be credited as the beginning of the campaign to desegregate baseball, then Wendell Smith's series in the *Courier* in 1939 took the campaign to its next phase.

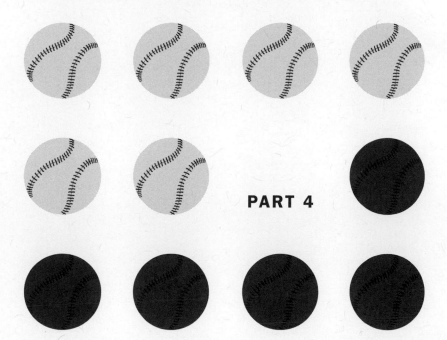

PART 4

CHAPTER 7

THE DOUBLE V CAMPAIGN

On August 23, 1939, Germany and the Soviet Union signed a nonaggression pact that said the countries would not attack one another. This allowed German chancellor Adolf Hitler to attack Poland without interference from its neighbor. Germany's invasion of Poland on September 1, 1939, and the grim realities of another European war would have a profound and lasting impact on the United States, which would be a very different country in 1945 than it had been in 1939. Whereas the United States and its leaders could ignore America's racial dilemma before the war, this was not possible after the war. More than two years passed between Germany's invasion of Poland and Japan's bombing of Pearl Harbor, which would force the United States into the war. During those twenty-seven months, as it became obvious that the United States would enter the war, black leaders pressured the Roosevelt administration for its assurances that blacks would not face the indignities and discrimination they did during World War I. During World War

II blacks fought both for their country on foreign soil and for racial equality on their own soil, resulting in race riots and in blacks being killed, beaten, or arrested on trumped-up charges. Baseball did not remain untouched by what was happening in the country.

The Nazi-Soviet pact embarrassed the CPUSA and the *Daily Worker*. U.S. Communists had steadfastly condemned fascism, which perpetuated racism — but now the Soviet Union was in alliance with the fascist government of Germany. The Soviet Union's pact with Germany told American conservatives all that they already suspected about Communists. Conservative politicians and journalists told the American people that Communists were no better than Nazis and that the social progressives and Far Left, which had grown substantially in the 1930s, could not be trusted. Congress passed the Smith Act in 1940, making it illegal to advocate — or belong to any group that advocated — the violent overthrow of the government. Congress, in the midst of the anticommunist hysteria of the late 1940s and 1950s, used the Smith Act to punish radical Americans, not for advocating the overthrow of the government but simply for belonging to the Communist Party, supporting communism, or, as it turned out, knowing people who supported communism. As the anger burned inside the Communist-hating Westbrook Pegler of the *New York World-Telegram*, he became obsessed with red-baiting and directed the full fury of his widely syndicated column to ending what he perceived as creeping communism and took it upon himself to destroy all those — like President Franklin Roosevelt — who were sympathetic to progressive politics. Pegler, who had thus far written some of the most searing criticisms of segregated baseball, would become an enemy of the campaign to desegregate baseball. Whereas Pegler had once supported racial equality, he now became a critic of it, denouncing black newspapers as Communist sympathizers and black newspapers as unpatriotic.

The Nazi-Soviet pact led to increased suspicion of communism in America. Communists took a lower profile and would learn to tread carefully in the coming years as suspicions about Communists exploded into Red Scare hysteria.[1] Stunned by the developments in Europe, the *Daily Worker* became less strident in its editorials and articles. The newspaper wrote less about baseball after the nonaggression pact. The *Worker*'s comparisons between Nazi Germany and U.S. Jim Crow laws, once vivid features of the campaign, became rare. But the communist daily did not forget its little war with the baseball establishment, providing progress reports of how the campaign against segregated baseball was growing in numbers and voices. By early 1940 the *Worker* may have toned down its rhetoric in calling for the desegregation of baseball, but, at the same time, it also expanded its view of the issue. This meant challenging anyone who defended racial equality in sports and praising those who supported it.

Daily News columnist Ed Sullivan, a sportswriter turned gossip columnist who would later become nationally famous for his television variety show, wrote that black athletes should be satisfied "with the spiritual thrill" that comes from playing sports and not be concerned with playing professionally. Lester Rodney responded with a mock telegram to Sullivan that said his salary would hereby be withdrawn so that he, too, could enjoy the "spiritual thrill" of hard work without being compromised by money. Rodney bristled that Sullivan needed to be lifted by the scruff of his neck and dragged to a home where a black family was starving and "let him explain to the unemployed man and his son how to bring that smile to the somewhat peaked face of their wife and mother with 'spiritual'" thrills.[2] The *Worker* reported that radio broadcaster Sam Balter, in a radio program sponsored by the Phillies Cigar Company, said no team in the National Football League had drafted Kenny Washington of UCLA, who was one of the best college halfbacks in the country. Balter called the discrimination against Washington "a source of bitter disillusionment to me . . . on behalf of American sports fans who believe in fair play and equal opportunity." He compared the discrimination in professional football to that in baseball. "The professional baseball leagues have decided that, with spring training in the Southern part of the country," he said, "there are matters of delicacy that make it necessary to refuse Negro baseball stars the right to play what is called the American pastime."[3]

In February 1940 the *Worker* published Jimmy Powers's open letter to Bill Terry, manager of the New York Giants, telling him he could improve his team and increase the crowds at the Polo Grounds by signing Satchel Paige and Josh Gibson. "Get yourself a batch of Satchel Paiges and Josh Gibsons and other truly great ball-busters. You'd find the Polo Grounds jammed with new and enthusiastic rooters," Powers said. Stan Kurman wrote in the *Worker* that it was unlikely Terry, given that he had expressed his opposition to desegregation, would be the one to break the color line but that if enough people pressured the team's front office, even Terry would have to go along. In March 1940 the *Worker* reported that the Young Communist League had pledged to collect names on petitions to send to the baseball establishment. The newspaper wanted black ballplayers at spring training. A couple days later the newspaper said that fifty-five unions in the New York Trade Athletic Association had "voted unanimously to launch a petition drive for a million signatures to end baseball's discrimination against Negro players this year."[4]

In April the *Worker* announced that the Committee to End Jim Crow in Baseball had been organized by the Trade Union Athletic Association, which was composed of more than thirty American Federation of Labor (AFL) and Congress of Industrial Organizations (CIO) unions with a reported membership of three hundred thousand. A month later a *Chicago Defender* editorial said it hoped the creation of the committee would expand nationally. This, it said, required more involvement on the part of black newspapers. But the black press, it added, had thus far done little to challenge the color line. "The Negro sports editors are strangely silent. Yet, here is a battle, which, if won, will have a great influence in smashing jim-crowism all along the line," the *Defender* said. "This is a victory which can be won. Let's get going. Negroes in the Big Leagues in 1940! Make baseball an American sport governed by American fair play tenets. Black-out jim-crow on the ball field." The editorial then directly addressed the ownership of the Chicago White Sox, which played in the black section of South Chicago. "White sox on black feet," it said, "can give Comiskey a pennant winner." The NAACP publication, the *Crisis*, also reported the committee's creation.[5]

Whenever a prominent mainstream sportswriter called for the end of segregated baseball, it was likely quoted in the *Worker* or in a black newspaper. But this did not happen often — and certainly not often enough for the issue to develop any traction. Therefore, most Americans knew little or nothing about black baseball. When stories were written about black players, they rarely went beyond caricature, and rarer still did stories mention the color line. "A Negro ball game is not a staid and stolid demonstration of fielding and hitting," Dan Daniel wrote in 1934. "It embodies comic relief impossible in white games because no Caucasian can play baseball with the rhythmic quality inherent in the black race."[6] Ted Shane wrote an article about Satchel Paige in the *Saturday Evening Post* that praised Paige as one of the greatest pitchers of all time, as good or better than Walter Johnson, Christy Mathewson, Lefty Grove, or Bob Feller. "Why," Shane asked, "haven't I heard of Satchel Paige before?" Shane then answered his own question, "Well, you see Satchel is colored." The article had the headline "Chocolate Rube Waddell." The article, while praising Paige's considerable talent, quoted the pitcher in black dialect, referred to his "apelike arms" and his "Stepinfetchit disingenuousness." After the article appeared Lucius Harper of the *Chicago Defender* said Paige deserved better than being characterized as a "Chocolate 'Rube' Waddell," the talented but erratic and often drunk former big league pitcher. Harper was critical of Shane for quoting Paige in black dialect, though, he acknowledged, Shane had at least mentioned Paige. "We prefer to overlook these literary sallies," Harper said, "and give him due credit for 'putting the case of Negro baseball' up to a vast white audience."[7]

To white journalists Paige, given his talent, his eccentricities, and his capacity for self-promotion, was a curiosity worth occasionally writing about. "His weird eight-hair pompadour stood up stiffly about his flattened black Brillo-hair, like a caricature of a frightened man," Bob Considine wrote. When Considine asked Paige about the playing conditions in black baseball, the columnist quoted Paige in dialect: "We don't carry no trainer with us, nobody to baby us like them big league fellers get. We rub each other's arms when they so', and pour hot water on so' arms. Wso'est arm I ever had. I just took three days off from pitchin' and walked around town. At night I poured hot water on it, and it got okay," Paige said. "We don't get no babying. We work, drive in a car all night, and work the next day. And play more baseball in two days than those big league fellers play in a month." When Paige was asked about the ban on Major League teams signing blacks, Paige replied that if blacks were not allowed on white teams, there should be a black team in the Major Leagues. If that happened, the black team would "show those boys some baseball."[8]

The *Worker* reported that articles in the *Saturday Evening Post* and in other magazines and newspapers demonstrated that the campaign to desegregate baseball was becoming a mainstream issue.[9] Representative Vito Marcantonio, of New York, who represented the radical Left, and Richard B. Moore of the National Negro Congress, a communist organization, spoke on behalf of racial equality as part of "End Discrimination in Sports Day" during the World's Fair in New York City on July 7. The *Worker* reported that more than ten thousand people signed their names to a petition calling for the end of segregated baseball.[10] Marcantonio began his political career as Fiorello La Guardia's campaign manager when the future mayor was elected to Congress in 1924. La Guardia was reelected in 1926, 1928, and 1930 before losing in 1932. In 1933 La Guardia became mayor of New York City. Marcantonio won election to Congress as a Republican in 1934. Marcantonio split with the GOP and was supported by a broad coalition of groups, including the American Communist Party. Marcantonio was reelected several times as a member of the American Labor Party.[11] Marcantonio pressured President Franklin Roosevelt to use his wartime executive powers to end Jim Crow.[12]

Although sympathetic on race issues, the Roosevelt administration failed to confront the country's race problem because it failed to grasp the depth of the problem, or simply because it did not know what to do about it.[13] Black America trusted the Wilson administration during World War I and then deeply regretted it. Blacks knew they again would be called upon to serve but, having learned their lesson from World War I, wanted assurances their service to the country would not be ignored. In October 1940, however, the White House released a statement that confirmed that segregation was the official policy of the War Department. "This policy has proven satisfactory over a long period of years, and to make changes would produce situations destructive to morale and detrimental to preparations for national defense," it said. "For similar reasons, the War Department does not contemplate assigning colored reserve officers other than those of the medical corps and chaplains to existing combat units of the regular army."[14]

Influential blacks expressed their impatience with FDR's tacit support of discriminatory policies in the army. In a speech Max Yergan, president of the National Negro Congress, expressed his disappointment with the Roosevelt administration's failure to confront racial discrimination. The administration would not even criticize lynching laws for fear of alienating southern Democrats. "I wish to raise the sharpest protest against the President's approval of the principle of segregation and discrimination." Yergan then asked, "What did blacks in America want?" He then answered, "We want security in employment; freedom to exercise our constitutional right to vote and relief from the debasing discrimination imposed upon us in the public special life of our country," Yergan wrote. "To ask for or accept less than this minimum standard of Americanism would be unworthy of the Negro people."[15]

In the decade or so preceding the war, progressive-thinking men and women in the Roosevelt administration addressed the "race issue" to a degree not done since Reconstruction.[16] According to Swedish sociologist Gunnar Myrdal, author of *An American Dilemma*, the New Deal was important to blacks because "for the first time in the history of the nation" the federal government did "something substantial in a social way without excluding the Negro." *Pittsburgh Courier* editor Robert Vann, economist Robert Weaver, and National Urban League chairman Eugene Kinckle Jones became advisers to the administration in 1933. From 1933 to 1945 a number of other highly regarded blacks such as educator Mary McLeod Bethune and lawyer William Hastie also advised the administration on race-related issues. These individuals became known as the "black New Dealers." Their influence was more than symbolic; it exceeded anything blacks had had in previous administrations. W. E. B DuBois recognized that progress in race relations, however limited or overdue, was made during the New Deal.[17] This progress was a direct result of the strength and determined efforts of black newspapers.

Myrdal acknowledged the black press's influence in the campaign for greater racial equality in the United States. But no matter how often the black press attacked racial discrimination, or how much influence it had in the black community, it lacked the political influence to effect significant reform. "If the protests were to succeed, the mainstream press — the white press — would have to discover racial discrimination," Gene Roberts and Hank Klibanoff wrote in their book, *The Race Beat*, "and write about it so candidly and so repeatedly that white America outside the South could no longer look the other way. Then they would see segregation, white supremacy, and black disenfranchisement as being at odds with the American conscience . . . and demand change." As long as white newspapers ignored America's "racial dilemma," there would not be progress. No major newspaper or magazine had a bureau in the South. The *New York Times* rarely wrote about either civil rights or racial equality, and when it did, the stories appeared on inside pages. Only once between 1935 and 1940 — in a story that mentioned A. Philip Randolph — did a story with the name of a prominent black activist appear on page 1.[18]

Randolph had long been a critic of American apartheid and an advocate of radical politics. During World War I the U.S. government suspended the mailing privileges of his magazine, the *Messenger*, calling it the "most dangerous" of black publications.[19] The *Messenger* then became the organ of the Brotherhood of Sleeping Car Porters and Maids, which Randolph created to secure better wages and working conditions from the Pullman Railway Company. The Pullman Company attacked Randolph as a Communist and an agitator but ultimately recognized the union and increased the salaries of porters and maids. In 1936 Randolph served as the first president of the National Negro Congress. By 1941 Randolph, like many other blacks, had grown impatient with the federal government's inaction on discrimination. Randolph decided that if Roosevelt was going to ignore the nation's black people, it was necessary for blacks to raise their voices so that they could not be ignored. Randolph announced a march in Washington DC, where, he said, tens of thousands of blacks would demand an end to job discrimination in the hiring of blacks in defense industries. In response FDR signed Executive Order 8802 on July 25 barring discrimination in defense industries and creating the Committee on Fair Employment Practice to investigate violations. Southern politicians condemned the executive order, mainstream newspapers opposed it, and white employers ignored it. Despite this John Hope Franklin called the executive order the most significant document affecting blacks since the Emancipation Proclamation. In late 1941 there were few blacks employed in the defense industry. Four years later tens of thousands were employed in the defense industry, and perhaps a hundred thousand worked in the iron and steel industries.[20]

As the United States prepared to enter World War II, blacks found that racial attitudes in the military had changed little since World War I. On December 7 Dorie Miller, who was serving on the battleship USS *West Virginia* while it was stationed at Pearl Harbor, was collecting laundry when Japanese airplanes attacked. Miller ran to the deck, where he began carrying wounded sailors to safety. He was then ordered to care for the ship's mortally wounded captain. Miller then manned a .50-caliber Browning antiaircraft gun and began firing the gun until it ran out of ammunition. Neither the FDR administration, the U.S. Navy, nor the mainstream press recognized Miller's act of valor. But black newspapers did. The *Pittsburgh Courier* used Miller's heroism to assail the navy's discriminatory policies. "Is it fair, honest or sensible that this country, with its fate in the balance, should continue to bar Negroes from service except in the mess department of the Navy," the *Pittsburgh Courier* said on January 3, 1942, "when at the first sign of danger they so dramatically show their willingness to face death in defense of the Stars and Stripes?" The *Courier* and other newspapers vigorously campaigned for Miller to receive the Congressional Medal of Honor. On May 27 the navy awarded Miller the Navy Cross, its highest honor.[21]

On January 31, 1942, almost two months after the bombing of Pearl Harbor, the *Courier* published a letter from James G. Thompson, a twenty-six-year-old cafeteria worker at the Cessna Aircraft Corporation in Wichita, Kansas. Thompson said he was hopeful he would have the opportunity to help his country win the war. But Thompson wondered why he, as a black American, should put his life in harm's way without being accorded the privileges that white Americans had. He asked the following questions: "Would it be demanding too much to demand full citizenship rights in exchange for the sacrificing of my life?" "Is the kind of America I know worth defending?" "Will America be a true and pure democracy after the war?" "Will colored American suffer still the indignities that have been heaped upon them in the past?" Thompson said blacks should contribute to the country's victory to protect democracy in Europe but that they should not be satisfied with simply making the world safe for democracy. He said that black Americans should commit themselves to achieving democracy for themselves on U.S. soil. Thompson said that democratic countries had adopted the *V* for victory sign to unify their efforts to defeat fascism, racism, and totalitarianism. "If this V sign means that to those now engaged in this great conflict, then let we colored Americans adopt the double V for a double victory," Thompson said. "The first V for victory over our enemies from without, the second V for victory over our enemies from within."[22]

Thompson's letter, "which arguably is the most famous ever run by a black paper," according to Patrick Washburn, author of *The African-American Newspaper: Voice of Freedom*, had a profound impact on black America. In response to the letter, the *Courier* launched the Double V campaign. Unlike W. E. B. DuBois's "Closed Ranks" editorial during World War I, black Americans were unwilling to bargain in good faith on the vague promise that they might receive greater civil liberties at the end of the war. Black journalists wrote that any editor who called on blacks to "close ranks," as DuBois had a generation earlier, would lose the respect of black readers. If blacks were going to put their lives on the line to defend American democracy against German fascism, they simply wanted what was their birthright. "Be it said once more that black Americans are loyal Americans," the *Crisis* editorialized, "but let there be no mistake about the loyalty, it is loyalty to the democratic ideals as enunciated by America. . . . If all the people are called to gird and sacrifice for freedom, and the armies to march for freedom, then it must be for freedom for everyone, everywhere, and not merely for those under the Hitler heel."[23]

In early April the navy said it would end its policy of restricting blacks to positions of servitude. In telegrams to FDR and Secretary of the Navy Frank Knox, Max Yergan characterized the navy's announcement as "a bold, patriotic action in smashing age-old color restrictions which have prevented the Negro people from full service in the United States Navy."[24] Within a few months nearly a hundred thousand blacks had joined the navy.[25] Although the navy's announcement constituted progress, black leaders and editors were not satisfied. Walter White of the NAACP asked, "What point is there in fighting and perhaps dying to save democracy if there is no democracy to save?" Black newspapers called on their readers to pressure their congressmen to end discrimination in the armed services.[26] For black and sympathetic white sportswriters, democracy could begin with baseball. Dan Parker of the

Daily Mirror wrote that the navy had recently lifted its ban on blacks after the heroic efforts of Dorie Miller. It was now time for baseball to lift its ban on blacks. The black man, Parker said, "has proved himself good enough for the Navy, what must he do to demonstrate that he is fit enough in Organized Baseball?"[27]

Although the army and navy admitted blacks, this did not mean they were treated the same as whites. Black newspapers reported that the Red Cross would not accept blood from black soldiers. The organization changed its practice after it was convinced scientifically that black blood was no different from white blood.[28] Black newspapers regularly reported cases of racial disturbances at military bases such as Fort Dix in New Jersey, Fort Bragg in North Carolina, Fort Benning in Georgia, and Mitchell Field in New York. When a white police officer struck a black soldier with a nightstick in early January 1942 in Alexandria, Louisiana, a riot followed, and twelve black soldiers were shot. A few weeks after the black soldiers were shot in Louisiana, a mob of whites in Sikeston, Missouri, dragged a black man accused of raping a white woman from a jail cell, tied him to a car, dragged him at a high speed, and then hanged him before throwing gasoline on him and lighting him on fire. An editorial cartoon in the *Baltimore Afro-American* showed Adolf Hitler and a Japanese soldier grinning as they watched the man's lynching. The cartoon's caption read, "Defending America Our Way."[29]

Race relations were only marginally better at defense plants in northern cities. As more and more blacks moved to Detroit, however, so did racist organizations like the Black Legion, which had been inspired by the Ku Klux Klan. Detroit also became home for frothing demagogues like Father Charles Coughlin, who ranted against Jews, J. Edgar Hoover, and Wall Street on his popular radio program. The Reverend J. Frank Norris and the Reverend Gerald L. K. Smith preached white superiority.[30] Race relations worsened as blacks moved into previously white urban neighborhoods. When dozens of black families prepared to move into the Sojourner Truth Housing Project in Detroit on February 28, they were attacked by a white mob that began throwing stones at the families and destroying their belongings. When blacks defended themselves, things turned violent. Black newspapers reported that 1,500 Michigan state troopers and 350 Detroit police officers battled blacks at the Sojourner Truth project. In a front-page story on March 14, the *New York People's Voice* quoted Roy Wilkins, assistant secretary of the NAACP, who said that blacks were "fed up with talk of democracy and now demand some action." The *California Eagle* of Los Angeles editorialized that race relations "are not getting better."[31] In fact, things in Detroit would get a lot worse. A year later Detroit became the site of the most serious race riot in the United States in a quarter century.

The Roosevelt administration was clearly concerned about race relations. The administration believed it needed the cooperation of blacks to win the war. It also was aware from its monitoring of the black press that black newspapers had grown increasingly critical of discrimination both in the military and in civilian life. FDR instructed Attorney General Francis Biddle to meet with black editors. During World War I Woodrow Wilson had used the Espionage Act to jail his critics and suppress publications that criticized the war effort. Black editors and publishers were concerned that FDR might do the same. Editors learned that the FDR administration — unlike the Wilson administration — was willing to listen. When John Sengstacke, editor of the *Defender*, met with Biddle, the attorney general showed him a number of articles that reported racial disturbances at military bases. Biddle complained that the stories were hurting the war effort. Sengstacke disagreed. Sengstacke told Biddle his newspaper wanted to support the war effort, but administration officials would not return his phone calls; therefore, he had to rely on other sources for his stories and editorials. Biddle and Sengstacke received a compromise whereby government officials would be more accommodating, and the *Defender* would support the war effort as much as possible. With Biddle's assurance Sengstacke told other black publishers that there would be no Espionage Act. FBI director J. Edgar Hoover and other conservatives were disappointed that the administration did not take stronger action against the black press. Hoover, acting on his own, tried to intimidate black newspapers. According to one black editor, it was "a rare day" when FBI officials did not visit his newsroom. Hoover also investigated the black press without the administration's approval. When Hoover asked FDR for permission to prosecute black journalists, he was denied. An undeterred Hoover then commissioned a study that concluded that a number of black newspapers, including the *Pittsburgh Courier, Chicago Defender, Baltimore Afro-American, Michigan Chronicle* (Detroit), *Oklahoma City Black Courier*, and *New York People's Voice,* were seditious and had ties with the Communist Party. The study was sent to the White House, but the administration ignored it.[32]

With his reactionary right-wing ideology, Hoover had a kindred spirit in Westbrook Pegler, who did not have to answer to FDR or anyone else. As blacks exerted themselves, Pegler responded by heaping his considerable scorn upon those newspapers who called for racial equality. Pegler openly expressed his scorn of the "Double V" campaign.[33] If Communists wanted racial equality, then, according to Pegler, there was something suspicious about racial equality. If black editors called for racial equality, they, too, were probably Communists. The *Chicago Defender* acknowledged that the campaign to include blacks in baseball had been called "Red." "But that is natural," it said. "Everything that systematically and consistently tends to better conditions for our people is now challenged along the 'Red Scare' line."[34] In April 1942 Pegler concluded after a cursory investigation of the *Courier* and *Defender*, the two most circulated black newspapers, that the newspapers were subversive. The NAACP responded by writing Pegler's newspaper, the *New York World-Telegram.* "The Negro press has urged loyal support for the war effort," the NAACP said. "It has never been critical of the war effort, but only of the way in which Negro American citizens are being denied an opportunity by their country."[35] In at least two different columns in June, Pegler criticized the "inferiority" of black newspapers, which, he said, treated whites with hostility, though the white press was "unscrupulously fair and sympathetic to the Negro."

If this was so, Ludlow Werner, editor of the *New York Age*, responded, why did white newspapers "deny qualified Negroes the opportunity to work on their newspapers?" Werner questioned Pegler's assertion that the white press had used "restraint" and "responsibility" in its reporting of the Detroit race riot. White newspapers used restraint because whites were responsible for the riot, Werner said. S. W. Garlington of the *People's Voice* criticized Pegler, who had defied "any colored editor to cite a single paragraph of anti-Negro copy in a New York paper in the last ten years." Such a statement was defensible on the grounds that white newspapers said so little about blacks, but that silence could hardly be construed as balanced. Black stories, when they were covered, which, Garlington added, was not often, were published in the back of the newspaper amid the obituaries and classifieds. The *New York Times*, it said, had also covered the military in great depth but did not mention that the military practiced segregation. Of white-owned New York dailies, only the *Daily Worker* and *P.M.* reported the Sikeston, Missouri, lynching, the Fort Dix race riot, or the Detroit race riot.[36] Throughout the rest of the war black editors had to defend their patriotism when conservative politicians and columnists charged that black newspapers endorsed communism. "Far from being parlor pinks," *Ebony* editorialized, "most Negro publishers are arch conservatives in their thinking on every issue with one exception — the race problem."[37]

One notable exception was Adam Clayton Powell Jr., who served on the New York City Council before being elected to the U.S. Congress. Powell said he became a journalist to correct false stereotypes about black people, to become a militant voice for black society, and to educate and arouse his readers to demand more democracy. In 1942 Powell created the *People's Voice*, which had the motto "A Militant Paper . . . Serving All People . . . The New Voice of the New Negro." Chuck Stone, who wrote for the *Chicago Defender* and later taught journalism at the University of North Carolina, said that the *People's Voice*'s biting, uncompromising militancy "has rarely been matched."[38] Its sports editor, Joe Bostic, was more confrontational than most of his fellow sportswriters. During the Christmas season in 1943, Bostic, in a letter called "No Room at the Yankee Inn," criticized the Yankees for their hiring practices that discriminated against blacks. Bostic won a writing award but was also banned from the team's press box.[39]

By the 1940s newspapers had become perhaps the most influential business in black America. Gunnar Myrdal characterized the black press as "the greatest single power in the Negro race." Readership reached the height of its popularity during the decade as weekly circulation rose into the millions. Black newspapers had a common goal of racial equality in all parts of American life and served both to inform and to unify readers. Although that goal was shared by the Communists, influential black editors were reluctant to work too closely with the Communists. The black press and the NAACP, while sharing a common distrust of communism, forged their mutual interests. Editors recognized the NAACP's contribution for greater civil rights. NAACP leaders wrote columns that regularly appeared in black newspapers that informed readers of pending laws and lawsuits intended to confront racial discrimination. The NAACP, in turn, praised black newspapers for their contributions to civil rights. "When there is no need for the NAACP," NAACP counsel Thurgood Marshall later said, "there will be no need for the Colored press."[40]

Black newspapers knew they could expect little or no support from the white press. If the black press had to confront racial discrimination alone, it was, therefore, necessary for publishers, editors, and other journalists to work together. During the spring of 1942 the NAACP called for a conference of black editors. This came as a result of growing concern that there was increasing pressure on the Roosevelt administration to suspend black newspapers from the mail.[41] Meanwhile, a number of black sportswriters created the American Sports Writers' Association during a meeting in late March at the Hotel Theresa in New York City.[42] The American Sports Writers' Association was an organization in name only. Each member may have supported the desegregation of baseball, but they did not support one another. Instead of working together toward a common goal, they constantly sniped at one another, offering not support or encouragement but petty criticisms for anyone who confronted the color line.

On March 21 Joe Bostic shared a dream that he had become a broker for Major League teams, which had come to him to buy players to replace the big leaguers who had left for the armed services. The New York Yankees paid twenty-five thousand dollars for third baseman Ray Dandrige. The Giants paid eighty-five thousand for Jake Spearman and Dave "Showboat" Thomas, Dick Seay, and Jesse Williams of the Kansas City Monarchs. Larry MacPhail of the Brooklyn Dodgers picked up pitchers Jonas Gaines, Hilton Smith, and Henry McHenry for eighteen thousand dollars. The Cleveland Indians needed a top pitcher to replace Bob Feller, and Bostic sold him Satchel Paige. The Detroit Tigers got Sammy Hughes to fill the vacancy left by all-star second baseman Charlie Gehringer. Bostic sold the entire Homestead Grays team to Jerry Nugent to replace his lowly Philadelphia Phillies and the Baltimore Elites to Clark Griffith, owner of the Senators. But then Bostic was interrupted by four men. A government agent charged him with operating a trust and served him an injunction requiring him to cease and desist. A second man, who identified himself as Kenesaw Mountain Landis, told Bostic he was ruining "the great American game . . . by introducing a democratic theme into the lily-white setup." The third and fourth men, Tom Wilson, president of the Negro National League, and J. B. Martin, president of the Negro American League, said that if black players went to the Major Leagues, the two men would lose their investments. "I protested that the Landis setup was a monopoly, too, and an un-American one at that . . . ," Bostic wrote. "But they'd hear none of it and together, they tossed me out onto the sidewalk."[43]

A few days before the column was published, the Chicago White Sox granted Jackie Robinson and pitcher Nate Moreland, who had pitched for the Baltimore Elite Giants before playing in Mexico, an afternoon workout with the team during its spring training in Pasadena, California. The blacks had been accompanied by *Pittsburgh Courier* correspondent Herman Hill. Although Robinson had a sore leg, he impressed White Sox manager Jimmy Dykes, who told reporters that he was worth fifty thousand dollars to any Major League team. Dykes told the players there was no written rule prohibiting blacks from playing in the Major Leagues. But, he added, there was "an unwritten law." Dykes said managers wanted to sign black players but did not have the authority. Commissioner Landis and the team owners were responsible for the color line, Dykes said. Years later, however, Herman Hill, the *Pittsburgh Courier*'s West Coast correspondent who was present at the workout, wrote that Dykes had "refused to pose for pictures with Jackie and Nate" and that "several White Sox players hovered around menacingly with bats in their hands."[44]

Robinson and Moreland, who were both expected to be drafted into the army, were discouraged by the response they received at the White Sox training camp. "I can play in the Mexican National league," Moreland said, adding that he could not play in the Major Leagues even if he fought to defend the country.[45] In its story the *Worker* reported that a number of big league managers such as McKechnie and Durocher had expressed interest in signing blacks. When Dykes returned to Chicago, he was ordered to the commissioner's office, where he was rebuked.[46] In a short time Durocher, too, would have to answer to the commissioner for his comments. By this time the *Worker* had put responsibility for the color line squarely on Landis. On May 6, 1942, a month before Lester Rodney was inducted into the army, he wrote a letter to the commissioner, which was published in the *Worker* and reprinted in black newspapers. Rodney wrote that the commissioner would probably ignore the letter because he had already ignored petitions with "millions of names" that had been sent to his office calling for the end of the color line, the numerous columns from white sportswriters who supported blacks in baseball, and the statements from dozens of ballplayers and managers who said they had no objection to blacks in baseball. Nevertheless, Rodney said he wrote the letter for others to read. "You, the self-proclaimed 'czar' of baseball, are the

man responsible for keeping Jim Crow in our national pastime. You
are the one who, by your silence, is maintaining a relic of the slave
market long repudiated in other American sports," Rodney said. "You
are the one refusing to say the word which would do more to justify
baseball's existence in this year of war than any other single thing. You
are the one who is blocking the step which would put baseball in line
with the rest of the country," Rodney wrote. "There can no longer be
any excuse for your silence, Judge Landis."

Rodney told Landis the commissioner had time and again told the
American public that he was the final authority on baseball. If Landis
opposed discrimination, why then did he not end it in baseball? But if
he supported discrimination against blacks, then his views ran contra-
dictory to those of the American people. Rodney said that blacks — like
Joe Louis and Dorie Miller — had earned the respect of the American
people. President Roosevelt had called for the end of discrimination in
the workplace. Rodney asked Landis how he could continue to allow
discrimination in baseball. Rodney said that managers like McKechnie,
Dykes, and Durocher had said that they would sign blacks if they were
allowed. Rodney said that a growing number of white sportswriters
and mainstream newspapers — including, most recently, the *Louisville
Courier-Journal* — had joined those who wanted an end to the color
line. "Baseball, in this war, should set an example of democracy. What
about it, Mr. Landis?" Rodney wrote. "Yes, what about it, Mr. Landis?
. . . The American people are waiting for you," Rodney said. "You're
holding up the works."[47]

The *Defender*, which reprinted Rodney's letter, reported that a committee of black activists in Chicago met at the Hotel Grand in Chicago
to discuss how best to pressure Landis and the baseball establishment.
The committee included William Harrison, who was named acting
chairman; Fay Young, sports editor of the *Chicago Defender*; C. Francis
Stradford, attorney and former president of the National Negro Bar
Association; and attorney William L. Patterson, the other cochair, who
had long been active in the NAACP and in radical politics with his

friends Paul Robeson and Heywood Broun. Patterson rejected Broun's invitation to join the Socialist Party and, instead, joined the Communist Party, where he contributed to the *Daily Worker*. Patterson served on the defense counsel in the murder trial of anarchists Nicola Sacco and Bartolomeo Vanzetti and then worked on the defense of the Scottsboro Boys. In his autobiography Patterson said the *Worker* had actively campaigned for the desegregation of baseball. "I myself had pushed the campaign vigorously," Patterson said. Patterson and his committee agreed to intensify the campaign by taking their case to the commissioner's office. "To this end, we would confront one of the Big League owners or Baseball Commissioner Kenesaw Mountain Landis, or both," he said. "I was asked to handle this phase."[48]

The committee anticipated Landis would put responsibility for the color line on team owners, who would, in turn, put responsibility on managers, who would say they could not sign blacks because of the gentlemen's agreement banning blacks. The committee also said managers and ballplayers had gone on record saying they did not oppose blacks in the big leagues. In addition, the committee questioned baseball's argument that the mixing of blacks and whites was not possible because of the segregation policies of hotels. Young said that members of the Ohio State University's mixed track team all stayed in the same hotel during a meet in Des Moines, Iowa. The committee invited several of the city's prominent politicians, ministers, and journalists to its next meeting, including Bernard J. Sheil, then the senior auxiliary bishop of the Chicago Roman Catholic Archdiocese of Chicago. When Sheil met with the committee, he said that he supported its efforts and said he would do what he could to arrange a meeting with Landis. "Of course I am with you," Shiel said. "This situation is not only a disgrace to democracy but it is harmful to the national morale. Now it is the time to show real American spirit and to demonstrate in action the democracy for which we are fighting."[49]

Shiel, by then, had earned a reputation for his support of civil rights. Shiel, who excelled at baseball while growing up, reportedly declined a tryout with both the Chicago White Sox and the Cincinnati Reds to enter the priesthood. He had personal knowledge of the talent of some of the black players. "I have played ball with some of the great Negro players who should have reached the big leagues," he said.[50] Shiel later organized the Catholic Youth Organization and used sports to draw lower- and middle-class Catholics, blacks, and Jews away from other less-worthy pursuits. Once when Shiel criticized bigotry in a speech, a woman in the audience responded by calling him a "Nigger lover" and "Jew lover" and then spat in his face. Shiel also was a longtime supporter of radical politics, including labor unions such as the CIO. In 1939 he accepted the invitation of John L. Lewis, president of the CIO, to speak with him at a rally. Before the event a friend told Shiel that "the minute you step on the platform, you lose your chance to become archbishop." Shiel responded, "I wasn't ordained a Catholic priest in order to become an archbishop."[51]

In late May Ches Washington of the *Courier* wrote his own letter to Landis, where he said that the navy had created separate training bases for its black soldiers, and therefore the Major Leagues could create a farm league of black teams. The better players could then transition into organized professional baseball. Washington wrote that Wendell Smith's interviews had demonstrated there was little objection to desegregation among Major League ballplayers and managers. He said that white sports columnists had reported there were black players with the ability to play in the big leagues. Big league teams already had black trainers who made their own accommodations where there were segregation laws. The addition of black players, he said, would also improve attendance at big league games. Crowds of fifty thousand had attended the annual East-West games. Washington concluded by referring to a recent game between the Kansas City Monarchs and a white team fronted by Dizzy Dean. Washington asked, "Did you read about the Kansas City Monarchs drawing 30,000 in Chicago last Sunday against Dizzy Dean's major league all stars and beating the stars, 3–1?"[52]

On May 30, 1942, Satchel Paige and the Monarchs defeated a team that included former big leaguers and current big leaguers who were in the armed services, including Dizzy Dean, Bob Feller, Zeke Bonura, and Cecil Travis, before a crowd of twenty-nine thousand at Wrigley Field. Two days later, on June 1, the Monarchs won again in front of a crowd of twenty-five thousand at Griffith Stadium.[53] On June 5 Paige, now pitching for the Homestead Grays, beat the Dean all-stars at Forbes Field in Pittsburgh. The crowd of twenty-two thousand was the largest of the year at Forbes Field. The mixed-race exhibition games drew bigger crowds than most big league games, and black and white fans sat together without incident. Landis banned a July 4 game between the Paige all-stars and the Dean all-stars that was scheduled to be played in Chicago. Landis, according to David Pietrusza, obviously was not pleased that the black all-stars had defeated the white all-stars and that the crowds had been bigger than for Major League games. He wanted to ensure that this could not happen again.[54] Fay Young wrote that Landis's reaction revealed the commissioner's true feelings on the issue. "As long as Paige can pitch against a white team of former major leaguers and beat them it is 'sour grapes' to white-haired Judge Landis," Young said.[55]

Eddie Gant of the *Defender* criticized Landis for canceling the exhibition games. "We believed all the time that the judge disliked colored players and colored baseball," Gant said, "and this we think only serves to convince us beyond a reasonable doubt. The judge really tipped his hand this time." Gant added that white sportswriters such as Powers and Rodney had "courageously fought to pry open the 'closed door.'" In Chicago, however, he added, all white sportswriters with the exception of Lloyd Lewis had "remained silent on the subject." Gant believed, as did other black journalists, the color line would fall if more and more white sportswriters challenged it. As long as the conspiracy of silence persisted, so too would segregation. Dave Farrell of the *Worker*, who signed his columns "Scorer," wrote that sportswriters may not have been writing about the issue, but this did not mean that they were not discussing it. During one Major League team's road trip, a sportswriter told his colleagues that they should all call for the end of the color line. "Opposition developed," Farrell said, "but out of the discussion came an agreement that the entire situation was contrary to the spirit of the United States Constitution."[56]

The U.S. Communist Party was closely associated with organized labor — particularly the more radical organizations such as the CIO and IWO. Throughout June the *Worker* chronicled the involvement of labor unions and influential whites in the campaign to end segregation in baseball. On June 2 the New Jersey District of the International Workers Order, representing fifteen thousand members, sent a resolution to Landis's office. On June 4 National Maritime Union members voted unanimously to appeal to Landis. On June 5 the *Worker* reported that Bishop Shiel said he would personally appeal to Landis to end the color line. On June 6 the New York Industrial Union Council of the CIO, representing a half-million trade unionists in 250 locals, approved a resolution demanding the end of the color line in baseball. On June 16 the Ford Local of the United Automobile Workers of America, representing eighty thousand members, sent a resolution to Landis. On June 17 the *Worker* quoted Brooklyn city councilman Peter Cacchione as saying that Jim Crow in baseball was doomed. By the end of the month the *Worker* reported that the IWO had begun distributing twenty thousand buttons with the words "Score Against Hitler, Lift Ban on Negro Players" to its rank and file across the country. On June 28 the *Worker* called June "the month of the greatest advance in the campaign for the end of Jim Crow in organized baseball."[57]

As demands for equality increased, so did the inflammatory rhetoric of racists such as Senator Theodore Bilbo and Representative John Rankin of Mississippi, who filibustered attempts to create antilynching laws and referred dismissively to blacks as "persons of Ethiopian descent." In a newspaper column poet Carl Sandburg criticized Rankin for his race-baiting and praised the contributions of the CIO and organized labor in the effort to bring racial equality in society and in baseball, in particular. Sandburg wondered what impact the desegregation of baseball might have on Rankin and others like him. "What shortstops and center fielders designated in the Emancipation Proclamation as 'persons of Ethiopian descent' Congressman Rankin may be watching if he goes to see a game," Sandburg said, "is beyond present telling." Sandburg recognized, like other white progressives, that change was inevitable in postwar America. "As this war goes on," Sandburg wrote, "we are going to hear more and more — and definitely not less and less about race issues and the color line."[58]

Joseph D. Bibb wrote in the *Pittsburgh Courier* that the North conceded to the South on matters of race because whites did not want to fight one another over blacks. Therefore, blacks were denied opportunities. This was as true for baseball as it was in other pursuits. "The colored man has always been made the goat. He is denied an opportunity to make the good money," Bibb said, "and draw the fabulous salary that has been paid to the big league stars purely because his presence in the national game might offend the southerners." The United States could not continue to deny the issue at home that had brought the world to war. He called for intensifying the campaign to desegregate baseball because of the impact that integration would have on the rest of society. "That is why colored Americans must crusade, protest and contend without ceasing," Bibb said. "Here and there, we gain a painful inch as we relentlessly hurl ourselves against a multitude of woes and evils."[59] Three months later Bibb expressed optimism about postwar America. "When the war ends the colored of America will be better off financially, spiritually, and economically," he said. "War may be hell for some, but it bids fair to open up the portals of heaven for us."[60]

Jack Saunders of the *Philadelphia Tribune* said baseball was not separate from American society — and that social conditions would impact what happened in baseball. He said that the issue would ultimately be settled in the South, where big league teams trained in the spring and where much of Minor League ball was played. This, Saunders said, would not change as long as the South was governed by racists like Rankin and Georgia governor Eugene Talmadge. Saunders said there could not be racial equality in baseball until there was racial equality in America and that progress toward equality depended on the Roosevelt administration. "If President Roosevelt had issued an ultimatum out-lawing jim-crowism and discrimination the width and breath of these United States of America," he said. "But President Roosevelt has yet to issue an ultimatum and Governor Talmadge would probably see himself strung up from the highest Georgia pine before he'd admit Negroes are half as good as mongrel dogs."[61]

One white sportswriter, Will Connolly of the *San Francisco Chronicle*, said southern players would protest any attempt to bring blacks into baseball, but they would accept integration eventually. "We can't go on coddling the dear old South forever," he said, "and allow it to shape the course of baseball's destiny." Connolly, however, added that few blacks had the ability for the Major Leagues or even the high Minors. Connolly, while admitting to knowing little about black baseball, concluded that blacks stood as little chance of playing in the big leagues as an English cricket player or, for that matter, as Bob Feller or Joe DiMaggio did playing cricket in England. Because there were so few blacks good enough for the big leagues, Connolly wondered why organized baseball was so opposed to desegregation. "This causes me to wonder why organized baseball put a restraining hand against Negroes in the first place," Connolly wrote, "and made such an unhappy issue of it to the detriment of the sport and the embarrassment of those who try to reconcile political equality with social."[62]

Roy Campanella, a twenty-year-old catcher of the Baltimore Elite Giants, had played enough games against white Major Leaguers to know he was as good or better than they were. The white ballplayers knew it as well as he did. In his autobiography, *It's Good to Be Alive*, Campanella said that during July 1945 he went to a Philadelphia Phillies game with his wife at Shibe Park. When Campanella and his wife got to the ballpark, it was still an hour before the game. The players and managers were on the field. Campanella saw Phillies manager Hans Lobert, whom he knew because Lobert had seen Campanella play at Shibe Park. Acting on an impulse, Campanella asked Lobert if he would speak to him.

"Hello, Campy," Lobert said. "What are you doing away from the Elites?"

"An off day," Campanella said, and then he told Lobert he had heard talk that the big leagues were considering allowing black players. "You can use a catcher," Campanella said, "and I'm a good catcher. I can help this club!"

Lobert suggested that Campanella call Gerry Nugent, the team's owner. "There's a pay phone out there in the lobby," Lobert said. "Why don't you go out and call Mr. Gerry Nugent, the president of our club? You can tell him I suggested you give him a ring. He's in his office."

After Campanella identified himself to Nugent's secretary, he was connected. "Mr. Nugent, this is Roy Campanella," he said. "I was wondering if maybe you could give me a tryout. I have been keeping tabs on the Phillies, and it strikes me that you could use not only some catchin', but hitting too."

Nugent told Campanella that he was familiar with the ballplayer's ability. He told Campanella there was an unwritten rule about blacks in organized baseball. Nugent thanked Campanella for calling, and that was the end of the conversation. When Campanella hung up the phone, he said he had a sinking feeling in his stomach. "I felt real bad for a minute, I knew I had no right to. After all, what did I expect? Did I expect Hans Lobert and owner Gerry Nugent to go busting the bars down for me — right there and then? I hadn't lost anything by that call. And maybe one day . . . well, maybe one day . . ."

Campanella did not call Nugent again. "I figured I had been a fool even to hope that I would be given a chance to play major league baseball," Campanella said in his autobiography. "Organized baseball was in another land. The frontiers were well guarded. No one of my race could sneak in."[63]

Campanella's memory was faulty, but the gist of the story was probably true. In 1945 the Phillies were owned by Robert Carpenter and managed by Ben Chapman and not Hans Lobert. It is unlikely that Campanella would have approached a racist like Chapman in hopes of integrating the big leagues. In 1942 Nugent was the team's president, and he had already gone on record in 1933 as supporting integration. In 1939 Doc Prothro, who was then the Phillies' manager, told the *Courier* that he would sign black players, "if given permission." If Lobert had indeed told Campanella that his team could use a catcher of Campanella's ability, he certainly had a reason. The team's regular catcher was Bennie Warren, who hit .209 for the season with just seven home runs and twenty runs batted in. The Phillies finished the season in last place with a 42-109 record, 62.5 games out of first place.

In all likelihood, any conversation between Campanella and either Lobert or Nugent or both occurred in late June or early July. The *Worker* broke the story on July 13 that a black catcher, whom it did not identify, had told one of its reporters that the Phillies were scouting him. A few days later the *Worker* published a profile of Campanella. Nat Low described Campanella "as a manager's dream," a twenty-year-old power hitter with exceptional defensive skills. It quoted Philadelphia Athletics and then Boston Red Sox slugger Jimmy Foxx as telling Campanella he would be a star in the Major Leagues. Low incorrectly reported, however, that Campanella had already had a tryout with the Phillies. The Phillies, the article said, told him to wait "until something turns up." The newspaper quoted Campanella as saying, "I'm sure I could do OK in the majors." When asked if he was wary of racial discrimination from other big league players, the catcher responded, "I've played against many big leaguers who have come from the South and have never had anything but friendliest relations with them. We'd get along perfectly if we were given the chance."[64]

On July 21 Hy Turkin of the *New York Daily News* incorrectly reported that the Phillies had become the first big league team to give a tryout to a black player since John McGraw "tried to 'palm off a sunburned Cuban.'" Bob Considine also wrote that Campanella had been "promised a tryout by the Phils."[65] Nugent, however, denied that the team gave a tryout to Campanella. Nugent said the team would be interested in looking at any player as long as they were not already signed with another team. Lobert, the story said, was unavailable for comment.[66] There is no evidence that the Phillies gave Campanella a tryout. Campanella may have mentioned his account of what happened at Shibe Park to Nat Low, who then reported it in his column in the *Worker*. It is impossible to say if it was Campanella or Low, or both, who exaggerated the details. On August 1 the *Pittsburgh Courier* interviewed Campanella, who contradicted earlier stories that said he had had a tryout with the Phillies. Campanella said he had contacted Nugent to regret the error. During his conversation with Nugent, Campanella asked the owner for a tryout. Nugent told him that the team would sign him if he was good enough. Before the team would give a tryout, however, Nugent explained, either Lobert or one of the team's scouts would have to recommend him. "I'd love the chance to see how I'd make out. If it ever happened that I was the first Negro to break in the big tent, I realize I'd be on the spot," Campanella said. "But the wolves could howl and the fans and the players could do whatever they wanted but the only thing that would stop me would be that I just would not be good enough."[67]

CHAPTER 8

"THE GREAT WHITE FATHER" SPEAKS

On June 22, 1942, Conrad Komorowski of the *Daily Worker* interviewed Kenesaw Mountain Landis for an hour and a half in the commissioner's office at 333 North Michigan Avenue in Chicago. Komorowski said he began the interview by asking Landis if he had any comment about the resolution passed by eighty thousand Ford workers condemning Jim Crow in the Major Leagues. Landis responded with a "No comment." Komorowski asked Landis more questions, and the commissioner responded to each with a "No comment."

"Why do you refuse to comment?" Komorowski asked.

"You fellows say I'm responsible," Landis said.

"Aren't you?" Komorowski responded.

"You fellows say I am," Landis answered.

"If you are not, why don't you defend yourself?" Komorowski said.

Landis initially did not respond to the question, then, Komorowski reported, "tried to pass the buck" to the team owners.

"Why don't you put them on the spot?" Landis asked.[1]

Landis, according to David Pietrusza, realized that his "no comment" would be criticized.[2] Landis then began talking more freely, admitting that he felt a lot of pressure to open up baseball to blacks. "There is no man living," Landis said, "who wants the friendship of the Negro people more than I." If that were so, Komorowski persisted, why did he not end the color line? Landis responded by saying, "No comment."

"And that," Komorowski reported on June 24, "is the answer — thus far — of the head of organized baseball in a nation at war for freedom, equality and democracy."[3]

On June 25 Nat Low wrote an open letter to Landis, saying that the commissioner's "no comment" contrasted with the Declaration of Independence's words that "all men are created equal." The letter also said that Landis stood in contrast to big league managers who said they were willing to sign blacks if they could. "You stand in opposition to the very reasons for which we are fighting this grim, bloody war. Millions of human beings throughout the globe are fighting, bleeding, and dying for the very thing you are denying to 12,000,000 Negro Americans," the letter said. "So I repeat, Judge Landis, your brusque 'No comment' cannot and will not be accepted by the American people. They will demand ever louder and ever stronger that you lift the ban on Negro baseball players in the big leagues."[4]

A. C. MacNeal of the *Chicago Defender* wrote that Landis had been presented with "a reasonable demand to remove a 'tradition' which says that the only way a Negro can play in the big leagues is to pass for a Cuban or Indian." MacNeal then added that Landis was in a position to take action against the color line but feared "to do anything which might disturb the entrenched 'tradition.'" MacNeal wrote that as more and more white big leaguers were drafted into the army, Major League teams would be forced to sign black players to fill their rosters. "Why wait?" he asked. *New York Sun* columnist Frank Graham quoted Jimmy Dykes as saying he was so short of quality ballplayers, he was considering giving his coaches gloves. The *Worker* reported that Dykes could find a number of talented ballplayers in the Negro leagues. Low said the newspaper would begin a series of articles on black ballplayers good enough for the Major Leagues. In mid-July members of the Industrial Workers of the World distributed thousands of leaflets outside theaters showing the premiere of the film *Pride of the Yankees*, the biography of the late New York Yankees slugger Lou Gehrig. The leaflets, which called for the end of segregated baseball, included a quote by Gehrig that said, "I have seen and played against many Negro ballplayers who could easily be stars in the big leagues. I could name just a few of them, like Satchel Page, Buck Leonard, Josh Gibson and Barney Brown, who should be in the Majors." The leaflets identified Landis as the man "responsible for the continuation of the un-American ban."[5]

Landis could have continued to ignore criticism in the *Worker*. The newspaper had little influence in mainstream America. But for whatever reason, Landis decided he needed to defend himself. What apparently provoked him was seeing Durocher's quote where he said he had seen many blacks who were good enough to play in the Majors. "I certainly could use a Negro ball player if the bosses said it was all right," Durocher said. *Worker* sportswriters taunted Landis by mailing him quotes like Durocher's and newspaper clippings that reported how black teams had defeated white teams. This may have been how Landis learned about the Durocher quote and why he responded three years after the quote first appeared in the *Pittsburgh Courier*. If the Communists had hoped to goad Landis into action, they achieved their objective. Why did Landis single out Durocher when other players and managers had expressed that same opinion? Perhaps because Durocher, like the *Worker* and organized labor, had long been a source of irritation for the commissioner. Landis perhaps felt he simultaneously could exert his authority over Durocher and deny culpability for the color line.

On July 15 Landis ordered Durocher to his office. After the meeting Landis told reporters the manager had denied making such a comment to the *Worker*. Durocher made the comment to Wendell Smith. Landis then addressed the issue with a statement. "Certain managers in

organized baseball have been quoted as saying the reason Negroes are
not playing organized baseball is (that the) commissioner would not
permit them to do so. Negroes are not barred from organized baseball
by the commissioner and never have been in the 21 years I have served.
There is no rule in organized baseball prohibiting their participation
and never has been to my knowledge," Landis said. If Durocher or
another manager wanted to sign one black players or twenty-five black
players, "it was all right with me. That is the business of the managers
and the club owners. The business of the commissioner is to interpret
the rules of baseball and enforce them."[6] As both commissioner and
a federal judge, Landis was used to having the last word. As a judge,
he understood the importance of nuance. It was true that he did not
bar blacks from baseball. It also was true that baseball did not have a
written law barring black players. And finally, it was true that Landis
had nothing to do with creating the color line. It predated him by
more than a generation. But Landis had a lot to do with maintaining
the color line. If Landis truly believed his announcement would be
the last word on the issue, he was mistaken. Not since Jake Powell's
"nightstick" remark did a comment so energize the forces that wanted
baseball desegregated.

Between games of a doubleheader between the Chicago Cubs and
Brooklyn Dodgers the next day at Wrigley Field, Landis discussed the
issue further with reporters, denying that there was any "rule, formal or
informal, or any understanding, written, subterranean or sub-anything"
against the hiring of black baseball players. Landis repeated his statement that teams were free to sign black players.[7] Fay Young reported
that Landis's interview was briefly interrupted by an announcement
that there would be a Satchel Paige Day at Wrigley Field on July 26.
Young recognized the irony of the juxtaposition of Landis's denial of
the color line and the announcement of a day of honor for black baseball's greatest pitcher, who was barred from white baseball because of
a rule Landis said did not exist. Young said that "one could write until
the sun sets on the following day of the exploits of black men whose

names could have headlined the sports pages if given a chance in the major leagues." He called Landis's statement "bosh."[8]

A week later Young said baseball was no different from the rest of the country. President Roosevelt had ordered an end to discrimination in defense contracts, yet discrimination continued — even as America was fighting a war over democracy. "Yet we are supposed to have full American rights. We are supposed to be able to go as far as our ability can take us," Young said. "But we are the 'supposingest' race on earth." Young again questioned Landis's sincerity. If baseball did not have a color line, he said, there would be blacks in baseball. "Since no Negroes are barred," Young asked, "what keeps them out? That's a question that Landis ought to answer." Eddie Gant of the *Chicago Defender* said, "It will be a long time before there are blacks in the big leagues." Lucius Harper said Landis's comment denied the existence of a color line, "but the old line is still there." Harper said the question of who was responsible for the color line had been on the minds of blacks and liberal whites for years. Buster Miller of the *New York Age* said Landis made his statement only after receiving considerable criticism. He made it clear that the individual teams — and not his office — were responsible for the color line.[9]

The *Pittsburgh Courier*, in an unsigned editorial, called Landis's statement baseball's "Emancipation Proclamation." Ches Washington said that Landis had forced the issue on owners. In addition, Wendell Smith wrote that a number of sportswriters had "pounded away on the issue" for years. "Now 'The Great White Father' of Baseball has finally spoken," Smith said. "The work of these veteran writers has not been in vain. Landis has left the issue to the owners and the fans. The end is in sight." Smith called on baseball fans to put pressure on the baseball establishment. Smith also recognized the contributions of Jimmy Powers, Dan Parker, and Lloyd Lewis. Washington quoted Vincent Flaherty of the *Washington Times-Herald* for calling for the end of segregated baseball. "Some day the colored star will make his way in either the National or American league," Flaherty said. "When?

That's something else Judge Landis might answer. When it happens, you can look for greatly increased attendance figures from all fronts." Clark Griffith told Ches Washington that there should be different leagues for blacks and whites. The *Courier* also quoted Harry Keck of the city's other black weekly, the *Sun-Telegraph*, as saying Landis was asking "the public to swallow a big sugar-coated pill" when the commissioner said there was no color line prohibiting blacks in baseball.[10]

Under the headline "The Judge Spoke, but He Did Not Say Anything," Joe Bostic wrote that Landis had not said anything that might be held against him. "Any close analysis of the statement made by Landis reveals a studied attempt to avoid any commitment of where he stands morally on the question," Bostic said. As a federal judge, he added, Landis learned "to say exactly what he meant but also to consider the delicate shading of (the) meaning of the words and phrases used." Therefore, Landis had said the owners could hire "one or twenty-five Negroes" for their team. "He took care not to say should or to make any statement as to what his opinion was of the unstated but terrifically effective ban now in force," Bostic said. There probably was not a written agreement prohibiting blacks from baseball, the sportswriter added. "That would be incriminating in the event of any investigation," Bostic said. "The problem is never discussed at any official gatherings because the views expressed might go on record. But, dammit, let's stop kidding, statement or not, there aren't any players on the team and anybody who thinks it's accidental also believes the Aesops fables." Bostic said Landis did not say anything significant; his statement was significant merely because his statement was reported in newspapers throughout the country.[11]

On July 17 Joe Cummiskey, sports editor of *P.M.*, wrote that Landis told him he was "sick and tired" of taking the blame and wanted to make it clear the issue was the responsibility of owners and managers. Cummiskey added that Landis "has been a long time arriving at this official statement." Cummiskey suggested that Landis made his statement because of growing pressure from outside baseball. Cummiskey said Landis's statement put pressure on teams to sign black players: "Why wouldn't it be a good idea for those owners and managers who have said on and off the record in the past that they wouldn't bar Negroes as long as they could make the grade" to give blacks an opportunity? *P.M.* sportswriters Jim Russell and John Lewy said Landis's announcement had resulted in an increased attendance among whites, including big league scouts, at Negro league games. "Nothing better could have happened," "Soldier Boy" Semler, owner of the New York Black Yankees, said. "Of course, lots of white teams would draw better if they had colored players, but right now we're happy to have attention." Abe and Effa Manley, owners of the Newark Eagles, praised Landis for his "fair-mindedness," saying desegregation would provide "white people a chance to see the best colored performers in the league."[12]

Dan Parker criticized Landis's statement as "hypocritical." Parker reported a piece of history rarely found in mainstream newspapers. Blacks, he said, had once played in the big leagues. Parker quoted a 1918 column by Hugh Fullerton that mentioned that Fleet Walker had played in the big leagues in 1884. The column included the quote from Walker's pitcher, Tony Mullane, who praised Walker's ability but said he refused to take signals from a black man. According to Parker, the color line did not happen naturally but was the result of racial discrimination. Blacks were not barred, Parker suggested, but they were not admitted either. "There is no good reason why, in a country that calls itself a Democracy, intolerance should exist on the sports field," Parker said, which he called the "most democratic of all meeting places."[13] Hy Turkin, who replaced Powers, who had joined the navy, wrote that Durocher's comment "may carve a larger niche in baseball history" than anything he did as a player or a manager. He said Landis had declared there was no rule keeping blacks out of baseball after his office received a million letters, telegrams, and phone calls. "Landis' statement is epochal," Turkin said, adding, "It is also false." Turkin then responded to one of the baseball establishment's arguments that said that southern ballplayers would quit if they had to play with or against blacks. Turkin told baseball to call the ballplayers' bluff. "Don't believe it!" Turkin said. "A microscopic minority of major leaguers could earn $10,000 or so per season doing anything besides pitching and hitting."[14]

New York Post columnist Stanley Frank wrote that baseball could not continue ignoring the calls for blacks in baseball, but it also could not allow teams to sign blacks without understanding the ramifications. He called the color line "a large stick of dynamite with a fuse suddenly ignited by a smoldering fire of public agitation," Frank said. "It is an issue too vital to ignore and too hot to handle without asbestos gloves and a fireproof shield of realism." Frank used fear to justify keeping blacks and whites separate. If blacks were allowed in baseball, he said, "southern ball players will brandish sharp spikes with intent to cut and maim Negro infielders; that there will be an unprecedented wave of murderous bean-balls thrown at Negro batters; that jockeying from the benches will decend to subhuman levels of violence." Southerners, he claimed, were conditioned to act violently toward blacks. Nat Low said Frank's comment was obviously not based on either personal experience or the history of interracial competition in the United States. "The ominous threats of spikings and fights is just the concoctions and perhaps wishful thinking of the sports columnist of the 'liberal' *Post*," Low said.[15]

Dan Burley of the *Amsterdam News* said that even if Frank was right, this should not keep blacks out of the big leagues. Blacks could take care of themselves, he said; they were doing so every day on battlefields in Europe and in Asia. Joe Bostic wrote Frank a letter agreeing with him. Frank quoted from the letter a few days later. Frank began the column by writing that Bostic had criticized the "bleeding hearts" who lacked the perspective for understanding the consequences if blacks were brought into big league baseball. "I was gratified to see a white writer who wasn't trying to raise a lot of false hopes or trying to be a rabble rouser," Bostic wrote. "It seems to me that it's mighty important at this time that a few people keep their shirts on or else the race angle will get so bitter that all the good that sports have done thus far in aiding inter-racial good will be tossed out the window." Frank said he was "utterly" and "sincerely in favor" of desegregating the big leagues. "But," he added, "not under conditions prevailing now."[16]

Joe Williams, who opposed desegregation, criticized Landis, for bringing baseball's dirty little secret into the open. Williams said that Landis had typically admonished privately those who dared question the color line. But this time Landis had gone straight to the press, Williams said, leaving sportswriters to wonder how he really stood on the issue. "What he told the Dodgers' manager was nothing new, but up to then it has all been behind closed doors," said Williams, suggesting that was where the issue belonged. *New York Journal American* columnist Bill Corum said he had received a letter from a reader asking him what he thought of Landis's statement. Corum responded that blacks should be allowed in the Major Leagues but only if they were good enough, adding that he knew of no black players with Major League ability. He said the day would come when blacks would become players in the Major Leagues, but "I don't quite see the point of attempting to stir up a rumpus about it right now," he added. A few days later Corum expressed his unqualified support for Landis, calling on baseball to have a day to honor the commissioner, saying that "no living man has done more for the old game than the old judge."[17]

The *New York Times* responded to Landis's statement with its customary silence. Ira Seebacher of the *New York Morning Telegraph* said that the *Times*'s reaction reflected the newspaper's editorial policy on issues like race. The *New York Daily News*, by contrast, Seebacher said, "happens to be taking a democratic stand on the matter." Seebacher questioned whether Landis was being truthful when he said baseball had no rule prohibiting blacks. "It is difficult to believe that Landis who has been, and still is, so keenly aware of every trick, every secret, every bit of skullduggery attempted in baseball, should not know that there is a tacit agreement among club owners and managers to bar Negroes from the game." Nat Low said he looked for Landis's statement in the *Times* but found nothing in the day's newspaper, or the day after that or the day after that, "nary a word, not a single mention of this vitally important statement by the head of organized baseball." The *Times*, however, Low said, reported on the third race at Jamaica, on a four-round preliminary fight at Queensboro Arena, and on a Minor League Baseball game in Peoria, Illinois. "We didn't think that the *Times* would stoop so low as to completely ignore the statement on Jim Crow in baseball," Low said. He said that if the *Times* thought it could suppress the bigger story, it was mistaken. The campaign would not stop, he said, "until the day of final victory when Negro players take their rightful places alongside the DiMaggios."[18]

Dave Egan of the *Boston Daily Record* wrote that he hoped his fellow sportswriters in Boston and elsewhere would criticize Landis for his statement calling for the end of the color line. This did not happen. "I waited for the bombs to burst around his shaggy old head, waited for the fearless journalists to haul off and ask the Judge who in the hell he thought he was kidding, waited for somebody to say that his statement was a cruel contradiction of fate," Egan said. But, he added, he saw nothing in the newspapers. Egan said sportswriters were not shy about writing about national and international issues they knew nothing about. But this was something else. Sportswriters were aware of the color line. They knew that Landis was being dishonest. "One might be pardoned for thinking that someone, somewhere would comment on the remarks of the Judge; would point out that the old gentleman was talking through his thoroughly disreputable hat," Egan wrote. "But everybody, everywhere, keeps an uncomfortable silence and allows the statement of the judge to pass unchallenged, like a saboteur in the night." White sportswriters knew black soldiers were wearing American uniforms and fighting and dying for their country. "I do not think they are fighting for the right to sit behind chicken wire in Southern ball parks, to live forever in slums," Egan said. "I do not think that they are dying in order that stupid discriminations may continue. And I am discouraged because the baseball writers of Boston failed to seize this opportunity and strike a blow, however feeble, for democracy."

Egan then continued with his indictment of racial discrimination with the following: "We are fighting, as I understand it, for the rights of under-privileged peoples everywhere. We weep for the teeming masses of India. Down the years, we must have contributed millions to the suffering Armenians. We have room in our souls to pity the Chinese, and the Arabs, and the brave Greeks," Egan said. "Could we, by any chance, spare a thought for the Negro in the United States? Do we, by any chance, feel disgust at the thought that Negro athletes, solely because of their color, are barred from playing baseball?" If baseball was America's national sport, Egan asked, why were talented ballplayers kept out? Blacks were, however, allowed to participate in other sports. "They can find opportunities in the despised sport of boxing. They can find it on the cinder paths and at the race tracks. But they cannot find it in the baseball parks, and I suggest that our national sport should be the very first to discourage discrimination and start practicing democracy." The *Chicago Defender* published the column. Wendell Smith thought so highly of the column that he kept it among his clippings and personal papers. According to Smith, Egan was unpopular with his colleagues because he confronted them with the race issue.[19]

The *Daily Worker*, which also published Egan's column, said Landis's statement had signaled the beginning of the end for the newspaper's long campaign against the color line. Low praised the newspaper for its contribution to the campaign. The newspaper also published congratulatory telegrams from black newspapers, including Detroit's *Michigan Chronicle*. "The organized and relentless campaign against the color ban in the Major League baseball conducted by the *Daily Worker* deserves national recognition for the favorable results it has achieved," it said. "Please accept our congratulations on your home run for democracy." Dan Burley said the *Worker* "deserves all the congratulations in the world. It is a great victory for the Negro people and all people." Low said that victory would not be complete until big league owners signed black stars. This, he said, was inevitable because of the clarity and finality of Landis's statement. The *New York Age*, however, said that any owner who said he was interested in signing blacks was "merely kidding the Negro ballplayers and the public." The *Age* also told its readers not to expect blacks to be signed anytime soon, adding, "The present campaign is a publicity stunt of the *Daily Worker* and nothing more."[20]

Neither Landis nor baseball executives would have further comment on the issue. Joe Cummiskey sent telegrams to big league executives asking their response to Landis's statement. But their responses were hardly encouraging. Clark Griffith said that blacks and whites should have separate leagues. Bob Quinn of the Boston Braves said that he was aware of no agreement by big league executives prohibiting blacks. Alva Bradley of the Cleveland Indians said that Landis spoke "for baseball on subjects you refer to." Given the responses, *P.M.* concluded that "it's going to be Jim Crow as usual in baseball." The newspaper said that none of the New York City teams had responded to its inquiry. It reported that Ed Barrow, president of the New York Yankees, was "unsympathetic" on the issue, telling Leon Straus, chairman of the New York CIO Sports Committee, "This is not the time to bring it up." Straus issued a press release that said, "The present war is being fought to put an end to social and racial discrimination. . . . Anyone who declares he is unsympathetic with the cause of ending discrimination against the Negro people must be judged unsympathetic to the war aims of the American people." The Associated Press quoted James T. Gallagher, general manager of the Chicago Cubs, who said, "Everybody in this country should be doing something of more value to the nation as a whole than stirring up racial hatred." Bill Benswanger, president of the Pittsburgh Pirates, who had already expressed an interest in signing black players, told the Associated Press he agreed with Landis. "There is not and never has been, to my knowledge, anything to ban Negroes from baseball," he said. "I know nothing of any agreement in the major leagues to ban Negroes. I have gone on record before on this matter, and I hope I still have a free mind and a free conscience."[21]

Nat Low saw an opportunity and seized it. On Thursday, July 23, the newspaper wired a telegram to Benswanger that reminded him he had once said if the question of admitting colored baseball players into organized baseball became an issue, he would support it. "In light of Judge Landis' recent ruling," the telegram asked, "would you sign up Negro stars for the Pirates?" Benswanger replied, "I stand by my statement of 1939." On July 24 Low telephoned Benswanger, whose team was in Brooklyn for a series with the Dodgers. Benswanger, according to Low, repeated what he had said in the telegram. During the conversation Low asked Benswanger if he had ever seen Negro league stars like Josh Gibson, Ray Brown, or Roy Campanella. Benswanger said he had attended Negro league games for several years and thought some of the players had the ability to play in the big leagues. Low then asked if Benswanger would give a tryout to players like Sammy Hughes and Dave Barnhill. Benswanger paused and answered, "I will be glad to have them try out with the Pirates."[22]

Low and Benswanger met for forty-five minutes at Benswanger's suite at the Hotel New Yorker. Low again reported that he asked Benswanger if he stood by the statement he made in 1939. Benswanger said he did. Low quoted Benswanger as saying, "My team needs ballplayers and we are willing to give these Negro stars a chance like anybody else." Low's story said that Benswanger had agreed to give a tryout to Barnhill of the New York Cubans and Hughes and Roy Campanella of the Baltimore Elite Giants at the team's ballpark, Forbes Field, on August 4. The *Worker* then sent telegrams to Hughes, Barnhill, and Campanella. The newspaper said it had received replies from the ballplayers. Low would accompany them to the tryout. The Associated Press and the United Press credited Low for breaking the story. "Negro men are American citizens with American rights," Benswanger said in the story. When the public address announcer told the crowd at a Negro league doubleheader at Yankee Stadium that Pittsburgh would give a tryout to Barnhill, Hughes, and Campanella, the stadium erupted in applause. The *Worker* reported that New York state legislator

Morris Mintz of Manhattan called Benswanger to congratulate him. The *Worker* predicted that all of the big league teams would bring blacks to their spring training camps the next spring.[23]

As was often the case, the newspaper's forecast proved overly optimistic, if not naive. But, as the story developed, Benswanger, for whatever reason, distanced himself from Low's account of their conversation. Benswanger said he had been misquoted. When other reporters interviewed him, he said there were inherent difficulties with signing blacks. He told the Associated Press that he had not discussed specifics with Low. The *New York Daily News* quoted Benswanger as saying it was necessary for any black player to have the ability to play in the big leagues. "If we hire and then drop a colored player who doesn't quite make the grade," he said, "I suppose we'll automatically be accused of discrimination." In addition, Benswanger also said he would not order manager Frankie Frisch to release a white player to make room for a black player.[24] Benswanger, contrary to what had been reported in the *Worker*, said that no date had been agreed upon for the tryout.[25] Benswanger said Low had asked him when the team would return from their road trip, and he had answered August 4. "But no mention was made of any players showing up on that date for trials," Benswanger said. The *Pittsburgh Press*, perhaps to discredit Low, identified the sportswriter as working for "the official Communist newspaper." The *Press* said nothing else about the possibility the Pirates might end the color line. If this happened, it would electrify a city with a rich tradition of black baseball. The *Pittsburgh Post-Gazette* reported a brief Associated Press account on Benswanger's announcement but said nothing else.[26] Benswanger subsequently criticized Low and the *Worker* in an interview with Wendell Smith. "The sports editor of the *Daily Worker* put words in my mouth," Benswanger said. "I am not going to let the *Daily Worker* name the players who are to get a trial." Benswanger said he would accept the recommendations of black sportswriters who were knowledgeable of the Negro league. "They know talent when they see it," he said, "and I don't need the advice of the *Daily Worker*." Benswanger said he would not sign players without the permission of their teams.[27]

Fay Young questioned Benswanger's sincerity. If Benswanger was serious about signing black players, he would pay for their travel to Pittsburgh, Young said. In addition, Major League rosters were restricted to twenty-five players, and no team would replace a white player with a black player. Even if Benswanger had really wanted to desegregate baseball, he did not realize the inherent difficulties in doing so. "Benswanger doesn't have to ride South in segregated coaches," Young said. "He doesn't have to eat in or near the kitchen sink in depot restaurants. He doesn't have to sit in separate sections in auditoriums and the back end of street cars." And finally, Young said, Benswanger was foolhardy if he believed that he alone could bring blacks into baseball. If he signed a black, he would do so against the wishes of the baseball establishment. Young said he had heard that owners had discussed the issue at a meeting and then agreed to destroy the transcript of the meeting.[28]

One columnist suggested that the innovative Larry MacPhail, the president of the Brooklyn Dodgers, who introduced night baseball, was the most likely to challenge baseball's color line.[29] But MacPhail's attitudes on race were strictly in accordance with those of other baseball executives. MacPhail criticized Landis after thinking the commissioner had grown soft on segregation. MacPhail told reporters that there were no blacks in baseball for a number of reasons. First, there was no demand. Second, there were no blacks who could make it in the big leagues. Third, integration would ruin black baseball. Fourth, blacks did not want to play in the big leagues. And finally, baseball had an agreement forbidding the signing of blacks.[30] MacPhail told the Associated Press that Negro league officials told him they did not support desegregation because it would ruin black baseball. "The way they look at it is that there aren't too many players of major league caliber in the Negro National and American leagues, so, if they should lose their best players to the majors, their own clubs would be hurt at the gate," he

said. MacPhail bluntly contradicted Landis by saying, "Any statement
that there is no agreement, formal or informal, barring Negroes from
playing in organized baseball is 100 percent hypocrisy."[31] Art Carter
of the *Baltimore Afro-American* asked pointedly: "Which one is telling the truth — Landis or MacPhail?"[32] J. B. Martin, president of the
Negro American League, said he supported desegregation and did not
know what Negro league officials MacPhail had talked to.[33] Effa Manley, owner of the Newark Bears, said the big leagues signed dozens of
players from the Minor Leagues every day but that the Minor Leagues
did not go out of business. She also questioned MacPhail's assertion
that there were few, if any, black ballplayers with the ability to play in
the big leagues and that black owners would block attempts to sign
Negro league players. "That is without a doubt the most stupid thing
I have ever heard," she said. But MacPhail was correct. Black owners
opposed desegregation. But they did not admit it, or else they would
have been condemned as being opposed to racial progress. They tried
to navigate the issue if asked. R. S. Simmons, owner of the Chicago
American Giants, said that black baseball should quit thinking about
playing in the "white man's big league" and build up black baseball.
"Any hope to play in the big leagues was simply quixotic," Simmons
said. "I dare say that when it happens there will not be a person living
who will witness it."[34]

If owners opposed desegregation for business reasons, Joe Bostic
said he did so for practical reasons. Bostic said he was "lukewarm" to
the idea of blacks in the big leagues. He said that desegregation would
destroy the Negro leagues and with it one of the more important black
businesses. Second, why should black players willingly submit themselves to "the humiliation and indignities associated with the problems
of eating, sleeping and traveling in a layout dominated by prejudice-
ridden southern whites!" And finally, Bostic said he was not convinced
the quality of play was any better in the big leagues than it was in the
Negro leagues. He suggested that the winner of this year's World Series
play the winner of a series between the Kansas City Monarchs and the

Homestead Grays. "From the idealist and democratic point of view we say 'yes'" to blacks in the big leagues. But "from the standpoint of practicality," Bostic said, the answer was, "'no.'"[35]

The Reverend Raymond Campion, the white rector of the largely black St. Peter Claver's Catholic Church in Brooklyn, criticized MacPhail for claiming if the best players left the Negro leagues, black baseball would suffer. Campion also said the Major Leagues constantly took players from the Minor Leagues and that the Minor Leagues continued to survive.[36] Campion wrote MacPhail asking him to sign black players. "There is a strong and powerful movement on foot to obtain just treatment for colored persons in all walks of life. One of the outstanding causes of complaints among colored people has been the fact that the major professional baseball leagues have not opened their ranks in recent years to colored persons," Campion said. "Nevertheless, among colored people there is a wide spread impression that the magnates of the major leagues have an unwritten gentleman's agreement to bar colored players." MacPhail, contradicting his earlier statement, responded to Campion by saying that blacks were kept out of baseball because white leagues and black leagues simply existed separately to their own benefit. He then blamed Communists and other social progressives for exploiting the issue. "Unfortunately the discussion of the problem has been contaminated by charges of racial discrimination — most of it vicious propaganda circulated by professional agitators who do not know what they are talking about," he said. "It is particularly unfortunate, it seems to me, that charges of racial discrimination should muddy the waters of any such discussion. It is doubtful whether recent publicity has contributed anything constructive in the best interests of Negro athletes or players." Campion told reporters he had spoken to MacPhail, who had expressed an interest in meeting with him.[37]

On August 6 the *Sporting News* broke its silence with the editorial "No Good from Raising Race Issue." J. G. Taylor Spink defended segregation by using the same arguments of MacPhail, Griffith, and others. "There is no law against Negroes playing with white teams, nor whites with colored clubs," he said, "but neither has invited the other for the obvious reason they prefer to draw their talent from their own ranks." Spink acknowledged that blacks competed against whites before integrated crowds in other sports, but baseball, which he called "a peculiar creature," was different because of the spirited nature of the heckling. Spink, like Stanley Frank, argued that mixing races on a ball field or in the bleachers of a ballpark would result in a race riot. "It is not difficult to imagine what would happen if a player on a mixed team, performing before a crowd of the opposite color, should throw a bean ball, strike out with the bases full or spike a rival," Spink said. "Clear-minded men of tolerance of both races realize the tragic possibilities and have steered clear of such complications because they realize what would happen." If race riots at ballparks were inevitable, why did Spink not include any examples? Spink, like MacPhail, also blamed the Communists for stirring up trouble, referring to them as "agitators" who were using the issue for their own benefit. "There are agitators ever ready to seize an issue that will redound to their profit or self-aggrandizement," Spink said, "who have sought to force Negro players on the big leagues, not because it would help the game, but because it gives them a chance to thrust themselves into the limelight as great crusaders in the guise of democracy." In his column Spink said desegregation would ruin the Negro leagues. Without the Negro leagues, there would be nowhere for blacks to get the training to play in either the Major Leagues or the Minor Leagues. This was perhaps the first time in his decades as editor that Spink had demonstrated any interest in either black ballplayers or in black baseball. Spink then quoted Bostic, who wrote that blacks were "lukewarm" to the idea of playing in the big leagues.

But Bostic had not said that blacks were "lukewarm" to the deseg-regation. Bostic said that he personally was lukewarm to desegrega-tion. Bostic's column, by itself, angered readers who wanted an end to the color line. When Bostic was misquoted in the *Sporting News*, he responded with a column in which he defended himself against being a "fascist," an "Uncle Tom," or a "stooge for the Negro baseball interests."[38] Bostic was not the only sportswriter who wanted to see a game between the champions of white and black baseball. Joe Cummiskey suggested that Satchel Paige and the Kansas City Monarchs play the New York Giants or the Brooklyn Dodgers "in a real, concrete step toward ripping away the barrier that has been keeping Negro stars out of organized baseball." Until that happened Cummiskey urged Pittsburgh and other teams "to go hunting for Negro talent and offer them something besides a condescending pat on the back." The Phillies, in particular, who were in last place and had drawn a mere ten thousand for a doubleheader against the Dodgers, had a lot to gain by signing a player like Roy Campanella. "A move like that," Cummiskey said, "would convince me and a lot of other people that Landis' speech wasn't just a lot of empty words."[39]

A number of mainstream newspapers, including the *Chicago Sun*, *St. Louis Star-Times*, and *Des Moines Register*, published columns calling for desegregation. *Star-Times* columnist Sid Keener wrote that big league owners had continued to prohibit blacks but had allowed exhibition games between black and white teams. The *Register* said Major League Baseball, while "disclaiming prejudice, has maintained its lily-white character while other major sports not only accepted but frequently featured Negro athletes." Bill Cunningham of the *Boston Herald* warned of a "Confederate crackdown" if blacks were signed but concluded, "Be that as it may, give them a chance — let 'em up there and see if they can't hit." Andy Razaf, the lyricist of "Stumpin' at the Savoy," "Honeysuckle Rose," and "Ain't Misbehavin'," also called for baseball to drop its color line. "How can club owners, if they are truly concerned with the best interests of Negro players, their race and the morale of our country," Razaf asked, "willfully continue to make a mockery of the things for which black and white boys are fighting and dying?"[40]

The *Worker* and black newspapers continued to develop the story, while mainstream sportswriters returned to reporting the results of the third race at Jamaica. John Foster, sports editor of the *Cleveland Call and Post*, said that Cleveland Indians president Alva Bradley told him that the Indians would consider signing blacks. Foster interviewed Bradley after Cleveland manager Roger Peckinpaugh said he had no objections to signing blacks, adding, however, that such a decision would ultimately have to come from the team's president. The *Worker* reported that Phillies president Gerry Nugent reportedly told *Pittsburgh Courier* sportswriter Randy Dixon that his team was willing to sign black ballplayers. "The major leagues have played Chinese players, and they are yellow. They have also played Indians, and they are red, so what has color got to do with it? A ball player is a ball player, and that is what counts," Nugent said. "Yes, I would use a Negro baseball player on my club." Nat Low said he called Nugent to confirm the story in the *Courier*. Nugent told Low he had no objection to signing blacks. He then added that any decision to sign blacks would ultimately have to come from Hans Lobert, the team's manager. The *Philadelphia Tribune* reported that a committee, which included local representatives of the National Negro Congress, the NAACP, the Civic League, the *Philadelphia Afro-American*, and the *Philadelphia Tribune*, would meet with Nugent to discuss his team giving a tryout to at least one black player.[41]

The *Worker* reported that Clarence "Pants" Rowland, president of the Los Angeles Angels in the triple-A Pacific Coast League, confirmed reports that he would give blacks a tryout with his team in the spring. "Three Negro players came up to me last week, and I told them it was a little late in the season for newcomers now, but I'd be glad to give them a chance in the spring," Rowland said. When the ballplayers asked Rowland if there was a ban against black players, he replied that there was not. The *Baltimore Afro-American* reported that the Pacific Coast League might be the first in organized baseball to drop the color line.[42] But Victor Collins, president of the Hollywood Stars, another Pacific Coast team, said the hiring of blacks would require approval of the team's stockholders. The *Los Angeles Tribune*, a black newspaper, reported that *Pittsburgh Courier* sportswriter Herman Hill had asked for a tryout for Nate Moreland but that Collins had rejected it because it was not "a matter of significant importance to warrant calling a meeting of the stockholders." The publicity surrounding the respective announcements of Landis and Benswanger had not yet resulted in a tryout but had translated into big crowds at Negro league games. The newspaper reported that thirty thousand spectators, including several big league scouts, attended a doubleheader between four teams — the Kansas City Monarchs, New York Cubans, Baltimore Elite Giants, and Philadelphia Stars. Newsreel and newspaper photographers, according to one story, were particularly interested in Campanella, Hughes, and Barnhill, who, Low reminded readers, were scheduled for tryouts with Pittsburgh. Low called Monarch pitcher Satchel Paige's pitching the "real thrill of the day." Before the game, as photographers took his picture, Paige responded, "I've been playing baseball for 16 years, but I've never seen so much fuss made over Negro teams in my life."[43]

Bob Considine wrote that "not in our time has there been such a hullabaloo over the discrimination against Negro players in baseball." White fans had little knowledge of the talents of black stars. But, Considine said, anyone who watched Paige pitch would be convinced there were indeed black players capable of playing in the big leagues. According to Considine, Paige's name was always mentioned when someone raised the subject. Considine described Paige as "a curious soul, given to fiery red roadsters, tearing cigarettes in two before lighting up and such primitive remedies for sore arms as pouring kettles of hot water on the ailing member. He is a nest of superstition, but he doesn't kid himself much about baseball." Considine said that Paige made two thousand dollars for pitching in the game. Paige admitted he was probably too old to pitch in the big leagues. However, he said, there were at least a dozen blacks who could play in the big leagues. "He knows enough baseball to realize that he's been around too long," Considine said, "and that he has wasted too much fragrance on too many desert airs to step into the big show now, if opportunity knocks."[44]

In an interview with the Associated Press, Paige said that even if a big league team were interested in him, none could meet his salary demands of thirty-five thousand dollars a year. Paige acknowledged that the mixing of blacks and whites would create problems. "All the nice statements in the world from both sides aren't going to change Jim Crow," Paige said. He suggested that instead of allowing individual teams to sign blacks, there should be a team composed entirely of black players in one or both of the Major Leagues.[45] Considine responded to Paige's quote by printing a letter from Sam Lacy, whom he described as "one of the better-known colored sportswriters." Lacy said that Paige's best days were behind him, and therefore Paige was free to say what he wanted because he knew he would be unlikely ever to pitch in the big leagues. Lacy said that Paige's income would indeed fall if he was to pitch in the big leagues, but desegregation would open the door to other Negro league stars. Lacy criticized Paige's proposal for the creation of a colored team to play in one or both of the big leagues. "There can be no compromise with prejudice," Lacy said. "A separate club for Negroes is no more logical than a separate team for Italians, Irishmen, Germans, Poles, Lithuanians or Jews. . . . No one asked the Norwegians, Cubans or French to organize themselves into formidable groups before being admitted to major competition."[46]

Paige, as Bostic had, found himself under attack in black newspapers for appearing to accept Jim Crow. Ludlow Werner, editor of the *New York Age*, said Paige was no better than an "Uncle Tom." Buster Miller said that white newspapers gave prominent blacks a lot of attention if they appeared to endorse segregation. "It strikes me as darned peculiar that Negroes holding opposite views are never interviewed or quoted at all," Miller said, adding, "Isn't that strange?" Paige tried to address the criticism in the middle of the annual East-West Classic. When he was called in to pitch, he went not to the mound but to a microphone, where he told the crowd that he had been misquoted. Art Carter, sports editor of the *Baltimore Afro-American*, called Paige's denial a "pointless statement." In his biography of Paige, Larry Tye wrote that the pitcher, given his reputation, had probably said what he was quoted in the AP article. The baseball establishment used Paige's statement to counter the argument for desegregation. As Spink manipulated Bostic's words and Joe Williams would later manipulate Sam Lacy's words, Eddie Collins, general manager of the Boston Red Sox, repeated Paige's comment by saying that desegregation was unnecessary because black ballplayers were prospering so well in their own league.[47]

The August 4 date in Pittsburgh came and went without a tryout. A week earlier the *Worker* had trumpeted the significance of the announcement, but when the day arrived, the newspaper said nothing. The Associated Press and the United Press also had each reported that Campanella, Hughes, and Barnhill would have a tryout. Metropolitan dailies had also picked up the story. There is no telling how many people had read about it. But then there was nothing else said about it — not in the *Daily Worker* and not in the mainstream press. Art Carter wondered aloud, "August 4 has come and gone and those promised tryouts to Roy Campanella, Sammy Hughes and Dave Barnhill with the Pittsburgh Pirates are still in the whispering stage. Verily, the democracy-in-the-majors fight is still at a standstill, with the owners, colored and white, standing in the shade waiting for the other fellow to take the initiative."[48] Fay Young blamed Campanella and Hughes for scuttling the opportunity because they had left the Elite Giants to play with the Cleveland Buckeyes in an exhibition game against white players. Too many players acted more like independent contractors than professional ballplayers because they jumped from team to team, Young said. He criticized the Negro leagues for lacking standard rules that restricted player movement. He said black baseball would never be taken seriously by white baseball until it got its house in order.[49] Doc Kountze, in an article distributed by the American Negro Press, disagreed. "The very fact," he said, "that colored baseball has to organize their own leagues and their own clubs in order to gain major league recognition is one of the unpleasant situations of our democracy."[50]

On August 1 Wendell Smith reported that Benswanger had given him permission to recommend four players who would be given a tryout at a future date. Smith said the announcement culminated in the newspaper's "long campaign for the integration of Negro ballplayers into the major leagues." Benswanger repeated that he had told the *Worker* he supported blacks in baseball but had not approved a tryout on August 4 or on any other date. Low, Benswanger said, "put words in my mouth." Benswanger said the team would consider the names of players recommended by the *Pittsburgh Courier* but not by the *Worker*. The *Courier* later announced it had selected Josh Gibson and outfielder Sammy Bankhead of the Homestead Grays and shortstop Willie Wells and pitcher Leon Day of the Newark Eagles. The *New York Times*, among other newspapers, published an Associated Press account that reported the players would get a tryout with the Pirates. The story said the team's farm director, who would supervise the tryouts, would be busy with the team's Minor League teams until the season ended.[51]

The Associated Press reported that Cleveland Buckeyes manager Parnell Woods said that the Cleveland Indians had advised him that the team would give tryouts to Woods and two other ballplayers, Sammy Jethroe, who was currently leading the Negro National League in hitting, and pitcher Eugene Bremmer. The Indians, the story said, were the second big league team to announce tryouts for black players.[52] On September 1, however, two Cleveland players were killed when a truck crashed into the back of their car. Four other players were seriously injured, including Bremmer.[53] Art Carter reported that both Benswanger and Bradley had promised tryouts to black ballplayers but had not yet followed with any specific dates.[54] Eddie Gant of the *Chicago Defender* said that "the question of giving colored players a tryout in the big leagues is getting hopeless with each week's new development." The Pirates had said it would give tryouts to Gibson, Bankhead, Day, and Wells, but not until the end of September. This "is the end of the baseball season," Gant said. "We would like to know what good will be accomplished at the time."[55] Major League teams could expand their rosters from twenty-five to forty players on September

1. This raised the possibility that a team might add a black player. But rules prohibited teams from adding players except for trades, waivers, and purchases from the Minor Leagues. The Negro leagues, however, were unaffiliated with organized baseball.

In mid-September Larry MacPhail met for an hour and a half in his office on Montagu Street with a delegation that included Father Raymond Campion, assemblyman William T. Andrews, Fred Turner of the NAACP, Dan Burley, and Joe Bostic. MacPhail told the committee there were black players with the ability to play in the big leagues. "It's not necessary to try them out," he said. "They're ready and willing to go into the majors." Blacks, he said, should have opportunities in baseball and elsewhere in the United States. MacPhail then proposed that the Dodgers play the Kansas City Monarchs after the season ended. MacPhail said that the players would receive 60 percent of the gate, while the remaining 40 percent would go to the war effort.[56] In response to the meeting, Dan Burley characterized as "hopeful" the possibility that the color line would end. Burley said all the promises from other owners on "tryouts" were simply "ballyhoo," adding, "Look for MacPhail to do something concrete."[57] MacPhail's promise, however, reeked of the worst kind of cynicism. On September 27 MacPhail entered the army. He knew he was going into the army, and he knew there would be no game because baseball rules restricted the number of players that could play on the same team in exhibition games.

MacPhail, like his mentor, Branch Rickey, was both smart and innovative. Unlike Rickey, MacPhail was also a heavy drinker who became belligerent when drunk. The Brooklyn Dodgers' ownership had finally had enough of MacPhail and his temper. Shortly after MacPhail left for the army, he was fired and later replaced by Rickey. MacPhail and Rickey could hardly have had different personalities. MacPhail had maintained good relations with the city's sportswriters by picking up their bar tabs. The midwestern Rickey preferred talking to drinking and moralizing to fighting. When Rickey arrived in New York, the city had three of the sixteen big league franchises and nine mainstream dailies. Brooklyn also had its own newspaper, the *Eagle*. Only the liberal afternoon newspaper, *P.M.*, gave the issue of racial equality more than a passing nod.[58] A number of sportswriters ridiculed Rickey for his moralizing and for his long-winded press conferences, which were called "Cave of the Winds."

By the end of September the possibility that this would finally be the year that the Major Leagues would admit blacks had become, according to sportswriter Ric Roberts, "an unfulfilled hope." Roberts reported that he had written thirty baseball executives and prominent sportswriters for their comments on the possibility of baseball's becoming desegregated. He received few responses. Roberts said that some of the older baseball men, including Clark Griffith, Connie Mack, and others, believed the campaign to integrate baseball "is a Communist plot to overthrow baseball." The others, Robert said, had nothing to say, "making it logical to assume that they are against the plan to get colored Americans into the big leagues." Spink took issue with Roberts for writing in his letter that the editor had called for "continuous discrimination against colored Americans in the major leagues." Spink said he had reread his editorial and found no such phrase. Although Spink did not use those precise words, Roberts said the inference of his editorial was clear. Spink clearly objected to the desegregation of blacks and whites in baseball and recommended that blacks and whites remain segregated. In addition, Roberts said that Spink lived and worked in St. Louis, which had the only segregated Major League ballpark. Spink and most mainstream sportswriters objected to desegregation, Roberts said, which made it easy for the baseball establishment to ignore the pressure to sign blacks. "We have forged a bridgehead in 1942," Roberts wrote. "Maybe we will effect a march next spring — perhaps the most tumultuous spring any generation of Americans ever saw. The failure of aging veterans to stand up, and the drafting of youngsters for army duty may make it mandatory to use our boys next year or let baseball die."[59]

In a piece with no byline, the *Chicago Defender* reported that the season had ended without any resolution on the question of blacks in organized baseball. It said that no team had fulfilled its promise to try out black players. The article said that MacPhail had no intentions of having the Yankees play a black team. The article blamed Campanella and Hughes for jeopardizing their tryouts by leaving their team without permission to play in an exhibition game. The article criticized Wendell Smith for being so naive as to believe Benswanger. Smith, it said, was nicknamed "Windy" because of his propensity for talking and took credit for arranging a tryout with the Pirates that had yet to — and probably never would — materialize. It said Smith had selected players who were too old and ignored better-qualified players. "The day will come when Negroes may get a tryout in the major leagues," the article said. "We didn't go into any conniption fit about it this year because the 'applesauce' being dished out was sour."[60]

Dan Burley also criticized Smith for grandstanding and for thinking the issue could be solved simply by having an owner agree to give any black player a tryout based on his recommendation. "'Windy's' usefulness has ceased," Burley wrote. Burley said that the *Worker* had been far more involved in the campaign than Smith. Burley also chided Joe Bostic and other sportswriters who were ambivalent on whether blacks should play in the Major Leagues. Such views were shortsighted, he said. "All the fans want to see are Negro players in big league lineups," Burley said, "and that is about as clear as I can make it." Burley later said Bostic's defection from the "united front against discrimination" had done harm to the campaign because baseball executives were using Bostic to defend their position. Burley said that white sportswriters had complained to him about Bostic. "What's the matter with that fellow Bostic? We're against Jim Crow in big league baseball, but as fast as get around and knock down barriers, that guy Bostic gumshoes around and messes things up again," Burley said. "We have been met by owners with quotations from Joe Bostic, who has been accepted by them as an authority on whether Negroes should be admitted to the big leagues."[61] Doc Kountze expressed his concern about the squabbling between black sportswriters over who was doing the most in the campaign to integrate baseball. This, he said, was the time for the black baseball writers' association to unite to end segregated baseball.[62]

Clark Griffith had thus far been an unlikely candidate to break baseball's color line. But this did not stop the Committee to End Jim Crow in Baseball in Washington DC from taking the campaign to him. The *Worker* reported that three thousand people, including Satchel Paige and Josh Gibson, had signed a petition calling on Griffith to sign black players to improve his struggling team. Griffith, the newspaper said, did not have the money of other owners and, therefore, could sign black players for less money than it would cost to buy white players from other big league teams. In addition, if he signed black players, it would improve his team and increase gate receipts at Griffith Stadium because of its proximity to black neighborhoods. The story said that a mass meeting had been scheduled to urge an end to the color line on October 16 at the Lincoln Temple Congregational Church at Eleventh and R streets. Griffith had been invited to speak, the story said. Griffith did not respond, nor did he attend the rally. In his speech Burley told black baseball stars to go directly to Major League spring training camps and ask for a tryout.[63]

The *Worker* reported that membership in the Committee to End Jim Crow in Baseball now included dozens of prominent politicians, labor leaders, civil rights leaders, college administrators, journalists, writers, and actors, including Representative Vito Marcantonio; Representative Elmer J. Holland; New York lieutenant governor Charles Poletti; New York City councilman Peter Cacchione; A. Philip Randolph, president of the Pullman Porters Union; Walter White of the NAACP; Max Yergan, president of the National Negro Congress; and actor John Garfield. It also included white sportswriters such as Dan Parker, Hugh Bradley, Louis Bromfield, Joe Cummiskey, Nat Low, and Hy Turkin and black sportswriters such as Dan Burley, Wendell Smith, Joe Bostic, Chappie Gardner, and Max Werner. The *Worker* reported that the annual meeting of Major League executives would be held in Chicago on December

3. The newspaper called on Major League Baseball to end the color line and asked readers and labor unions to contact teams to demand that they sign black players. The newspaper reported that the Los Angeles Union Council, representing one hundred thousand workers, urged big league baseball to "remove any ban against Negro players and to also invite Negro players to tryouts with their respective clubs" during spring training. The resolution continued by saying, "Such discrimination is anti-democratic and denies to a large section of our citizens the very equality and status for which we are waging a total war."[64]

CHAPTER 9

BLACK EDITORS MAKE THEIR CASE FOR DESEGREGATION

On December 1 Commissioner Kenesaw Mountain Landis and the rest of the baseball establishment met at the Palmer House in Chicago for Major League Baseball's annual meetings where league and team executives discussed possible trades and rule changes, resolved issues and disputes, and addressed the continuing problem with the woeful Philadelphia Phillies, which continued to borrow money from Major League Baseball to make its payroll. As baseball executives traveled to Chicago, they also were keenly aware their discussions would be affected by issues outside of their control. World War II affected everything, and baseball was no exception. Major League Baseball had to consider the real possibility that gas rationing and other wartime restrictions might curb travel, force the cancellation of spring training, or perhaps even shorten the season. After the attack on Pearl Harbor, Landis wrote President Roosevelt, telling him that baseball was prepared to cancel the season if necessary. Roosevelt responded with his

"Green Light" letter, telling Landis it was in the best interests of the country "to keep baseball going."[1]

The presence of so many baseball executives under one roof provided a distinct opportunity for those wanting an end to the color line. Before the meeting began, *Chicago Defender* publisher John Sengstacke, who was also president of the Negro Publishers Association, and editor Metz T. P. Lochard wrote Pittsburgh Pirates owner Bill Benswanger, asking that the issue be added to the agenda. "In the interest of national unity and morale in these crucial war days, we believe that you should act to place this important question before the current meeting by insisting that it be placed on the agenda," the letter said. Benswanger did not respond.[2] William Harrison, chairman of the Chicago-based Committee to End Jim Crow in Baseball, sent a telegram to Landis, asking to be included on the agenda. "There is a scarcity of baseball players," Harrison said. "We are fighting very hard for democracy abroad and we would like to have some democracy at home." There was no response. Terry Kendal, president of Local 719, United Auto Workers of the Congress of Industrial Organizations, notified Landis in a telegram that a committee of CIO members would appear at 11:00 a.m. the next day to make the case for admitting blacks into baseball. Landis did not respond.[3]

At 11:00 a.m. the next day, the CIO committee interrupted a meeting of baseball executives from both leagues. When Leslie O'Connor, Landis's executive assistant, answered the door, he was told the committee wanted to present its case. O'Connor disappeared back inside the room and then, after a long period of time, said it might be possible if there was time. Kendal told O'Connor that if his committee was not given a hearing, it would take up the issue with the Committee on Fair Employment Practice. O'Connor closed the door and repeated what he had been told to those inside the room. Without discussion Landis gave O'Connor his response. O'Connor opened the door, responded with a sharp no, and then closed the door.[4] The United Press International reported that the attempt of the CIO to make its case before baseball

executives was considered "a failure." The *Sporting News* reported that
Kendal admitted his committee had acted improperly. He said it would
not drop the issue but would use a more conventional approach the
next time.[5]

Fay Young, who quoted from the telegram his newspaper had sent
Benswanger, said owners "sidestepped the question of admitting
Negroes in the big leagues." When Young tried to discuss the issue with
owners, they would not talk with him. Young then sought information
from white sportswriters, but none were willing to talk to him, either.
One sportswriter, speaking on condition of anonymity, told Young
that Clark Griffith believed that black baseball needed to clean up its
own league before requesting to become a part of white baseball. The
reporter told Young that the baseball establishment said Communists
were behind the effort to desegregate baseball. When Young asked the
reporter "how the *Defender* and millions of baseball fans of color could
be classed as Reds simply because they demanded a fair deal for all," the
reporter answered that this was simply what team executives believed.[6]

Joe Cummiskey of *P.M.* wrote that Major League officials had been
forced to look directly at their own prejudices and had quickly looked
away. He said the nation's sportswriters had done the same thing, adding that public opinion would eventually force both baseball and the
writers who covered it to accept blacks in baseball.[7] Bob Considine
wrote that integration would be good for baseball and also good for
the business of baseball. He said that it also would be the right thing
to do. "No one can doubt there has been brutal discrimination against
Negroes in baseball," he wrote. Nat Low praised Considine. Blacks
could soon have the opportunity to play in the Major Leagues "if more
columns like yours are written on the subject," he said. Low characterized baseball's response to the CIO committee as "a disgrace."[8] Buster
Miller wrote in the *New York Age* that the ghost of Jefferson Davis had
obviously been in the room with the baseball executives.[9]

On the first day of the meetings, Low wrote a column asking labor
unions to send telegrams to Landis and owners at the Palmer House

demanding that blacks be allowed in baseball. A day later the *Daily Worker* reported the 60,000-member National Maritime Union, the 20,000-member United Office and Professional Workers of America, the 40,000-member New York chapter of the IWO, and other unions had sent telegrams. A day after that, the *Worker* reported that one of the largest unions in the country, the 500,000-member Greater New York CIO, had sent a telegram demanding the end of discrimination against blacks. The 75,000-member Transport Workers Union also sent a telegram to Landis. Other unions sent their telegrams to individual owners. The 20,000-member International Workers Order of Western Pennsylvania telegrammed Benswanger, asking him to fulfill his promise to give a tryout to black players. The 20,000-member New England International Workers Organization sent a telegram to Eddie Collins, general manager of the Boston Red Sox.[10]

After Landis and baseball executives closed the door on the CIO committee, business continued as usual. When the meeting was finished, Chicago Cubs president Philip Wrigley, the chewing gum magnate, told the committee he was sympathetic to their demands. Wrigley, who had become an honorary member of the CIO after paying the initiation dues of the stewards on the ships used in transporting his gum, invited the Chicago Committee to End Jim Crow in Baseball to discuss the issue in his office in the Wrigley Building.[11] Wrigley told the group they "had the floor." William Patterson told Wrigley that black spectators did not want to patronize baseball games if they were not allowed to play on big league teams. Patterson told Wrigley about the talent in black baseball. Wrigley listened patiently, but, according to Patterson, he was afraid to commit.[12]

Wrigley told the committee there "are men in high places who don't want" blacks in baseball. He said he was not one of them. "I know it's got to come," he said. "But I don't think the time is now." Wrigley said the public needed to be educated so they would accept blacks. "What must be done is to get people talking. If there was sufficient public demand at this time I would put a Negro on my team," Wrigley said.

Patterson responded by saying the desegregation of the big leagues would improve morale and unity among blacks in both baseball and society. "If Negroes are taken into the big leagues without proper public support, I'm afraid some fights will take place," Wrigley responded. "What I'm afraid of is a riot." Wrigley concluded by telling the committee that his door was always open to them.[13] Sol Vail, chairman of the 155,000-member National Athletic Commission, International Workers Order, sent Wrigley a telegram challenging his statement that the American public was not ready for blacks in baseball. He said Americans had no qualms about blacks fighting with whites in North Africa and Europe. "Mr. Wrigley, many of our boys, Negro and white, are giving their lives on the sands of North Africa and around the world so that democracy may live. They are carrying on our fight against Hitlerism and its vile ideology of race superiority," Vail said. "You and other club owners have the opportunity of serving your country in a very important manner at this critical time. In the name of our organization, I urge you to hire Negro ball players in the major leagues now."[14]

On February 7 the Chicago Joint Council of Packinghouse Workers organized a meeting at Forum Hall on East Forty-Third Street that supported a resolution calling for the integration of blacks into the Major Leagues. Organizations that endorsed the resolution included the CIO council, the NAACP, the Urban League, and a collection of religious, civic, and social organizations. Hundreds attended the meeting. The resolution was sent to the offices of Commissioner Landis and President Roosevelt. If Landis and baseball executives such as Grace Comiskey, who owned the White Sox, and Philip Wrigley, who owned the Cubs, ignored the resolutions, the committee said it would consider a boycott of Major League games. The speakers included Robert Travis, vice president of the Illinois CIO; alderman Benjamin Grant; I. P. Florey of the Chicago Industrial Union; and Fay Young.[15]

In Brooklyn Father Raymond Campion called on baseball to address its shortage of talented players by signing blacks during a speech at the

Columbus Club in Brooklyn at a meeting of the Irish-American Committee for Interracial Justice. Campion said that Larry MacPhail "had missed a glorious opportunity to strike a blow" against discrimination. "It is utterly wrong, unfair, un-American, un-Democratic, un-Christian to deny a Negro the opportunity to earn a decent living because of the dark shade of his skin," Campion said.[16] To Campion and others, the hypocritical MacPhail was gone — and since MacPhail apparently had no interest in signing black players, maybe his successor, Branch Rickey, would. Cummiskey reported Campion said he wanted to sit down with Rickey.[17] Dan Burley said Rickey had not yet been asked whether he would sign blacks. His response, Burley added, "will be anxiously awaited."[18] The *Worker* made a direct appeal to Rickey. When the Dodgers' star outfielder, Pete Reiser, entered the military service on January 1, the newspaper told Rickey to sign outfielder Sammy Bankhead of the Homestead Grays. "How about it, Mr. Rickey?" the newspaper said.[19]

There was little evidence from Rickey's time as vice president of the St. Louis Cardinals to foreshadow that he would become baseball's great emancipator. But, according to Rickey's biographer Lee Lowenfish, the longtime baseball executive's life in baseball had demonstrated his willingness to challenge conventional baseball. By the time Rickey moved to Brooklyn, he had revolutionized baseball by creating a farm system that controlled a number of Minor League franchises and thus kept the Cardinals stocked with outstanding players by restricting their movement to other organizations. Critics, including his fellow owners, denounced Rickey's farm system as a slave plantation. Landis, who ordered Rickey to end his Minor League monopoly, did not like Rickey. Landis's criticism of Rickey included the following: "that hypocritical preacher" and "that Protestant bastard (who's) always masquerading with a minister's robe."[20] New York sportswriters found Rickey and his morality lessons tiresome. When he returned from the service, Jimmy Powers missed few opportunities to chide Rickey for his long-winded sermons and his low salaries. Powers referred to him as "El Cheapo."[21]

Rickey, who believed he stood a little closer to God than others did, cared little whether owners or sportswriters liked him. He ultimately succeeded in part where others failed because he saw opportunities where others did not. Unlike some of his colleagues, who may have privately wanted to sign blacks, Rickey, motivated by both economic and moral reasons, had both the courage and the confidence to confront his fellow owners. To Rickey, Lowenfish said, "the continued example of racial discrimination in the United States was, at best, an embarrassment to the American war effort and, at worst, a politically indefensible, sustained injustice." Rickey knew that A. Philip Randolph had threatened a march on Washington DC to protest discrimination. Rickey was aware of the race riots of the past summer. He opposed racial discrimination. But, if he were to confront it, he would move slowly. "Yet for all his genuine indignation at race discrimination," Lowenfish wrote, "Rickey remained a very conservative man, fearful of any leftist, collectivist, or — worst of all — Communist agitation of the race issue."[22]

Baseball had long argued black players did not have the ability to play in the big leagues. As more and more Major Leaguers left their teams for the armed services and the quality of Major League ball became weaker month after month, so did the argument that there were no blacks with big league talent. But even if a team signed a black, it would be problematic to bring him to spring training in Florida, where Jim Crow laws made it illegal for blacks and whites to play with or against one another or stay in the same hotels or eat in the same restaurants. During its annual meetings, the baseball establishment announced that because of travel restrictions by the Department of Transportation, teams would no longer train in Florida, but instead camps would be restricted to north of the Ohio and Potomac rivers and east of the Mississippi. Because northern cities did not have the same rigid segregation laws as in Florida, this removed a significant obstacle of desegregation. "There is no excuse," Dan Burley said, "for the majors not thinking seriously about doing something about hiring

Negroes." Burley instructed black players to go to the nearest spring training site and confront the issue. "There can be no 'ifs' and 'buts' about it," Burley said. "Negro ballplayers must be admitted to the big leagues this year."[23]

In January 1943 the American Negro Press wire service reported that Clarence "Pants" Rowland, manager of the Los Angeles Angels, the top Minor League team in the Chicago Cubs organization, who played in the Pacific Coast League, had been scouting black players. Rowland had expressed particular interest in Nate Moreland, a right-handed pitcher who lived in Pasadena. Moreland had had a tryout with Jackie Robinson a year earlier with the White Sox in Pasadena. According to another account, Rowland announced that he had approved tryouts for three black players: Moreland, Chet Brewer, and Howard Easterling. Two weeks later, under pressure from his fellow owners, Rowland reportedly canceled the tryout. Soon after, *Oakland Tribune* sports editor Art Cohn chided Oakland's Minor League team, the Oaks of the Pacific Coast League, for rejecting blacks. Owner Vince Devincenzi reportedly ordered his manager, Johnny Vergez, to give tryouts to Brewer and Olin Dahl, but the manager refused and the issue was dropped. The *Defender* reported that Kenny Washington, the former All-American halfback of UCLA, asked for a tryout with both the Los Angeles Angels and the Hollywood Stars of the Pacific Coast League but was rejected by both teams because of "the color of his skin."[24]

Robert Smith of the *Defender* reported that no Los Angeles sportswriter — except for Gordon Macker of the *Daily News* — had anything to say about the efforts to desegregate baseball. In addition, Smith also reported that journalists Halley Harding, sports editor of the *Los Angeles Tribune*, and Herman Hill of the *Pittsburgh Courier* had asked owners and managers to try out black players, but their requests had been rebuffed. Both men took the issue to the Los Angeles County of Supervisors and the Los Angeles City Council. Both bodies voted to support the journalists' request. Local 887, United Automobile Workers, CIO, Union of North American Aircraft, sent a resolution to the

Pacific Coast League urging that blacks be given tryouts in the name "of the Four Freedoms for which American boys of all races, colors and creeds are fighting and dying." Smith reported that CIO workers and members of the community would protest outside Wrigley Field in Los Angeles on May 23 before a game between Los Angeles and Hollywood. The *Defender* published a photograph of protesters carrying picket signs outside the ballpark.[25]

Ultimately, baseball would not become desegregated until one owner had the courage to challenge Landis and the cabal of baseball executives who supported segregation. After replacing MacPhail after the 1942 season, Rickey brought up the issue during a meeting with the Dodgers' board of directors in early 1943. "You might turn up something," George V. McLaughlin, president of the Brooklyn Trust Company, the bank that financed the Dodgers, said, "so go ahead." But McLaughlin also wanted Rickey to understand the possible consequences. McLaughlin told Rickey that integrating baseball would not work if it were done to change American society. McLaughlin also warned Rickey that he had to find the right type of player. If Rickey signed a ballplayer who was perceived as temperamental or uppity, the decision would end in failure.[26] Rickey and the board vowed to one another they would not discuss the issue even with their own families.[27] Thus began Rickey's Manhattan Project, where he would secretly scout players of color. "As usual," Lowenfish wrote, "the persuasive executive was able to enlist a wide variety of people in his important cause, making sure, however, that he kept secret his main motive: breaking the color line in the major leagues." He recruited Robert Haig, a former fraternity brother who now taught political economy at Columbia University, to learn what he could about talented ballplayers in South America. Rickey contacted Jose Seda, a New York University physical education graduate student, to keep him aware of promising ballplayers in Puerto Rico. Rickey also sent one of his top scouts, Tom Greenwade, to evaluate ballplayers playing in Mexico.[28] Rickey himself attended Negro league games and the annual East-West Classic.

While Rickey was given permission to proceed with his secret plan to desegregate baseball, Bill Veeck, according to an often repeated story, tried to buy the Phillies with the objective of signing players from the Negro leagues. In his autobiography, *Veeck — as in Wreck*, he said he tried to buy the Phillies from Gerry Nugent in late 1942. After buying the team, Veeck, then the owner of the Milwaukee Brewers of the American Association, said he would sign black players after conferring with black sportswriter "Doc" Young of the *Chicago Defender* and white promoter Abe Saperstein, who were both knowledgeable about black baseball. While Veeck could not afford to buy the Phillies with his own money, he said he had possible financing from two sources — Phillies Cigars and the CIO. Veeck said he discussed his plan with Landis, whom he had known through his father, Bill Veeck Sr., who had been president of the Chicago Cubs. When Veeck contacted Nugent, he learned the team had been sold to the National League. Upon inquiring to Ford Frick, Veeck learned the league had sold the team to the lumber dealer William Cox. "Word reached me soon enough," Veeck said, "that Frick was bragging all over the baseball world — strictly off the record, of course — about how he had stopped me from contaminating the league."[29]

Veeck's story became an accepted part of the pre–Jackie Robinson narrative because the story, given Veeck's history, appeared credible. In 1947 Veeck ended the color ban in the American League by signing Larry Doby and then other blacks, including Satchel Paige. In addition, Veeck often challenged conventional baseball and the baseball establishment. Finally, Landis and Frick supported segregation; therefore, their response appeared reasonable. Author Jules Tygiel reported the Veeck story in his 1983 book, *Baseball's Great Experiment*. In 1996, however, Tygiel publicly doubted the story. "Most of us who have worked in the field of baseball integration," Tygiel said, "have always naively, and even professionally, taken Veeck at his word although his report was totally unsubstantiated by any supporting evidence." David Jordan, who had

written extensively on baseball, also found significant problems with
Veeck's account. "There was no interference in a Veeck deal by either
Landis or Frick," Jordan said. "Veeck, nothing if not a storyteller, seems
to have added these embellishments, sticking in some guys with black
hats, simply to juice up his tale."[30]

Jordan, Larry Gerlach, a professor of history at the University of Utah
and then president of the Society for American Baseball Research, and
John Rossi, professor of history at La Salle University in Philadelphia,
questioned the credibility of the Veeck account and the integrity of
Veeck himself in an article in the SABR publication the *National Pastime*. "The major difficulty with this oft-told story," Jordan, Gerlach,
and Rossi wrote, "is that it is not true." They criticized writers and
particularly historians for being so careless to accept Veeck's account
without "the most rudimentary research to see if it checked out." They
said that Veeck had made a number of fundamental factual errors such
as confusing Doc Young, who was sports editor of the *Cleveland Call
and Post*, with *Defender* sports editor Fay Young.[31]

Jordan, Gerlach, and Rossi said if Veeck had done what he said he
did, he would have left behind a trail. During the fall of 1942 Veeck told
reporters he met with Nugent to discuss buying the Phillies. Jordan et al.
said that Nugent confirmed the meeting but said Veeck did not express
interest in buying the team. If Veeck had discussed his intentions, the
Philadelphia Tribune, the city's black weekly, would have reported it,
and the newspaper said nothing. In fact, no black newspaper said
anything about Veeck's plan to buy the team. Such silence, Jordan et
al. said, was "significant" because it demonstrated the incredulity of
Veeck's story. If Veeck really had been thwarted in his bid to buy the
Phillies, as he claimed, it would certainly have been reported at the
time or when Veeck bought the Indians in 1946. Finally, Jordan et al.
wrote that if Veeck had really done as he said, somebody would have
mentioned it before Veeck did in 1962. "It is inconceivable that Veeck's
Phillies project would not have become a matter of public currency.

At least within the world of Negro baseball," Jordan et al. wrote. "That the black press refrained from reacting with great vehemence to the betrayal of Veeck by the white authorities . . . is simply not believable."[32]

Jordan, Gerlach, and Rossi suggested Veeck manufactured his story based on other accounts, such as the column written by Joe Bostic, who shared his dream of acting as a broker between black players and big league teams, or Paige's interview with the Associated Press, when he suggested that there should be a black team in the Major Leagues. Jordan et al. said that Veeck "no doubt" saw the articles, and they "piqued his fertile imagination. He would put together such a team!" Jordan et al. also said neither Fay (or Doc) Young nor Saperstein ever mentioned in print any conversation with Veeck about his interest in buying the Phillies. In addition, Jordan et al. doubted the CIO would have been interested in buying the Phillies. "A bankrupt baseball team seems an odd investment for the CIO," they said. Jordan et al. then took their argument beyond questioning Veeck's facts to questioning his character. They speculated Veeck created the story because of his jealousy of Rickey who had, in essence, beaten him to the moon. According to Jordan et al., Veeck, who was ill at the time he worked on the book with author Ed Linn, saw this as his last opportunity to get out his side of the story. "He probably felt that this book was to be his last chance to poke the baseball powers in the eye, to steal some credit from Rickey, and to polish his own place in baseball history," Jordan et al. wrote.[33]

Given the credentials of the authors and the strength of their evidence, the article made a compelling argument that Veeck invented the story of buying the Phillies and replacing the team's untalented white ballplayers with talented black ballplayers. But given close scrutiny, it became apparent that the article's conclusions were based too little on research and too much on assumption and character assassination. In a letter to the *National Pastime*, Mike Gimbel, a member of SABR, condemned the publication for "printing this scurrilous article" and the authors for their "mean-spirited" attacks on Veeck. Gimbel

questioned Jordan et al. for their conclusion that if Veeck had really
been prevented from buying the Phillies, he would have protested the
injustice openly. If Veeck had complained to reporters, Gimbel said,
his career in organized baseball would have been over.[34]

In an article in the *Baseball Research Journal*, another SABR publication, Tygiel, while continuing to harbor doubts about Veeck's story,
criticized the article written by Jordan, Gerlach, and Rossi. Tygiel, like
Gimbel, considered the assertion that Veeck, fearing he might die, created the story as a chance to polish his image an ad hominem attack. In
addition, Tygiel argued that simply because there was no evidence to
directly support Veeck's account did not mean the account was false. In
doing so, Jordan, Gerlach, and Rossi committed the rhetorical fallacy
of trying to prove a negative. Tygiel also questioned Jordan et al. for
their conclusion that the silence in the press was "significant" because
if Veeck had been serious about his attempt to desegregate baseball,
he would have spoken to the press, and if he had done so, someone in
the press would have reported it.[35]

Tygiel also questioned Jordan et al.'s assertion that Veeck's account
had never been independently corroborated. In 1949, Tygiel said, the
Chicago Defender reported that Fay Young discussed a meeting he had
seven years earlier where Veeck had discussed his interest in buying
the Phillies. In 1953 Doc Young wrote about a story he had heard about
Veeck's plan to buy the Phillies and sign blacks. In 1954 Saperstein told
the *Philadelphia Independent* that Veeck had planned to buy the Phillies,
take the team to spring training, and, on opening day, replace the team
with black players. Two years later the *Independent* again quoted Saperstein as saying that Veeck and he spoke to Landis, who had then sent
them to Frick. Furthermore, Tygiel criticized Jordan et al. for saying
it was "inconceivable" that any attempt to desegregate baseball would
have been a matter of public interest.[36] In fact, Jordan et al.'s argument
demonstrated a certain naïveté, if not ignorance, about the workings
of journalists. It suggested that reporters are aware of everything that
happens and that they report everything they hear and see. A lot of

white sportswriters knew about the campaign to desegregate baseball but said nothing. What if a sportswriter learned about Veeck's interest in signing blacks, questioned Veeck about it, and Veeck either denied it or asked the reporter not to publish the story? Wendell Smith — and perhaps Sam Lacy — withheld information about the signing of Jackie Robinson until Rickey gave his approval. Given the false alarms during the last few months of 1942, it also is possible a reporter, having heard that Veeck might buy the Phillies with the intention of signing black players, did not publish the story until he received more substantive information. Or the possibility exists that journalists were simply unaware of Veeck's plan.

Veeck, in fact, probably would not have confronted the baseball establishment after learning the Phillies had been sold. Tygiel said that Veeck did not want to risk alienating the commissioner in case he had another opportunity to buy a Major League team. Furthermore, Jordan, Gerlach, and Rossi summarily dismissed the notion that Veeck would try to get financing from either the Phillies Cigars or the CIO. Such a plan, instead of being laughable as Jordan et al. considered it, was perfectly reasonable, if not inspired. Phillies Cigars had a record of supporting integration. It had sponsored Sam Balter's radio program in 1940 calling for an end to the color line in the National Football League. Jordan et al. derisively asked why the CIO would be interested in "a bankrupt baseball team." What if a bankrupt team provided the CIO, which was heavily involved in the campaign to desegregate baseball, the best opportunity to desegregate baseball? It also made sense for Veeck to consult Saperstein, a booking agent who had particular knowledge of black players, including Paige. In the conclusion of his article, Tygiel agreed that Veeck was a storyteller, but this did not mean he was lying. Veeck talked a lot but, given his flair for dramatics, knew how to keep a secret and, in fact, understood the element of surprise. Although there is no definitive evidence to verify the Veeck story, there is enough circumstantial evidence that it cannot be dismissed as quickly and derisively as Jordan et al. did. Their essay failed to confirm their assertion that Veeck created his story two decades after it supposedly happened. In addition, Jordan et al., instead of clarifying a matter of dispute, further confused it by, according to Tygiel, making the same mistakes they accused other writers and historians of making.[37]

By early 1943 a decade had passed since the *Pittsburgh Courier* published its symposium on race as a result of Heywood Broun and Jimmy Powers calling for the end of the color line. Rickey may have discussed the issue with the Dodgers' board of directors behind closed doors, and Ford Frick may have laughed at Veeck behind closed doors. However, the optimism palpable during the summer of 1942 had disappeared. Richard Robinson of the American Negro Press wrote that there was a noticeable lull in the campaign to desegregate baseball because, in part, owners of black and white teams had little interest in ending the color line. Black owners did not want to lose the stars that had resulted in record attendance. If attendance fell in black baseball, white owners would also lose money. Robinson noted that white sportswriters had given the story cursory attention the previous summer but had since "closed the book on the subject." Black sportswriters should have followed Bostic's suggestion and urged black players to go to spring training and force the issue. "The owners of big league teams," Robinson said, "are not going to make the first gesture."[38]

The baseball establishment frequently made the argument that desegregation would cause race riots. Whereas blacks and whites had long played baseball against one another without incident, either on the field or in the stands, racial tensions between blacks and whites on military bases or in crowded cities continued to obstruct discussions about integration. On June 20, 1943, an argument between a black man and a white man led to a fistfight in Detroit, which then escalated into the worst race riot in a quarter century. By the time order was restored, twenty-five blacks and nine whites were dead, and hundreds of thousands of dollars worth of property had been destroyed. President Roosevelt sent six thousand soldiers to patrol the city.[39] According to Earl Brown, reportedly the only black reporter working for *Life*, "Crowds of whites . . . hunted and killed any of the easily visible black prey which chanced onto their territory." Civil rights leader Roy Wilkins said people in Detroit were using the riot as an excuse to "murder Negroes . . . in cold blood."[40] Detroit officials blamed the riot on the NAACP and the *Michigan Chronicle*, a black weekly. The governor saw no reason to investigate the brutality against blacks. U.S. Attorney General Francis Biddle, who had told black journalists the Roosevelt administration was not interested in prosecuting black newspapers, suggested to FDR that blacks be prohibited from moving to communities in Detroit where they could not be controlled.[41]

Six weeks later in Harlem a black soldier was shot by police after intervening in the arrest of a black woman. Rumors spread that the soldier had been killed. As a result, hundreds of blacks, angry at their living conditions, began torching and looting businesses owned by white, predominantly Jewish, merchants.[42] Whereas in other riots black leaders had criticized the disproportionate response of law enforcement agencies, black leaders in New York insisted that the violence was not a race riot but an act of "hoodlumism." Black leaders praised Mayor Fiorello La Guardia and the New York City Police Department for acting quickly to control the riot without overreacting.[43] Adam Clayton Powell Jr. said the disorder was the result of "blind, smoldering and unorganized resentment against Jim Crow treatment of Negro men in the armed forces and the unusual high rent and cost of living forced upon Negroes in Harlem."[44] Powell organized a committee that later met with La Guardia. As a result of the 1943 race riot, La Guardia announced his own alternative to the "Double V" campaign. He created the Mayor's Committee on Unity, naming as its chair Charles Evans Hughes Jr., the son of a former presidential candidate and Supreme Court justice, to study the causes of prejudice, exploitation, and discrimination in the city. "One of the Unity Committee's early studies was on baseball," La Guardia biographer Thomas Kessner wrote.[45] La Guardia later created the Mayor's Committee to Integrate Baseball to investigate the possibility of desegregating baseball.

By the summer of 1943 Lacy had left the *Washington Afro-American* after a dispute with his editor and became national editor of the *Chicago Defender*. In a front-page story on July 24, Lacy reported he had interviewed Paul Robeson after the prominent singer and lecturer had performed at the U.S. Naval Training Station at Great Lakes, Michigan. Lacy reported white and black sailors had responded with thunderous applause to Robeson, who then signed hundreds of programs. Robeson told Lacy he thought a better world awaited black America following the end of World War II, but that some whites would oppose any progress toward racial equality. "I am fully aware of the fact that the anti-Negro elements in this country will seize the opportunity to discredit Negroes wherever and whenever they can when the present war is over," Robeson said. "But I am also aware of the fact that America cannot hope to be a great nation in the world as it shapes up after the war unless she makes up her mind to do the right thing."[46] In several months Lacy and Robeson, who both supported racial equality in sports and society, would find themselves in the middle of the fight for the desegregation of baseball.

As sports editor of the *Washington Afro-American*, Lacy had the authority to write whatever he wanted. But that changed when he moved to Chicago. Whenever Lacy asked Fay Young to write sports stories, he said he was rebuffed. This did not prevent Lacy from, in his own words, thinking about "this desegregation business."[47] While Lacy was living in Washington DC, he had been frustrated in his attempts to contact Landis. Lacy's move to Chicago put him in the same city as the commissioner. Lacy continued contacting Landis. Finally, Lacy received the answer he had long awaited. Landis told Lacy he would meet with him on November 17.[48] During the meeting Landis told Lacy he could make the case for desegregation at the annual baseball meetings at New York City's Roosevelt Hotel in December. Landis sent the invitation to the Negro Newspaper Publishers Association.[49]

According to Lacy and Landis biographer David Pietrusza, the association then double-crossed both Lacy and Landis by inviting Robeson to make the argument for blacks in baseball.[50] Lacy, however, believed Landis had suggested Robeson, a Communist, to associate the campaign to desegregate baseball with communism. Lacy called the addition of Robeson to speak to the conservative owners foolish. "I knew that was a kiss of death because at that time, Paul was considered by many a communist," Lacy said. To Lacy, Landis could allow the black publishers to make their case yet leave the impression to the press and public that the campaign to desegregate baseball was a communist front by inviting one of the country's best-known black Communists. On November 30, a few days before the meeting, Joe Cummiskey said it was "great news" that baseball executives would consider the question of signing black players. "But," he added, "I also hope that the upshot will be more than a gesture."[51] Landis would ensure that any consideration of the issue would be a gesture and nothing more. Mainstream sportswriters would ensure that the issue received little consideration.

Landis and Robeson briefly chatted with one another before the meeting began in a conference room on the second floor of the Roosevelt Hotel on Friday, December 3. They then walked to the conference room, where they posed for photographs. The delegation of baseball executives included Landis, league presidents Frick and Harridge, and representatives from each of the sixteen Major League teams. The Negro Newspaper Publishers Association's delegation included John Sengstacke of the *Chicago Defender*, Ira Lewis and Wendell Smith of the *Pittsburgh Courier*, Dan Burley of the *Amsterdam News*, Louis E. Martin of the *Michigan Chronicle*, C. B. Powell of the *Amsterdam News*, William O. Walker of the *Cleveland Call and Post*, and Howard H. Murphy of the *Baltimore Afro-American*. The nonjournalists in the room included Robeson and Father Raymond Campion of Brooklyn. William Patterson and Ishmael Flory, executive secretary of the left-wing Negro People's Assembly and editor of its publication, the *New World*, accompanied Robeson but were not allowed in the conference room.[52] Robeson, Sengstacke, Lewis, and Murphy each addressed the executives. Reporters were barred from the meeting, except for the black journalists who were allowed. But as was Landis's practice, he did not close the transom door to the room. He was aware reporters were listening; others in the room were not.[53]

Shortly before eleven o'clock Landis opened the meeting with the following comment: "I want it clearly understood that there is no rule, nor to my knowledge, has there ever been, formal or informal, or any understanding, written or unwritten, subterranean or sub-anything, against the hiring of Negroes in the major leagues." Wendell Smith wrote that "the sound of Landis' voice" pierced the smoke-filled room as the commissioner "put on record" his stand regarding Negro players in the Majors. "With that off his chest," Smith continued, "the rock-jawed, fiery boss of baseball explained that he had personally invited Negro representatives to the meeting, marking the first time such an opportunity has been granted." Landis then introduced Robeson by calling him "a great man in public life, a great American."[54] Robeson, the once great defensive end at Rutgers University and now great baritone of the theater, told the executives he had seen for himself how integration had improved race relations. When he played football at Rutgers University, Robeson said, southern universities threatened to cancel games if he took the field. But the games were played, and there were no incidents. Robeson said that when he was cast to play Othello on Broadway, he was told that white audiences would not accept a black man in the role. But, he added, he played before full houses, and the response was overwhelmingly positive. Robeson said he understood why owners might be concerned about what might happen if baseball became desegregated. But, he said, such fears were "groundless." When Robeson finished his speech, the owners enthusiastically applauded.[55]

John Sengstacke then called Landis's introductory remarks "a good starting point" but said that blacks remained segregated as "a different and inferior type of citizen." He said that baseball's color line, whether formal or otherwise, reflected the same kind of master-race argument practiced by Hitler's Germany. "If any American organization establishes barriers either for or against any class of citizens, the security of all classes is placed in constant and potential jeopardy," Sengstacke said. This, he said, "strikes at the very heart of democracy."[56] Ira Lewis then challenged Landis's comment that there was no agreement prohibiting blacks from baseball. "We believe there is a gentlemen's agreement, that no Negroes players be hired," Lewis said. "I ask you, gentlemen, in the name of the America we all love, in the name of the democracy that we associate with the word America, that you undo this wrong . . . and let our national pastime be a game for all the boys in America."[57]

Howard H. Murphy concluded the publishers' presentation by submitting a four-point program that organized baseball (1) accept qualified black players into organized baseball; (2) make it possible for black players to move from the Minor Leagues to the Major Leagues without prejudice or discrimination; (3) employ the same process for black players as was currently used for white players to sign black players from schools, sandlots, and semipro clubs; and (4) release a statement declaring blacks eligible for tryouts with ballclubs.[58] When Murphy finished the baseball executives responded with sustained applause. Landis asked if there were any questions from the forty or so baseball executives. But there was only silence. "Strangely, not one offered a query," Wendell Smith reported. "They sat there for approximately one minute and finally Landis said, 'I guess that's all gentlemen.'" But it probably was not so strange after all. Landis had instructed the executives to keep quiet. "Don't interrupt Robeson," Landis told the owners before the meeting. "Let's not get into any discussion with him."[59]

Dissatisfied with the response, or lack therefore, Smith later tried to interview executives but received only more silence. "After the meeting it was almost impossible to get a statement from any of the owners," Smith said. Smith then approached Landis. "I can't speak for the owners at all," Landis told Smith. "Really, there is absolutely nothing I can tell you." When Smith approached Ford Frick, he responded by saying, "I really think they were impressed by the presentation. But I can't say what will happen." William Harridge, the president of the American League, refused to comment. Baseball rejected the publishers' proposals by issuing a statement that said, "Each club is entirely free to employ Negro players to any and all extent it pleases. The matter is solely for each club's decision, without restriction whatsoever."[60] Clark Griffith issued his own statement saying that segregation was better for both black and white leagues. In addition, he questioned the motives of those activists calling for the desegregation of baseball. "Why should propagandists be bringing it up at this time?" Griffith said.[61]

The meeting between black publishers and Major League Baseball was historic. But there was little or no sense of that in the coverage in the mainstream press. The *Sporting News* published a photograph of Robeson, Wendell Smith, and Stanley Frank of the *New York Post*. Dan Daniel reported that a delegation of blacks had spoken to the owners. "The Negro delegates were told by Landis that there was no baseball rule against the signing of members of their races," Daniel said, "and there the matter was left, just where it had been." John Drebinger of the *New York Times* reported the "Negro question was tactfully handled" by Landis, who issued a statement that said that teams were free to hire black players.[62] Sportswriters, though reluctant to say anything about the race issue in their columns and articles, felt comfortable enough to make jokes about it. Someone wrote a note next to the agenda item on a bulletin board in the hotel's press room that said, "Landis enters black market." The sportswriters all had a chuckle about that, Joe Cummiskey said. Cummiskey wrote that his columns calling for desegregation had brought at least one sharp response. "One scribe, revered by myself and all men who write baseball, gave it that old oldie about, 'Well, if you want them to play in the Majors, why don't you hire them for work in your office?' When I told him we did, he had no answer."[63]

In a column on January 8, 1944, Fay Young said the baseball establishment and mainstream sportswriters had thus far responded with silence to the issue. "Since Landis' declaration, the newspaper baseball writers haven't had anything to say on the matter other than a plain cold statement," he said. "'Same old soup warmed over' is what some of them have said to us. Some have declared their intentions to touch heavily on the subject." But thus far, they had said little, he said. He did not expect any owner to confront the color line. The first owner to sign a black player, Young wrote, "will do so over the pressure of other owners and managers and men high in government."[64] Wendell Smith said the baseball establishment expressed its opinion on the issue by giving the delegation the silent treatment.[65] In an editorial the *Baltimore Afro-American* said that the executives who listened to the presentation had to be aware they had lost many of their best players to the war and could strengthen their teams by signing blacks. "No club owner questioned the ability of colored players to qualify," it said. "Teams from the colored leagues have bested the white professionals too often." Paul Robeson said there was "every reason to believe that before the next season starts, Negro players will be in the major leagues." Of Robeson's many crusades, his biographer Martin Bauml Duberman wrote that the former athlete's "participation in the campaign to desegregate major league baseball brought him special satisfaction."[66]

Sam Lacy, however, believed Robeson's presence at the meeting with baseball executives hurt the campaign to desegregate baseball. Lacy, who believed he had arranged the meeting with the baseball establishment and deserved a seat at the table, was furious at Landis and felt betrayed by his editor, John Sengstecke, for replacing him with Robeson. Lacy quit the newspaper and went to work for the *Baltimore Afro-American*, where he would remain for the next half century. In his first "Looking 'Em Over" column, Lacy wrote that he had suggested restricting the committee to the president of the black newspaper publishers organization, the only black congressman, and a representative of either the Urban League or the NAACP. What transpired was a committee that was too big and lacked knowledge of both the issue and the attitudes of big league owners. "The major league owners are almost fanatical in their dislike of communism," Lacy said. Lacy said that Landis reminded him of a cartoon he had seen of a man extending his right hand in a gesture of friendship while clenching a long knife in a left hand, which was concealed behind his back. Landis "told the

gullible colored folks" that he was going to give them a fair chance, Lacy
said, and then, in private, told owners that there was "a Communist
influence along with the torchbearers."[67]

Although the meeting had little impact on the attitudes of the
baseball establishment, it appeared to energize black journalists. John
Sengstacke urged black newspapers to increase pressure on teams in
organized professional baseball to sign black players. William Harrison
and William Patterson of the Chicago Committee to End Jim Crow
in Baseball met again with Philip Wrigley and gave Wrigley a list of
prospective black ballplayers who could play in the Major Leagues. The
meeting accomplished little. Wrigley said he would consider hiring a
scout to look at promising black players. Wrigley, however, said the
middle of a war was not the right time to change tradition. "Baseball
is not progressive," Wrigley said. "When everyone else finally adopts
something new, then baseball accepts it. Baseball hesitates to break a
custom whether it is using Negro players or removing the traditional
sleeves out of uniforms."[68]

The black baseball establishment tried to find middle ground where
it could support desegregation while ensuring its interests were served.
During the annual meetings of the Negro leagues, J. B. Martin, president of the Negro American League, said that when organized baseball began signing black players, white teams needed to compensate
black teams, as they did players from Minor League teams.[69] Black
sportswriters said white baseball had no obligation to do that until
black baseball standardized its rules so that the league was organized
more like white baseball. Because the Negro leagues did not recognize
contracts, organized professional baseball would not be obligated to
recognize contracts, either; therefore, Major League teams were under
no obligation to compensate black teams.[70] Black sportswriters said
owners needed to recognize their teams could sell their players to
big league teams for a considerable profit if they had standardized
contracts.[71] Black baseball needed a more reliable method of keeping
statistics. To that end, Wendell Smith offered to serve as the league's

statistician for five thousand dollars a year. Black baseball, no doubt tired of being ridiculed by Smith and other sportswriters, refused the offer.[72] It did not, however, reject Smith's suggestion and hired the Howe and Elias bureau to keep statistics — although, because of the peripatetic nature of black baseball, keeping reliable statistics remained problematic, if not impossible.[73]

As the war continued and more and more Major League ballplayers entered the armed services, owners ignored blacks but signed whites who were rejected for the armed services, either because they were too old or too young or could not pass the required physical. Clark Griffith gave a tryout to a Chinese ballplayer, signed Cuban players, and had one-legged Burt Shepperd pitch. One-armed outfielder Pete Gray played for the St. Louis Browns, and fifteen-year-old Joe Nuxhall pitched for the Cincinnati Reds. But Major League owners continued to ignore talented, able-bodied black ballplayers. "A one-armed man, Cubans, Chinese, Mexicans," Rollo Wilson sneered, "anyone except a colored man is welcomed in the big leagues at this time."[74] World War II caused a number of white Americans, including sportswriters, to change their attitudes on race. The irony of fighting bigotry abroad while denying racial equality at home became more and more obvious.[75]

World War II made it hard, though obviously not impossible, for the United States to ignore what Gunnar Myrdal called its "Negro problem." Myrdal, however, expressed optimism that the United States would move toward its promise of equality for all. "Not since Reconstruction has there been more reason to anticipate fundamental changes in race relations," Myrdal said. "Changes which will involve a development toward the American ideal." But Myrdal, who was neither American nor black, probably underestimated the depth of the Negro problem. Earl Conrad, who left *P.M.* to work for the *Defender*, called Myrdal naive. Conrad said America could not solve the problem without confronting it — and the country's white newspapers had neither the interest nor the courage to do this. If the white press addressed the issue of racial discrimination, this would force politicians to address it, Conrad said. But this would not happen. The white press, he said, was "either actively anti-Negro or it is silent. Either course is an attack on one-tenth of the nation."[76]

Black newspapers reported instances of racial discrimination involving black soldiers. In Little Rock, Arkansas, a white police officer shot and killed a black army sergeant on a city street. In Centerville, Mississippi, a white sheriff intervened in a dispute between a black soldier and a white military policeman, shooting and killing the soldier.[77] A *Memphis World* reporter said he had witnessed military policemen savagely beating a black soldier, who had been waiting in line at the city's train station. A policeman had said something to the solider and did not like the response, and immediately a number of police officers began pummeling the soldier.[78] A black chaplain resigned from the army in protest of the blatant racism in the armed forces. His chronicling of the abuses was published in the *Crisis*.[79]

The War Department responded to the complaints of black editors that negative stories about the treatment of black soldiers were partially the result of their being denied access to the military. A number of black journalists, including Billy Rowe, who would later accompany Jackie Robinson on his first spring training in baseball in 1946, were given credentials to serve as war correspondents. Walter White, executive secretary of the NAACP, returned to the United States in the middle of 1944 after a tour of military bases. In mid-July White delivered a searing condemnation of American racism in an address at the annual meeting of the NAACP in Chicago. He criticized the government for not passing antilynching laws, for not investigating the murder of black soldiers, and for not rebuking racist politicians like Senator James Eastland of Mississippi, who openly referred to blacks as "burr headed niggers." White said it was common practice that the military used court-martials to intimidate black soldiers. He said military bases continued to segregate blacks, even though Gen. Dwight D. Eisenhower, supreme commander of Allied troops, had ordered an end to it. White said the continued discrimination against blacks sent a destructive lesson to white children, who were being taught that America was fighting a war for democracy. America, White said, "could not play the Star-Spangled Banner without using the black and white keys."[80]

In early July 1944 one of America's most famous black athletes, Jackie Robinson, found himself in the middle of a racial incident that nearly resulted in his being sentenced to a military prison. Robinson, a lieutenant in the army, was riding on a military bus at Fort Hood, Texas, when he was ordered to the back. Robinson, knowing that segregation was prohibited on military buses, refused. Robinson and the bus driver exchanged harsh words. When the bus got to the base, Robinson was taken into custody by white MPs. An angry Robinson was indignant about being sent to the back of the bus and then by being interrogated by military authorities who refused to acknowledge him as an officer. Robinson was charged with insubordination and court-martialed. The *Pittsburgh Courier* and black newspapers publicized his prosecution. Robinson's attorney argued that there had been no violations of military law. Robinson later wrote that his arrest was "simply a situation in which a few individuals sought to vent their bigotry on a Negro they considered 'uppity' because he had the audacity to seek to exercise rights that had belonged to him as an American and as a soldier." Cleared of charges, Robinson could return to his unit. But his unit had been deployed to Europe, where it would engage in relentless combat for six months, sustaining heavy casualties. On November 28, 1944, Robinson was "honorably discharged from active duty."[81]

Three days earlier, on November 25, Kenesaw Mountain Landis died. The *Sporting News,* the nation's sports pages, and the baseball establishment buried Landis with full honors. In its obituary the *New York Times* said that Landis had been called baseball's "Abraham Lincoln" because he "had freed so many baseball slaves" when he put an end to the practice by Branch Rickey and other baseball executives of keeping scores of players under contract and hiding them in the Minor Leagues.[82] The comparison between Landis and Lincoln was, at best, ironic, because the man who did everything within his power to prohibit blacks from playing in baseball was portrayed as Lincoln, and Rickey, who ultimately made it possible for blacks to play in the big leagues, was portrayed as a plantation owner. Sportswriters speculated about the future of organized baseball without Landis, who had lorded over the sport for a quarter century. Questions arose over who would succeed him. The long list of possible candidates included, among other people, Ford Frick; Senator A. B. "Happy" Chandler, a former governor of Kentucky; FBI director J. Edgar Hoover; Robert Patterson, undersecretary of war; and Postmaster General James Farley. Few, if any, owners liked Landis personally, but "the Great White Father" had kept baseball segregated, and that was to his credit.

Others, however, recognized the commissioner's death provided an opportunity that had not existed since the campaign to end the color line had begun. Few knew the man who would become the architect of "baseball's great experiment" was Branch Rickey, who came from the baseball establishment. When Landis died, Lee Lowenfish wrote, "Rickey was thinking that one obstacle to his integration plan was now removed." When Sam Lacy learned the baseball establishment would have a special meeting in April in Detroit to select Landis's successor, he wrote Major League Baseball, suggesting a committee be created to consider bringing blacks into baseball. Lacy said he was willing to accept desegregation even if it were to happen slower than he wanted. "This is sort of a compromise for me as a colored man, in that it embraces certain elements of appeasement, but if it accomplished anything, I shall feel compensated in some measure for suggesting it," Lacy wrote. "Certainly, it will be a step in the right direction." Leslie O'Connor, who chaired the search for Landis's replacement, accepted Lacy's offer to address the owners.[83]

Landis's death also coincided with a changing America. Blacks and social progressives, particularly in New York, were increasingly using legislation to end discrimination. For the first time since Reconstruction, U.S. lawmakers, particularly in New York, took seriously discussions about racial equality. In March 1945 the New York legislature passed the Ives-Quinn Act, which banned discrimination in hiring and established a commission to investigate complaints.[84] Rickey was at spring training at Bear Mountain when he read that Governor Thomas Dewey had signed Ives-Quinn, which would go into law in July. "They can't stop me now," Rickey told his wife.[85] The *Chicago Defender* said the most profound and immediate result of Ives-Quinn could come in baseball. The law could end the color line in baseball and "mark one of the most forward steps in the long campaign by Negro and white sportswriters" and other activists to put blacks in Major League uniforms. In another editorial the *Defender* said the law would compel Major League teams to sign blacks. "If baseball is to continue its claim of being a great American game," it said, "it is time that it became all-American and used all players regardless of race, color or creed."[86]

When spring training opened Representative Samuel Weiss of Pittsburgh praised baseball for its contribution to the morale of the country and called on the national pastime to continue as it had, even as the war continued in Europe and Asia. Wendell Smith criticized Weiss for failing to acknowledge that baseball continued to discriminate against blacks. "Why won't Congressman Weiss launch an investigation and find out why professional baseball continues to bar Negro citizens?" Smith asked. In an editorial the *Courier* said that if big league owners ended the color ban, it would improve the game and make it truly a national pastime. If not, it said, "then they must bear responsibility for whatever extremists may do in their effort to break down the color bar. . . . American negroes have been patient, courteous and considerate. Now it is time for the white men who control this sport to be likewise."[87]

Representative Vito Marcantonio of New York introduced a resolution in the U.S. House of Representatives, authorizing the U.S. Commerce Department to investigate racial discrimination in Major League Baseball. "Baseball's America's greatest sport," Marcantonio said, "and it is silly to pretend that Negroes are not among the best players." Marcantonio called the color line "contrary to American sportsmanship."[88] He said the integration of baseball had long been a topic of conversation behind closed doors, and it was time to bring it into the open for debate in Congress. If the resolution was approved, it would force the baseball commissioner and other executives to testify in U.S. Congress.[89] Al Schaffer, Marcantonio's biographer, said that Marcantonio was "was more interested in frightening organized baseball into action than he was in any inquiry." To Schaffer, Marcantonio was aware of the movement to bring blacks into baseball and wanted to use his influence to raise the profile on the issue.[90]

Chicago Daily News columnist John P. Carmichael chided the congressman. "Marcantonio contends there are some Negro players good enough to make the big leagues," Carmichael wrote. "Being a representative presumably makes Marcantonio an expert in baseball and no doubt he would be managing the Yankees or some other club if he hadn't cast his lot in politics." The *Chicago Defender* told Carmichael that Marcantonio was no more an expert on baseball than the columnist was an expert on democracy. "Remember that little sentence in the Declaration of Independence about 'all men are created equal,'" the *Defender* continued. "Marcantonio thinks that applies to players, too."[91] A week later, on May 12, the *Defender* used the issue of racial discrimination in baseball to address the issue of racial discrimination in the United States. "Baseball's ban on Negroes is a black eye to Uncle Sam no less than a lynching in Georgia. Baseball is the No. 1 American sport," the editorial said. "Today, the world is looking to the United States as the democratic citadel, as the land of hope in a world of despair. As long as we ape Hitler's racial laws in our biggest sport, America is saying to the world: Aryan supremacy is fine for us, but not for Germany."

Ives-Quinn raised the profile on racial discrimination in New York State by the spring of 1945. In New York City progressive politics and labor unions were popular, and progressives had the ear of influential lawmakers like Mayor La Guardia. Marcantonio, who once served as La Guardia's campaign manager, lived in Brooklyn. Membership in the Committee to End Jim Crow in Baseball included most, if not all, of the city's influential social progressives, including city council members such as Peter Cacchione of Brooklyn and Benjamin Davis Jr. of Harlem. "The trade union movement took it a big way and so did millions of white baseball fans and progressives," Davis wrote in his autobiography. "Many big league baseball players expressed support, thereby depriving big league magnates of the bogus contention that white players would not play on the same team with Negro players." Davis later wrote about his deep sense of pride in being a part of the campaign to desegregate baseball.[92]

La Guardia, who had decided not to run for reelection, wanted to secure his record on civil rights by desegregating baseball. He created the Mayor's Committee to Integrate Baseball as part of the Mayor's Committee on Unity. La Guardia then urged the city's three Major League teams, the Yankees, Giants, and Dodgers, to pledge their support.[93] Horace Stoneham, president of the Giants, rejected La Guardia's advances as a political stunt. Branch Rickey and Larry MacPhail both agreed to support the committee.[94] Rickey met a number of times with La Guardia. To Rickey, Ives-Quinn meant that if he did not integrate baseball on his own, he might be forced to do so on someone else's terms. He did not want to appear as if he had been coerced by the mayor. Rickey, who was as savvy as anyone when it came to the politics of the game, wanted to present himself as the man who desegregated baseball on his own terms. Rickey understood the sense of urgency, but, as a scholar of the Bible, he also understood there was a time for everything. And, with so much at stake, he did not want to rush — or be rushed. Rickey did not reveal anything about his plan to La Guardia. He did, however, share his secret with Brooklyn's popular play-by-play announcer, Red Barber, who had been raised in Sanford, Florida. When Rickey told him, Barber considered quitting but remained with the team.[95]

During the summer of 1942, when the color barrier was cracking, MacPhail had the opportunity to deliver a decisive blow to segregated baseball but then lied about his interest in organizing a game between the Yankees and the champions of the Negro leagues. Shortly after MacPhail was named president of the Yankees in early 1945, he was interviewed by Richard Dier of the *Baltimore Afro-American*. MacPhail expressed his optimism that Ives-Quinn would lead to the desegregation of baseball. "I am opposed to discrimination against colored ball players in the major leagues," MacPhail said in the March 24 story, "but the job is to convince the majority of the sixteen owners along these lines. They do not think in terms of discrimination. To them it is matter of dollars and cents, and you've got to show them that the hiring of colored players is profitable." MacPhail said that owners had discussed the issue in 1935 but had dismissed it because there had been no interest in desegregation from anyone outside baseball. Dier praised MacPhail as a friend of desegregation. "It's good to have such a strong and influential baseball figure on our side. Broadsides aimed at discrimination in baseball should not be fired his way," Dier wrote. "He has a tough enough job trying to convince others in this sport that his convictions are not only a part of democracy but that they will pay off dividends too."

The campaign to desegregate baseball had developed far beyond black newspapers and the *Daily Worker* to mainstream politicians and journalists. By April 1945 Vito Marcantonio had addressed the issue in Congress, Charles Perry had done so in the state legislature, Peter Cacchione and Ben Davis Jr. had addressed the New York City Council, and Fiorello La Guardia had done so from the mayor's office. Rickey, unbeknownst to others, was moving forward his plan to desegregate baseball. There also was pressure mounting in Chicago. And in Boston a Jewish city councilman, Isadore Muchnick, had told the city's two Major League teams that he would reject the teams' permit to play Sunday baseball if they continued to prohibit blacks from their roster. "I cannot understand how baseball, which claims to be the national sport . . . can continue a pre–Civil War attitude toward American citizens because of the color of their skins." Red Sox general manager Eddie Collins wrote Muchnick that no blacks wanted to play in the Major Leagues.

Muchnick then released Collins's reply to the press. Wendell Smith offered to recommend ballplayers for a tryout if Muchnick pursued the matter.[96] The councilman dropped his threat when the Red Sox and Braves assured him that blacks were free to try out for their teams.[97] The Red Sox and Braves reportedly told Muchnick they would give blacks a tryout.[98] A year later neither team had lived up to its promise, and Muchnick and Wendell Smith decided to confront the teams. Ten days earlier Joe Bostic confronted Rickey at the Dodgers' spring training camp, demanding that he give a tryout to two black players.

CHAPTER 10

"GET THOSE NIGGERS OFF THE FIELD"

Shortly after Joe Bostic left his home in Harlem at 7:30 a.m. on April 6, he discovered he had a flat tire. He had the tire patched, filled the car with gas, and called Terris McDuffie and Dave "Showboat" Thomas to let them know he was running late. Bostic then picked up the ballplayers and crossed over the George Washington Bridge. As Bostic drove, McDuffie recounted how he had beaten Major Leaguers in game after game. Today, if things went according to plan, the pitcher would face Major Leaguers again. At 11:50 Bostic, McDuffie, and Thomas arrived at the Brooklyn Dodgers' spring training camp at West Point Academy in Bear Mountain, New York. They got out of the car, and as they looked across a baseball field, they felt the chill of the early-spring wind. "A game was in progress and wintry blasts were sweeping Durocher Field," Bostic said. Bostic briefly chatted with *Daily Worker* sportswriter Nat Low, *Pittsburgh Courier* reporter Jimmy Smith, and Associated Negro Press photographer Harold Stovall. At 12:10 Bostic told Harold Parrott,

the Dodgers' traveling secretary, that he wanted to speak to Branch
Rickey about a tryout for the ballplayers. Parrott said that Rickey was
watching a game at another practice field and could not be disturbed.
When Bostic insisted, Parrott went to find Rickey. As Bostic waited
his eyes scanned the field. "I made a mental note," Bostic said while
watching the game. "Never saw such a nondescript bunch of ballplayers
in my life. Those performing in the game should be easy pickins' for
the likes of 'Showboat' and McDuffie."[1]

At 12:40 Parrott returned with Bob Finch, Rickey's top assistant.
Bill Roeder of the *New York World-Telegram* had joined the ballplayers
and sportswriters. Finch said tryouts were given only to players who
had either been invited by the team or been recommended by one of
the team's scouts. Bostic asked why the team had never seen a black
player who had been good enough to be recommended. Finch had no
answer. Finch insisted that Rickey and the rest of the men in charge of
the Brooklyn organization were men of goodwill. Finch then talked at
length about how he had confronted discrimination at a USO club in
St. Louis. "Then came one of the most amazing of all our experiences,"
Bostic said. "Finch, visibly upset by the Negro plight, broke down and
cried like any child. As tears streamed down the elderly man's face, we
hardened newspapermen stood there speechless." Finch said Rickey
wanted to discuss the issue with Bostic and the ballplayers over lunch.
"Here is the first break in the clouds," Bostic thought. "If he can be
talked to, he can be sold." If Rickey or Durocher, Brooklyn's manager,
could see McDuffie or Thomas play, Bostic thought, the ballplayers
would be signed.[2] But Rickey was livid about the interruption and
livid about the presence of Nat Low, who he assumed was behind the
interruption. He hated surprises and he hated Communists. Roeder
later wrote that Low's presence added "a sickening Red tinge . . . to
the invasion of the Brooklyn training camp at Bear Mountain."[3] The
Sporting News reported that the confrontation had "all the earmarks
of a definite pogram."[4]

At 2:20 Bostic and the ballplayers were escorted into a dining room. Rickey entered fifteen minutes later and made no effort to conceal what one writer would later describe as his "cold rage."[5] Bostic was surprised by Rickey's profanity-filled tirade. "This was my first meeting with the man," he said, "and I had read all those stories about his religion so I was plenty surprised." Rickey, which should not have surprised Bostic, talked and talked and talked, finally issuing a stern reprimand. "I'm more for your cause than anybody else you know," he said, "but you are making a mistake using force, dictating in this matter. . . . It will fail because this is a manner of evolution, not revolution. It is a matter of education. You are defeating your aims."[6] Rickey's quote would be widely reported in mainstream newspapers. Rickey agreed to give the ballplayers a tryout the following day. He asked assurances that nobody in the room discuss the particulars of the meeting with the press.[7]

When the men emerged from the conference at 4:00 p.m., Rickey told awaiting reporters the team would give a tryout to McDuffie and Thomas the next day. Rickey was asked if this was a response to the Ives-Quinn antidiscriminatory law.[8] Rickey denied that Ives-Quinn or anything else would influence who would or would not wear a Brooklyn uniform. "I will look at ball players of any age, color or creed," Rickey said, "and I will do it whenever I please." Rickey then asked himself, "Does this include Colored players?" and then he answered his own question: "I'll say it does." Rickey told reporters that he had had two conversations with New York City mayor Fiorello La Guardia about the issue.[9] Rickey also told reporters he was interested in the advancement of black players and was considering leasing his own ballpark, Ebbets Field, to black teams. "Why, I might even be interested in ownership of a franchise."[10] Rickey, either knowingly or not, tipped his hand with his remark about being interested in becoming involved with black baseball. In a month he would announce that he would be part owner of a black team in a newly organized black league.

Bostic told reporters he planned to take the players to the training camps of the other New York City teams, the Yankees and the

Giants. When Rickey asked why they had selected Bear Mountain, Low answered that the Dodgers' seventh-place finish the previous year had demonstrated the team's need for quality ballplayers. He insisted that McDuffie and Thomas could improve the team. "These two players are better than those you have out there on the field," Low said. "I know they can help you better your team." An indignant Rickey snapped, "A more debatable statement I never heard."[11] Rickey was probably right about McDuffie and Thomas, neither of whom probably was good enough to play in the Majors. But Rickey was hardly in a position to be choosy. Brooklyn finished the 1944 season with a record of 63-91 — more than forty games behind first-place St. Louis and only a game and a half ahead of last-place Philadelphia, which had the worst record in the Major Leagues. To put this in perspective, Brooklyn had been one of the worst teams in a season when most of the best players were in the armed services. Brooklyn, therefore, was a bad team coming off a bad season in a particularly bad year for baseball.

Leonard Cohen of the *New York Post*, an evening newspaper, probably wrote the first account of the story. Cohen wrote that Brooklyn was selected because it was the weakest of the three New York City teams. He also said the confrontation put Rickey on the spot. If Rickey allowed the tryout, Bostic and the Communists would make names for themselves. If Rickey rejected the tryout, he would be reviled as an obstructionist. Cohen said the "situation was rife with possibilities" — though he did not specify in particular what that meant. He did, however, say that baseball did not have a written rule prohibiting blacks. He also said that some black players, like Satchel Paige, made more money in the Negro leagues than they could in the big leagues. But Paige was an anomaly. Few black players made as much as a lowly paid Major Leaguer. Cohen also said that there were no blacks in baseball because none had ever requested a tryout. "If a colored player didn't ask for a tryout, the majors had a perfect out," Cohen said, adding, "An unwritten law was thus observed." This statement also was wrong. Roy Campanella had, of course, approached the Philadelphia Phillies. Joe

Cummiskey of *P.M.* ridiculed Cohen for repeating baseball establishment's lie that there was no written law banning blacks from the game.
Cummiskey called Cohen's statement "hogwash." If there was no ban,
he asked, why were there no blacks in baseball?[12]

Al Laney of the *New York Herald Tribune* was the only other sportswriter to cover the confrontation at Bear Mountain. Laney took delight
in writing how the talkative Methodist deacon had been left speechless. "It would have been a real pleasure to be at Bear Mountain yesterday. . . . To catch Brother Rickey thus with his guard down was an
extraordinary achievement. The situation had elements of immortal
comedy," Laney said. With sarcasm dripping over his words, Laney
wrote that Rickey was sitting in the sunshine, constantly chewing on
a cigar while contemplating how he had cut the team's payroll to "an
irreducible minimum and was running over in his mind what he would
later say to the press in a few thousand well chosen words. Content-
ment and peace were with Brother Rickey." Then, according to Laney,
the sky darkened and the heavens shook. "Rickey, as soon as the facts
penetrated through the sweet dream he was dreaming, sputtered and
then he continued to sputter for more than an hour. Normally, Brother
Rickey is by no means addicted to sputtering," Laney said, adding, "But
he had to give himself time. So he turned the two Negro players and
three newspaper men" over to one of his assistants. Laney reported that
Rickey met with Bostic during the lunch meeting but would not commit to giving the players a tryout while speaking at great length about
his belief in democracy and justice for everyone. This, Laney said, was
typical Rickey double-talk. "But Bostic pushed him right into a corner
and demanded an answer," Laney said. "Rickey said he was being pressured. He said it would be all right, maybe if the newspaper men didn't
know about it. But now they did. Finally, he came through and agreed
to give McDuffie and Thomas a tryout the following day."[13] Laney, who
was not at the closed-door meeting, depended for his information on
someone who was present at the lunch meeting with Rickey.

Bostic and the ballplayers arrived at Bear Mountain the next day shortly after noon. As Bostic waited for Rickey, he sat with photographer Harold Stovall in the dining hall. "It seemed that everybody in the inn was staring at us," Bostic said, "as though we were freaks from another world." Bostic's noon meeting with Rickey was no more pleasant than his meeting the previous day. Rickey was furious that Bostic had leaked the tryout. "I was thoroughly raked over the coals for breaking the agreement not to tell anybody about the tryout so that it would be held in comparative privacy," Bostic said. "I didn't feel too much concern for I was aware that the white light of publicity would accomplish more for Negro players than all the silent pacts in the world."[14] Rickey then made little attempt to conceal his contempt toward Bostic to the waiting reporters. "The fact that several newspapers in New York knew of this tryout . . . indicates that this thing was staged," Rickey said. The *Sporting News* reported that Bostic violated a "pledge" he had made with Rickey to withhold the details of the tryout. "First, the matter was supposed to be kept secret, so that all papers could have the story at the same time," the *Sporting News* reported. "Second, no photographers were to be present."[15]

Bostic admitted to calling Laney and Jack Smith of the *Daily News*. He also said he had called Cohen and Joe Cummiskey. When other writers asked why they, too, had not been called, Bostic responded with a short, but revealing, answer. "I didn't think you would be interested," he said. The *Sporting News* reported that Rickey, even though Bostic had violated his pledge, "went ahead with his part of the agreement."[16] To Rickey's credit, he put his professional obligation to improve his team over his personal feelings. If Rickey could turn the Brooklyn Dodgers into winners by signing blacks, he was willing to give that a try.[17] Rickey asked Bostic if the sportswriter would object if the tryout was closed to team personnel. Bostic replied that he would. Bostic said he demanded that the tryout be open to reporters because "this was a tremendous break and silence would completely neutralize its value." Rickey agreed that the tryout would be open to all journalists — except photographers.[18]

For years black sportswriters had listened to the promises of baseball executives, and nothing had come of those promises. Bostic decided to put Rickey on the spot, and Rickey called Bostic's bluff. Bostic now found himself on the spot. For Bostic's strategy to succeed, or even to have a chance of succeeding, it required that the talents of McDuffie and Thomas be so obvious that no one could deny them. But neither McDuffie nor Thomas had such talent. Newspaper accounts reported that McDuffie was thirty-two and had gone 18-6 with the Newark Eagles in 1944. Thomas, the stories said, was thirty-four and had hit .328 for the Cuban All-Stars.[19] Even if the statistics were accurate—and it was later learned they were not—McDuffie and Thomas were both past their prime. Thomas, in another account, was forty and McDuffie nearly thirty-five.[20] Bostic later said that he selected the two ballplayers because they were "willing to face the wrath of the man."[21] The ballplayers also were chosen, in part, because most of the better players were at spring training with their respective Negro league teams or playing in Mexico. Even though Rickey had been pressured into the tryouts, he treated the ballplayers like any other prospects and even supervised the tryout himself. McDuffie and Thomas, wearing Brooklyn uniforms, began warming up at 12:45 p.m. McDuffie wore number 9, while Thomas wore number 14.[22] While McDuffie warmed up, Rickey worked with two pitching prospects, Vic Lombardi and Claude Crocker. Others present included Bob Quinn, coaches Charlie Dressen and Clyde Sukeforth, and team manager Leo Durocher. Brooklyn pitchers Frank Wurm, John Gabbard, and Ralph Branca threw batting practice to Thomas. Rickey worked privately with McDuffie.[23] McDuffie said it was the first time in his career that he had received any coaching.[24]

The tryouts lasted forty-five minutes to an hour, depending on press accounts. When McDuffie and Thomas were finished, Rickey released his personal observations. Jack Smith of the *New York Daily News* said that Rickey issued such a report "on every youngster in camp."[25] Rickey was unimpressed with Thomas. "On what he showed me I could not be impressed in him if he were 24 instead of 34." The quote, which was included in the Associated Press account, was widely repeated. Rickey was more charitable toward McDuffie, who, he said, had good control, a good fastball, and a good curve but lacked an effective changeup.[26] According to the *Daily Worker* and *Pittsburgh Courier*, the report included a promising quote from Rickey, who said, "I want to see more of this pitcher."[27] The quote, however, was not included in stories appearing in the mainstream dailies, which stressed that McDuffie was too old to be a prospect. Rickey's report said Claude Crocker, who was nineteen and had pitched in two games for Brooklyn in 1944, had a lot more potential than McDuffie, who was more than a decade older.[28] Rickey's report included a quote by manager Leo Durocher who said that he had a dozen ballplayers in camp with more talent and that thirty-two-year-olds with no professional experience did not interest him.[29] Durocher's comment was misleading. The ballplayers each had been playing professionally for years. They had simply been doing it in the Negro leagues.

Daily Mirror columnist Dan Parker bristled at Durocher's comment, knowing, as Durocher did, that Major League teams, including the Dodgers, had 4Fs and forty-year-olds. Parker wrote that Durocher "could have thought of a more convincing excuse" for rejecting Thomas and McDuffie because Brooklyn had three players on its roster in their forties. Parker predicted baseball's color line would continue to be questioned as big league teams continued to put inferior players in uniforms. The issue, Parker said, "will bob up often this year to plague the sidestepping baseball magnates who are ill prepared to duck it with those comic opera ball clubs they're putting on the field." Eight days later Parker returned to the tryout, calling it "a pleasant little phantasy [*sic*]." Rickey, Parker said, "unloosed some of his sugary platitudes" and ordered that the black prospects be treated with a certain amount of caution. "All amenities were observed," Parker said. "However, when it came to photographing the two players in Dodger uniforms, the line was drawn."[30]

After the tryouts concluded Bostic released a statement that expressed his satisfaction. "Today's extensive tryout, given Terris McDuffie and Dave Thomas by the Dodgers, represents a constructive and significant step in the effort to have Negro players in the major leagues. I feel it represents the first concrete step toward realization of that goal. . . . I am completely satisfied with the conduct of the tryout and feel confident that the rest of the job can be accomplished in a comparatively short time." Bostic's statement was widely reported. The *Sporting News*, however, reported that Rickey was not satisfied with what had transpired and would not allow another tryout under such circumstances. Jim McCulley of the *Daily News* disagreed with Bostic that the issue could be settled in a relatively short time. "I, for one, doubt it, and I am far from being alone in that viewpoint," he said, adding that he "was not prejudiced one way or another." McCulley said blacks would not be welcome in the Major Leagues until there were profound changes in society. McCulley repeated the old argument that it was the players — and not the owners — who kept blacks out of baseball. A few owners, he said, would sign black players if they did not think it would upset the players. McCulley said he had been recently talking with a group of Major League players and baseball executives. "It wasn't a heated discussion in which violent prejudices reared up. It was a quiet discussion," he said. "And then someone asked the question: 'Well, if the door were opened to Negro ballplayers, how many of them could make the grade?' The answer was: 'About a half dozen at the most.'"[31]

New York sportswriters Bill Lauder of the *Herald Tribune*, Gus Steiger of the *Daily Mirror*, and Jack Smith of the *Daily News* each wrote detailed articles about the tryout.[32] Lauder wrote that it was business as usual elsewhere on the field. "There were no unusual actions by any of the Dodgers present or by Rickey. They all went through their jobs as they have daily since arriving in camp," Lauder said. "McDuffie was just another pitcher, except that the newspaper men added to the scenery." There was no evidence if Bill Roeder, who was present for Bostic's confrontation, returned to report on the tryout. The *World-Telegram* ran a brief account with no byline. The *Journal American* published brief stories on April 7 and April 8. Roscoe McGowen of the *New York Times* was at West Point but said nothing about the tryout. The *Times* instead ran an Associated Press account.[33] The *Sun* also had a reporter at the training camp but said nothing. *Times* sports columnist Arthur Daley did not mention the tryout. The *New York Morning Telegraph* also said nothing. In his April 7 column *Post* columnist Leonard Cohen repeated that McDuffie and Thomas had asked for a tryout, which he had reported the day before. But Cohen said nothing in particular about the tryout.

The story of the tryout of McDuffie and Thomas was covered for a day by the mainstream press before it disappeared from the sports pages. Bill Roeder later characterized it as "a publicity stunt." According to Bostic, it was more than that. "It was the psychological breaking of the conspiracy of silence," Bostic said. But mainstream dailies tried to suppress the story by not reporting it, he said. "They might just as well have tried to hold off a tidal wave," Bostic said. He said that history was made at Bear Mountain, whether some sportswriters acknowledged it or not. Bostic characterized the tryout as "the turning point in a great battle . . . to open the doors of the great American game of baseball to all American citizens, including Negroes." He called the tryout of McDuffie and Thomas "the most momentous single adventure in the fight for Negroes into the major leagues."[34]

Nat Low also did his best to capture the story's historical significance. "Another milestone in the long campaign to bring Negro players into the major leagues was passed today," he said, "when for the first time in the history of baseball two Negro players received tryouts with the Brooklyn Dodgers." Low reported that those present included Rickey, Durocher, and other Brooklyn officials, players, and reporters as well as a number of enlisted men stationed at West Point. During the try-out the size of the crowd of onlookers increased. Low asked one of the GIs watching what he thought of McDuffie. "Looks damned good to me," the soldier said. "Do you think he'll be signed up?" Another soldier asked Low if there was a rule prohibiting blacks from the Major Leagues. When Low told him there was not, "the soldier shook his head perplexedly and wondered how come there never had been a Negro in the majors." When McDuffie began throwing, Clyde Sukeforth cautioned him against throwing too hard in the beginning of his workout. Rickey stood behind McDuffie and asked him to throw a series of different pitches. Once McDuffie was loose, his pitches smacked "resoundingly into Sukeforth's mitt." Rickey, Low said, called McDuffie's control "amazing." When the workout ended at 2:30, Rickey and his coaches met briefly before Rickey issued a lengthy statement that said, in reference to McDuffie, "I want to see more of this pitcher." Two weeks later Low asked why Rickey had not yet contacted McDuffie. Rickey, Low said, could immediately improve the team by signing Negro leaguers. "Our patience at the delay in ending the infamous Jim-crow ban in baseball is wearing out," he said. If the Dodgers, Giants, and Yankees did not sign black players, Low said, they would be in violation of Ives-Quinn.[35]

Jimmy Smith of the *Courier* called the tryout the most "progressive step" baseball had taken in signing black players and said it had been the result of two days of negotiations between Rickey, Bostic, and himself. He did not mention Low. An accompanying sidebar reported a conversation between Rickey and McDuffie, where the Brooklyn executive had asked the prospect how much money he would want to sign with the Dodgers. McDuffie said he did not have a figure in mind. Rickey then asked McDuffie how much he was making with the Newark Eagles. Rickey reportedly asked McDuffie if he would pitch for his Negro league salary, and McDuffie said he would. Rickey then told McDuffie that this did not mean he would sign him for either Brooklyn or one of its farm teams but that "he had something in mind that would profit McDuffie and himself, if newspapers would leave this matter alone." Wendell Smith wrote that McDuffie and Thomas accomplished something that no black player had ever done. "It was, without a doubt, a great step forward, and one that will go down in history," he said. Wendell Smith praised Rickey for his courage to "give the players a chance." Smith credited Bostic and Jimmy Smith with making the tryout possible. While pointing out that he did not want to appear critical of Bostic, he said the sportswriter made a mistake by selecting McDuffie and Thomas, who were, according to Smith, "in the afternoon of their baseball careers." Rickey, Smith said, "could see for himself that the players were not good enough for the major leagues."[36]

S. W. Garlington of the *Amsterdam News* praised the "unfailing courage" of Bostic. "After years of agitation in the Negro Press and a segment of the namby-pamby liberal press," Garlington said, Bostic forced the issue into the mainstream press. Garlington described the coverage in the New York press as "evasive." He took particular issue with white sportswriters who either ignored the story or said the tryout would not achieve anything substantial. Garlington called on black sportswriters to put pressure on mainstream sportswriters. Garlington said black sportswriters needed to become more involved. He accused them of "sabotaging the possibility of desegregation with their silence." An indignant Sam Lacy criticized Garlington. "Invariably the guy who doesn't know what he's talking about is the one among us, somehow or other, gets himself quoted in the white press," said Lacy, who wondered if Garlington had "ever read a colored paper." Lacy said that black sportswriters on all the better-known black weeklies had been "banging away at the subject of discrimination in big-league baseball."[37]

Amsterdam News columnist Jerome Mehlman wrote that if those blacks sportswriters most involved in the effort to sign black players — namely, Bostic, Dan Burley, Sam Lacy, and Fay Young — would work together to identify players with the talent to play in the big leagues, the "results would be much more gratifying than those achieved by taking a couple of old timers to a big league magnate for a feeble tryout."[38] Fay Young said that if Bostic had consulted with sportswriters who followed black baseball, he would have selected a player like Buck Leonard of the Homestead Grays. Young also criticized Bostic for expressing his satisfaction. A forty-five-minute tryout had accomplished little. "It might suit Bostic," Young said. "But it doesn't suit the rest of us. Not by a jug full." Young said that sportswriters were too concerned with "who will get the credit" for breaking baseball's color line and not with putting pressure on Major League Baseball teams.[39] Bostic later defended himself against his critics. "The grandstand manager," he said, "always knows how someone else should have blazed a trail after it has been blazed."[40]

When Bostic was confronting Rickey at the Brooklyn training camp, Boston city councilman Isadore Muchnick was putting pressure on the Red Sox and Braves. A year after threatening to revoke the teams' Sunday permits if they did not consider black ballplayers, neither team had given a tryout to black players. Muchnick repeated his threat.[41] In a letter dated March 16, 1945, Collins wrote the councilman, saying his team had never practiced discrimination during his twelve years in Boston. Blacks, he said, were simply not interested in organized baseball. "It is beyond my understanding," Collins said, "how anyone can insinuate or believe that all ballplayers, regardless of race, color, or creed, have not been treated in the American way as far as having an equal opportunity to play for the Red Sox."[42] Collins said that blacks preferred to play in the Negro leagues.[43] Collins added, however, that the team would consider a tryout for any black player who wanted one. Muchnick asked Smith to find three ballplayers. Smith chose Jackie Robinson, Sam Jethroe, and Marvin Williams. Jethroe and Williams were established Negro leaguers. Robinson was beginning his first season in the Negro leagues. Smith brought the three to Boston at the *Courier*'s expense. Muchnick then received Collins's word that the Red Sox would give the players a tryout on April 12, four days before the team would leave Boston to begin its regular season in New York.[44]

Smith later said Muchnick represented a black district in Boston and became involved in the issue to secure his reelection. "I saw this little piece in the paper where he was running for re-election in a predominantly Negro area and was having quite a time getting re-elected," Smith later said. Smith said he called Muchnick and suggested he put pressure on the city's baseball teams to desegregate their teams.[45] But this was not true. Muchnick, not Smith, prompted the Boston tryout. Writers Stephen Norwood and Harold Brackman said that Muchnick's district was more than 99 percent white, and he was so popular he had run unopposed in his heavily Jewish district, where he had a long record as a civil rights advocate. Muchnick had pressed for school desegregation and the creation of educational programs to address racism.[46] Glenn Stout, an author and Red Sox historian, agreed. "A sense of justice, not political expediency, motivated Muchnick to take on baseball's color line," he said.[47]

The Red Sox ignored Muchnick, Smith, and the ballplayers. There was no tryout on April 12. Smith reported that the ballplayers vowed to stay in Boston. He criticized Collins and Braves general manager John Quinn as "uncompromising despots." Robinson told Smith he, too, was prepared to make a stand. "We consider ourselves pioneers," Robinson said in words that became prescient. "Even if they don't accept us, we are at least making the way easier for those who follow. Some day some Negro player or players will get a break. We want to help make that day a reality."[48] It became apparent the Red Sox would delay the tryout until they could leave town to start the season. Mainstream sportswriters also ignored Smith and the ballplayers. Dave Egan of the *Daily Record* broke the silence with a column on the morning of April 16. It chided Collins by telling him he was "living in *anno domini* 1945, and not in the dust covered year 1865. He is residing in the city of Boston, and not in the city of Mobile, Alabama. . . . [T]herefore we feel obligated to inform you that since Wednesday . . . three citizens of the United States have been attempting vainly to get a tryout." Egan added the three would be at Fenway Park that morning for their tryout, "to inquire whether or not those words were written in good faith, to ask an opportunity, if not with the Red Sox, then with the worst and the weakest of its farm clubs." Egan's column caught Collins on his way out of town. "Had the Red Sox been able to delay the tryout for one day," Stout said, "it likely never would have taken place."[49]

Muchnick, Smith, and the ballplayers arrived at Fenway Park at

10:30 a.m. and were met by Collins and manager Joe Cronin. Collins escorted the ballplayers to the dressing room. Cronin watched the tryout from the Red Sox dugout.[50] Coaches Hugh Duffy and Larry Woodall put the ballplayers through an hour-and-a-half workout at the near-empty ballpark. The Red Sox obviously were not serious about the tryout. Boston prospects, who were still in high school, pitched batting practice. Smith called it demeaning to put the Negro league stars with a bunch of kids.[51] Robinson agreed. "It would be difficult to call it a tryout because they had these kid pitchers throwing," Robinson remembered. "I sort of laughed within myself at what I felt was the uselessness of the venture. I didn't feel anything would come of it."[52] Robinson, however, impressed Duffy, who said, "Too bad he's the wrong color." Muchnick said that Cronin told him that he, too, was impressed with Robinson. "He said to me, 'If I had that guy on my club, we'd be a world beater.'"[53] Smith reported that Cronin told him he was impressed with Robinson and Williams. "He did not say, however, that he would sign either of the players," Smith wrote. Shortly after the tryout, Cronin broke his leg and, recovering in the hospital, was unavailable for further comment.[54] Even if Cronin was interested, and he probably was not, it is unlikely that Red Sox owner Tom Yawkey would have allowed it. None of the ballplayers ever heard from the Red Sox.

Unlike what had transpired at Bear Mountain, the Boston newspapers had advance notice of the tryout at Fenway Park. Smith hoped they would cover it.[55] But this did not happen. Smith attributed the lack of coverage to the death of President Franklin Roosevelt on April 12. In truth, the Boston press simply had no interest in reporting the story. No Boston daily carried more than a perfunctory note about the tryout. The *Globe* published an Associated Press story that reported that Muchnick had said blacks should have equal opportunity in baseball, and the team responded by saying that no black player had ever asked for a tryout. A day later the newspaper ran a brief story with no new information.[56] The *Herald* published a brief wire-service story that said little beyond that the ballplayers had reported to Collins, who sent them to the Red Sox dressing room to be issued uniforms. Hugh Duffy was quoted as saying the ballplayers seemed like "fine fellows," but he could not say whether they were good enough for the Red Sox by watching only one workout. Associated Press accounts appeared in a number of other metropolitan newspapers. The *Sporting News* buried a two-paragraph story deep inside its April 19 issue that said, "Three Negro players — first of their race ever given a tryout by a major league team — worked out at Fenway Park April 16." If the tryout of the three black players — whom the *Sporting News* did not mention by name — was such a historic event, why did the publication not provide more details about it? Doc Kountze of the *Boston Guardian* called it "one of the biggest letdowns" he experienced in his sportswriting career.[57] Kountze remembered asking a Red Sox official if he thought segregation should end in baseball. When Kountze pressed him, the secretary said the team would never sign a black player and then motioned his finger in the direction of Yawkey's office.[58]

Boston sportswriters may have provided few, if any, firsthand accounts of the tryout. But this does not mean sportswriters were not at Fenway. Stout surmised that Wendell Smith, Joe Cashman of the *Daily Record*, and Clif Keane and Jack Barry of the *Globe* were present.[59] Although these sportswriters reported little about what happened, Keane later reported what he heard. "I can distinctly remember during the workout somebody yelling 'get those niggers off the field,'" he said. "I can't recall who yelled it."[60] Keane later said it had either been Yawkey, Collins, or Cronin. What, if anything, was said and who, if anyone, said it remains a mystery. Decades later Will McDonough of the *Globe*, once described by a colleague "as an unapologetic mouthpiece for the wealthy, silver-haired white men who own the bats, the balls, and the stadiums," bristled when asked about the story. He said Keane "made the whole thing up." McDonough said he had checked the *Globe*'s microfilm and said that Cronin was not at the ballpark because he had taken an earlier train to go to New York for the start of the season. In addition, McDonough said, Keane was covering a golf tournament at the time of the tryout. Stout, too, checked the microfilm and found no story on a golf tournament in the *Globe*. Eyewitnesses at the time, however, put Cronin at Fenway Park. Stout said there is no way of knowing if anyone yelled the racial epithet at the ballplayers. One fact is beyond debate. The Red Sox were the last team to have a black player on its roster when it signed "Pumpsie" Green in 1959. The blame for this has justifiably gone to Yawkey and those he hired. But Stout said the blame should not end with the Red Sox management. "Boston's increasingly cooperative local press corps never asked Yawkey to explain those standards, nor did it question why the Red Sox failed to trade for an African-American player or hire an African-American in any capacity," Stout wrote. "The press accepted answers from Red Sox representatives without skepticism, even though press members knew that many of Yawkey's employees . . . were openly racist."[61]

Although neither tryout at Bear Mountain or Fenway Park led to the immediate signing of a black player, it signaled an increasing assertiveness on the part of black journalists, who had once told their readers to reject the confrontational strategy of the Communists. In an editorial the *Chicago Defender* said that people of good conscience had fought to end the color line in baseball for ten years. There had been countless newspaper and magazine stories urging baseball to sign black players. Countless delegations had taken the issue to the offices of team owners and league executives but with no effect. "Of promises there have been many," the editorial said. "But not a single baseball club owner or official has kept faith. . . . The big leagues evidently won't play ball with democracy." The editorial called on Americans to raise their voices, to organize picket lines, to distribute more petitions, and to put pressure on their elected officials. Twenty blacks protested outside Yankee Stadium before the opening-day game between the Red Sox and Yankees. Their signs read, "If we can pay, why can't we play?" and "If we stop bullets, why not baseballs?" Both Joe Cummiskey of *P.M.* and Dan Parker of the *Daily Mirror* criticized the protest. Parker said Wendell Smith's deliberate approach would ultimately be more successful than "the spectacular-picketing-stunts-and-tryouts-before-cameramen employed by others engaged in the campaign. Picketing, etc., get more publicity but they leave resentment." An indignant Larry MacPhail defended his team against the demonstrations outside his team's ballpark by saying it had black employees. "We have colored employees in the grounds department, in the concessions department, and in the offices," he said.[62]

For decades owners had a commissioner who, like them, was a segregationist. If they wanted baseball to remain segregated, it was necessary for them to select a successor to Landis who believed as they did. During the meetings, owners selected Senator A. B. "Happy" Chandler of the segregated state of Kentucky as baseball's next commissioner. Chandler's decision drew immediate criticism from the black press. "It appears that his choice was the most logical one to suit the bigoted major league operators, of which there is a heavy majority on hand," Lacy wrote.[63] Bostic questioned the decision of putting the onetime governor of a segregated state into the commissioner's office. *Sporting News* editor J. G. Taylor Spink sent Chandler a copy of Bostic's criticism and included his own 1942 editorial "No Good from Raising Race Issue," obliquely noting that it had "taken care of the situation." MacPhail wrote Chandler, describing the race issue as "increasingly serious and acute." He warned the commissioner that "the three New York clubs are in a critical position right now. . . . [W]e can't stick our heads in the sand and ignore the problem. If we do, we will have colored players in the minor leagues in 1945 and in the major leagues shortly thereafter."[64]

When Chandler was asked about the color line, he responded by saying, "I have no knowledge of discrimination."[65] Shortly thereafter, in an interview with Ric Roberts of the *Pittsburgh Courier*, Chandler recognized that other sports did not discriminate against blacks. He recognized that blacks were allowed in other sports but not in baseball. "If it's discrimination you are afraid of, you have nothing to fear from me," Chandler said. Then, perhaps sensing Roberts's skepticism,

Chandler added he could be taken at his word. "When I feel I am right, there is no middle ground or compromise."[66] An excited Roberts called Wendell Smith, telling him, "Get your streamers out!"[67] In an interview with the *Chicago Defender*, Chandler repeated his opposition to the color line in baseball. "I do not believe in barring Negroes from base-ball, just because they are Negroes," Chandler said.[68] Chandler was no less resolute in an interview with the United Press. "I believe Negroes should have a chance like everyone else," he said. "The arrangements are yet to be worked out, but I believe that this is a free country and everybody should have a chance to play its favorite pastime." Nat Low, however, was not ready to get out the streamers. "Actions, Mr. Chan-dler," he said, "speak louder than words."[69]

During the owners' meeting Sam Lacy proposed that a committee be created to investigate desegregating the Major Leagues. The owners approved the proposal. Within a few weeks Major League Baseball had appointed the following to serve on the committee: Lacy, Rickey, Larry MacPhail, and Philadelphia magistrate Joseph H. Rainey. In June the committee's objectives were announced: to create a better relationship between black and white professional baseball, to explore the merits for the inclusion of blacks in organized white baseball, to determine how best to include blacks in white baseball, and to create a player pool of black players who could be drafted by Major League teams. The com-mittee would add a member of the Baseball Writers' Association and a representative from the Negro leagues. The Negro leagues declined the request.[70] Rainey, who would have to travel from Philadelphia, told Lacy that whenever a meeting could be arranged when Lacy, Rickey, and MacPhail could all be present, he would make the trip. But whenever Rickey proposed a meeting, MacPhail said he could not attend. This blocked the committee's progress. Rickey and Lacy eventually met a few times in Rickey's office.[71] When Lacy expressed his frustration, Rickey said, "Well, Sam, maybe we'll forget about Mr. MacPhail. Maybe we'll just give up on him and let nature take its course."[72]

In early May Rickey created another layer of obfuscation — and angered black journalists — by announcing he would own a team in Gus Greenlee's newly formed United States League. Greenlee, who had had to sell his franchise, wanted to rejoin the Negro leagues but was rebuffed. In January he announced he had created his own league, the United States League, to compete with the Negro National and Negro American leagues. John Shackleford, a Cleveland attorney, was appointed the league's president. Rickey began his May 7 press conference by saying he would not discuss the color line. Rickey then launched into an attack on the Negro leagues, which he said were leagues in name only. "There is, at the present time, so far as I know, no league association of clubs that has a constitution of rules and regulations. There has been no uniform contract for players; every player is a free agent at the end of the current season. No club or league anywhere is incorporated." He added that there was no schedule, no incorporated franchises, no league financing, no fixed admission prices, no provisions for distribution of receipts, no definition of duties of league officials, and no written procedures to discipline players or managers.[73] Rickey said his team would be called the Brooklyn Brown Dodgers.[74] Rickey called the United States League a "legitimate Negro League," which he said might one day become a part of organized baseball.[75] Rickey said the Brown Dodgers would play their home games at Ebbets Field.[76]

To black sportswriters, who had heard too many broken promises and seen their hopes dashed too many times, Rickey's speech appeared to be more of the same old thing, delivered by yet another white baseball executive, smiling condescendingly and telling them that he was acting in their best interests. Rickey appeared to be interested not in integrating baseball but in making it more segregated and, like Larry MacPhail and Clark Griffith and others, in taking his cut off the top and leaving black baseball with the scraps. Blacks had heard this story before and knew how it ended. Ludlow Werner, editor of the *New York Age*, later wrote that when he listened to Rickey, he thought, "It would be a hot day in December before Rickey would have a Negro wear the uniform" of a team in organized baseball. Fay Young questioned Rickey for trying to "assume the role of Abraham Lincoln." He added that "we want Negroes in the major leagues if they have to crawl to get there . . . but we won't have any major league owners running any segregated leagues for us."[77]

Julius Adams of the *Amsterdam News* wondered about the practicality and the timing of the announcement. "Surely, there is no reason for setting up another jim crow league since there is so much emphasis on breaking down the color barriers that keep Negroes out of the big time show," Adams said. Jerome Mehlman called Rickey's announcement "another blow against the Negro gaining entrance into the big time." But Mehlman speculated that Rickey had plans to move baseball slowly toward desegregation. If desegregation required that blacks first be accepted by the white public, as so many white executives had said, then maybe this was what Rickey had in mind, Mehlman said. If blacks played at Ebbets Field while the Dodgers were on the road, white spectators could then grow accustomed to seeing blacks at Ebbets Field. Once that happened, Rickey could sign black players for the Dodgers without creating too much of an issue. "If that is the Deacon's real reason for renting out the park," Mehlman said, "it isn't a bad one."[78] But this had been going on for decades and had not resulted in desegregation.

White sportswriters had little to say about Rickey's announcement—presumably because it had to do with black baseball and was, therefore, a black story. Dan Parker, however, questioned Rickey's motives. Parker said black owners were curious why Rickey had suddenly shown such an interest in black baseball now that the issue of admitting blacks into the big leagues was "getting too hot to handle in a forthright manner." Parker said Negro league owners, in particular, were angered by Rickey's announcement because they stood to lose the most if blacks were allowed into organized baseball. "The owners of the Negro ball clubs, who are satisfied with the good thing they have,"

Parker said, "are as much opposed to the agitation to tear down racial barriers in the national pastime as are the club owners in Organized Baseball."[79]

Rickey's announcement also drew criticism from his fellow Major League owners. Clark Griffith chided Rickey for wanting to be the "dictator" of black baseball. He said Rickey was trying to destroy the Negro National and American leagues.[80] Lacy called Griffith's response laughable because the Washington owner had for years said that before blacks could be admitted into organized baseball, they needed to create a league with a strong organization. Was that not what Rickey was doing?[81] Wendell Smith called Griffith "one of the most bitter opponents of the forces advocating the admission of Negro players in the major leagues." Griffith, according to Smith, was to baseball what racist politicians such as John Rankin and Theodore Bilbo were to American society. Griffith recruited ballplayers from Cuba, Mexico, and Venezuela, but ignored blacks because he made so much money renting his ballpark to black teams. "He'll do everything he can to perpetuate segregated baseball, but he won't lift one finger to help a Negro player get into the majors," Smith wrote. "The only fighting he'll do on the subject is against the people who are trying to get Negroes into the majors. . . . He is no friend. No one who helps perpetuate discrimination and segregation is a friend of the Negro."[82]

Having created a smoke screen, Rickey sent his best scouts — George Sisler, Clyde Sukeforth, and Wid Matthews — to search for players presumably for the Brown Dodgers. In reality, unbeknownst to the scouts, Rickey had no intention of owning the Brown Dodgers. Just as Jackie Robinson would be the right person to desegregate baseball, Rickey would be the right person to make desegregation possible. He was the president of a struggling team playing in a city with a large black population. Rickey also understood the economics of signing the best black players for little money. But Rickey also had a strong moral streak. He had a chance to do what was morally right and maybe even win a pennant. Rickey also had keen instincts, knowing when to do something and when to do nothing, knowing whom to tell and whom not to tell. He knew he needed the support of the public but knew he had to keep his plans to himself until the time was right. As president of a mediocre team, Rickey perhaps had less to lose. As someone who was challenging America's fundamental sin, its custom of racial discrimination, Rickey knew the stakes were high. Therefore, he could not leave anything to chance. Rickey knew he would have to find the right person, and that did not necessarily mean the best player. To Rickey, it was not enough for the ballplayer to have the ability to play in the big leagues; the chosen one had to have the right education, character, and temperament.

After the Fenway Park tryout, Wendell Smith, instead of returning to Pittsburgh, went to Brooklyn for a meeting with Rickey. Rickey wanted to hear about the tryout directly from Smith. During the conversation Smith recommended Robinson. Rickey knew about Robinson's talent as a football player, according to Smith, but did not know he also excelled at baseball. Rickey asked a lot of questions about Robinson and told Smith he would contact him again. Soon after Rickey told Smith he would be sending Clyde Sukeforth to "look at that young man from the West." At some point Smith began to think that Rickey had different plans for Robinson. "This may be more extensive than you visualize," Rickey told Smith. "I don't know exactly how this is going to turn out." Smith once asked Rickey if he was interested in signing Robinson for the Dodgers. Rickey did not answer. "He didn't say yes and he didn't say no," Smith remembered.[83]

From the beginning of the search, all roads led to Robinson. Robinson was a four-sport athlete at UCLA, had competed against whites in college, and had worked with whites in the army. Rickey knew that white America would not accept Robinson if he was like former heavyweight boxing champion Jack Johnson, whom whites perceived as arrogant and who was often accompanied by white women. Robinson was an introvert who was neither promiscuous nor a heavy drinker. But the investigation into Robinson revealed his temper, often triggered by racial slights, and that worried Rickey, who was conscious of the fact that a lot of people believed as Stanley Frank and J. G. Taylor Spink did — that integration would cause race riots. Ever since Robinson was a young boy in Southern California he fought with those who yelled racial epithets against him. Unlike other blacks he refused to accept that he was inferior to whites. Robinson had never been on an athletic field where he was inferior to anyone as an athlete, and he refused to accept that he was inferior as a person. At UCLA Robinson challenged whites who treated blacks as second-class citizens and sneered at blacks who accepted second-class treatment. Because of his sensitivity to racial slights, he earned a reputation as a troublemaker. His court-martial had done nothing to contradict that. Smith tried to assure Rickey that Robinson was not belligerent. Smith knew otherwise and told Robinson to watch his conduct because Rickey was scouting him for the Brown Dodgers. Rickey and Smith regularly corresponded, cryptically referring to Robinson as "the young man from the West."[84]

Lacy also had a high opinion of Robinson. In a preseason article in *Negro Baseball*, Lacy identified several Negro league players with big league potential. He called Robinson "the ideal man" to break the color barrier because he had played with and against whites. Robinson had confidence but did not have Jack Johnson's arrogance.[85] Lacy said there were probably no blacks who could go directly from the Negro leagues to the Major Leagues. But, he said, the average black player, given the same coaching and development that white players received in the Minor Leagues, would become as good or better than a white Major Leaguer.[86] After meeting with Rickey, Lacy had a sense that Rickey had a sincere interest in bringing blacks into baseball.[87] He had no such confidence in MacPhail. In response to Richard Dier's flattering article of MacPhail in late March, Lacy lashed out at both Dier and MacPhail. He called MacPhail's statement that there had been no outside interest in desegregation in the 1930s "hogwash." Lacy said he had copies of columns he had written protesting the color line and receipts of letters sent registered mail to Commissioner Landis and team owners. Lacy said that if MacPhail was so interested in ending discrimination in baseball, why did he not sign a black player for the Yankees? "To my way of thinking, Colonel MacPhail's crime is worse than that of his contemporaries. He knows there's something wrong and claims that something should be done about it, yet he declines to do anything," Lacy said. MacPhail, Lacy added, was like a doctor who found a child who had been hit by a hit-and-run driver and lay suffering on the street. "Although he knows the child needs immediate attention," Lacy said, "he refuses it because no other doctor has responded to the call."[88]

La Guardia found himself under increasing political pressure from the Left to end baseball's color line. The *Daily Worker*, encouraged by the tryouts in Bear Mountain and in Boston, urged readers to contact the Dodgers, Giants, and Yankees.[89] Labor unions kept up their demands. The Committee to End Jim Crow in Baseball included an increasing number of influential social progressives who had La Guardia's ear. The New York City Council included Peter Cacchione and Benjamin Davis Jr. In mid-April Davis called for the Mayor's Committee on Unity to become a permanent committee and thus have more authority to investigate complaints of discrimination. Davis then introduced a resolution ordering the State Commission on Discrimination "to investigate the question of racial discrimination in professional baseball and to bring about a discontinuance of such practices."[90] New York state legislator Philip J. Schupler openly criticized Rickey for not having blacks on his roster. Schupler told Rickey that it would be in his best interests and in the team's best interests to sign black players. By doing so he would improve the Dodgers, Schupler said, "but you would also increase the prestige of the Brooklyn ball club by showing that you really believe in the letter and spirit of Ives-Quinn."[91]

During the summer Dan Dodson, a New York University sociologist who was executive director of the Mayor's Committee on Unity, which had been organized to investigate violations of Ives-Quinn, met individually with Rickey, MacPhail, and Horace Stoneham, president of the Giants. Stoneham dismissed Dodson because he thought the mayor was making the integration of baseball an election-year gimmick. MacPhail rejected Dodson as "a professional do-gooder" with no knowledge of baseball.[92] Rickey, too, initially was skeptical of the committee because he thought it was influenced by Communists and other social progressives. Before his meeting with Dodson, Rickey did a background check to make sure the sociology professor was not a closet left-winger. By the end of their meeting, Rickey trusted Dodson enough to confide in him. Rickey told Dodson he was planning to sign at least one black by the beginning of the next season. Although this pleased Dodson, he knew La Guardia wanted the issue resolved before he left office. Dodson suggested that Rickey move up his timetable to the end of the current season.[93] With so much at stake, Rickey did not want to rush — or be rushed. He wanted Dodson to stall La Guardia so the Brooklyn executive could sign as many blacks as possible before the color line was broken.

The Committee to End Jim Crow in Baseball, which had received letters of support from Eleanor Roosevelt, Paul Robeson, Peter Cacchione, and Democratic mayoral candidate Brig. Gen. William O'Dwyer, made it known to La Guardia and the city's three Major League teams that the issue deserved immediate attention. In early August the Committee to End Jim Crow in Baseball, chaired by Ben Goldstein, announced it would organize a march on August 18 from 136th Street to 155th Street to support the desegregation of baseball. Demonstrations would then follow before games outside Ebbets Field and the Polo Grounds. According to one report, thousands were expected to attend, including actors, screenwriters, legislators, and trade unionists.[94] The committee canceled the protest after La Guardia assured them he was committed to addressing the issue. The Sporting News suggested La Guardia had told the committee that the demonstrations would "do more harm than good."[95] On August 11 La Guardia announced that he had asked a number of prominent New Yorkers to serve on the Mayor's Committee to Integrate Baseball, including Rickey; MacPhail; state

supreme court justice Jeremiah T. Mahoney, the former president of
the Amateur Athletic Union; Daniel E. Higgins of the New York City
Board of Education; Edward Lazansky, former presiding justice of the
appellate division in Brooklyn; Arthur Daley, sports columnist for
the *New York Times*; state supreme court justice Charles Colden of
Queens; Professor Robert Haig of Columbia University; entertainer
Bill "Bojangles" Robinson; and the Reverend John Johnson of St. John's
Episcopal Church, who chaired the committee.[96] La Guardia told the
committee to study the issue of discrimination in baseball. La Guardia
met with the committee almost two weeks later.[97]

For the second time Lacy found himself excluded from a committee
to address the color line. Lacy expressed no opinion about the committee or its members in print. Dan Burley, however, said the committee
kept the issue on the sidelines, "while a group of big shots . . . soaks
up a lot of publicity, eats and drinks up a lot of free food and winds
up with as long list of resolutions that will be promptly pigeonholed."
Rollo Wilson questioned the selection of Bojangles Robinson, who
had never done anything to "improve the conditions of any members
of his own race." The Committee to End Jim Crow in Baseball considered the tap-dancing Robinson an apolitical and outdated symbol of
black America.[98] The selection of Arthur Daley also merited criticism.
New York City had several mainstream sportswriters — including Dan
Parker, Hy Turkin, and Joe Cummiskey — who had taken an interest
in the issue. Daley, on the other hand, never had — and never would.
By serving on the committee, Daley could have used the bully pulpit
of his column to address and advance the committee's agenda. His
silence served segregated baseball by depriving readers from being
educated about the issue.

Less than a week after the committee's first meeting, Jackie Robinson
arrived at Rickey's office on Montagu Street, thinking he would be
offered a contract with the Brown Dodgers. After a lengthy conversation, Rickey let Robinson know the real reason. Rickey then tested the
ballplayer's temperament, challenging him by shaking a finger in his

face and yelling racial epithets at him. Angrily, Robinson responded, "Mr. Rickey, do you want a ballplayer who's afraid to fight back?" Rickey then answered, "I want a player with guts enough not to fight back." After a three-hour meeting, Rickey signed Robinson to a contract after receiving the athlete's assurances that for the next three years he would have to restrain himself from responding to any verbal or physical confrontation, on or off the field. Rickey told Robinson that if he lost his temper, it would vindicate those who believed blacks were too emotional to play in organized baseball. By the end of the meeting Rickey signed Robinson to a contract with the organization's top Minor League team, the Montreal Royals. It included a bonus of thirty-five hundred dollars and a salary of six hundred dollars a month. Rickey insisted that Robinson keep the news to himself.

On September 8 Wendell Smith, acting on Rickey's suggestion, reported that there had been a meeting between Rickey and Robinson to discuss black baseball, but there had been no discussion of "the possibility of Robinson becoming a member of the Brooklyn Dodgers' organization." Smith said the purpose of the meeting was not revealed. He said neither Robinson nor Rickey was willing to discuss why Rickey had requested such a meeting with Robinson, who was playing in his first year in the Negro leagues. "It appears the Brooklyn boss has a plan in his mind that extends farther than just the future of Negro baseball," Smith said.[99] Neither black nor white sportswriters followed up on the story.[100] Smith's column also included an attack on the Negro leagues. Smith, at this point, said he knew Rickey had signed Robinson, but — at Rickey's behest — kept the news to himself. The journalist later said that he would do whatever Rickey asked if it led to the integration of the game — and that included suppressing the biggest story of his career.[101]

Rickey then asked a friend, journalist Arthur Mann, to write a magazine story on Robinson to be published simultaneously with the announcement that the ballplayer had been signed to play for the Royals. Decades later baseball historians Jules Tygiel and John Thorn found photos of Robinson practicing with two other players in September. The

photos were to accompany Mann's story. When the Dodgers played a
series of exhibition games against a team of top Negro league players,
Rickey took the opportunity to speak with at least three pitchers: Don
Newcombe, Roy Partlow, and Johnny Wright.[102] On October 17, 1945,
catcher Roy Campanella also had a meeting with Rickey, who, without
explanation, asked Campanella not to sign a contract with anyone
until he was contacted again. Campanella assumed Rickey wanted
to sign him for the Brown Dodgers. A few days later the Elite Giants
were playing against Jackie Robinson and the Kansas City Monarchs.
During a game of gin rummy after the game, Robinson said, "I hear
you went to see Mr. Rickey."

"How did you know?" Campanella asked.

"I was over there myself," Robinson answered.

Robinson asked Campanella if he had signed with Rickey. Campanella said he had not, but told Robinson that he had agreed to Rickey's
instructions that he would not sign with anyone until he had again
heard from Rickey. Robinson then told Campanella that he had signed
with Brooklyn's AAA team, the Montreal Royals. "It's a secret," he said.
"Mr. Rickey told me to keep it quiet, so you got to promise me not to
tell anyone." A couple days later Montreal announced it had signed
Robinson. Robinson went to spring training the following March with
the Royals; meanwhile, Campanella waited to hear from Rickey. Finally,
in early March, Rickey sent Campanella a telegram, asking him to
report to Brooklyn's Minor League team in Nashua, New Hampshire.[103]
Campanella played the 1946 and 1947 seasons in the Minor Leagues
before breaking into the Major Leagues in 1948 at the age of twenty-
six. Over the next decade, Campanella became the dominant catcher
in the National League, winning the league's Most Valuable Player
award three times.

On October 7 Rickey wrote Mann, telling him to postpone the piece
because he hoped to sign a few other blacks, including Campanella.[104]
If Rickey was going to get first crack at signing blacks, he wanted to
sign as many as possible — and if he was going to do that, he needed his

plan to stay a secret.[105] Larry MacPhail, who was unaware of Rickey's plans, unknowingly contributed to his rival's subterfuge by becoming the story himself. In early September MacPhail said the Yankees were not interested in signing blacks. "I have no hesitancy in saying that the Yankees have no intention of signing Negro players under contract or under reservation to Negro clubs," MacPhail said. "It is unfortunate that groups of professional political and social drumbeaters are conducting pressure campaigns in an attempt to force Major League clubs to sign Negro players." In addition, MacPhail said blacks lacked the ability to play in the Major Leagues. MacPhail supported his view by quoting Sam Lacy, who, he said, had written, "I am reluctant to say that we haven't single man in the ranks of colored baseball who could step into the major league uniform and disport himself after the fashion of a big leaguer."[106] MacPhail also said that desegregation would not be in the best interests of black baseball because it would cause the demise of the Negro leagues, which would leave teams bankrupt and players unemployed. MacPhail's concern for black baseball was transparent. If black baseball suffered, MacPhail would receive less money from teams renting Yankee Stadium. MacPhail made no attempt to reduce black baseball's financial problems by charging less to rent Yankee Stadium, Neil Lanctot wrote.[107]

Lacy attacked MacPhail in print for taking his quote out of context. Lacy said MacPhail had not used his entire quote. Lacy said if black players were given the same coaching in the Minor Leagues as white players, many would develop into big league prospects. Furthermore, Lacy said, he had also written that he had little doubt that black players were equal to or better than many of the Major Leaguers on the war-depleted rosters. Lacy called racist MacPhail's belief that black men were incapable of playing in the big leagues.[108] The Committee to End Jim Crow in Baseball, which had to believe that MacPhail was referring to them with his reference to "professional political and social drum-beaters," wrote La Guardia, asking that MacPhail be removed from the Mayor's Committee to Integrate Baseball and that La Guardia "appoint instead a few progressive minded Americans, particularly those who are actively working for the elimination of Jim Crow in Baseball."[109] MacPhail remained on the committee.

In early October the mayor's committee issued a preliminary report that identified some of the problems and difficulties related to deseg-regation. The report's conclusions, however, were largely encouraging. There was "little doubt that New York City's baseball public would certainly support the integration of Negroes on the basis of their abili-ties," it said. "There was never a more propitious moment than the present, when we are just concluding a terrible World War to suppress the theory of racial superiority, to put our house in order." La Guardia planned to devote his Sunday, October 18, radio program to the issue.[110] Rickey found himself in a dilemma. It had been his idea to create the committee. But Rickey did not want people to think he had signed Robinson because of politics. Rickey told La Guardia that he would have an announcement to make and asked the mayor to postpone his speech. La Guardia agreed. A few days later and nearly two months after Robinson had sat in his office, Rickey instructed him to fly to Montreal for a press conference.

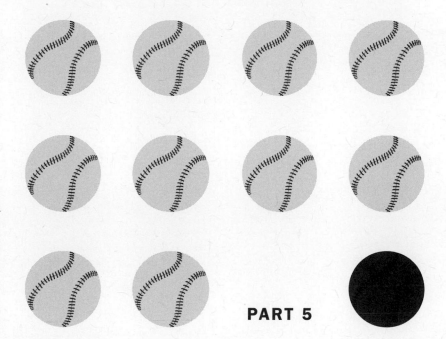

PART 5

CHAPTER 11

ROBINSON BECOMES

THE CHOSEN ONE

In the early afternoon of Tuesday, October 23, 1945, Hector Racine, president of the Montreal Royals, the Brooklyn Dodgers AAA team, told reporters he had a big announcement to make at 5:00 p.m. at the team's offices at Delormier Downs in Montreal. He said nothing else, leaving reporters wondering and rumors flying. The *Montreal Star* speculated that the city would get a Major League team. According to another story, the Royals would fire manager Bruno Betzel and replace him with retired Yankees slugger Babe Ruth.[1] About two dozen sportswriters, newscasters, and photographers were waiting when Racine entered the room as scheduled with Romeo Gavreau, the team's vice president; Branch Rickey Jr., director of Brooklyn's farm system; and a broad-shouldered black man, who was introduced as Jackie Robinson, formerly of the Kansas City Monarchs of the Negro leagues. Branch Rickey Sr. remained in Brooklyn.

Racine announced that the International League team had signed

Robinson, ending professional baseball's seemingly impenetrable color line. In just a few words, Racine forever changed baseball and American society. Stunned silence followed. Then there was chaos as camera bulbs flashed and a number of reporters moved forward with questions, while others rushed to phones to alert their newspapers and radio stations. When order was resumed, Racine explained that the team had signed Robinson because he was "a good ballplayer." But, he said, the team had also signed Robinson because it was a "point of fairness." According to Racine, blacks earned their right to play alongside whites in baseball after serving their country during World War II. "Negroes fought alongside whites and shared the foxhole dangers, and they should get a fair trial in baseball."[2] Racine added that there were no guarantees for Robinson. Like any other ballplayer, Racine said, Robinson would have to earn his uniform the following March at spring training in Daytona Beach, Florida.[3] When reporters asked Robinson how he felt, he described himself as "a guinea pig in baseball's racial experiment."[4]

In his initial account of the press conference, filed within hours of Montreal's announcement, Sid Feder of the Associated Press reported that Robinson was the first black "ever to be admitted into organized baseball." He mentioned Robinson's athletic success at UCLA and said Robinson had been signed by Rickey Sr. after a three-year, twenty-five-thousand-dollar search throughout the United States, Mexico, and Latin America. The article said that Rickey Sr. expected to sign as many as twenty-five other black ballplayers with the intention of developing them for the Major Leagues. Feder also included remarks made at the conference by Racine, Robinson, and Rickey Jr., or "the Twig," as he was nicknamed. "I can't begin to tell you how happy I am that I am the first member of my race in organized ball," the article quoted Robinson as saying. "I realize how much it means to me, to my race and to baseball. I can only say I'll do my best to come through in every manner."[5]

Rickey Jr. told reporters his father knew he had "the alligator by the tail" and was prepared for whatever might come. He predicted that his father would be severely criticized "in some sections of the country where racial prejudice is rampant." He also said the organization was prepared for the possibility that a number of southern players might quit in protest. "Even if some players quit," he said, "they'll be back after a year or two in a cotton mill."[6] Philadelphia Athletics pitcher "Bobo" Newsom of Hartsville, South Carolina, made the following jab at the tightfisted Rickeys: "A ball player would make more money in a cotton mill if young Rickey pays the same kind of dough his father" does. Rickey Jr.'s comments angered southerners such as Billy Werber, a onetime Major League third basemen who had grown up in Maryland. Werber wrote Rickey Sr., telling him that his son's reference to "ballplayers from the South is a definite insult to every Southern boy." It was wrong, Werner said, to expect southern ballplayers to accept blacks on the ball field or anywhere else.[7]

Other southerners criticized the signing of Robinson. The United Press reported that Rogers Hornsby, a Texan who had retired after a Hall of Fame career as a player, said that desegregation would never work. Hornsby said that baseball players lived and traveled together, and it was unfair for Rickey to force the mixing of races on southern ballplayers. George Digby, a scout with the Boston Red Sox, said, "I think it's the worst thing that can happen to organized baseball. I don't think anyone should go in and start a lot of trouble." Dick Callahan of New Orleans, an eighteen-year-old pitching prospect who had just been signed by Digby, said he did not think integration was a good idea. Cincinnati Reds catcher Johnny Riddle of Clinton, South Carolina, and Pittsburgh Pirates coach Spud Davis of Birmingham, Alabama, said that desegregation was "all right as long as (blacks) are with some other team." Dixie Walker, the popular Brooklyn outfielder from Alabama, also said he did not object as long as Robinson played for Montreal and not Brooklyn.[8] Detroit Tigers first baseman Rudy York of Cartersville, Georgia, however, said he hoped "Jackie makes good." The NAACP sent York a letter praising him for his "spirit of fair play worthy of a great athlete in America's national game."[9]

W. G. Bramham, the president of the Minor Leagues, who lived in Durham, North Carolina, told the *Sporting News* that it was in the best interests of blacks to have their own league. "It is my opinion that if the Negro is left alone and aided by his unselfish friends of the white race, he will work out his own salvation in all lines of endeavor," he said. "It is those of the carpet-bagger stripe of the white race, under the guise of helping, but in truth using the Negro for their own selfish interests, who retard the race." The *Chicago Defender* called Bramham "stupid" for saying that gullible blacks had to be protected from "carpetbaggers" like Rickey. In an editorial the newspaper called the opinions of Walker, Hornsby, and Digby "prejudiced."[10] Sam Lacy said the wire services and mainstream newspapers had sought the reactions of only southern ballplayers, which gave the impression that all, or at least most, ballplayers were opposed to desegregation.[11] Nat Low also criticized the wire services for quoting only southern ballplayers, "deliberately ignoring the hundreds of stars from both the South and the North who have in the past voiced their approval" for integration."[12] This, as Lacy and Low correctly pointed out, left readers with the impression that ballplayers, in general, and southerners, in particular, opposed the signing of Robinson.

The northern press avoided responsibility for America's racial dilemma by perpetuating the myth that racism was solely a southern problem and that the color line was perpetuated only by southern sensibilities. Newspapers said that opposition to Robinson was restricted to the South, using, as William Simons pointed out, language such as "the Southern attitude," "the Southern interest," "those in the South," and "the baseball constituency which hails from the South." In an editorial the *Washington Post* said baseball requires that ballplayers have contact with one another — in the dugouts, in the clubhouse, and while traveling. It cautioned that mixing black players with southern players "might tend to aggravate prejudice or resentment where it already exists." The *Boston Herald*, for instance, wrote that northern fans would welcome Robinson but that southerners would be ready to create "a most harrowing situation."[13] The *Herald* did not tell its readers about Robinson's failed tryout with Boston a little more than six months earlier, nor did it include that owners of northern teams — such as Tom Yawkey of the Red Sox and Larry MacPhail of the New York Yankees — were among the baseball establishment's biggest segregationists.

The baseball establishment had long perpetuated the democratic myth in baseball even though blacks were prohibited. Montreal's announcement brought together these conflicting ideas, putting league executives and team owners in a difficult position. Baseball executives opposed desegregation but were reluctant to say so publicly. So they simply said nothing. Commissioner Happy Chandler, National League president Ford Frick, and American League president Will Harridge were "unavailable for comment." Philadelphia Athletics owner and manager Connie Mack, Cincinnati Reds owner Powell Crosley, and Detroit Tigers general manager Jack Zeller also had no comment. Rickey received telephone calls from a number of owners, including Mack, Griffith, and Sam Breadon of the St. Louis Cardinals, telling him, "Branch, you're gonna kill baseball bringing that nigger into baseball." Rickey replied, "You run your ball club and I'll run mine."[14]

Boston Red Sox general manager Eddie Collins denied there had ever been a color line. He said that the Red Sox had given Robinson a tryout but had not been interested in signing him.[15] Collins told the *Boston Daily Globe*, "Very few players can set off a sandlot or college diamond into a major league berth."[16] Whether purposely or not, Collins suggested Robinson had been signed by the Brooklyn Dodgers and not by the Minor League Montreal Royals. He also denigrated black baseball by comparing it to the ball played on sandlots. New York Giants president Horace Stoneham told reporters that baseball's primary responsibility was to returning GIS — and not to black players. Larry MacPhail criticized Rickey for taking players from the Negro leagues without compensating the teams.[17] Baseball executives expressed their opposition by criticizing Robinson's ability or by saying the signing of blacks would take positions away from returning servicemen. Others tried to discredit Rickey's method of signing Robinson or said that Rickey had been prompted less by righteousness than by political pressures. William Simons said that opponents of integration largely kept their opinion to themselves. "Rather than attacking integration directly," he said, "opponents typically utilized more circuitous stratagems. Critics sought to avoid the stigma of illiberalism."[18]

Rickey responded to charges he had signed Robinson without informing the Kansas City Monarchs. The Negro leagues were not in fact a league, he said, and thus had no legally binding contract with Robinson.[19] Jack Hand of the Associated Press asked Rickey if he had been coerced into signing Robinson by political pressures. Rickey said he considered only Robinson and the Brooklyn organization when he signed the ballplayer. "No pressure groups had anything to do with it," he said. "In fact, I signed him in spite of such groups rather than because of them." Writing from New York, AP writer Gayle Talbot quoted Rickey, who said he had given a lot of thought to racial discrimination since his days coaching baseball at Ohio Wesleyan in the early 1900s. Rickey recalled that during one road trip, the team's only black ballplayer, Charles "Tommie" Thomas, was denied a room at a hotel. Rickey said he asked the hotel clerk if the ballplayer could sleep on a cot in his room. Later that evening Rickey said he looked over at Thomas and saw he was rubbing his skin, saying, "Black skin. Black skin. If only I could make them white."[20] Rickey said the scene had haunted him ever since. "I vowed that I would always do whatever I could to see that other Americans did not have to face the bitter humiliation that was heaped upon Charles Thomas," Rickey said.

Thomas confirmed the story.[21] But Rickey rarely spoke about the Thomas story in the years preceding his decision to sign Robinson. In the days, months, and years to come, Rickey told the story often. "The Charlie Thomas story, though based in fact, is vintage Rickey," Jules Tygiel said. "The allegory is almost biblical and the sermonlike quality of the tale invites skepticism. Many people place little stock in the episode as the primary rationale for his actions. Even if one accepts the Charlie Thomas story at face value, it does not fully explain why the Dodger president chose to challenge the color barrier four decades later." To *Worker* sportswriter Bill Mardo, Rickey was an opportunist who sat on the sidelines while others fought the good fight and then desegregated baseball when he saw that it was inevitable. Despite this, Mardo credited Rickey for supporting desegregation and Robinson once he got behind the issue. "There was the pre-Robinson Rickey who stayed shamefully silent for much of his baseball life," Mardo said. And there was the other Rickey, he added, "whose extraordinary business and baseball sense helped him seize the moment, jump aboard the Freedom Train as it was getting ready to pull out of Times Square, catch social protest at its apex, and then do just about everything right once he signed Robinson."[22]

A popular and still prevailing misconception gives Rickey most, if not all, of the credit for the signing of Robinson. This perception took shape in the hours, perhaps even moments, after Montreal signed Robinson. Rickey co-opted the story in his own image, ignoring the contributions of politicians, activists, and journalists. The mainstream press made little or no attempt to interpret the information beyond what Rickey or his associates fed it. This left readers to believe it was Rickey and only Rickey who deserved credit for desegregating baseball. The Associated Press filed a number of articles in the hours and days after Montreal's announcement. Robinson was not interviewed for any of the stories. None mentioned the decadelong campaign to integrate baseball in the black and communist press. Black baseball fans knew otherwise. With rare exception, only in the black and communist press would readers get a sense of the story's context. And only in the black and communist press would readers get a sense of what the story meant to America.

When black America learned that the Brooklyn organization had signed Robinson, the world, as it had been, stopped for a moment, and all things denied for so long seemed possible. Unlike mainstream newspapers that said little after the initial story, black newspapers played up the story on their front pages and on their sports pages for weeks.[23] Black newspapers commented on the story in articles, editorials, and columns. They included interviews with and photographs of Robinson. While hyperbolically praising Rickey as another Abraham Lincoln, the black press also recognized there was more to the story than Rickey and Tommie Thomas. For Wendell Smith and the *Pittsburgh Courier*, the news had been a long time coming. The *Courier* filled its next issue with ten stories and three photographs of Robinson. Two of the stories covered much of page 1. In one of the stories Rickey insisted that this was only the beginning of a movement for fairer play in baseball. "This is a movement that cannot be stopped by anyone," he said. "They may be able to detain it for a while, but not for too long. The world is moving on and they will move with it, whether they like it or not." The other story, which carried Robinson's byline though it was ghostwritten by Smith, said that the ballplayer had initially doubted Rickey's sincerity, but concluded after their August meeting that he was not being signed simply as a "gesture" and was going to be given a chance to make an impact. "If I make the team, I will not forget that I am representing a whole race of people who are pulling for me," he said. He pledged that if he were to be a guinea pig, he would be "the best guinea pig that ever lived, both on the field and off."[24]

In an editorial the *Chicago Defender* wrote that the signing of Robinson was more than just an opportunity for the ballplayer; it was an opportunity for all blacks. Fay Young called the news "a step toward a broader spirit of democracy in baseball and will do much to promote a friendlier feeling between the races."[25] According to Representative Adam Clayton Powell Jr., who represented Harlem, this was "a definite step toward winning the peace, and now that this gentleman is in the International League, the other leagues will not be able to furnish any alibis." Roy Wilkins, who would later become executive secretary of the NAACP, asserted that the signing of Robinson meant that blacks "should have their own rights, should have jobs, decent homes and education, freedom from insult, and equality of opportunity to achieve."[26]

The *Amsterdam News* called the news "a drop of water in the drought that keeps faith alive in American institutions."[27] Dan Burley praised Robinson for his courage. Robinson would have to endure unspeakable insults and threats, but Burley expressed that he was the right man for the experiment.[28] *New York Age* editor Ludlow Werner wrote that a lot of Americans were hoping that Robinson would fail. Werner added that Robinson "would be haunted by the expectations of his race. . . . Unlike white players, he can never afford an off day or off night. His private life will be watched, too, because white America will judge the Negro race by everything he does. And Lord help him with his fellow Negroes if he should fail them."[29]

In a front-page story in the *Baltimore Afro-American,* Robinson told Michael Carter that he understood that the eyes of millions of blacks would be on him. "I feel sort of as if everyone was looking at me. I feel that if I flop, or conduct myself badly — on or off the field — that I'll set the advancement back a hundred years," Robinson said. "Why, I feel that all the little colored kids playing sandlot baseball have their professional futures wrapped up somehow in me." Robinson told Carter that he owed a debt of gratitude to black Americans who had pressured baseball for years. "I owe this to the colored people who helped make it possible, and I hope I shall always have their good will." Robinson also recognized the contributions of black journalists. "It's a press victory, you might say," he said. Writing in the same issue, Sam Lacy mentioned his long involvement in the effort to end segregated baseball. The *Courier* reminded its readers that it had long fought for the inclusion of blacks in organized baseball. The newspaper published a letter from Robinson to Wendell Smith. "I want to thank you and the paper for all you have done and are doing in my behalf," he wrote. "As you know I am not worried about what the white press or people think as long as I continue to get the best wishes of my people."[30]

The *Daily Worker* reported it had joined arms with blacks to end segregation. Mike Gold reminded readers of the newspaper's ten-year campaign against baseball's color line. He told his readers that the newspaper would fight on against discrimination in America until Jim Crow was "ruined, finished, destroyed in every dirty root and fibre." The newspaper quoted Walter White of the NAACP and New York City councilman Benjamin Davis Jr., who praised baseball for its progress in race relations. Brooklyn councilman Peter Cacchione said that the people of his city were happy that Robinson had signed with Montreal but would be happier "when he is playing for the Dodgers in Ebbets Field." Nat Low praised Davis and Cacchione for introducing end–Jim Crow baseball resolutions in the New York City Council. Low called for the creation of Jackie Robinson fan clubs to fight the reactionaries in baseball, politics, and the press who wanted Brooklyn and Montreal to stop what they had started.[31] Dan Dodson of the Mayor's Committee on Unity expressed his "keen satisfaction" with the signing of Robinson. The Committee to End Jim Crow in Baseball congratulated Rickey and called on other owners to sign blacks. "This is only the beginning," it said, "since our committee will not cease its activities until the hiring of Negro players is a customary practice."[32]

There was no such enthusiasm in the mainstream press. Phil Gordon of the *Daily Worker* criticized the New York dailies. The *Times*'s account, he said, was "cold and antagonistic." The *Times*'s story with no byline appeared in the sports section and included nothing of substance beyond the basic details of the press conference. Arthur Daley praised Rickey for his moral courage but wondered if the Brooklyn executive was not "rushing things too rapidly," given that there were so many southern ballplayers and a number of southern Minor Leagues.[33] Daley did not mention that there had been no blacks in baseball for decades, the existence of a color line, or the campaign of black and Communist sportswriters to end it. He also did not mention that he served on the Mayor's Committee to Integrate Baseball or that such a committee even existed. New York City's sportswriters were among the most knowledgeable and respected in America. They also were among the most influential and best known in the history of sportswriting. They knew the Negro leagues had players who could start for any team in the big leagues. They probably knew that the signing of Robinson had ramifications far beyond baseball. They had all written column after column about baseball as a metaphor for greater things. Yet when Montreal announced it had signed Robinson, these men responded not with enthusiasm or even curiosity, but with aggravation or even silence.

Since 1933 no mainstream sportswriter had criticized segregated baseball as often as Jimmy Powers. Yet when the moment arrived, Powers called Robinson's chances of making it in organized ball "a 1,000-to-1 shot." Does this mean that Powers's columns calling for integration were disingenuous? Or, as Wendell Smith would later suggest, that they were simply a craven attempt to appeal to black readers in Harlem? Perhaps, but not necessarily. Powers had an undisguised contempt for Rickey. When Rickey signed Robinson, Powers found himself caught between his dislike of Rickey and his dislike of segregation. Powers's disdain for Rickey won out. Dan Parker had also long called for desegregation in his columns. When Montreal announced it had signed Robinson, Parker wrote that he never understood why blacks had been kept out of professional baseball when they had succeeded so well in college athletics. "Why a good respectable Negro athlete shouldn't fit just as well into organized baseball as he does into college football, basketball, boxing, or cricket," he said, "is something I have never been able to figure out."[34] When interviewed about Robinson's chances, Red Smith of the *Herald Tribune* responded with the following platitude: "There is more democracy in the locker room than on the street."[35]

Dan Daniel, the longtime president of the New York Baseball Writers' Association, had long reflected the views and the opinions of the baseball establishment. In his column in the *World-Telegram*, Daniel predicted a grim future for Robinson, who would face the hatred of southern players and racial discrimination on trains and in restaurants and hotels. Daniel added that Robinson lacked the ability to play in the high Minors. "The dope," he said, "is that he will not make the grade." Daniel's colleague at the *World-Telegram* Joe Williams also was dubious — not only about Robinson's ability but also about Rickey's motives.

Williams suspected Rickey had signed Robinson because of politics and not because of his ability. As a southerner, Williams said, he had seen blacks make advances, but their progress had been impeded by "pressure groups, social frauds and political demagogues." He said he hoped Robinson had been signed because of his ability. "For in the end," he said, "the young man must stand or fall on his ability."[36]

Williams observed that "there is no doubt there have been Negroes capable of playing big league baseball in the past, and that there will be many more in the future," adding, "And I would be guilty of sheer stupidity and hypocrisy if I failed to concede there has been discrimination." He could have included specific cases of discrimination or identified the names of blacks who had been denied the opportunity of playing in the big leagues. Williams did not mention that the baseball establishment had prohibited blacks and that sportswriters had aided and abetted the baseball establishment. Williams then quoted Sam Lacy as saying there were no blacks ready for the Major Leagues. Lacy later said he meant that black ballplayers might require socializing with whites in the Minor Leagues before playing in the big leagues. MacPhail, Williams, and others tossed around that quote, Lacy said, "whenever it served their purpose." The *Sporting News* published Williams's column.[37]

The *Worker*'s Phil Gordon said that Joe Cummiskey of *P.M.* and Al Laney of the *Herald Tribune* wrote "stirringly sympathetic" articles.[38] Cummiskey provided a chronology of the events that led to the signing of Robinson, including the creation of the Mayor's Committee to Integrate Baseball and the fact that Rickey had had many talks with Dan Dodson. Cummiskey asked Rickey about the response he had received. "I have been flooded with telegrams and letters and phone calls," he said. "Only one was bitterly derogatory. The writer called me a 'nigger lover and hoped I'd wind up in a cotton mill.'" Cummiskey said he had received a letter from a serviceman, Sgt. Paul Ganapoler, who was stationed in New Jersey, who said he had attended UCLA with Robinson. He said Robinson excelled in the classroom and in any sport he tried. The UCLA football team played a number of games in the South, and there were no fights or even scuffles. Ganapoler criticized Dixie Walker, who "should begin to realize what the hell this war was about," he said. Ganapoler said he wrote a letter of commendation to Rickey and asked *P.M.* readers to do so.[39]

Laney wrote that there had been a lot of discussion about bringing blacks into baseball for months and that everyone thought that Rickey was against it. Unlike most white journalists, Laney understood that the signing of Robinson transcended the sports page. He quoted Roy Wilkins, who said that Robinson would forge a greater respect between the races. He also interviewed Robinson, who told him, "I know that I will take a tongue beating. That I can take it. At least I think I can take it. And I am due for a terrible riding from the bench jockeys around the International League circuit if I am good enough really to play with Montreal all summer." Laney understood that the issue would have a profound meaning for black men and women. He tried to capture the story in the words of black baseball fans. Jimmie Odoms told him that Robinson would have to face the ugliness that came his way, beginning at spring training in Florida. "This boy Robinson's got to take it. I hate to think what he got to take. They'll find plenty of ways to give it to him" during spring training in Daytona Beach, Florida, Odoms said. "And he's got to take it. Otherwise, it don't make no sense signing him."[40] Laney then added his own observation, "Without further preliminaries it may be said that, if there are baseball players who will refuse to play with or against this personable, intelligent sensitive man, they must, indeed, be blinded by prejudice."[41]

J. T. Winterich of the *Saturday Review* praised Laney for "exploring all sides of the issue as a good reporter." Winterich noted that integration was "absolutely inevitable if America is going to live up to its high protestations of democracy. And there is no better place it begin it than on a baseball diamond." Winterich's article said that if Robinson succeeded, he would go further toward ending racial discrimination than either pianist Hazel Scott or Broadway singer and activist Paul

Robeson. Robeson, Winterich wrote, had once "made an eloquent plea for the admission of Negro players into big-time baseball." Winterich quoted the conclusions of La Guardia's committee to integrate baseball that said "sheer prejudice and tradition have heretofore motivated the exclusion of Negroes from organized ball." Other national news magazines — such as *Time, Newsweek, Life, Look, and Opportunity* — reported that Robinson had signed with Montreal but failed to examine what it meant beyond baseball.[42]

The *Sporting News*, which had long acted as defender and apologist of baseball's color barrier, published several related stories, ranging in content from shallow to substantive. In the second paragraph of the main story, Al Parsley provided this revealing description of the ballplayer: "Robinson is definitely dark. His color is the hue of ebony. By no means can he ever be called a brown bomber or a chocolate soldier." The article did, however, look beyond Robinson's skin color. "There were things about Jack Robinson that impressed you that he was a gamester," the article said. "He talked with the easy fluency of an educated man." Robinson, it said, was going to barnstorm with a team of black all-stars to South America and was then expected to be married in January. An adjoining sidebar reported that twenty blacks played in the Minor Leagues during the 1887 season. The story included the anecdote that Adrian "Cap" Anson had pulled his team off the field rather than play against a Newark, New Jersey, team with a battery of catcher Fleet Walker and pitcher George Stovey. It also added that Anson had blocked John Montgomery Ward's attempt to sign Stovey. The issue included a separate story on Fleet Walker, whom it identified as the first black player in the Major Leagues. The story chronicled Walker's life and mentioned a number of other black players who had played in the nineteenth century.[43] But it did not mention why no blacks had played in the twentieth century.

J. G. Taylor Spink wrote that the signing of Robinson "touched off a powder keg in the South, unstinted praise in Negro circles, and a northern conviction that the racial problem in baseball is as far from a satisfactory solution as ever." Spink had opposed desegregation — and the reality of integration did little to change his mind. Spink dismissed Robinson's chances of success by saying that if he were white and six years younger, he might make Brooklyn's AA team in Newport News, Virginia. Spink called the press coverage "out of proportion to the actual vitality of the story." Having criticized Robinson, Spink then wrapped himself in the cloak of phony liberalism, criticizing those southern ballplayers who had opposed integration. "The *Sporting News*," he said, "is convinced that these players of Southern descent who gave out interviews blasting the hiring of a Negro would have done a lot better by themselves and baseball if they had refused to comment."[44]

Dan Daniel agreed with his editor that the story "had received far more attention than it was worth," because, after all, Robinson was not the first black to play in organized professional baseball. Daniel echoed the party line of organized baseball by saying that ability and nothing else had kept blacks out of organized baseball. Rather than directly criticize the signing of Robinson, Daniel said that Rickey had been motivated by pressure groups. Daniel called the signing of Robinson a move to "solve a problem which has been agitated by high-pressure groups more than Negro baseball circles themselves." Daniel twice quoted Rickey's saying that Robinson did not now have the ability to play in the big leagues.[45] Robinson had signed a Minor League contract.

According to Daniel, the signing of Robinson also was "unquestionably" an effort by Rickey to comply with Ives-Quinn. In an interview with Rickey, Daniel asked the Brooklyn president why he had not signed any blacks when he had been president of the St. Louis Cardinals and why he had allowed Sportsman Park to remain segregated. Rickey said he regretted not doing more to end the ballpark's racist policy. He said he did not think much about integration until he moved to Brooklyn and began watching black teams play. "I decided that something had to be done about the Negro players in relationship to the major leagues in general, and those in New York in particular," Rickey said. "I signed Robinson despite the misguided labors of pressure groups."[46] Daniel reported that Rickey might be challenged in court by the Kansas City Monarchs because Rickey did not compensate the team. Because of this, the Brooklyn executive was vulnerable to criticism.

Journalists quoted Larry MacPhail and Clark Griffith, who tried to portray themselves as defenders of black baseball.[47] MacPhail told the *Brooklyn Eagle* that if the Negro leagues lost their best players to organized baseball, which he considered "comparatively few," then the Negro leagues would fold, and the rest of black ballplayers would lose their livelihoods.[48] Griffith denounced Rickey for raiding the Negro leagues. "In no walk of life can one person take another's property unless he pays for it," Griffith said. "We have no right to destroy" the Negro leagues, he said.[49] When Griffith was told the Negro leagues used Major League ballparks to play their games, Griffith responded, "We'd be fine ones to do that and then steal their best players."[50] The article did not mention that Griffith, MacPhail, and other owners greatly profited from renting their ballparks to black teams. If Griffith and MacPhail hoped to ingratiate themselves to black owners, it did not work. Black newspapers, in particular, "reflected a disdain for obstructionists who clothed themselves in the rhetoric of racial justice," William Simons wrote.[51]

MacPhail and Griffith were right about one thing. If the Negro league owners supported Rickey, they would sign black baseball's death warrant, as their best stars would jump to organized professional baseball. If owners sued Rickey, they would be accused of obstructing desegregation. The *Sporting News* quoted Negro American League president J. B. Martin as saying, "I admire Branch Rickey for his courage, but the method of signing Robinson raises some problems." The Monarchs, which had an agreement, however informal, with Robinson, found themselves squeezed by Rickey and the black press. Tom Baird, the team's owner, briefly considered filing a lawsuit to block Robinson's contract with Montreal. In a patronizing column *Brooklyn Eagle* columnist Tommy Holmes claimed that it was blacks and not whites who stood in the way of integration. In his column, however, Holmes called Robinson "an ideal candidate to crash though the invisible color line in what, from time to time, has been called our national pastime." After being criticized in the black press, Baird changed his mind, saying that he had urged the national pastime to sign blacks and therefore would not challenge any player's contract with a team in organized baseball. The *Pittsburgh Courier* said it would not have approved of the raiding of black players by the Brooklyn organization if these had not been extraordinary circumstances. The newspaper told Baird that he may have had a legal and moral justification for challenging Rickey but advised him to drop the matter. The signing of Robinson, the newspaper said, "transcended everything else at this particular time."[52]

Mainstream sportswriters did not want to criticize the signing of Robinson or appear as obstructionists. They believed, however, it was fair to criticize whether Robinson was good enough for the Major Leagues — even though he had been signed by a Minor League team. If others were willing to question Robinson's ability, this gave sportswriters the freedom to express their opinion without having to take responsibility for it. The United Press quoted one of Robinson's former coaches who said that Robinson was better in football, basketball, and track than he was in baseball. "Jackie didn't try too hard at baseball," he said.[53] When Cleveland Indians pitcher Bob Feller, who had fronted exhibition games between black and white all-stars, was asked about Robinson, he said he believed that Satchel Paige and Josh Gibson were good enough for the big leagues but not Robinson. Robinson had "football shoulders" and could not hit an inside pitch, Feller said, adding, "If he were a white man, I doubt if they would consider him big-league material. . . . I hope he makes good. But I don't think he will."[54] Feller defended himself by saying that when he had faced Robinson, he had held him hitless.[55]

But a few weeks before Montreal's announcement, Robinson had a double in two at-bats against Feller. Robinson told *New York Post* columnist Jimmy Cannon that he had played two games against Feller but doubted if Feller knew who he was. "If you lined up ten of us," Robinson said, "I'll bet he couldn't pick me out of the bunch."[56] In a letter to Wendell Smith, Robinson said he had doubts about his fielding but not his hitting. "The few times I faced Feller has made me confident that the pitching I faced in the Negro American League was as tough as any I will have to face if I make it at Montreal," Robinson said.[57] Feller found himself under attack from the black press. Feller, who believed he had done a lot to advance racial equality with his interracial tours, remained sensitive about the criticism. He said Robinson never forgave him and once criticized the pitcher in front of a roomful of reporters for what he said in 1945.[58] If Robinson held a grudge toward Feller, there is no evidence of it in any of the Robinson biographies. Robinson and Feller entered the Baseball Hall of Fame together in 1962. In the weeks before the ceremonies Robinson learned that Feller and he were going to be guests at a dinner of Boston sportswriters. Robinson's plane landed before Feller's at the Boston airport, but Robinson waited to congratulate the pitcher. "It's a pleasure to go hand in hand with you," Robinson told him.[59]

Satchel Paige had been Feller's counterpart in a number of games and was always mentioned whenever someone talked of integration; therefore, Paige believed he would be the one who would break the color line. When sportswriters asked Paige if Rickey had made a mistake, the pitcher, while greatly disappointed, praised Robinson. "They didn't make a mistake in signing Robinson," he said. "They couldn't have picked a better man."[60] Paige, however, was disappointed. Other black players believed they were better than Robinson, too. But there was little criticism of Robinson from black players. Hy Turkin of the *New York Daily News*, writing in the *Negro Digest*, agreed with a lot of black players that Robinson, who had played just one season in the Negro leagues, was not the best available black player. He was, however, according to Turkin, "the greatest prospect" and would be given a fair shot at making it in organized baseball. He said there would be no conspiracy against Robinson and he would have the support of baseball fans. "No matter what the prejudices of club owners has been," Turkin said, "the sports fan always tends to lean toward the underdog."[61]

Robinson, of course, was not merely confronting baseball tradition; he was confronting something even more formidable — Jim Crow. A day after the announcement, Tommy Holmes wrote that Robinson's first challenge would come during spring training in Daytona Beach. "Anyone who has ever traveled that far South can't help but wonder just how things can be arranged. Fundamental things such as where he will sleep and where he will eat," Holmes said. "Not to mention what traveling accommodations they'll let him have in deepest Dixie."[62]

In Daytona Beach, where the Brooklyn organization would go for spring training, the *Evening News* published wire-service stories about the signing of Robinson, but had no local reaction beyond reporting that Rickey would be arriving in town in a couple days to discuss his spring training plans. Twenty miles to the west of Daytona Beach, the *Deland Sun-News* published a United Press account that said Daytona Beach city officials were surprised to learn that Robinson would join the rest of the Brooklyn organization during spring training. The *Sun-News* sports editor told the *Chicago Defender*, "Opinion here is divided on whether it will work or not." But the same editor had no comment in his own newspaper. Newspapers in nearby Florida cities — such as Jacksonville, Sanford, and Orlando — suppressed the news. The *Miami Herald* ran the story across the front page of its sports section and included an Associated Press photograph of Robinson signing his contract.[63]

Daily newspapers, whether in Florida or elsewhere in the South, either gave the story minor play or ignored it. They relied for their information on wire-service stories and included no reaction in columns or editorials. The *Louisville Courier-Journal*, *Charlotte Observer*, and *Atlanta Journal* each published columns about the signing of Robinson. A column with no byline in the *Courier-Journal* expressed approval of the signing of black ballplayers but not if they already were under contract to another team. In the *Charlotte Observer*, columnist Jake Wade criticized Rickey Jr. for saying that the announcement would be criticized in the South, where "racial prejudice is rampant." Times have changed, Wade said, and so had southern views about blacks. He expected no negative reaction to the announcement. *Atlanta Journal* sports columnist Ed Danforth suggested that liberal newspapers could ruin Robinson's chances. "Robinson probably will have a minimum of trouble getting along with his teammates," he said, "until the red-eyed press begins to challenge the official scorers on unfairness in giving base hits."[64]

Northern metropolitan newspapers gave the story more prominent coverage. But the stories, for the most part, came from wire-service accounts. In a column with no byline, the *Detroit News* blamed the persistence of the color line not on prejudice but on tradition. The column called Robinson a "credit to his race." The *Washington Post* said Robinson would stand as a test of whether "the recent laws and rulings aimed at the end of racial discrimination really reflect a change of popular feeling." *Post* columnist Shirley Povich wrote that Robinson was "good enough to make the grade in the International League, and perhaps in the majors."[65]

Frank Shaughnessy, president of the International League, which included the Montreal Royals, said he approved of the news conditionally. "It depends entirely on the individual player," he said. "If he's the right type, there's no reason in the world why he shouldn't find a place in organized baseball. I think Jackie Robinson is definitely the right type."[66] Stories in the mainstream press portrayed Robinson as unthreatening, as someone who would not stir up racial issues. He was described as the "right type of fellow," "right boy," or "a credit to the race." Americans had rejected the loud and flamboyant heavyweight champion Jack Johnson but had accepted the quiet Joe Louis. To Rickey, Robinson had to be viewed as "the right type" of black, "one," according to William Simons, "who sought to affirm, not challenge."[67]

Rickey, with the assistance of a cautious press, manipulated the coverage of the story and shaped it in his image. With the exception of the Ives-Quinn law, readers saw little in their newspapers to conclude that anyone but Rickey had anything to do with Robinson's signing.

Most newspaper readers got little sense that the signing of Robinson was anything but a sports story. Few reporters working for mainstream newspapers sought reactions from either black or white activists who had crusaded for greater civil liberties — or even from black activists in their own cities. Newspapers did not mention that the baseball establishment had kept blacks out of the national pastime for decades or that the United States itself practiced segregation against its black people. Even for those newspapers that reported it, the story was off the sports pages in a few days. America missed the irony that the national pastime would be integrated in Canada.

When Hector Racine announced that his team had signed Robinson, he told reporters the ballplayer had been assigned to Montreal because the city, being the northernmost city in professional baseball, would provide a sanctuary relatively free of the discrimination in America.[68] The signing of Robinson was met with unqualified praise in Montreal. The *Daily Star* called the story "one of the most revolutionary moves in baseball since Abner Doubleday started this pastime." The *Herald* added, "Those who were good enough to fight and die by the side of whites are plenty good enough to play by the side of whites." Dink Carroll of the *Gazette* wrote that Japanese propaganda had stressed that blacks were discriminated against in America. He said that the war had forced the United States to question its color line. "It is a social problem that has been facing the American people," he said, "and the signing of young Jack Robinson to a Royals contract here yesterday is bound to have an effect upon it." In another column the next day, Carroll said that Montreal fans did not seem to appreciate the story's significance because they did not have the same history of racial discrimination. "This reaction surely proves the absolute absence here of an anti-Negro sentiment among sports fans," Carroll wrote, "which is what Mr. Rickey doubtless had in mind when he chose Montreal as the locale for his history-making experiment."[69]

Robinson could win over the hearts of baseball fans if he proved himself; however, it was a far more daunting task to change the minds of those with deep-seated prejudices. Rickey sent his trusted assistant, Bob Finch, to organize a tolerance program in central Florida, hoping to convince citizens that integration was not being forced upon them. As Rickey himself put it, he was interested not in overturning segregation but in giving a black man an opportunity to play in the national pastime. In an odd twist, before leaving for Florida, Finch learned for himself what it meant to be restricted because of his skin color. When Robinson returned to New York from Montreal, Finch went to the ballplayer's Harlem hotel. When Finch tried to go upstairs to Robinson's room, the clerk told him whites were not allowed in the hotel. A porter was then sent to Robinson's room. Robinson and Finch then met outside the hotel.[70]

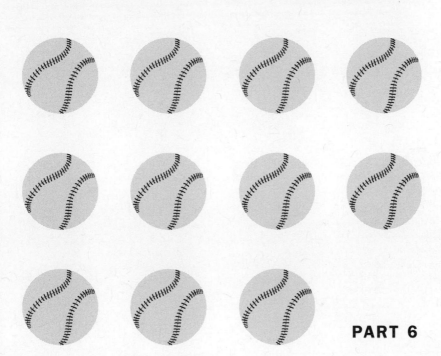

PART 6

CHAPTER 12

"I NEVER WANT TO TAKE
ANOTHER TRIP LIKE THIS ONE"

Before sportswriters left en masse for spring training, the New York chapter of the Baseball Writers' Association held its twenty-third annual meeting at the Waldorf-Astoria Hotel on February 3. The all-white crowd included twelve hundred journalists, owners, managers, players, politicians, and other dignitaries. Speeches were made and awards were handed out. But, as always, the evening was judged by the entertainment. Harold Burr of the *Brooklyn Eagle* wrote, "The fast-moving program was one of the best in the chapter's history." The *Sporting News* called the songs and skits "the best yet." *New York Times* columnist Arthur Daley agreed. "The burlesque was so broad that the scribes were able to risk bringing into the cast of characters as delicate a subject as Jackie Robinson," Daley said. "But it was all such lampoonery that no one's feelings really were hurt."[1] To make his point, Daley included the dialogue of a skit that opened at a mansion with a butler — or, as the columnist described him, "a darky" in satin knee breeches, wearing a Montreal uniform.

Before the butler, a sportswriter in blackface, exited the stage, he referred to his boss, Commissioner "Happy" Chandler, by saying, "Looks lak de massa will be late dis ebning."

The Chandler character, played by sportswriter James Kahn, entered with four other colonels, including *Sporting News* editor J. G. Taylor Spink. Chandler then clapped his hands and called, "Robbie! Robbie!"

When the butler, Jackie Robinson, entered, he said, "Yassuh, Massa. Here Ah is."

Chandler then replied, "Ah, there you are, Jackie. Jackie, you ole woolly headed rascal. How long yo' been in the family?"

"Long time, Kunl, marty long time," the butler said. "Eber since Massa Rickey done bots me from da Kansas City Monarchs."

"To be sure, Jackie, to be sure," Chandler said. "How could ah forget that Colonel Rickey brought you to our house." Then, in an aside, Chandler said, "Rickey, that no good carpetbagger! What could he be thinking of?"[2]

In another skit, Arthur Mann, who wrote a lot of the skits and often parodied Rickey in the shows, noted the signing of Robinson with the spiritual "Glory Massa Rickey." When Rickey, who was in Florida preparing for the beginning of spring training, heard about the digs directed at Robinson and himself, he snapped, "That's nonsense."[3]

Wendell Smith also saw nothing funny about the parody of Robinson. He reprinted the skit and then unleashed an attack upon the New York sportswriters. "They are not for equality in sports and they gave vent to their feelings in this vicious manner," he said. "They weren't courageous or brave enough to express their feelings in their respective newspapers (that might affect circulation), so they put on this dastardly act behind closed doors," he said, adding, "The parts were played by well-known writers of the New York chapter of the association, but their names were not made public for fear of being reprimanded. Therefore, the entire blame for that 'Nazi Opera' must be heaped upon the entire body." There was no such sense of outrage in the New York City press because such racist stereotypes were acceptable. "This brand of racism, rarely given a second thought," Jules Tygiel wrote, "spoke for an age in which as 'invisible men,' blacks could feel no pain and well-intentioned whites had little sense of the harm they afflicted."[4]

Smith kept in contact with Rickey during the off-season. On December 19 Smith wrote Rickey telling him he would be covering Montreal's spring training for the *Courier* and offered his services. In his reply on January 8, Rickey asked Smith if he would go to Florida early to find room and board for Robinson and another black player, whom he identified as a pitcher named Wright. Rickey asked Smith if he would watch over the ballplayers in Sanford and Daytona Beach, "because much harm could come if either of these boys were to do or say something or other out of turn." On January 14 Smith wrote Rickey that he was pleased the Brooklyn executive intended to sign other black players. "I am most happy . . . that you are relying on my newspaper and me, personally, for cooperation in trying to accomplish this great move for practical Democracy in the most amiable and diplomatic manner possible." Smith added that he knew a family in Sanford who might have room for Robinson and Wright. Smith also suggested the ballplayers could avoid travel difficulties if he acted as their chauffeur. Rickey paid Smith fifty dollars a week, which was equal to his *Courier* salary. The *Courier* assigned photographer Billy Rowe to accompany Smith. In his letter to Rickey, Smith said the *Courier* and he were committed to advancing the "cause of Democracy in this country, so ably championed by you."[5]

On January 29 Montreal announced the signing of twenty-seven-year-old right-handed pitcher Johnny Wright of the Homestead Grays. Wright went 31-5 for the Grays in 1943 and then had two shutout victories against the Birmingham Black Barons in the Negro League World Series.[6] Wright, while serving in the navy, reportedly had the lowest earned run average of any pitcher in armed-forces baseball. The *Worker*, which had named Wright as a Montreal prospect in mid-November, said the pitcher had thrown well against the Dodgers in an exhibition game in 1945. *Worker* sports editor Bill Mardo looked ahead to spring training. "Within a month the eyes of America will be focused on the playing field at Daytona Beach," he wrote. "As Jackie Robinson turns in those spectacular plays of his at shortstop; as John Wright blazes across his fast ball underneath the hot Florida sun at that precise moment will the hypocrisy and stupidity of jimcrow be mirrored across America in letters big enough for even the most narrow-minded to understand." Mardo chided the New York press for not reporting Wright's signing. "Why in hell didn't the other papers play it up big? I ain't never seen no Negroes playin' big-league ball. Sure this is news. Big news." Mardo noted sarcastically, "You sure this guy Wright ain't a Communist?"[7]

During the off-season Rickey quietly negotiated with city officials in Daytona Beach to allow Robinson and Wright to play in the city's ballpark, but segregation laws were to be enforced elsewhere. Daytona Beach was a progressive city by southern standards. It had black bus drivers, a black middle class, and a black political presence. It also was the home of a black college, Bethune-Cookman, whose founder and president, Mary McLeod Bethune, was one of the more influential blacks in the United States. She was friends with Eleanor Roosevelt and had been one of the so-called black New Dealers during the Roosevelt administration. In addition, Daytona Beach had a baseball field in the black section of town. But the city lacked the necessary resources to accommodate the Brooklyn organization, which included a large number of war veterans. Spring training began in Sanford, which was about forty miles southwest of Daytona Beach, and then moved to Daytona Beach when enough prospects were sent home. Sanford converted a military training field into an athletic complex with enough ball fields for the organization's two hundred ballplayers.[8] The white players stayed at a lakefront hotel near the training camp. Robinson and White stayed with private families in the segregated section of town.

Sanford, which had a Klan presence, was more typical of southern towns than Daytona Beach. While Wendell Smith praised Sanford for its hospitality, he probably did that to try to convince his readers and perhaps himself that the racial climate was better than it was.[9] Sam

Lacy said he never felt comfortable in Sanford.[10] Mardo provided this description of the town: "Sanford's got the smell. The Smell of the South, the silent, lazy and ominous smell of a million lynchings that weren't good enough for the pretty palms. Strange Fruit Hangin' on the Poplar Trees." If you walked away from the nice houses on the clean streets with the pretty palms, Mardo said, you would be in the black part of town. "Here's where the Negroes live. Here's where every street is a shanty-town. Here's where you walk by and the Negroes look up at you quickly and then away again. Here's where they live and die," he said, adding, "some sooner than others."[11]

On February 28 Jackie and Rachel Robinson, who had been married less than two weeks, waited to board an American Airlines airplane at a Los Angeles airport to fly to Daytona Beach. Jackie knew a lot of things could go wrong in Florida, and some of them could go extremely wrong. Robinson, who was forever scarred by his court-martial at Fort Hood in Texas, was aware of the bigotry in the South, but he probably did not know the sheer depth of it. Rachel had never been to the Deep South, but she had heard the stories. "I was worried because I had heard so many stories about the treatment of Negroes in the Deep South," she said. "I knew how quickly Jack's temper could flare up in the face of a racial insult." If that happened, she did not know whether they both might be "harmed or killed, or, at best, we might jeopardize this opportunity to wipe out segregated baseball."[12]

When Montreal announced it had signed Robinson, all that had seemed impossible for black America seemed possible. The war had made black Americans more emboldened, and the signing of Robinson had given wings to their hopes. As blacks stood resolute, a growing number of whites in the North and in the South stood with them, drafting legislation to end lynching and unleashing stinging attacks on Jim Crow. In his 1945 book, *Rising Wind*, Walter White wrote that the time had come for the United States to reject racism. The country, he said, "could choose between a policy of appeasement of bigots — which, of course, she gives every indication now of following or she can live up to ideals and thereby save herself." To sociologist Howard Odum, the South and the North now faced the possibility of their greatest conflict since Reconstruction. "A small group of Negro agitators and another small group of white rabble-rousers are pushing this country closer and closer to an interracial explosion," Virginius Dabney, editor of the *Richmond Times-Dispatch* wrote. "Unless saner counsels prevail, we may have the worst internal clashes since Reconstruction, with hundreds, if not thousands, killed and amicable race relations set back for decades."[13]

Black newspapers filled their front pages with stories that told readers things were not getting better and were maybe even getting worse. White Americans, particularly those living in the South, would not waive generations of discrimination, regardless of how valiantly blacks had fought in Europe or how well reasoned the arguments for racial equality. On October 11, two weeks before Montreal announced it had signed Robinson, Jesse Payne, a black teenager, was in custody in a state prison in Raiford, Florida, near Tallahassee, for allegedly attacking the five-year-old niece of a sheriff in Madison. Payne was transferred back to Madison for arraignment and trial, where he was left in an unguarded and unlocked jail. In the middle of the night, a mob dragged him from his cell, shot him to death, and left his body on a highway several miles away. According to news stories, the sheriff, who lived next to the jail, watched the mob as it removed Payne. Two grand juries failed to indict the sheriff.[14] Two weeks before Payne's murder, a sixty-year-old black man living near Live Oak, Florida, was removed from his car, pistol-whipped, lynched, and dumped into a river. The suspects, including a police chief, were not indicted.[15] After crosses were burned outside the homes of several families near Miami, Thurgood Marshall, the chief counsel of the NAACP, asked the U.S. attorney general to investigate.[16]

In the months following the end of World War II, there was an escalation of violence against blacks, who were lynched "to teach them their place." In Columbia, Tennessee, a few days before the Robinsons left for spring training, a black woman and her son, who had recently been discharged from the navy, complained to a white merchant about a radio that had not been properly repaired. The merchant resented the complaint and shoved the woman. Her son then pushed the merchant through the store's window. A number of white townspeople, including a police officer, attacked the mother and son, who were arrested and charged with assault. The town's sheriff, hearing that a mob was forming and a rope had been acquired, smuggled the two blacks out of town. This did not resolve the tension. During the night gunshots were fired between blacks and whites. Hundreds of white law enforcement officers and townspeople converged on the black section of Columbia the next day, destroying homes, businesses, and churches and beating up and arresting black citizens. A hundred blacks were jailed, and two were shot while in custody.[17]

The Robinsons' trip from Los Angeles to Daytona Beach, meanwhile, turned into a grueling thirty-six-hour odyssey. They would twice be bumped from planes and replaced with whites. They would be denied entrance at a whites-only restaurant in the New Orleans airport. As the Robinsons rode on a bus from the Florida Panhandle, they were ordered to the back by the driver, who called Jackie "boy."[18] When the Robinsons finally arrived at the bus station in Daytona Beach, Wendell Smith and Billy Rowe were waiting for them. "Well, I finally made it," Robinson angrily snapped. "But I never want to take another trip like this one."[19] After Rachel went to bed, Jackie spent much of the night spitting out anger, telling Smith and Rowe, "Get me out of here!" Smith and Rowe tried to calm him down. They told Robinson he could not give up, regardless of what he had just been through and regardless of what lay ahead. Smith and Rowe told Robinson he would have to suffer certain indignities so other blacks could follow him into baseball. "We tried to tell him what the whole thing meant and that it was something he had to do," Rowe said.[20] Robinson and Wright reported to their first day of practice in Sanford on March 4, joining other Montreal prospects on a makeshift practice field described by *Brooklyn Eagle* columnist Tommy Holmes as "a huge, vacant lot, as bumpy as a cow pasture." Seven spectators and maybe a dozen or so sportswriters and photographers were in attendance. "It could be readily seen that Cecil B. DeMille had nothing to do with the setting for the debut of Jackie Roosevelt Robinson," Holmes said. "There was no fanfare and no curious, milling crowd." The Associated Press also said the workout failed to create much excitement or interest. Bill Mardo laughed at this description. "It was a thrilling day," he remembered. "The day belonged to decent-minded people who understood that discrimination against a man because of his skin hurt the nation as a whole." In his column Mardo chided Florida newspapers for not being at the field. Under a headline that said, "Florida Papers 'Forgot' Negro Workouts," Mardo wrote, "I suppose some people and some papers would need an atom bomb bursting about their heads before admitting that this world of ours does move on."[21]

After Robinson's first day of practice, he was interviewed by reporters. In one of his autobiographies, *I Never Had It Made*, Robinson described a contentious exchange with reporters. Robinson said that sportswriters suggested that he was trying to oust the Dodgers' popular shortstop, "Pee Wee" Reese. Robinson said he told them he was trying to earn a spot on the triple-A Royals. "This confrontation with the press was just a sense of what was to come," Robinson said. "They frequently stirred up trouble by baiting me or jumping into any situation I was involved in without completely checking the facts."[22] In fact, white sportswriters rarely, if ever, treated Robinson with hostility. Rather, they ignored him and the bigger story of the desegregation of baseball. Wendell Smith also suppressed information. But his reasons for doing so were different.

After the second day of practice, Smith and Rowe were sitting on the front porch of the home where they were staying when a white man approached. The man said he had been sent to deliver a message from a meeting of a hundred townspeople. "We want you to get the niggers out of town," the messenger said.[23] There would be trouble unless Robinson and Wright were "out of town by nightfall," he added.[24]

Smith called Rickey, who ordered the journalist to take Wright and the
Robinsons to Daytona Beach immediately. Smith said nothing about it
in his column. He wanted to convince *Courier* readers that all was well
in Florida — despite the reality.[25] *Sanford Herald* sports editor Julian
Stenstrom never mentioned Robinson in the columns or articles he
wrote that spring. In the decades ahead, however, he repeatedly told
his readers that Sanford "paved the way for professional baseball's color
line to be broken" and criticized anyone who said otherwise.[26]

Montreal opened camp in Daytona Beach on Wednesday, March
6. Robinson played four innings at shortstop during a seven-inning
scrimmage against Brooklyn's substitutes, failing to get a hit in either
of two plate appearances.[27] It was just a scrimmage in front of a few
nonpaying spectators. But to Sam Lacy, "It marked the first time in
history that a colored player had competed in a game representing
a team in modern organized baseball."[28] When Lacy looked out at
the field, he saw progress. He knew that Robinson was under pressure. Robinson had injured his arm and had not yet begun to hit. But
Robinson was not the only one squirming under the Florida sun. In
his "Looking 'Em Over" column on March 11, Lacy called Robinson
"a man in a goldfish bowl. . . . It is easy to see why I felt a lump in my
throat each time a ball was hit in his direction those first few days;
why I experienced a sort of emptiness in the bottom of my stomach
whenever he took a swing in batting practice," he wrote. Lacy said he
became personally involved in the story that spring. He could not help
it. "It came from my heart. I did feel it," he said. "I was emotionally
involved in everything."[29]

The March 19 issue of *Look* included a profile of Rickey, who, the
writer, Tom Cohane, said, had become "baseball's 'great emancipator.'"
Like Lincoln before him, Rickey vowed that if he got the opportunity
to make the world right, he would do it. Robinson provided him that
opportunity. Rickey said his decision to sign Robinson was based not
on economics or politics; it was purely spiritual. "I cannot face my God
much longer knowing that His black creatures are held separate and

distinct from His white creatures in the game that has given me all I can call my own," he said. Cohane suggested that the signing of Robinson would result in smaller crowds at Ebbets Field. "The Dodgers are now a 'black' baseball team," he wrote. Cohane quoted unnamed baseball experts as saying that Robinson was not good enough for the big leagues or even the International League but would probably play in a lower Minor League.[30] Jimmy Powers and Dan Parker used Cohane's piece to resume their attack on Rickey. Powers criticized the characterization of Rickey as another Abraham Lincoln who has "a heart as big as a watermelon and loves all mankind." Powers said progress was being made in the South without the interference of liberal do-gooders, like Rickey — who, in fact, was hardly liberal. Parker said the signing of Robinson was not baseball's Emancipation Proclamation, as Rickey portrayed it, but a publicity stunt, as the *Sporting News* called it. In a far more defensible statement, Parker said Robinson had not been living up to expectations.[31] He again expressed his doubts that Robinson would ever play in the Major Leagues.[32]

Wendell Smith responded viciously to Parker and Powers — as he had the New York baseball writers a month earlier. Smith described the columns as "smutty," "smelly," "vicious," "putrid," "wacky," and "violently prejudiced." According to Smith, Powers and Parker campaigned for desegregation because they wanted to ingratiate themselves to black readers and not because they believed in racial equality. "They prostituted the gullible population of Harlem by publishing burning stories on the great injustice that was being done to Negro players by the majors," he said. "They published pictures of these black baseball orphans and accused the majors of perpetuating a system that 'has no place in American life.' And, as they ranted and raved and blustered like inspired abolitionists of the underground railroads, the circulation of their respective papers soared to a new high in Harlem."[33] Unlike Powers and Parker, Smith said, southern sportswriters had been fair in their coverage of Robinson. If saying nothing meant the same as being fair, then southern writers were indeed fair — but the two words

should not be used interchangeably. Bill Mardo criticized the New York
dailies for practicing what amounted to a blackout of the story. Mardo
ridiculed Powers for his "cheap talk," writing, "It was much cheaper of
you, Mr. Powers, wasn't it, to blast Rickey and his small-salary policies,
than to level against the big-bankrolled Larry MacPhail, who prefers
to pay fairly good wages to his white players but not a single penny
for the hiring of Negroes to the Yankee organization." The *Washington
Afro-American* quoted the Mayor's Committee to Integrate Baseball
as calling Powers's column "untrue," "vicious," and "insidious." The
committee said that Powers's statement that whites and blacks "cannot
compete against each other in sports without the danger of a race riot
is against the evidence of well-proved facts."[34]

On Sunday, March 17, Robinson played his first spring training
game. Four thousand spectators, nearly a quarter of whom were black,
jammed into City Island Ballpark in downtown Daytona Beach. When
the Daytona Beach newspapers referred to the game decades later,
articles said the city had relaxed its segregation laws and allowed blacks
and whites to sit together. This did not happen.[35] Yet the mere fact that
so many blacks and whites shared a ballpark demonstrated once again
the fallibility of the race-riot argument. Robinson and Wright played
several more games that spring at City Island Park without incident. But
no other city allowed Robinson to play. Before the Brooklyn Dodgers
left for a series of games in South Florida, the city of Miami, wrongly
believing that the team would bring Robinson and Wright, announced
the Dodgers would have to leave behind its black ballplayers because
its ballpark was restricted. "I don't want to embarrass any ball club,"
a city official told New York Giants player-manager Mel Ott. "But if
they come here they can't play and that's flat."[36] Paul Waner, a hitting
star of the Pittsburgh Pirates in the 1920s and 1930s who was now a
part owner and manager of Miami's Minor League team, said he would
challenge his city's segregation law and find a way whereby blacks could
attend ball games. "I don't care if I have to build (bleachers) and pay
for them myself," he said.[37]

But one of baseball's grand old men was not as progressive. When sportswriters asked Connie Mack, owner and manager of the Philadelphia Athletics, what would happen if Brooklyn brought Robinson to West Palm to play the Athletics at West Palm Beach, Mack answered sharply: "I wouldn't play him. I used to have respect for Rickey. I don't any more." Mack later took the comments "off the record," and the remark received no publicity.[38] Red Smith, who was present at the interview, remembered Mack's tirade. "You wouldn't want that in the paper, would you, Connie?" asked Stan Baumgartner of the *Philadelphia Inquirer*. "I don't give a goddamn what you write," Mack replied. "Yes, publish it." Don Donaghey of the *Philadelphia Bulletin* recognized the explosiveness of the comments and convinced Mack to take them off the record. Smith did not mention anything in print about the incident, although he later said, "I decided that I'd forgive old Connie for his ignorance." When Smith was asked later how he felt about the story of baseball's first integrated spring training, he answered, "I don't remember feeling any way except having a very lively interest in a good story."[39] If he indeed had such a lively interest in the story, why did he not write anything about it? Ira Berkow wrote in his biography of Smith that the columnist was sympathetic to the race problem but did not think it should be challenged in print.

Wendell Smith said Dick Young of the *Daily News*, who was beginning his long career as a beat writer, and Gus Steiger of the *Daily Mirror* were among the few sportswriters who expressed interest in the Robinson story. "They were constantly querying me," Smith remembered. "Every day they'd talk to me. After all, I was living with Jackie and he was the big story." If Young was interested in the story, he kept it to himself during the spring of 1946 but also during Robinson's rookie year with Brooklyn in 1947. When Young was asked why he did not mention Robinson's race when he played his first game on opening day, he said that the ballplayer had not done anything that merited attention. This, according to Jonathan Eig who wrote *Opening Day: The Story of Jackie Robinson's First Season*, was "like saying Neil Armstrong did nothing but plant a flag and collect rocks when he landed on the moon." Young never acknowledged the racial angle to the story during the season of 1947. "Whether the cause was racism or simple stubbornness," Eig wrote, "Young, for all his intelligence and for all his skills as a reporter, wasn't able to see past the events on the baseball diamond and make sense of them for his readers."[40]

White sportswriters working for mainstream newspapers treated the Robinson story during the spring of 1946 "as a passing event," Sam Lacy said. Most sportswriters kept their racial attitudes to themselves, or at least out of print. Black sportswriters were allowed in the press box at City Island Park. Billy Rowe later reported that when Smith entered the press box, a sportswriter with the *Brooklyn Eagle* sneered, "'This was a good job until Mexicans, Cubans, and Negroes started cluttering up the diamond.' His statement wasn't that mild, but this is a family paper. Don't write your senator, write the *Eagle*." By the end of the spring, Robinson had put his struggles behind him and had played his way onto the Montreal team as it headed north to begin the season. Johnny Wright also started the season with the Royals but was released after having control problems. Jules Tygiel wrote that the 1946 spring training foreshadowed what lay ahead in the civil rights movement. "What stands out in retrospect is the extent in which baseball's first integrated spring training unveiled a strategy for later civil rights advocates," Tygiel said. "Aided and abetted by sympathetic whites, a handful of individual blacks shouldered the physical risks inherent in a policy of direct confrontation with the institutions of Jim Crow. In the face of opposition from local public officials, baseball's integration coalition refused to retreat."[41]

On opening day of the 1946 season, Robinson had four hits, including a home run. Joe Bostic, who had left the *New York People's Voice* to become sports editor of the *Amsterdam News*, wrote, "The most significant sports story of the century was written into the record books as baseball took up the cudgel for democracy and an unassuming but superlative Negro boy ascended the heights of excellence to prove the rightness of the experiment. And prove it in the only correct crucible for such an experiment — the crucible of white hot competition." Bill Mardo wrote that the day "belonged to Jackie Robinson . . . and all the progressive forces who fought so tirelessly to drive a wedge into baseball's jimcrow ban." Robinson finished the season as the International League's leading hitting and led the Royals to the league championship. After Montreal's championship game a crowd of French Canadians cheered as they chased after Robinson as he left the ballpark. "It was probably the only day in history," Sam Maltin wrote in the *Pittsburgh Courier*, "that a black man ran from a white mob with love instead of lynching on its mind."[42]

Toward the end of the baseball season, a committee of Major League executives and owners, which included Ford Frick, Sam Breadon, Philip Wrigley, William Harridge, Larry MacPhail, and Tom Yawkey, drafted a document that reiterated the opposition to desegregation by stating that the campaign to integrate baseball was being led by "political and social-minded drumbeaters . . . who know little of baseball and of its operation. They single out Professional Baseball because it offers a good publicity medium." The document stated that segregation was good for black and white baseball. If blacks were allowed into the Major Leagues, it said, the value of Major League teams would decrease.[43] Rickey was outraged when the report was distributed to all owners. No action was taken on the report, and most of the copies were destroyed. Rickey went public with the report during a speech at Wilberforce College in Ohio in 1948. While Rickey called for continued progress in civil rights for blacks, he again attacked communism. "Now there is a Communist effort to get credit for 'forcing' us to sign Robinson, but I warn you to be on your guard against this thing," he said. "The American public is not as concerned with the first baseman's pigmentation as it is with the power of his swing, the dexterity of his slight, the gracefulness of his fielding or the speed of his legs."[44]

When Robinson took the field with the Brooklyn Dodgers on opening day of the 1947 season, it was the first time a black had worn a big league uniform in more than six decades. Yet there was little sense of that history in the New York press. The *Brooklyn Eagle* did not mention Robinson in its game story. In his column Tommy Holmes wrote that it was the first time that "an acknowledged Negro" had taken the field in the Major Leagues. Gus Steiger did not mention Robinson's race in the *Daily Mirror* but did include the curious observation that the ballplayer "showed a decided strangeness with big league pitching." Red Smith said nothing of substance. Arthur Daley did not write about how Robinson did that game; instead, he tried to assure his readers that Robinson was the "right type" of black man — deferential and quiet, one who never questioned his place. "The muscular Negro minds his own business and shrewdly makes no effort to push himself," Daley said. "He speaks intelligently when spoken to and already has made a strong impression."[45]

Sportswriters typically avoided references to Robinson's race. But as had happened with the Jake Powell story a decade earlier, circumstances forced the issue onto the sports pages. On April 22 the Philadelphia Phillies, led by manager Ben Chapman, directed a torrent of racist language from their dugout so vulgar it offended members of their own team. Chapman, according to one reference, gave his players orders to call Robinson anything they wanted, the more objectionable the better.[46] Chapman once again had crossed the line of what was acceptable in a profession where such lines were broad. Newspaper articles and columns mentioned that Chapman had been traded from the Yankees after making anti-Semitic remarks at fans. Walter Winchell, in his national radio broadcast, criticized Chapman. Dan Parker said that Robinson was "the only gentleman among those involved in the incident." Robinson, who had made a vow "not to fight back," later admitted that the taunts "brought me closer to cracking up than I ever had been." At one point, Robinson said, he could feel himself coming apart. "What, indeed, did Mr. Rickey expect of me? I was, after all, a human being. . . . For one wild and rage-crazed minute, I thought, 'To hell with Mr. Rickey's noble experiment.' . . . To hell with the image of the patient black freak I was supposed to create. I could throw down my bat, stride over to the Phillies dugout, grab one of those white sons of bitches and smash his teeth in with my despised black fist. Then I could walk away from it all."[47]

Chapman's verbal assault angered Robinson's teammates. Eddie Stankey called the Phillies "cowards," screaming at the team's dugout, "Why don't you yell at someone who can answer back!" Brooklyn outfielder Dixie Walker, who was friends with Chapman, confronted the Phillies' manager after the game. Branch Rickey later said that the Phillies' dugout served to unify the Dodgers. "Chapman did more than anybody to unite the Dodgers," Rickey said. "When he poured out that angry string of unconscionable abuse, he solidified and unified thirty men." In early May Stanley Woodward of the *New York Herald Tribune* reported that National League president Ford Frick had learned of a conspiracy among players on the St. Louis Cardinals, who agreed to go on strike rather than play against Robinson on May 6. Frick sent a letter to the Cardinals telling them that anyone participating would be suspended. When the Dodgers went to Philadelphia for a series beginning on May 9, Phillies general manager Herb Pennock, whom the Pittsburgh *Courier* had praised as "liberal" in 1933, told the Dodgers not to "bring the Nigger here with the rest of your team." Rickey told Pennock if the Phillies declined to play, the Dodgers would win by forfeit.[48] On May 10 newspapers reported that Robinson had been receiving death threats by mail.[49]

Jonathan Eig wrote that Woodward's column had an impact, albeit brief, on the coverage of the Robinson story. The *Sporting News* acknowledged that baseball had to accept that there were now blacks wearing big league uniforms. Jimmy Cannon of the *New York Post* addressed the bigots who opposed Robinson's presence in baseball. "There is a great lynch mob among us and they go unhooded and work without rope," Cannon said. "We have been involved in a war to guarantee all people the right to life without fear. . . . In such a world it seems a small thing that a man be able to play a game unmolested. In our time such a plea should be unnecessary. But when it happens we must again remember that all this country's enemies are not beyond the frontiers of our home land." Dan Parker said that baseball could no longer ignore the issue. "Sports writers have been studiously try- ing to avoid the racial angle in Baseball this spring, but, despite their best efforts, it keeps bobbing up. Obviously, it must be faced squarely, sooner or later," Parker said. "If it is our national pastime, embodying American ideals, let us proceed to conduct it along those lines with no more racial barriers in its playing fields than there are at its turnstiles."[50]

Patrick Washburn, in his study of the coverage of Robinson's rookie season in the *New York Herald Tribune*, *Daily News*, and *Times*, said the newspapers considered the Robinson story important during the ballplayer's first month in the Major Leagues. But after Woodward's story, newspapers avoided the "racial angle" for the remainder of the season. "This suggests that the editors felt they were adding to racial problems," Washburn wrote, "even though they were reporting only the facts, and therefore the responsible course was to delete anything that might inflame the situation further." There is reason to suggest that the race issue continued to make editors uncomfortable well into Robinson's career. Roger Kahn of the *Herald Tribune* wrote in his book *The Boys of Summer* that during 1952 and 1953 he had trouble from his "segregationist" editors if he submitted stories about racial incidents that involved Robinson. Kahn remembered receiving a telegram from an editor who told him, "Write baseball, not race relations."[51]

Sportswriters, whether for personal reasons or because of instruc- tions from their editors, wrote stories that made it appear race relations were better than they were — instead of publishing factual accounts of the verbal attacks and death threats faced by Robinson. In July *Boston Globe* sportswriter Clif Keane, who reported that a Red Sox official had yelled, "Get those niggers off the field!" during Robinson's 1945 tryout at Fenway Park, wrote that the relationship between Dixie Walker and Robinson had grown so close that Walker was giving the rookie batting tips. The story, which had no truth to it, was circulated among other columnists. Vincent X. Flaherty of the *Los Angeles Examiner* said that Walker had become Robinson's "best friend and chief advisor among the Dodgers." Rachel Robinson clipped the column and wrote the following on the margins: "Some sports writers will fall for anything."[52] Robinson, perhaps because he was a rookie, had the worst locker in the clubhouse, and the distance he felt between his teammates and him was more than spatial. He was both alone and lonely. Wendell Smith certainly knew this but revealed little of it to his readers. According to Smith, Robinson thought the St. Louis Cardinals were "a swell bunch of fellows." In another story Smith wrote that Robinson was treated no differently than anyone else on the Dodgers. "He is one of the boys," Smith said, "and treated that way by his teammates."[53]

In late June President Harry S. Truman delivered a speech on civil rights at the Lincoln Memorial during the thirty-eighth annual meeting of the NAACP. Truman's speech was the first time a president had addressed the organization or spoken so unequivocally about the inalienable rights for blacks. No president had ever addressed America's racial dilemma with such conviction. "Many of our people still suffer the indignity of insult, the harrowing fear of intimidation, and, I regret to say, the threat of physical injury and mob violence. The conscience of our nation, and the legal machinery which enforce it, have not yet secured to each citizen full freedom from fear," he said. "Our case for democracy should be as strong as we can make it. It should rest on the practical evidence that we have put our own house in order. For these compelling reasons, we can no longer afford the luxury of a leisurely attack upon prejudice and discrimination."[54] Truman later issued orders to end discrimination in the military and in federal hiring. Truman's commission on civil rights issued a report that addressed racism on a broad scale, condemning lynching and other serious forms of racism. The report, *To Secure These Rights*, mentioned that progress had been made in civil rights. It referred to Robinson and the possibilities inherent in "the presence of a Negro player on the Brooklyn Dodgers."[55]

Yet no story had more impact on the fledgling civil rights movement than the desegregation of baseball, and no single person had as much impact on race relations as Robinson. Roger Wilkins, the fifteen-year-old son of NAACP leader Roy Wilkins, later wrote that Robinson changed the lives of young blacks like himself. "He knew what the stakes were every time he danced off a base. If he failed, we failed," Wilkins said. "He knew what he was trying to do. And this man, in a very personal sense, became a permanent part of my spirit and the spirit of a generation of black kids like me because of the way he faced his ordeal."[56] Gil Jonas, then a teenager, used to sit in Ebbets Field and hear the profane language directed at Robinson. "I didn't know people could be that cruel," he remembered. But as the season progressed and Robinson proved himself, the racial taunts became quieter and less frequent. "I watched people who were hard-hearted or antagonistic ... and they changed. It was palpable. It changed so completely, and it changed me over the course of the season. Just watching the pain this guy felt." Poet Langston Hughes, who lived in New York City, marveled at what was happening. "Anyhow, this summer of our Lord 1947, the Dodgers are doing right with Jackie Robinson at first," Hughes said. "And maybe if the Dodgers win the pennant, a hundred years from now history will be made."[57]

The Dodgers won the pennant, and Robinson's long, painful season ended with vindication. In late September J. G. Taylor Spink, who had once opposed segregation and dismissed Robinson's talent, selected Robinson as the *Sporting News*'s Rookie of the Year. Spink said that Robinson's race had no impact on his selection. "The sociological experiment that Robinson represented, the trail-blazing that he did, the barriers he broke down, did not enter into the decision," Spink wrote. "He was rated and examined solely as a freshman player in the big leagues — on the basis on his hitting, his running, his defensive play, his team value." Dixie Walker, who had stridently objected to Robinson's promotion to the Dodgers, told Spink that nobody else on the team had contributed more to its success than Robinson. "He is everything that Branch Rickey said he was when he came up from Montreal," Walker said.[58] Major League owners had long said that blacks did not have the talent to play in the big leagues. But Robinson had changed that. Segregationists had long said white players, particularly southerners, would not accept blacks as teammates. But Walker's quote refuted that.

Robinson's race might not have made a difference to the *Sporting News*. But it certainly made a difference to black sportswriters and other journalists who had clamored long and loudly about how racial discrimination contradicted the American ideal of democracy. Wendell Smith had been closer to the Robinson story than anyone else. Smith reported St. Louis's strike threat and Philadelphia's profane bench jockeying, but, for the most part, he preferred to report what went right and not what went wrong, even if he had to shave part of the story.[59] All was well in the Brooklyn dugout and on the train the team took on road trips. Robinson was just one of the guys, Smith repeated over and over. Smith criticized Jimmy Cannon's description of Robinson as "the loneliest man I have ever seen in sports." Smith also criticized the *Daily Worker* after it published a column giving Communists credit for the signing of Robinson. "The truth of the matter is that the Communists did more to delay the entrance of Negroes in the big leagues than any other single factor," Smith wrote. He said that owners had refused to discuss the issue as long as Communists were connected with it.[60] This angered Rodney, who wrote Smith, reminding him of the letter he had once written praising the *Worker*. "I fired off a letter," Rodney said. "I recalled that when we had worked together in 1939, he had written me a letter congratulating us." Rodney told Smith that if he criticized the *Worker* again, the newspaper would embarrass him by reprinting the earlier letter.[61]

Smith ghostwrote Robinson's newspaper columns and subsequently his first autobiography. Smith later described himself as "Robinson's Boswell."[62] In 1948 Smith, based on his work on the Robinson story, was hired by the *Chicago American*, making him one of the first black sportswriters to work for a mainstream daily. As a sportswriter for the *American*, he qualified for membership in the Baseball Writers' Association, where he received his long-sought press card. After Smith contributed to winning the campaign to desegregate baseball, he later was successful in ending segregation in Florida's spring training camps.[63] In 1993 Smith became the first black sportswriter inducted into the J. G. Taylor Spink writers' wing of the Baseball Hall of Fame for his "meritorious contributions to baseball writing." Five years later Sam Lacy also was honored with the Spink award for his long career that included his efforts to desegregate baseball. Smith and Lacy had reached the top of the association that had once banned them.

In recent years Rodney's contribution to the desegregation of baseball has been recognized. In early 2010 ESPN aired a program on Rodney's significance to both baseball and society. Gerald Horne, professor of history and African American studies at the University of Houston and an author of a number of books on race relations, said, "Rodney was early in teaching an audience that sports was a significant sociological force." When Rodney died in December 2009, Dave Zirin, sports editor of the *Nation* and author of *A People's History of Sports in the United States*, called for Rodney's induction into the Spink wing of the Hall of Fame. Rodney "crusaded against baseball's color line when almost every other journalist pretended it didn't exist," Zirin said. "He edited a political sports page that engaged his audience in how to fight for a more just sports world." Rodney argued that sports had an impact on the world outside its lines of play. His writing captured how Robinson "helped inspire the struggle for civil rights, especially in the South," Zirin said.[64]

Rodney once told Zirin about an exhibition game in Atlanta, where so many blacks had come to see Robinson, Campanella, and Don Newcombe that there was not enough room in the segregated stands. When Robinson, Campanella, and Newcombe took the field, black fans roared their approval, while white fans booed. As the game progressed, more and more white spectators cheered the black players, and the booing quieted. Rodney said players like Robinson and Campanella were part of the civil rights movement before it had a name. Campanella once told Rodney, "Without the Brooklyn Dodgers, you don't have *Brown v. Board of Education*." Rodney, at first, expressed skepticism. "All I know," Campanella continued, "is we were the first ones on the trains, we were the first ones down South not to go around the back of the restaurant, first ones in the hotels. We were like the whole integration thing."[65] Social progressives had a significant political influence when Rodney left the United States to serve in the armed services in 1942. But by the time he returned, the expansion of the Soviet Union had created a fear of communism in the United States that the Far Right exploited to advance their political agenda. During the Red Scare of the late 1940s and early 1950s, right-wing hysteria destroyed communism and Communists. Blacklists ended the careers of countless actors, directors, and screenwriters in Hollywood. Vito Marcantonio was called un-American and voted out of Congress. Benjamin Davis Jr. was sentenced to jail for violating the Smith Act. Robinson reluctantly appeared before the House Un-American Activities Committee to respond to Paul Robeson, who had said that if the United States and the Soviet Union went to war, blacks should not enlist in the U.S. armed services because they had long been discriminated against in the United States while given equality in the Soviet Union. Robeson later had his passport revoked for his support of communism. The Red Scare left the *Worker* and communism in tatters. Rodney left the Communist Party in 1958 in protest of its failure to condemn the atrocities of Joseph Stalin.[66] Rodney made his mark in the story of the campaign to desegregate baseball. But like many revolutionaries, he ended up in the background.[67]

When Robinson's three-year pledge to Rickey ended, he no longer had to restrain himself. He could become his own man. He ran aggressively on the bases and no longer turned his other cheek when baserunners ran into him or pitchers threw at him. He argued with opponents, umpires, and sportswriters. As a result, he found himself criticized in the press because he had become the "wrong type" of black. The *Sporting News* suggested that Robinson's temperament made him un-American and was responsible, in part, for the death threats against him. "They will resent and repel with all their force the agitator, the sharper with an angle, the fellow who is less than an American because he chooses to be a rabble rouser," the publication said. When Robinson complained about being booed, Spink accused the ballplayer of being an ingrate. "Would it be more fitting and gracious if you repaid the game," Spink wrote, "not only by your playing skill, but by words of good will instead of any bitterness?"[68]

When Robinson complained about his treatment in the press, his old friend Wendell Smith, whose relationship with Robinson had cooled, also accused Robinson of ingratitude. Smith said Robinson owed everything to the press. "Mr. Robinson's memory, it seems, is getting shorter and shorter. That is especially true in the case of the many newspapermen who have befriended him through his career."[69] Smith and Robinson, who had been through so much together, died a month apart in 1972. Billy Rowe had been with Smith when Jackie and Rachel Robinson got off the bus in Daytona Beach in 1946. Smith and Rowe had spent the night telling Robinson it was necessary for the ballplayer to sacrifice himself for the hopes and dreams of black America. "He accepted it," Rowe said. "He realized how things were and that there were certain things he had to accept for it to work. He was part of the agenda to change baseball, to truly make it America's game."[70]

Arnold Rampersad wrote that Robinson gave blacks not just hope for the future but also the courage to confront it. "As their champion, Robinson had taken their hopes into the arena of baseball and succeeded beyond their wildest dreams. He had been stoical, but the essence of this story was the proven quality of his black manhood," Rampersad said. "To blacks, he passed now into the pantheon of their most sublime heroes, actual and legendary — the slave revolutionary Nat Turner and the abolitionist Frederick Douglass, the steel-driving John Henry and the roustabout Stagolee. Neither blacks not whites would be quite the same thereafter in America." When Robinson confronted baseball's color line, the U.S. Supreme Court's *Brown v. Board of Education* decision, the murder of Emmitt Till, and the Birmingham bus boycott were years away. Martin Luther King Jr. was still a teenager when Robinson played his first game in the Major Leagues. In 1962, a few days before Robinson was inducted into the Baseball Hall of Fame, King recognized that Robinson had made progress possible for millions of black Americans. "Back in the days when integration wasn't fashionable," King said, "he underwent the trauma and the humiliation and the loneliness which comes with being a pilgrim walking the lonesome byways toward the high road of Freedom. He was a sit-inner before sit-ins, a freedom rider before rides."[71]

Robinson forever changed both baseball and society, but he paid a terrible price for it. He died at the age of fifty-three. More than six decades after Robinson first took the field in a Brooklyn uniform and four decades after his death, Robinson remains the most important figure in baseball history, not because of his greatness as a player — although he was great — but because of the courage he demonstrated while playing and because, like one of Joseph Campbell's heroes, he willingly embarked on the hero's journey and sacrificed himself for something bigger. Robinson's career in the Major Leagues — beginning with his rookie season — transcended sport as no athlete has since. Robinson "revolutionized the image of black Americans in the eyes of many whites," Arnold Rampersad wrote. "Starting out as a token, he had utterly complicated their sense of the nature of black people, how they thought and felt, their dignity and their courage in the face of adversity. No black man ever shone so long as the epitome not only of stoic endurance but also of intelligence, bravery, physical power and grit. Because baseball was lodged so deeply in the average white man's psyche, Robinson's protracted victory had left an intimate mark there."[72]

In *Baseball's Great Experiment*, Jules Tygiel wrote, "The integration of baseball represented both a symbol of imminent racial challenge and a direct agent of social change. Jackie Robinson's campaign against the color line in 1946–47 captured the imagination of millions of Americans who had previously ignored the nation's racial dilemma."[73] Robinson's presence in a Brooklyn uniform forced many white sportswriters and millions of white Americans to examine what they had been conditioned to accept without question. In doing so, they took a hard look at the game and the society it represented and asked themselves if either the nation or the national pastime was living up to its professed values: fairness, justice, and equality. Others simply saw in Robinson a compelling story, a ballplayer unlike any they had seen before, and accurately reported that story. Given the requisite information, readers could then make their own judgments.

But a lot of sportswriters missed the biggest baseball story in history because of ignorance, fear, and prejudice, and because if they looked too closely at Robinson or listened too closely to what bigots were calling him, they were afraid of what they might see in themselves and what inner voices they might hear. Instead, they said little. To most sportswriters, Robinson's presence in a Brooklyn uniform meant that he had broken Major League Baseball's color barrier and ended segregation in baseball. There was, therefore, no more to be said about the issue. This myth would be perpetuated for years, if not decades. But Robinson had merely integrated one team. It would be more than a decade before the last Major League team, the Red Sox, would add a black player to its roster. Instead of calling for more blacks in baseball, most sportswriters remained silent. What is particularly revealing is not that white sportswriters failed to acknowledge what Robinson represented and what he accomplished but rather how sympathetic they remained toward the racists who stood in the way of baseball's becoming the game it promised to be.

In October 1994 Ray Robinson, a longtime sportswriter and author of many books on baseball, wrote a column for the *Sporting News* on Ben Chapman, who had died a year earlier. Of all the players or managers in the National League, Chapman had been Jackie Robinson's "chief malefactor, the most pernicious," Ray Robinson said. Robinson recalled a meeting several years earlier with Chapman, who regretted his actions nearly a half century earlier. "A man learns about things and mellows as he grows older," Chapman said. "I think maybe I've mellowed. Maybe I went too far in those days when I thought it was OK to try to throw guys off balance and upset them with jockeying. I'm sorry for many of the things I said. I guess the world changes and maybe I've changed too." Robinson wrote that Chapman "sounded sincere. . . . People can change. Whether in that brief exchange he was seeking some vague absolution for forgiveness from an intruder into his life, I do not know."[74]

Maybe Chapman changed. If so, he deserves credit for that. But what about Robinson and all the blacks that both preceded him and followed him? Where was the sympathy for them? An examination of the press and the campaign to desegregate baseball underscores the conclusions of the 1947 Hutchins Report, which heavily criticized the media of the day for failing to provide a flow of information and interpretation that would help readers understand the day's events.[75] A few years earlier Gunnar Myrdal said that white America had "an astonishing ignorance" about black Americans. White America, he said, was content with its stereotypes about blacks. According to Myrdal, whites did not "understand the reality and the effects of discrimination" faced by blacks. "There is no doubt, in the writer's opinion, that a great majority of white people in America would be prepared to give the Negro a substantially better deal if they knew the facts," Myrdal wrote. The future of race relations, he added, was, according to authors Gene Roberts and Hank Klibanoff, "in the hands of the American press."[76]

Black editors expressed their frustration that northern white editors, in particular, did not support racial equality and civil rights in their editorials and columns. Black editors knew they needed the support of white editors, but they also knew they could not afford to wait any longer for it. Black editors found themselves on their own, as they had historically. "What the white editors did not see was that Negro editors, perhaps without knowing it, were preparing new generations of their race for what would ultimately became the civil rights movement," Roberts and Klibanoff wrote. "The Negro press was ready for the future; it sensed it was on the cusp of one of the great stories in American history. How long would it take the white press to share the vision?" Twenty years after the Hutchins Report, the Kerner Commission wondered the same thing. "It is the responsibility of the news media to tell the story of race relations in America," the commission said. But the news media had failed to do that. "Although charged with the responsibility of keeping a close check on government, of rooting out injustice and of protecting the weak, the American press," one media critic said, "had not discovered the problems of the Black man in America, nor had it led in the struggle to solve the problems."[77]

The same was true during the campaign to desegregate baseball. Between 1933 and 1945 the *Daily Worker* and the black press confronted the issue of racial discrimination. But the campaign to desegregate baseball went largely ignored by the baseball establishment because it went largely ignored by the mainstream dailies. Americans accepted baseball's policy of racial exclusion because the baseball establishment denied the existence of a color line and the mainstream press accepted those denials because they were in on the lie. If prominent white sportswriters pressured baseball, the baseball establishment would have had to listen. But this did not happen. Wendell Smith observed that white sportswriters "didn't do much to advance our cause." Sam Lacy recalled that Smith and he approached sympathetic white sportswriters, hoping for their cooperation. Their pleas were ignored. *Worker* sportswriters also sought out mainstream sportswriters. Bill Mardo said some sportswriters opposed the color line but refused to challenge segregated baseball. "They didn't think they had the freedom, working for newspapers that reflected the culture of a white society," Mardo said, adding, "or they simply reflected the status quo of most whites." Most white sportswriters, Mardo added, were pessimistic or simply indifferent toward racism. "'You guys are wasting your time,' they told me.

'This country wasn't going to change. . . . Those club owners will never give in.'" The result of this was that most Americans were unaware of the campaign to end segregation in baseball. "As long as mainstream sportswriters maintained their silence, the color line remained firm," Mardo said. "Most newspaper readers didn't know there was a massive campaign to end Jim Crow in baseball."[78]

NOTES

1. WHITE SPORTSWRITERS AND MINSTREL SHOWS

1. *New York Times*, February 6, 1933; *Sporting News*, February 16, 1933; *New York Times*, February 6, 1933.
2. Editorials refer to columns representing the newspaper's point of view and appear on the editorial page. Columns are written by individual writers and represent their point of view.
3. *New York World-Telegram*, February, 6 1933.
4. *New York Daily News*, February 8, 1933.
5. Carroll, *When to Stop the Cheering?*, 9.
6. *New York Daily News*, February 8, 1933.
7. *Sporting News*, January 18, 1934.
8. *New York Evening Post*, February 7, 1933; *Sporting News*, February 9, 1933.
9. *New York Daily News*, February 1, 1933; *Sporting News*, February 9, 1933.
10. *Pittsburgh Courier*, February 11, 1933.
11. *Pittsburgh Courier*, February 18, 1933.
12. *Pittsburgh Courier*, February 25, March 4, 1933.

13. *Pittsburgh Courier*, March 11, 1933.

14. *Pittsburgh Courier*, March 18, 1933.

15. *Pittsburgh Courier*, February 25, March 4, April 1, 1933.

16. Wiggins, "Wendell Smith," 6–8.

17. *Amsterdam News*, February 15, 1933; *New York Age*, February 18, 1933.

18. *Chicago Defender*, February 25, 1933.

19. *Chicago Defender*, March 4, 11, 1933.

20. Tygiel, *Baseball's Great Experiment*, 22.

21. Crepeau, *Baseball*, 171–72.

22. Rogosin, "Black Baseball," 234.

23. Tygiel, *Baseball's Great Experiment*, 46.

24. *Pittsburgh Courier*, August 26, 1933; Lanctot, *Negro League Baseball*, 210.

25. Pride and Wilson, *History of the Black Press*, 138–39.

26. Washburn, "*Pittsburgh Courier*'s Double V Campaign," 81.

27. Wolseley, *The Black Press, U.S.A.*, 68; Wiggins, "Wendell Smith," 6.

28. Simons, "Jackie Robinson and the American Mind," 40.

29. Simons, "Jackie Robinson and the American Mind," 40.

30. Carroll, *When to Stop the Cheering?*, 2.

31. The committee was called different names such as the Citizens Committee to End Jim Crow in Baseball and the Committee to End Discrimination in Baseball.

32. Logan, "Negro and the Post-war World," 543–44.

33. Howe and Coser, *American Communist Party*, 362.

34. Rusinack, "Baseball on the Radical Agenda," 3.

35. Glazer, *Social Basis of American Communism*, 169.

36. Davis, "Summary for Angelo Herndon, Defendant," 7–10; *Washington Daily News*, April 11, 1933.

37. *Daily Worker*, August 29, 1933.

38. Tygiel, *Baseball's Great Experiment*, 30–31.

39. Rose, *Negro in America*, 20.

40. Ellison, *Invisible Man*, 3.

41. Orodenker, "Westbrook Pegler," 264; Fountain, *Sportswriter*, 247–49.

42. Ashe, *Hard Road to Glory*, 37; Sam Lacy, interview by the author, May 20, 1999; *New York World-Telegram*, October 26, 1945; P. Williams, *The Joe Williams Reader*, 203.

43. *Sporting News*, August 6, 1942; Ribowsky, *Complete History of the Negro Leagues*, 253.

44. Shirley Povich, interview by the author, July 8, 1996.

2. THE COLOR LINE IS DRAWN

1. Reidenbaugh, *"Sporting News'" First Hundred Years*, 14.

2. Seymour, *Baseball*, 350.

3. Reidenbaugh, *"Sporting News'" First Hundred Years*, 19.

4. Reidenbaugh, *"Sporting News'" First Hundred Years*, 162.

5. Voigt, *American Baseball*, 1:95–96; *Sporting News*, January 22, 1887.

6. Voigt, *American Baseball*, 1:95.

7. *Baseball Magazine*, March 1909, 30; October 1910, 67–70, in Voigt, *American Baseball*, 2:95.

8. Recent evidence suggests that a black player, William White, briefly played in the big leagues in 1879.

9. Tygiel, *Baseball's Great Experiment*, 10–12.

10. *Sporting News*, March 23, 1889, quoted in S. White, *Sol White's History of Colored Base Ball*, 137–38.

11. Peterson, *Only the Ball Was White*, 20–21.

12. Zang, *Fleet Walker's Divided Heart*, 37.

13. Ralph Frasca, "Walker Was a Great Favorite," 320.

14. *Toledo Blade*, September 19, 1883, quoted in Zang, *Fleet Walker's Divided Heart*, 38; *Sporting Life*, July 22, 1883; Zang, *Fleet Walker's Divided Heart*, 37.

15. Zang, *Fleet Walker's Divided Heart*, 39.

16. Zang, *Fleet Walker's Divided Heart*, 42, 43.

17. *Louisville Commercial*, May 2, 1884; *St. Louis Globe-Democrat*, May 2, 1884, quoted in Zang, *Fleet Walker's Divided Heart*, 42.

18. Zang, *Fleet Walker's Divided Heart*, 45.

19. *Sporting News*, March 23, 1889. See also S. White, *Sol White's History of Colored Base Ball*, 137–38.

20. *Sporting News*, May 14, 1887.

21. Zang, *Fleet Walker's Divided Heart*, 54.

22. Zang, *Fleet Walker's Divided Heart*, 55.

23. S. White, *Sol White's History of Colored Base Ball*, 137.

24. Zang, *Fleet Walker's Divided Heart*, 55.

25. S. White, *Sol White's History of Colored Base Ball*, 76–78; Zang, *Fleet Walker's Divided Heart*, 54, 56.

26. Peterson, *Only the Ball Was White*, 31–32.

27. Tygiel, *Baseball's Great Experiment*, 10, 12.

28. *New York Times*, September 12, 1887.

29. Rader, *Baseball*, 52.

30. *Washington Post*, July 22, 1890.

31. Logan, *Negro in the United States*, 50.

32. Woodward, *Strange Career of Jim Crow*, 96.

33. Zang, *Fleet Walker's Divided Heart*, book jacket.

34. Voigt, *American Baseball*, 1:279.

35. Woodward, *Strange Career of Jim Crow*, 98–104, 117–18.

36. *Atlanta Constitution*, December 31, 1902.

37. *Baltimore Sun*, March 16, 1901; *Sporting News*, March 23, 1901.

38. *Washington Post*, March 31, 1901; *Sporting Life*, March 23, 1901; *Baltimore American*, March 30, 1901.

39. *Baltimore Sun*, March 30, 1901.

40. *Chicago Tribune*, April 7, 1901; *Sporting Life*, April 20, 1901.

41. See *Washington Post*, May 19, 1901; and *Chicago Tribune*, May 19, 1901.

42. Undated newspaper clipping.

43. W. R. Wilson, "They Could Make the Big Leagues," 115, originally in *Crisis*, October 1934, 305–6.

44. Peterson, *Only the Ball Was White*, 59.

45. Lindholm, "William Clarence Matthews."

46. *Washington Post*, December 5, 1909; Gay, *Satch, Dizzy, and Rapid Robert*, 22, 24.

47. Ward, *Unforgivable Blackness*, 201, 217–18.

48. Rice, *Tumult and Shouting*, 248.

49. *Pittsburgh Courier*, November 3, 1945, quoted in Tygiel, *Baseball's Great Experiment*, 25.

50. Voigt, *American Baseball*, 1:278.

51. Tygiel, *Baseball's Great Experiment*, 25.

52. Lanctot, *Negro League Baseball*, 76.

53. *Washington Post*, May 16, 1912; *New York Times*, May 20, 1912; *Sporting News*, March 30, 1907; *Washington Post*, June 15, 1908.

54. Gay, *Satch, Dizzy, and Rapid Robert*, 23.

55. Knight, "Heywood Broun," 35.

56. Quoted in Henry, *American Carnival*, 78.

57. Fried, *Socialism in America*, 12.

58. Bernstein and Matusow, *Twentieth-Century America*, 1.

59. Pietrusza, *Judge and Jury*, 108.

60. Lanctot, *Negro League Baseball*, 214–15.

61. Moore, *Citizen Klansmen*, 1–3, 7.

62. Pietrusza, *Judge and Jury*, 410–13.

63. Lieb, *Baseball as I Have Known It*, 57–58.

64. Holtzman, *No Cheering in the Press Box*, 221.

65. Lanctot, *Negro League Baseball*, 76.

66. *Sporting News*, December 6, 1923.

67. Pietrusza, *Judge and Jury*, 412.

68. English, "Fred Lieb," 222.

69. Fountain, *Sportswriter*, 6.

70. Orodenker, "Westbrook Pegler," 266; Winchell, "Grantland Rice," 288.

71. Carroll, *When to Stop Cheering?*, 50.

72. Winchell, "Grantland Rice," 286.

73. Fountain, *Sportswriter*, 256.

74. Winchell, "Grantland Rice," 286.

75. Holtzman, *No Cheering in the Press Box*, 18, 23–24.

76. Holtzman, *No Cheering in the Press Box*, 218.

77. Curren, "John Kieran," 170; Crawford, "Arthur Daley," 92.

78. Garrison, *Sports Reporting*, 27.

79. Holtzman, *No Cheering in the Press Box*, 219.

80. Voigt, *American Baseball*, 3:98.

81. *Sporting News*, December 10, 1925, June 13, 1935.

82. Kelley, "Jackie Robinson and the Press," 138.

83. Crepeau, *Baseball*, 165; Kelley, "Jackie Robinson and the Press," 138.

84. *Sporting News*, November 5, 1931.

85. Crepeau, *Baseball*, 165.

86. Farr, *Fair Enough*, 74.

87. Crepeau, *Baseball*, 169, 170.

88. Rogosin, *Invisible Men*, 181.

89. Fountain, *Sportswriter*, 248.

90. Fountain, *Life and Times of Grantland Rice*, 250; Laucella, "Jesse Owens."

91. *New York Daily News*, February 14, 1995.

92. *Daily Worker*, August 15, 1936.

3. INVISIBLE MEN

1. Lacy and Newton, *Fighting for Fairness*, 24.

2. *Philadelphia Daily News*, April 9, 1997; *Washington Herald-American*, n.d., Baseball Hall of Fame, Cooperstown NY.

3. Lacy, interview, May 20, 1999.

4. Lacy, interview, February 17, 1995.

5. Lacy and Newton, *Fighting for Fairness*, 26–27.

6. Lacy, interview, June 24, 1996.

7. Lacy and Newton, *Fighting for Fairness*, 16, 29, 31.

8. Reisler, *Black Writers/Black Baseball*, 12.

9. *Baltimore Afro-American*, November 10, 1945; W. R. Wilson, "They Could Make the Big Leagues," 113–15.

10. Lacy and Newton, *Fighting for Fairness*, 99.

11. Reisler, *Black Writers/Black Baseball*, 2.

12. Carroll, *When to Stop the Cheering?*, 45.

13. Weaver, "Black Press," 303; Lacy, interview, June 24, 1996; DuBois, "Strivings of the Negro People," n.p.

14. Myrdal, *American Dilemma*, 908.

15. Wolseley, *The Black Press, U.S.A.*, 17–23.

16. Pride and Wilson, *History of the Black Press*, 85.

17. Wolseley, *The Black Press, U.S.A.*, 41–42.

18. Wolseley, *The Black Press, U.S.A.*, 42; Simmons, *African American Press*, 6; Pride and Wilson, *History of the Black Press*, 127.

19. Wolseley, *The Black Press, U.S.A.*, 27, 37.

20. *Chicago Defender*, June 13, 1942.

21. "Frank (Fay) Young," in *Dictionary of Literary Biography*, http://www.bookrags.com/biography/frank-a-fay-young/dlb/.

22. Reisler, *Black Writers/Black Baseball*, 57–59.

23. Rogosin, *Invisible Men*, 3.

24. S. White, *Sol White's History of Colored Base Ball*, 16.

25. S. White, *Sol White's History of Colored Base Ball*, 76–77.

26. S. White, *Sol White's History of Colored Base Ball*, 67, 77, 78.

27. Overmyer, *Effa Manley and the Newark Eagles*, 269.

28. Lanctot, *Negro League Baseball*, 24–25.

29. Rogosin, *Invisible Men*, 33.

30. Lanctot, *Negro League Baseball*, 9.

31. Woodward, *Strange Career of Jim Crow*, 114.

32. Simmons, *African American Press*, 29.

33. Pride and Wilson, *History of the Black Press*, 136–37.

34. Simmons, *African American Press*, 37.

35. Tuttle, *Race Riot*, 92–94.

36. Simmons, *African American Press*, 36.

37. Tuttle, *Race Riot*, 80–82, 91.
38. DuBois, "Fighting against Racism," 190.
39. Franklin, *From Slavery to Freedom*, 472.
40. Lindsey, *History of Black America*, 98.
41. Tuttle, *Race Riot*, 106–7.
42. Lewis, *W. E. B. Du Bois*, 56.
43. Tuttle, *Race Riot*, 217.
44. Lindsey, *History of Black America*, 100.
45. Franklin, *From Slavery to Freedom*, 478–79.
46. Franklin, *From Slavery to Freedom*, 479.
47. Woodward, *Strange Career of Jim Crow*, 114–15.
48. Woodward, *Strange Career of Jim Crow*, 115.
49. Wolseley, *The Black Press, U.S.A.*, 53.
50. Tuttle, *Race Riot*, 23.
51. Tuttle, *Race Riot*, 242.
52. W. White, "Chicago and Its Eight Reasons," 275.
53. Simmons, *African American Press*, 47.
54. Buni, *Robert L. Vann of "Pittsburgh Courier,"* 72–77.
55. Simmons, *African American Press*, 47.
56. Pride and Wilson, *History of the Black Press*, 136–37.
57. Wiggins, "Wendell Smith," 10.
58. Detweiler, *Negro Press in the United States*, 80.
59. Lenthall, "Covering More than the Game," 62–64.
60. Carroll, *When to Stop the Cheering?*, 28, 30, 36, 37, 60.
61. Rogosin, *Invisible Men*, 33.
62. Tygiel, *Baseball's Great Experiment*, 16, 20.
63. Peterson, *Only the Ball Was White*, 115.
64. Carroll, *When to Stop the Cheering?*, 48, 65; S. White, *Sol White's History of Colored Base Ball*, 153.
65. Carroll, *When to Stop the Cheering?*, 48.
66. Lester, *Black Baseball's National Showcase*, 5.
67. Lacy, *Fighting for Fairness*, 6, 23, 27, 31, 35.
68. Rogosin, *Invisible Men*, 6, 8; Rust, *"Get That Nigger Off the Field!"* 16.
69. Rogosin, *Invisible Men*, 25.
70. Carroll, *When to Stop the Cheering?*, 82, 83.
71. Ribowsky, *Complete History of the Negro Leagues*, 177.

72. Lester, *Black Baseball's National Showcase*, 2.

73. *Philadelphia Tribune*, August 7, 1941, quoted in Reisler, *Black Writers/Black Baseball*, 150–51.

74. *Baltimore Afro-American*, November 7, 1931; *Pittsburgh Courier*, March 7, 1936, quoted in Reisler, *Black Writers/Black Baseball*, 101.

75. *Philadelphia Tribune*, August 6, 1936, quoted in Reisler, *Black Writers/Black Baseball*, 149–51.

76. *Philadelphia Tribune*, August 6, 1936, quoted in Reisler, *Black Writers/Black Baseball*, 149–51.

77. *Baltimore Afro-American*, June 1, 1940, April 1, 1939.

78. Lacy and Newton, *Fighting for Fairness*, 45.

79. Lacy, interview, May 20, 1999.

80. DuBois, "Negro Editors on Communism," 700, 708.

81. Patterson, *Man Who Cried Genocide*, 142.

82. Carroll, *When to Stop the Cheering?*, 92; *Baltimore Afro-American*, April 1, 1939.

83. Tygiel, *Baseball's Great Experiment*, 39.

84. Peterson, *Only the Ball Was White*, 169.

85. Tygiel, *Baseball's Great Experiment*, 35; Wendell Smith Papers.

86. *Pittsburgh Courier*, May 11, 1938.

87. Wiggins, "Wendell Smith," 28.

88. Wiggins, "Wendell Smith," 11.

89. Smith Papers.

4. "AGITATORS" AND "SOCIAL-MINDED DRUM BEATERS"

1. The *Worker*'s Sunday edition was called the *Sunday Worker*. This book refers to all references to the newspapers as the *Daily Worker*.

2. Lester Rodney, interview by the author, November 11, 1997.

3. Tygiel, *Baseball's Great Experiment*, 37.

4. Carroll, *When to Stop the Cheering?*, 104–5; Rampersad, *Jackie Robinson*, 120; Patterson, "Against Jim Crow," 378.

5. Bill Mardo, interview by the author, November 18, 1997; Rodney, interview, November 11, 1997.

6. Rodney, interview, November 11, 1997; Naison, "Lefties and Righties," 140.

7. Klein, "Sports Reporting in New York City," 27.

8. Mardo, interview, November 18, 1997.

9. Fried, *Socialism in America*, 12.

10. Kessler, *Dissident Press*, 129.

11. Kennedy, *Over Here*, 46; Stevens, *Shaping the First Amendment*, 45.

12. *Debs v. United States*, 249 U.S. 211, 39 S.Ct. 252, 63 L.Ed. 566 (1919).

13. Conlin, *Radical Press in America*, 1:574; Pietrusza, *Judge and Jury*, 120–37.

14. Morgan, *Reds*, 78–80.

15. Buhle and Georgakas, *Encyclopedia of the American Left*, 148.

16. *Fighting Words*, xi, xiii.

17. Simon, *As We Saw the Thirties*, 218–19.

18. Howe and Coser, *American Communist Party*, 362.

19. Rusinack, "Baseball on the Radical Agenda," 3.

20. Naison, "Lefties and Righties," 136.

21. Glazer, *Social Basis of American Communism*, 169.

22. Silber, *Press Box Red*, 9–10.

23. *Daily Worker*, January 2, 1934, quoted in Silber, *Press Box Red*, 3–4.

24. *New York World-Telegram*, August 10, 1938, quoted in Silber, *Press Box Red*, 33–34.

25. *Daily Worker*, December 19, 1939.

26. Silber, *Press Box Red*, 20–22.

27. "View from Left Field."

28. *San Francisco Chronicle*, July 10, 2005.

29. Klein, "Sports Reporting in New York City," 20.

30. Quoted in Norwood and Brackman, "Going to Bat for Jackie Robinson," 119.

31. Rodney, interview, November 11, 1997.

32. Silber, *Press Box Red*, 55–56.

33. *Daily Worker*, August 23, 1936.

34. Silber, *Press Box Red*, 144–47.

35. Silber, *Press Box Red*, x, 56.

36. *Daily Worker*, August 30, 1936.

37. Rodney, interview, November 11, 1997.

38. *Daily Worker*, January 17, 1937.

39. Silber, *Press Box Red*, 64.

40. Rodney, interview, November 11, 1997.

41. Silber, *Press Box Red*, 62.

42. *Daily Worker*, April 18, 1937, September 13, 1938.

43. *Daily Worker*, February 15, 1937.

44. Silber, *Press Box Red*, 68.

45. Rodney, interview, November 11, 1997.

46. Lacy, interview, May 20, 1999; Rodney, interview, November 11, 1997.

47. *Daily Worker*, January 10, 1938.

48. Silber, *Press Box Red*, 34.

49. Rodney, interview, November 11, 1997.

50. Silber, *Press Box Red*, 36–37.

51. Rodney, interview, November 11, 1997.

52. Silber, *Press Box Red*, 35.

53. Silber, *Press Box Red*, 72.

54. *Daily Worker*, February 3, 1943.

55. *Daily Worker*, February 21, 1937.

56. "Striking Out Jim Crow," *Young Communist Review*, September 1939, quoted in Rusinack, "Baseball on the Radical Agenda," 113; Silber, *Press Box Red*, 72.

5. "*L'AFFAIRE* JAKE POWELL"

1. Rogosin, *Invisible Men*, 192.

2. Rogosin, "Black Baseball," 234.

3. *Nation*, August 6, 1938.

4. *Washington Post*, November 5, 1948.

5. *Dayton Journal*, November 5, 1948.

6. *Washington Post*, November 5, 1948.

7. *Dayton Journal*, November 5, 1948.

8. *New York Times*, June 15, 1936.

9. *Washington Post*, June 15, 1936.

10. *New York Age*, August 6, 1938; *Pittsburgh Courier*, August 27, 1938.

11. *Washington Post*, June 15, 1938.

12. *Sporting News*, November 10, 1948.

13. *Sporting News*, August 4, 1938; *Daily Worker*, August 2, 1938.

14. Ribowsky, *Complete History of the Negro Leagues*, 254.

15. *Sporting News*, November 17, 1948.

16. *Sporting News*, August 4, 1938.

17. *Portsmouth (OH) Times*, July 31, 1938.

18. *Chicago Defender*, August 6, 1938.

19. This Associated Press account was published throughout the country in newspapers such as the *Norfolk Virginian-Pilot*, July 31, 1938, and *Portsmouth (OH) Times*, July 31, 1938.

20. *New York Times*, July 30, 1938; *Washington Post*, July 31, August 1, 1938; *New York Herald Tribune* (Paris edition), July 31, 1938; *Dayton Daily News*, July 31, 1938; *Sporting News*, August 4, 1938.

21. *Dayton Forum*, August 5, 1938; *Baltimore Afro-American*, August 6, 1938; *New York Age*, August 6, 1938; *Pittsburgh Courier*, August 6, 1938; *Philadelphia Afro-American*, August 20, 1938, quoted in Crepeau, "Jake Powell Incident," 45; *Philadelphia Tribune*, August 4, 1938; *Chicago Defender*, August 13, 1946.

22. *Chicago Defender*, August 6, 1946.

23. *Norfolk Virginian-Pilot*, July 31, 1938.

24. *Daily Worker*, August 1, 1938.

25. *Chicago Daily News*, July 30, 1938; Pietrusza, *Judge and Jury*, 415–16; *New York Herald Tribune* (Paris edition), July 31, 1938.

26. *Pittsburgh Courier*, August 6, 1938.

27. *Norfolk Journal and Guide*, August 13, 1938.

28. *Chicago Defender*, August 6, 1938.

29. *Sporting News*, August 4, 1938.

30. *Los Angeles Times*, August 2, 1938.

31. *Chicago Daily News*, August 4, 1938; *Washington Post*, August 5, 1938.

32. *Washington Post*, August 5, 1938.

33. *Los Angeles Times*, August 15, 1938; *New York Post*, August 4, 1938; *Nation*, August 6, 1938; *Daily Worker*, August 2, 11, 13, 1938.

34. *Dayton Daily News*, July 31, 1938; *Dayton Journal*, August 17, 1938; *Dayton Forum*, August 5, 1938; *Chicago Defender*, August 6, 1938.

35. *Baltimore Afro-American*, August 6, 1938; *Norfolk Journal and Guide*, August 6, 1938; *Philadelphia Tribune*, August 4, 1938.

36. *Chicago Defender*, August 6, 1938.

37. *Chicago Defender*, August 6, 1938.

38. *Dayton Forum*, August 12, 1938.

39. *Chicago Defender*, August 20, 1938.

40. *New York Age*, October 1, 1938.

41. *Amsterdam News*, August 13, 1938. *New York Age*, October 1, 1938.

42. Crepeau, "Jake Powell Incident," 38.

43. *New York Age*, August 13, 1938.

44. *Chicago Defender*, August 20, 1938.

45. *New York Age*, August 20, 1938.

46. *Pittsburgh Courier*, August 13, 1938.

47. *New York Age*, August 20, 1938.

48. *New York Times*, August 17, 1938.

49. *Sporting News*, August 25, 1938.

50. *Washington Post*, August 17, 1938; *Sporting News*, August 25, 1938; *Daily Worker*, September 11, 1938; *Philadelphia Tribune*, August 25, 1938.

51. *Chicago Defender*, August 13, 1938.

52. *Chicago Defender*, August 6, 13, 20, 1938.

53. *Chicago Defender*, August 6, 1938.

54. *Chicago Defender*, August 27, 1938.

55. Crepeau, "Jake Powell Incident," 44.

56. *Chicago Defender*, September 17, 1938.

57. *Chicago Defender*, April 22, 1939.

58. Levitt, *Ed Barrow*, 314.

59. *Baltimore Afro-American*, February 11, 1939; *Chicago Defender*, March 25, April 8, 1939.

60. *Washington Post*, September 19, December 11, 1940.

61. *Washington Post*, November 1, 1944, April 11, 1945.

62. *Dayton Journal*, November 5, 1948.

63. *Washington Post*, November 5, 1948.

64. *Dayton Journal*, November 5, 1948.

65. *Washington Post*, November 5, 1948.

66. *Dayton Daily News*, November 6, 1948.

67. *New York Times*, November 5, 1948; *Dayton Daily News*, July 2, 1996.

68. *Chicago Defender*, November 13, 1948; Lacy, interview, July 10, 1996; Povich, interview, July 8, 1996; *Sporting News*, November 10, 1948.

69. *Sporting News*, November 17, 1948.

70. *Sporting News*, November 17, 1948.

71. Crepeau, "Jake Powell Incident," 36.

72. Crepeau, "Jake Powell Incident," 44–45; *Dayton Forum*, August 12, 1938.

6. MANAGERS AND BALLPLAYERS CALL FOR END OF COLOR LINE

1. *Pittsburgh Courier*, February 25, 1939.

2. *Pittsburgh Courier*, February 25, 1939.

3. *Pittsburgh Courier*, February 25, 1939.

4. *Pittsburgh Courier*, February 25, 1939.

5. *Pittsburgh Courier*, February 25, 1939.

6. Lovell, "Washington Fights," 370–72.

7. Boston, *1939 — Baseball's Tipping Point*, xv; *Washington Post*, April 7, 1939.

8. *Pittsburgh Courier*, March 11, 1939.

9. Smith, untitled article, Smith Papers, courtesy of the National Baseball Hall of Fame.

10. *Pittsburgh Courier*, July 15, 1939.

11. *Pittsburgh Courier*, July 15, 1939.

12. *Pittsburgh Courier*, July 22, 1939.

13. *Pittsburgh Courier*, July 22, 1939.

14. *Pittsburgh Courier*, July 29, 1939.

15. *Pittsburgh Courier*, July 29, August 5, 1939. Wendell Smith spelled the man's name *Red*. See Durocher and Linn, *Nice Guys Finish Last*, where it is spelled *Redd*.

16. *Pittsburgh Courier*, August 5, 1939.

17. *Pittsburgh Courier*, August 5, 1939.

18. *Pittsburgh Courier*, August 12, 1939.

19. *Pittsburgh Courier*, August 12, 1939.

20. *Pittsburgh Courier*, August 19, 1939.

21. Boston, *1939 — Baseball's Tipping Point*, 167–69.

22. *Chicago Defender*, August 19, 1939.

23. *Baltimore Afro-American*, August 5, 1939.

24. Tygiel, *Baseball's Great Experiment*, 28.

25. *Pittsburgh Courier*, September 9, 1939.

26. *Chicago Defender*, September 30, 1939.

27. *Pittsburgh Courier*, September 2, 1939.

28. *Pittsburgh Courier*, September 2, 1939.

29. *Pittsburgh Courier*, August 12, 1939.

30. *Pittsburgh Courier*, August 5, September 2, 1939.

31. *Chicago Defender*, September 9, 1939.

32. *Daily Worker*, March 26, 1939. See also Rusinack, "Baseball on the Radical Agenda," 96–97.

33. *Daily Worker*, July 23, 1939. See also Rusinack, "Baseball on the Radical Agenda," 104–5.

34. Rusinack, "Baseball on the Radical Agenda," 107–8.

35. *Daily Worker*, August 20, 1939.

36. *Baltimore Afro-American*, November 10, 1945.

37. Rampersad, *Jackie Robinson*, 163–64.

38. Stout, "Tryout and Fallout," 6.

39. Rust, *Get That Nigger Off the Field*, 6.

40. Smith, untitled article, Smith Papers.

41. Smith, untitled article, Smith Papers.

42. *Pittsburgh Courier*, January 14, 1939.

7. THE DOUBLE V CAMPAIGN

1. Rusinack, "Baseball on the Radical Agenda," 191–20.

2. *Daily Worker*, January 2, 1940. See also Rusinack, "Baseball on the Radical Agenda," 121.

3. Rusinack, "Baseball on the Radical Agenda," 122.

4. Rusinack, "Baseball on the Radical Agenda," 126–30.

5. *Daily Worker*, April 13, 1940; *Chicago Defender*, May 18, 1940; *Crisis*, June 1940.

6. Lanctot, *Negro League Baseball*, 227.

7. Shane, "Chocolate Rube Waddell," 26, 79–81; *Chicago Defender*, August 3, 1940.

8. *Washington Post*, July 22, 1941.

9. Rusinack, "Baseball on the Radical Agenda," 137.

10. *Daily Worker*, July 25, 1940, quoted in Rusinack, "Baseball on the Radical Agenda," 144.

11. Schaffer, *Vito Marcantonio*, 20–26, 52, 65.

12. *Daily Worker*, July 31, 1942.

13. Kirby, "Roosevelt Administration and Blacks," 286.

14. H. Wilson, "Jim Crow Army," 403–4.

15. Yergan, "Democracy and the Negro People Today," 391, 395.

16. Kirby, "Roosevelt Administration and Blacks," 268.

17. Myrdal, *America Dilemma*, 74; Kirby, "Roosevelt Administration and Blacks," 280; DuBois, "Race Relations in the United States," 42.

18. Roberts and Klibanoff, *The Race Beat*, 10–12.

19. Wolseley, *The Black Press, U.S.A.*, 63.

20. Franklin, *From Slavery to Freedom*, 494, 579–80, 593.

21. Washburn, *African-American Newspaper*, 145–46.

22. Washburn, *African-American Newspaper*, 143–44.

23. Washburn, *African-American Newspaper*, 144–47.

24. *New York Age*, April 8, 1942.

25. Aldridge, "Let's Look at the Record," 518.

26. Lewis, *W. E. B. Du Bois*, 466.

27. *New York Daily Mirror*, July 18, 1942.

28. Franklin, *From Slavery to Freedom*, 588.

29. Washburn, *African-American Newspaper*, 146.

30. E. Brown, "Detroit Race Riot of 1943," 451.

31. *California Eagle* (Los Angeles), April 9, 1942.

32. Washburn, *African-American Newspaper*, 155–59, 166–68.

33. Washburn, *"Pittsburgh Courier's* Double V Campaign," 80.

34. *Chicago Defender*, May 18, 1940.

35. *California Eagle* (Los Angeles), April 30, 1942.

36. *New York Age*, June 27, 1942; *New York People's Voice*, July 4, 1942.

37. Wolseley, *The Black Press, U.S.A.*, 55–56.

38. Wolseley, *The Black Press, U.S.A.*, 83.

39. Tygiel, *Baseball's Great Experiment*, 36.

40. Myrdal, *American Dilemma*, 924; Pride and Wilson, *History of the Black Press*, 155–56.

41. Washburn, *Question of Sedition*, 87.

42. *Philadelphia Tribune*, April 11, 1942.

43. *New York People's Voice*, March 21, 1942, quoted in Reisler, *Black Writers/Black Baseball*, 77–79.

44. Lanctot, *Negro League Baseball*, 232.

45. *Pittsburgh Courier*, March 21, 1946.

46. *New York World-Telegram*, July 27, 1942.

47. *Daily Worker*, May 6, 1942.

48. Patterson, *Man Who Cried Genocide*, 141–42.

49. *Chicago Defender*, May 30, June 13, 1942.

50. *Chicago Defender*, June 13, 1942.

51. Quoted in Gems, "Selling Sport and Religion," 300–312.

52. *Pittsburgh Courier*, May 30, 1942, quoted in Reisler, *Black Writers/Black Baseball*, 109–11.

53. *Daily Worker*, June 30, 1942.

54. Pietrusza, *Judge and Jury*, 417.

55. *Chicago Defender*, June 27, 1942.

56. *Chicago Defender*, June 13, 1942; *Daily Worker*, July 13, 1942.

57. *Daily Worker*, June 28, 1942.

58. *Washington Post*, August 2, 1942.

59. *Pittsburgh Courier*, July 25, 1942.

60. Washburn, *African-American Newspaper*, 145.

61. *Philadelphia Tribune*, July 25, 1942.

62. *San Francisco Chronicle*, July 27, 1942.

63. Roy Campanella, *It's Good to Be Alive*, 96–98.

64. *Daily Worker*, July 16, 1942.

65. *Washington Post*, August 1, 1942.

66. *Baltimore Afro-American*, July 28, 1942.

67. *Pittsburgh Courier*, August 1, 1942.

8. "THE GREAT WHITE FATHER" SPEAKS

1. *Daily Worker*, June 24, 1942.

2. Pietrusza, *Judge and Jury*, 418–19.

3. *Daily Worker*, June 24, 1942.

4. *Daily Worker*, June 25, 1942.

5. *Chicago Defender*, July 11, 1942; *Daily Worker*, July 14, 15, August 29, 1942.

6. *Pittsburgh Courier*, July 25, 1942.

7. *New York Herald Tribune*, July 17, 1942.

8. *Chicago Defender*, July 25, 1942.

9. *Chicago Defender*, August 1, 1942; *New York Age*, July 25, 1942.

10. *Pittsburgh Courier*, July 25, 1942.

11. *New York People's Voice*, July 25, 1942.

12. *New York P.M.*, July 19, 1942.

13. *New York Daily Mirror*, July 21, 1942.

14. *New York Daily News*, July 21, 1942.

15. *New York Post*, July 21, 1942; *Daily Worker*, August 10, 1942.

16. *Amsterdam News*, August 1, 1942; *New York Post*, July 28, 1942.

17. *New York World-Telegram*, July 27, 1942; *New York Journal American*, July 23, 1946, July 26, 1942.

18. *New York Morning Telegraph*, July 18, 1942; *Daily Worker*, July 22, 1942.

19. Smith Papers.

20. *Daily Worker*, July 18, 19, 22, 1942; *New York Age*, August 8, 1942.

21. *New York P.M.*, July 19, 20, 1942; *New York Herald Tribune*, July 18, 1942.

22. *Daily Worker*, July 26, 27, 28, 1942.

23. *Daily Worker*, July 27, 1942.

24. *New York Daily News*, July 26, 1942.

25. *Chicago Daily Tribune*, July 26, 1942.

26. *Pittsburgh Press*, July 27, 1942; *Pittsburgh Post-Gazette*, July 27, 1942.

27. *Pittsburgh Courier*, August 1, 1942.

28. *Chicago Defender*, August 1, 1942.

29. *New York P.M.*, July 17, 1942.

30. Pietrusza, *Judge and Jury*, 418.

31. *Washington Post*, July 28, 1942.

32. *Baltimore Afro-American*, August 1, 1942.

33. *Chicago Defender*, August 8, 1942.

34. *Philadelphia Tribune*, August 22, 1942.

35. *New York People's Voice*, July 11, 1942.

36. *New York World-Telegram*, July 20, 1942.

37. *Chicago Defender*, August 8, 1942.

38. *New York People's Voice*, August 8, 1942.

39. *New York P.M.*, July 27, 1942.

40. *Daily Worker*, August 4, 26, 28, 1942.

41. *Daily Worker*, July 29, 1942; *Philadelphia Tribune*, August 1, 1942.

42. *Daily Worker*, August 6, 1942; *Baltimore Afro-American*, August 4, 1942.

43. *Daily Worker*, August 3, 4, 7, 1942.

44. *Washington Post*, August 1, 1942.

45. *Chicago Defender*, August 15, 1942.

46. *Washington Post*, August 15, 1942.

47. *New York Age*, August 15, 1942; Tye, *Satchel*, 194.

48. *Baltimore Afro-American*, August 15, 1942.

49. *Chicago Defender*, September 26, 1942.

50. *Baltimore Afro-American*, September 19, 1942.

51. *Pittsburgh Courier*, August 1, 1942; *New York Times*, August 21, 1942.

52. *New York Times*, September 3, 1942.

53. *Chicago Defender*, September 12, 1942

54. *Baltimore Afro-American*, August 29, 1942.

55. *Chicago Defender*, August 29, 1942.

56. *Chicago Defender*, September 26, 1942.

57. *Amsterdam News*, September 19, 1942.

58. Milkman, *"P.M.": A New Deal in Journalism*, 155.

59. *Baltimore Afro-American*, September 26, 1942.

60. *Chicago Defender*, October 10, 1942.

61. *Amsterdam News*, August 8, September 12, 1942, January 23, 1943.

62. *Baltimore Afro-American*, September 19, 1942.

63. *Daily Worker*, September 1, 3, October 14, 16, 21, 1942.

64. *Daily Worker*, November 2, 1942.

9. BLACK EDITORS MAKE THEIR CASE FOR DESEGREGATION

1. Pietrusza, *Judge and Jury*, 432–33.

2. *Chicago Defender*, December 12, 1942.

3. *Daily Worker*, December 3, 1942.

4. *Chicago Defender*, December 12, 1942.

5. *Washington Post*, December 4, 1942; *Sporting News*, December 10, 1942.

6. *Chicago Defender*, December 12, 1942.

7. *Amsterdam News*, December 12, 1942.

8. *Daily Worker*, December 5, 7, 1942.

9. *New York Age*, December 12, 1942.

10. *Daily Worker*, December 2, 4, 5, 1942.

11. *Chicago Defender*, December 26, 1942.

12. Patterson, *Man Who Cried Genocide*, 143.

13. *Chicago Defender*, December 26, 1942.

14. *Amsterdam News*, January 16, 1943.

15. *Chicago Defender*, February 6, 1942, February 20, 1943.

16. *Amsterdam News*, December 26, 1942.

17. *Baltimore Afro-American*, December 12, 1942.

18. *Amsterdam News*, November 17, 1942.

19. *Daily Worker*, December 12, 1942.

20. Pietrusza, *Judge and Jury*, 361.

21. Tygiel, *Baseball's Great Experiment*, 50.

22. Lowenfish, *Branch Rickey*, 351–52.

23. *Amsterdam News*, January 13, 23, 1943.

24. *Chicago Defender*, December 12, 1942, May 15, 1943.

25. *Chicago Defender*, May 15, June 5, 1943.

26. Lowenfish, *Branch Rickey*, 326.

27. Mann, *Branch Rickey*, 212–14.

28. Lowenfish, *Branch Rickey*, 349.

29. Veeck and Linn, *Veeck — as in Wreck*, 173–75.

30. Tygiel, *Baseball's Great Experiment*, 40–41; Pietrusza, *Judge and Jury*, 422–23.

31. Jordan, Gerlach, and Rossi, "Baseball Myth Exploded."

32. Jordan, Gerlach, and Rossi, "Baseball Myth Exploded," 6.

33. Jordan, Gerlach, and Rossi, "Baseball Myth Exploded," 9, 11.

34. Tygiel, "Revisiting Bill Veeck," 112.

35. Tygiel, "Revisiting Bill Veeck," 112, 114.

36. Tygiel, "Revisiting Bill Veeck," 113, 112.

37. Tygiel, "Revisiting Bill Veeck," 114.

38. *Chicago Defender*, May 15, 1943.

39. Franklin, *From Slavery to Freedom*, 598.

40. E. Brown, "Detroit Race Riot of 1943," 451; Kessner, *Fiorello H. La Guardia*, 532.

41. E. Brown, "Detroit Race Riot of 1943," 452–53.

42. Tuttle, *Race Riot*, 267.

43. Kessner, *Fiorello H. La Guardia*, 532.

44. *New York Times*, August 3, 1943.

45. Kessner, *Fiorello H. La Guardia*, 532.

46. *Chicago Defender*, July 24, 1943.

47. Lacy and Newton, *Fighting for Fairness*, 40.

48. Lacy and Newton, *Fighting for Fairness*, 45; *Baltimore Afro-American*, January 8, 1944.

49. Pietrusza, *Judge and Jury*, 424–25.

50. Lacy and Newton, *Fighting for Fairness*, 45–46; Pietrusza, *Judge and Jury*, 425.

51. Lacy and Newton, *Fighting for Fairness*, 45; *New York P.M.*, November 30, 1943.

52. Duberman, *Paul Robeson*, 283.

53. Pietrusza, *Judge and Jury*, 425.

54. *Pittsburgh Courier*, December 11, 1943.

55. *Chicago Defender*, December 11, 1943.

56. *Chicago Defender*, December 11, 1943.

57. *Pittsburgh Courier*, December 11, 1943.

58. *Chicago Defender*, December 11, 1943.

59. Pietrusza, *Judge and Jury*, 426.

60. *Pittsburgh Courier*, December 11, 1943.

61. *Baltimore Afro-American*, December 11, 1943.

62. *Sporting News*, December 9, 1943; *New York Times*, December 4, 1943.

63. *New York P.M.*, December 2, 5, 1942.

64. *Chicago Defender*, December 11, 1943.

65. *Pittsburgh Courier*, December 11, 1943.

66. *Baltimore Afro-American*, December 11, 1943; *Chicago Defender*, December 8, 1944; Duberman, *Paul Robeson*, 282.

67. Lacy and Newton, *Fighting for Fairness*, 45, 46.

68. *Chicago Defender*, December 25, 1943.

69. *Baltimore Afro-American*, January 1, 1944.

70. *Chicago Defender*, December 19, 1942.

71. *Pittsburgh Courier*, December 18, 1943.

72. Carroll, *When to Stop the Cheering?*, 132.

73. Lanctot, *Negro League Baseball*, 142.

74. Lanctot, *Negro League Baseball*, 253.

75. Tygiel, *Baseball's Great Experiment*, 37; Barck and Blake, *Since 1900*, 749.

76. Tygiel, *Baseball's Great Experiment*, 7; Conrad, *Jim Crow America*, 73.

77. Rampersad, *Jackie Robinson*, 96.

78. N. Williams, "Beaten Half to Death," 486.

79. Reynolds, "What the Negro Soldier Thinks," 487.

80. W. White, "World Supremacy and World War II."

81. Rampersad, *Jackie Robinson*, 102–9.

82. *New York Times*, November 26, 1944.

83. Lowenfish, *Branch Rickey*, 359; Lacy and Newton, *Fighting for Fairness*, 42, 47.

84. Tygiel, *Baseball's Great Experiment*, 38.

85. Lowenfish, *Branch Rickey*, 359.

86. *Chicago Defender*, February 10, March 31, 1945.

87. *Pittsburgh Courier*, March 31, April 28, 1945.

88. *Chicago Defender*, May 5, 1945.

89. *Pittsburgh Courier* April 28, 1945.

90. Schaffer, *Vito Marcantonio*, 151.

91. *Chicago Defender*, May 5, 1945.

92. Davis, *Communist Councilman from Harlem*, 132–34.

93. *New York Daily Mirror*, April 7, 1945.

94. Lowenfish, *Branch Rickey*, 377.

95. Barber and Creamer, *Rhubarb in the Catbird Seat*, 69.

96. Norwood and Brackman, "Going to Bat for Jackie Robinson," 124.

97. *New York Post*, April 6, 1945.

98. *Pittsburgh Courier*, April 14, 1945.

10. "GET THOSE NIGGERS OFF THE FIELD"

1. *New York People's Voice*, April 14, 1945.

2. *New York People's Voice*, April 14, 1945.

3. Roeder, *Jackie Robinson*, 10.

4. *Sporting News*, April 12, 1945.

5. Rodney, interview, November 11, 1997.

6. *New York People's Voice*, April 14, 1945.

7. *Sporting News*, April 12, 1945.

8. *New York Post*, April 17, 945.

9. *New York Daily Mirror*, April 7, 1945.

10. *New York Herald Tribune*, April 7, 1945.

11. *Sporting News*, April 12, 1945.

12. *New York Post*, August 6, 1942; *New York P.M.*, April 8, 1945.

13. *New York Herald Tribune*, April 7, 1945.

14. *New York People's Voice*, April 14, 1945.

15. *Sporting News*, April 12, 1945.

16. *Sporting News*, April 12, 1945.

17. Lowenfish, *Branch Rickey*, 362.

18. *New York People's Voice*, April 14, 1945.

19. *New York Herald Tribune*, April 8, 1945.

20. Riley, *Biographical Encyclopedia*, 534–36, 775–76.

21. Lowenfish, *Branch Rickey*, 362.

22. *New York World-Telegram*, April 7, 1945.

23. *New York Herald Tribune*, April 8, 1945.

24. *New York P.M.*, April 12, 1945.

25. *New York Daily News*, April 8, 1945.

26. *New York Daily Mirror*, April 8, 1945.

27. *Daily Worker*, April 8, 1945; *Pittsburgh Courier*, April 14, 1945.

28. *New York Daily Mirror*, April 8, 1945.

29. *New York Daily News*, April 8, 1945.

30. *New York Daily Mirror*, April 13, 21, 1945.

31. *New York Daily News*, April 8, 1945; *Sporting News*, April 12, 1945; *New York Daily News*, April 8, 1945.

32. *New York Herald Tribune*, April 8, 1945; *New York Daily Mirror*, April 8, 1945; *New York Daily News*, April 8, 1945.

33. *New York Herald Tribune*, April 8, 1945; *New York World-Telegram*, April 8, 1945; *New York Times*, April 8, 1945.

34. Roeder, *Jackie Robinson*, 10; *New York People's Voice*, April 14, 1945.

35. *Daily Worker*, April 7, 8, 22, 1945.

36. *Pittsburgh Courier*, April 14, 1945.

37. *New York Amsterdam News*, April 14, 1945; *Baltimore Afro-American*, April 7, 1945.

38. *New York Amsterdam News*, April 14, 1945.

39. *Chicago Defender*, April 14, 1945.

40. *New York People's Voice*, April 28, 1945.

41. Stout, "Tryout and Fallout."

42. Tygiel, *Baseball's Great Experiment*, 44.

43. Rampersad, *Jackie Robinson*, 119.

44. Stout, "Tryout and Fallout."

45. Smith Papers.

46. Norwood and Brackman, "Going to Bat for Jackie Robinson," 124–25.

47. Stout, "Tryout and Fallout."

48. *Pittsburgh Courier*, April 21, 1945.

49. Stout, "Tryout and Fallout."

50. *Boston Herald*, April 17, 1945.

51. Smith Papers.

52. Roeder, *Jackie Robinson*, 14.

53. Rampersad, *Jackie Robinson*, 120.

54. *Pittsburgh Courier*, April 28, 1945.

55. Smith Papers.

56. *Boston Globe*, April 16, 17, 1945.

57. *Boston Herald*, April 17, 1945; *Sporting News*, April 19, 1945; Stout, "Tryout and Fallout."

58. Bryant, *Shut Out*, 26.

59. Stout, "Tryout and Fallout."

60. Tygiel, *Baseball's Great Experiment*, 44.

61. Stout, "Tryout and Fallout."

62. *Chicago Defender*, May 12, April 28, 1945; *New York P.M.*, April 18, 1945; *New York Daily Mirror*, April 19, 1945; *Washington Afro-American*, April 28, 1945.

63. Lacy and Newton, *Fighting for Fairness*, 47–48.

64. Tygiel, *Baseball's Great Experiment*, 42.

65. *Chicago Defender*, May 5, 1945.

66. *Pittsburgh Courier*, May 12, 1945.

67. Rogosin, *Invisible Men*, 199.

68. *Chicago Defender*, May 12, 1945.

69. *Daily Worker*, May 5, 1945.

70. *Baltimore Afro-American*, June 16, July 14, 1945.

71. Lacy and Newton, *Fighting for Fairness*, 57.

72. Tygiel, *Baseball's Great Experiment*, 42.

73. *Sporting News*, May 24, 1945.

74. Rowan and Robinson, *Wait Till Next Year*, 104; Rampersad, *Jackie Robinson*, 123; Tygiel, *Baseball's Great Experiment*, 47.

75. Rowan and Robinson, *Wait Till Next Year*, 104; Rampersad, *Jackie Robinson*, 123; Tygiel, *Baseball's Great Experiment*, 47.

76. Rowan and Robinson, *Wait Till Next Year*, 104; Rampersad, *Jackie Robinson*, 123; Tygiel, *Baseball's Great Experiment*, 47.

77. *New York Age*, November 3, 1945; *Chicago Defender*, May 26, 1945.

78. *Amsterdam News*, May 19, 12, 5, 1945.

79. *New York Daily Mirror*, May 10, 1942.

80. *Sporting News*, May 24, 1945.

81. *Baltimore Afro-American*, June 2, 1945.

82. *Pittsburgh Courier*, May 19, 1945.

83. Smith Papers.

84. Smith Papers.

85. *Negro Baseball*, April 1945, quoted in Tygiel, *Baseball's Great Experiment*, 63–64.

86. *Baltimore Afro-American*, September 29, 1945.

87. Lowenfish, *Branch Rickey*, 365.

88. *Baltimore Afro-American*, March 31, 1945.

89. *Daily Worker*, April 19, 1945.

90. *New York Times*, April 18, May 2, 1945.

91. *Baltimore Afro-American*, July 14, 1945.

92. Tygiel, *Baseball's Great Experiment*, 57.

93. Lowenfish, *Branch Rickey*, 377–78.

94. Heaphy, *Negro Leagues*, 195.

95. *Sporting News*, August 23, 1945.

96. *New York Times*, August 12, 1945; *Baltimore Afro-American*, August 18, 1945.

97. *New York Times*, August 23, 1945.

98. Lanctot, *Negro League Baseball*, 276–77.

99. *Pittsburgh Courier*, September 8, 1945.

100. Thorn and Tygiel, "Jackie Robinson's Signing," 86.

101. Lamb and Bleske, "Democracy on the Field," 53.

102. Thorn and Tygiel, "Jackie Robinson's Signing," 90–91.

103. Campanella, *It's Good to Be Alive*, 109–16.

104. Rampersad, *Jackie Robinson*, 129.

105. Thorn and Tygiel, "Jackie Robinson's Signing," 90–91.

106. *Baltimore Afro-American*, September 29, 1945.

107. Lanctot, *Negro League Baseball*, 277.

108. *Baltimore Afro-American*, September 29, 1945.

109. Kent Papers.

110. Lowenfish, *Branch Rickey*, 378–79.

11. ROBINSON BECOMES THE CHOSEN ONE

1. *Montreal Daily Star*, October 23, 1945; *Detroit Times*, October 24, 1945.

2. *Pittsburgh Courier*, November 3, 1945.

3. *New York Times*, October 24, 1945.

4. *Sporting News*, November 1, 1945.

5. *Philadelphia Inquirer*, October 24, 1945.

6. *New York Times*, October 24, 1945.

7. *Brooklyn Eagle*, October 24, 1945.

8. *New York World-Telegram*, October 24, 1945; *Detroit Times*, October 25, 1945; *Chicago Defender*, October 27, 1945.

9. *Baltimore Afro-American*, November 10, 1945.

10. *Sporting News*, November 1, 1945; *Chicago Defender*, November 10, 1945.

11. *Baltimore Afro-American*, November 10, 1945.

12. *Daily Worker*, October 26, 1945.

13. Simons, "Jackie Robinson and the American Zeitgeist," 85; *Washington Post*, October 27, 1945; Simons, "Jackie Robinson and the American Zeitgeist," 85.

14. Frommer, *Rickey and Robinson*, 112.

15. *Sporting News*, November 1, 1945; *Chicago Defender*, November 3, 1945; Tygiel, *Baseball's Great Experiment*, 80.

16. Simons, "Jackie Robinson and the American Zeitgeist," 80.

17. *Sporting News*, November 1, 1945; *Chicago Defender*, November 3, 1945; Tygiel, *Baseball's Great Experiment*, 80.

18. Simons, "Jackie Robinson and the American Zeitgeist," 79–80.

19. *Charleston News and Courier*, November 25, 1945.

20. *Miami Herald*, October 24, 1945.

21. Rampersad, *Jackie Robinson*, 24.

22. Tygiel, *Baseball's Great Experiment*, 52; Mardo, "Robeson-Robinson," 102–3.

23. Kelley, "Jackie Robinson and the Press," 139.

24. *Pittsburgh Courier*, November 3, 1945.

25. *Chicago Defender*, November 3, 1945.

26. *New York Herald Tribune*, October 25, 1945.

27. *Amsterdam News*, November 10, 1945. See also Weaver, "Black Press," 305–6.

28. *Amsterdam News*, November 10, 1945.

29. *Sporting News*, November 1, 1945.

30. *Baltimore Afro-American*, November 10, 1945; Robinson to Smith, Smith Papers.

31. *Daily Worker*, October 26, 1945.

32. *Amsterdam News*, November 3, 1945.

33. *Daily Worker*, October 26, 1945; *New York Times*, October 25, 1945.

34. *Pittsburgh Courier*, November 3, 1945.

35. *Sporting News*, November 1, 1945.

36. *New York World-Telegram*, October 25, 1945.
37. *New York World-Telegram*, October 26, 1946; Lacy, interview, May 20, 1999; *Sporting News*, November 1, 1945.
38. *Daily Worker*, October 26, 1945.
39. *New York P.M.*, October 28, 1945.
40. *New York Herald Tribune*, October 25, 1945.
41. Quoted in Winterich, "Playing Ball," 12.
42. Winterich, "Playing Ball," 12; *Time*, November 5, 1945, 77; *Newsweek*, November 5, 1945, 63–64; *Life*, November 26, 1946, 77; *Look*, November 27, 1945, 68; *Opportunity*, January 1946, 41.
43. *Sporting News*, November 1, 1945.
44. *Sporting News*, November 1, 1945.
45. *New York World-Telegram*, October 26, 1946.
46. *Sporting News*, November 1, 1945.
47. Simons, "Jackie Robinson and the American Zeitgeist," 81.
48. *Brooklyn Eagle*, October 24, 1945.
49. *Montreal Gazette*, October 25, 1945.
50. *Charleston Post and Courier*, October 25, 1945.
51. Simons, "Jackie Robinson and the American Zeitgeist," 82.
52. *Sporting News*, November 1, 1945; *Brooklyn Eagle*, October 24, 1945; Tygiel, *Baseball's Great Experiment*, 88.
53. *Philadelphia Inquirer*, October 25, 1945.
54. *Pittsburgh Courier*, November 3, 1945.
55. Feller and Gilbert, *Now Pitching Bob Feller*, 140–41.
56. Tygiel, Baseball's Great Experiment, 76.
57. *Pittsburgh Courier*, November 10, 1945.
58. Feller and Gilbert, *Now Pitching Bob Feller*, 140–41.
59. Rampersad, *Jackie Robinson*, 361–62.
60. Tygiel, *Baseball's Great Experiment*, 78–79.
61. *Negro Digest*, March 1946, 41–43.
62. *Brooklyn Eagle*, October 24, 1945.
63. *Daytona Beach Evening News*, October 24, 1945; *Deland Sun-News*, October 24, 1945; *Chicago Defender*, November 3, 1945; *Miami Herald*, October 24, 1945.
64. *Louisville Courier-Journal*, October 25, 1945; *Charlotte Observer*, October 25, 1945; *Atlanta Journal*, October 24, 1945.
65. *Detroit News*, October 26, 1946; *Washington Post*, October 27, 1945.
66. *Montreal Gazette*, October 25, 1945.

67. Simons, "Jackie Robinson and the American Zeitgeist," 94.

68. *New York Times*, October 24, 1945.

69. *Montreal Daily Star*, October 24, 1945; *Pittsburgh Courier*, November 3, 1945; *Montreal Gazette*, October 24, 25, 1945.

70. *Washington Post*, October 28, 1945.

12. "I NEVER WANT TO TAKE ANOTHER TRIP LIKE THIS ONE"

1. *Sporting News*, February 7, 14, 1946; *New York Times*, February 4, 1946.

2. *New York Times*, February 4, 1946.

3. Polmer, *Branch Rickey: A Biography*, 186.

4. *Pittsburgh Courier*, February 23, 1946; Tygiel, *Baseball's Great Experiment*, 93.

5. Smith to Rickey, December 19, 1945; Rickey to Smith, January 8, 1946; Smith to Rickey, January 14, 1946, Smith Papers.

6. Riley, *Biographical Encyclopedia*, 883–84.

7. *Daily Worker*, January 30, 1946.

8. Lamb, *Blackout*, 64, 71.

9. *Pittsburgh Courier*, March 2, 1946.

10. Lacy, interview, June 24, 1996.

11. *Daily Worker*, March 5, 1946.

12. Rowan and Robinson, *Wait Till Next Year*, 131.

13. W. White, "A Rising Wind," 60; Woodward, *Strange Career of Jim Crow*, 119–20.

14. *Chicago Defender*, February 23, 1946.

15. Lamb, *Blackout*, 61.

16. *Pittsburgh Courier*, November 17, 1945.

17. Lamb, *Blackout*, 9–11.

18. Rowan and Robinson, *Wait Till Next Year*, 134.

19. *Pittsburgh Courier*, March 9, 1946.

20. Billy Rowe, interview by the author, March 10, 1993.

21. *Brooklyn Eagle*, March 5, 1946; *Daytona Beach Morning Journal*, March 5, 1946; Mardo, interview, November 18, 1997; *Daily Worker*, March 8, 1946.

22. Lamb, *Blackout*, 86–87.

23. Rowe, interview, March 10, 1991.

24. Smith Papers.

25. *Pittsburgh Courier*, April 13, 1946.

26. Lamb, *Blackout*, 157.

27. *Daytona Beach Morning Journal*, March 7, 1946; *New York Times*, March 7, 1946.

28. *Baltimore Afro-American*, March 12, 1946; *Washington Afro-American*, March 23, 1946.

29. *Washington Afro-American*, March 11, 1946; Lacy, interview, May 22, 1995.

30. Cohane, "Branch Grows in Brooklyn," 70, 72, 75.

31. *New York Daily Mirror*, March 20, 1946.

32. *New York Daily News*, March 12, 1946.

33. *Pittsburgh Courier*, March 30, 1946.

34. *Daily Worker*, March 19, 1946; *Washington Afro-American*, March 23, 1946.

35. Lamb, *Blackout*, 105.

36. *Brooklyn Eagle*, March 13, 1946.

37. *Sporting News*, March 21, 1946.

38. Tygiel, *Baseball's Great Experiment*, 109.

39. Berkow, *Red*, 109.

40. Smith Papers; Eig, *Opening Day*, 201–2.

41. Lacy, interview, June 24, 1996; Lamb, *Blackout*, 146; Tygiel, *Baseball's Great Experiment*, 119.

42. *Amsterdam News*, April 27, 1946; *Daily Worker*, April 19, 1946; *Pittsburgh Courier*, October 12, 1946.

43. Maury Brown, "MLB Committee Fought to Keep Blacks Out Even after Robinson Signing," Biz of Baseball.com, http://bizofbaseball.com/index.php?option=com_content&view=article&id=4372:mlb-committee-fought-to-keep-blacks-out-even-after-robinson-signing&catid=26:editorials&Itemid=39.

44. Lowenfish, *Branch Rickey*, 396, 450–51.

45. *New York Times*, April 13, 1997.

46. Eig, *Opening Day*, 74.

47. Rampersad, *Jackie Robinson*, 172–73.

48. Rampersad, *Jackie Robinson*, 173–76.

49. Rampersad, *Jackie Robinson*, 176; Washburn, "New York Newspapers," 643.

50. Eig, *Opening Day*, 97.

51. Washburn, "New York Newspapers," 643; Kahn, *The Boys of Summer*, 135, quoted in Washburn, "New York Newspapers," 640.

52. Eig, *Opening Day*, 211.

53. Rampersad, *Jackie Robinson*, 182.

54. Truman, "Truman Speaking at NAACP Conference," Washington DC, June 29, 1947, Harry S. Truman Library and Museum, http://www.trumanlibrary.org.

55. Eig, *Opening Day*, 171.

56. Rampersad, *Jackie Robinson*, 179.

57. Eig, *Opening Day*, 77, 217.

58. *Sporting News*, September 17, 1947.

59. *Pittsburgh Courier*, May 24, 1947.

60. *Sporting News*, August 23, 1947.

61. Rodney, interview, November 6, 1997.

62. Smith Papers.

63. *Chicago American*, November 9, 1961. See also Carroll, "Wendell Smith's Last Crusade."

64. Weinbaum, "Rodney Pushed for MLB Integration"; Zirin, "More than a Sportswriter."

65. Zirin, "More than a Sportswriter."

66. Duffy, "Red Rodney."

67. Weinbaum, "Rodney Pushed for MLB Integration."

68. Rampersad, *Jackie Robinson*, 238, 271, 280.

69. Rampersad, *Jackie Robinson*, 206–7.

70. Lamb, *Blackout*, 177.

71. Rampersad, *Jackie Robinson*, 7, 187.

72. Rampersad, *Jackie Robinson*, 186–87.

73. Tygiel, *Baseball's Great Experiment*, 9.

74. *Sporting News*, October 31, 1994.

75. See Commission on Freedom of the Press, *Free and Responsible Press*.

76. Roberts and Klibanoff, *The Race Beat*, 6.

77. Roberts and Klibanoff, *The Race Beat*, 23; Martindale, *White Press and Black America*, 3.

78. Smith Papers; Lacy, interview, February 17, 1995; Mardo, interview, November 18, 1997.

BIBLIOGRAPHY

PRIMARY SOURCES

Kent, Rockwell. Papers. Smithsonian, Reel 5167. Frames 669, 670. Washington DC.

Rickey, Branch. Papers. Ohio Wesleyan University, Delaware OH.

Smith, Wendell. Papers. National Baseball Hall of Fame, Cooperstown NY.

SECONDARY SOURCES

Aldridge, Madeline L. "Let's Look at the Record." In vol. 4 of *A Documentary History of the Negro People in the United States*, ed. Herbert Aptheker. New York: Citadel, 1974.

Aptheker, Herbert, ed. *A Documentary History of the Negro People in the United States*. Vols. 3–5. New York: Citadel, 1973, 1974, 1993.

Ashe, Arthur. *A Hard Road to Glory: A History of the African-American Athlete, 1919–1945*. New York: Amistad, 1988.

Barber, Red, and Robert Creamer. *Rhubarb in the Catbird Seat*. Garden City NY: Doubleday, 1968.

Barck, Oscar, Jr., and Nelson Blake. *Since 1900*. New York: Macmillan, 1967.

Beasley, Maurine. "The Muckrakers and Lynching: A Case Study in Racism." *Journalism History* 9, no. 3 (1982): 876–89.

Berkow, Ira. *Red*. New York: New York Times, 1986.

Bernstein, Barton J., and Allen J. Matusow, eds. *Twentieth-Century America: Recent Interpretations*. San Diego: Harcourt Brace Jovanovich, 1972.

Bleske, Glen L. "Heavy Hitting Sportswriter Wendell Smith." *Media History Digest* 13 (1993): 38–42.

Boston, Talmage. *1939 — Baseball's Tipping Point*. Houston: Bright Sky, 2005.

Branch, Taylor. *Parting the Waters: America in the King Years, 1954–1963*. New York: Simon and Schuster, 1988.

Brooks, Thomas. *Walls Come Tumbling Down: A History of the Civil Rights Movement, 1940–1970*. Englewood Cliffs NJ: Prentice-Hall, 1974.

Brown, Earl. "The Detroit Race Riot of 1943." In vol. 4 of *A Documentary History of the Negro People in the United States*, ed. Herbert Aptheker. New York: Citadel, 1974.

Bryant, Howard. *Shut Out: A Story of Race and Baseball in Boston*. Boston: Beacon, 2003.

Buhle, Paul, and Dan Georgakas. *Encyclopedia of the American Left*. Urbana: University of Illinois Press, 1992.

Buni, Robert. *Robert L. Vann of the "Pittsburgh Courier": Politics and Black Journalism*. Pittsburgh: University of Pittsburgh Press, 1974.

Campanella, Roy. *It's Good to Be Alive*. Boston: Signet, 1959.

Campbell, Christopher P. *Race, Myth, and the News*. London: Sage, 1995.

Capecci, Dominic J., and Martha Wilkerson. "Multifarious Hero: Joe Louis, American Society, and Race Relations during World Crisis, 1935–1945." *Journal of Sport History* 10 (Winter 1983): 5–25.

Carroll, Brian. "Beating the Klan: Baseball Coverage in Wichita before Integration, 1920–1930." *Baseball Research Journal* 37 (2008): 51–61.

———. "A Tribute to Wendell Smith." *Black Ball: A Negro Leagues Journal* 2 (Spring 2009): 4–11.

———. "Wendell Smith's Last Crusade: The Desegregation of Spring Training." In *The Cooperstown Symposium on Baseball and Culture*, ed. William Simons, 123–35. Jefferson NC: MacFarland, 2001.

———. *When to Stop the Cheering? The Black Press, the Black Community, and the Integration of Professional Baseball*. New York: Routledge, 2007.

Cohane, Tim. "A Branch Grows in Brooklyn." *Look*, March 19, 1946.

Commission on Freedom of the Press. *A Free and Responsible Press: A General Report on Mass Commission*. Chicago: University of Chicago Press, 1947.

Conlin, Joseph R. *The Radical Press in the United States, 1880-1960*. Vol. 2. Westport CT: Greenwood, 1974.

Conrad, Earl. *Jim Crow America*. New York: Duell, Sloan, and Pearce, 1947.

Crawford, Scott A. G. M. "Arthur Daley." In *Twentieth-Century American Sportswriters*, ed. Richard Orodenker. Detroit: Gale Research, 1993.

Crepeau, Richard. *Baseball: America's Diamond Mind, 1919-1941*. Orlando: University Presses of Florida, 1980.

——. "The Jake Powell Incident and the Press: A Study in Black and White." *Journal of Baseball History* (Summer 1986): 32–46.

——. "Landis, Baseball, and Racism: A Brief Comment." *Baseball Research Journal* 38 (Spring 2009): 31–32.

Curren, William. "John Kieran." In *Twentieth-Century American Sportswriters*, ed. Richard Orodenker. Detroit: Gale Research, 1993.

Davis, Benjamin, Jr. *Communist Councilman from Harlem*. New York: International Publishers, 1969.

——. "Summary for Angelo Herndon, Defendant, before Fulton County Petit Jury." In vol. 3 of *A Documentary History of the Negro People in the United States*, ed. Herbert Aptheker. New York: Citadel, 1973.

Detweiler, Frederick G. *The Negro Press in the United States*. Chicago: University of Chicago Press. 1922.

Dorinson, Joseph, and Joram Warmund, eds. *Jackie Robinson: Race, Sports, and the American Dream*. Armonk NY: M. E. Sharpe, 1998.

Duberman, Martin Bauml. *Paul Robeson*. London: Pan Books, 1989.

DuBois, W. E. B. "Fighting against Racism." In vol. 3 of *A Documentary History of the Negro People of the United States*, ed. Herbert Aptheker. New York: Citadel, 1973.

——. "The Migration of Negroes." In vol. 3 of *A Documentary History of the Negro People of the United States*, ed. Herbert Aptheker. New York: Citadel, 1973.

——. "Negro Editors on Communism." In vol. 3 of *A Documentary History of the Negro People in the United States*, ed. Herbert Aptheker. New York: Citadel, 1973.

——. "Race Relations in the United States." In *Negro in Depression and War: Prelude to Revolution, 1930-1945*, ed. Bernard Sternsher. Chicago: Quadrangle Books, 1969.

——. "Strivings of the Negro People." *Atlantic Monthly*, August 1897. http://www.theatlantic.com/magazine/archive/1897/08/strivings-of-the-negro-people/5446/.

Duffy, Peter. "Red Rodney: The American Communist." *Village Voice*, June 10, 1997.

Durocher, Leo, and Ed Linn. *Nice Guys Finish Last*. New York: Simon and Schuster, 1975.

Eig, Jonathan. *Opening Day: The Story of Jackie Robinson's First Season*. New York: Simon and Schuster, 2007.

Ellison, Ralph. *Invisible Man*. 2nd ed. New York: Vintage, 1995.

English, J. Douglas. "Fred Lieb." In *Twentieth-Century American Sportswriters*, ed. Richard Orodenker. Detroit: Gale Research, 1993.

Farr, Farris. *Fair Enough: The Life and Times of Westbrook Pegler*. New Rochelle NY: Arlington House, 1975.

Feller, Bob, and Bill Gilbert. *Now Pitching Bob Feller*. New York: Harper Collins, 1990.

Fetter, Henry D. "The Party Line and the Color Line: The American Communist Party, the *Daily Worker*, and Jackie Robinson." *Journal of Sport History* 28 (Fall 2001): 375–402.

Fighting Words: Selections from Twenty-Five Years of the "Daily Worker." New York: New Century, 1949.

Fountain, Charles. *Sportswriter: The Life and Times of Grantland Rice*. New York: Oxford University Press, 1993.

Franklin, John Hope. *From Slavery to Freedom: A History of Negro Americans*. Vol. 3. New York: Alfred A. Knopf.

Frasca, Ralph. "Walker Was a Great Favorite with the Crowd: Racial Prejudice and Press Coverage of the First Black Major League Baseball Player." In *Take Me Out to the Ballgame*, ed. Gary Gumpert and Susan J. Drucker. Cresskill NJ: Hampton, 2002.

Frazier, E. Franklin. *The Negro in the United States*. New York: Macmillan, 1949.

Fried, Albert. *Socialism in America*. Garden City NY: Doubleday, 1970.

Frommer, Harry. *Rickey and Robinson: The Men Who Broke Baseball's Color Barrier*. New York: Macmillan, 1982.

Garris, Bruce. *Sports Reporting*. Ames: Iowa State University Press, 1993.

Gay, Timothy. *Satch, Dizzy, and Rapid Robert: The Wild Saga of Interracial Baseball before Jackie Robinson*. New York: Simon and Schuster, 2010.

Glazer, Nathan. *The Social Basis of American Communism*. Westport CT: Greenwood, 1974.

Gumpert, Gary, and Susan Drucker, eds. *Take Me Out to the Ballgame: Communicating Baseball*. Cresskill NJ: Hampton, 2002.

Heaphy, Leslie A. "Dan Burley: Journalist and Musician." *Black Ball: A Negro Leagues Journal* 2 (Fall 2009): 4–9.

———. *The Negro Leagues, 1869–1960*. Jefferson NC: MacFarland, 2002.

———. "A Tribute to Sam Lacy." *Black Ball: A Negro Leagues Journal* 1 (Fall 2008): 6–11.

Henry, Neil. *American Carnival: Journalism under Siege in an Age of New Media*. Berkeley and Los Angeles: University of California Press, 2007.

Hogan, Lawrence. *Shades of Glory: The Negro Leagues and the Story of African-American Baseball*. Washington DC: National Geographic, 2006.

Holtzman, Jerome. *No Cheering in the Press Box*. New York: Henry Holt, 1995.

Holway, John. *Voices from the Great Negro Baseball Leagues*. New York: Dodd, Mead, 1975.

Horne, Gerald. *Black Liberation/Red Scare: Ben Davis and the Communist Party*. Newark: University of Delaware Press, 1994.

Howe, Irving, and Lewis Coser. *The American Communist Party: A Critical History*. New York: Da Capo, 1974.

Hutchinson, Earl Ofari. *Blacks and Reds: Race and Class Conflict, 1919–1990*. East Lansing: Michigan State University Press, 1995.

Inabinett, Mark. *Grantland Rice and His Heroes: The Sportswriter as Mythmaker in the 1920s*. Knoxville: University of Tennessee Press, 1994.

Jordan, David M., Larry R. Gerlach, and John P. Rossi. "A Baseball Myth Exploded: The Truth about Bill Veeck and the '43 Phillies." *National Pastime: A Review of Baseball History* 18 (November 1998): 3–13.

Kahn, Roger. *The Boys of Summer*. New York: Signet Books, 1973.

Kelley, William. "Jackie Robinson and the Press." *Journalism Quarterly* 53 (Spring 1976): 137–39.

Kennedy, David. *Over Here: The First World War and American Society*. New York: Oxford University Press, 1982.

Kessler, Lauren. *The Dissident Press: Alternative Journalism in American History*. Beverly Hills: Sage, 1984.

Kessner, Thomas. *Fiorello H. La Guardia and the Making of Modern New York*. New York: McGraw-Hill, 1989.

Kirby, John. "The Roosevelt Administration and Blacks: An Ambivalent Legacy." In *Twentieth-Century America: Recent Interpretations*, ed. Barton J. Bernstein and Allen J. Matusow. New York: Harcourt, Brace, Jovanovich, 1972.

Klein, Robert. "Sports Reporting in New York City, 1946–1960, by Two of the Era's Greatest and Most Influential Reporters — Arthur Daley and Lester Rodney." *Nine: A Journal of Baseball History and Social Policy Perspectives* 6 (Fall 1997).

Knight, Bill. "Heywood Broun." In *Twentieth-Century American Sportswriters*, ed. Richard Orodenker. Detroit: Gale Research, 1993.

Lacy, Sam, and Moses Newton. *Fighting for Fairness: The Life Story of Hall of Fame Sportswriter Sam Lacy*. Centreville MD: Tidewater, 1998.

Lamb, Chris. "*L'affaire* Jake Powell: The Minority Press Goes to Bat against Segregated Baseball." *Journalism and Mass Communication Quarterly* 76 (Spring 1999): 21–34.

———. "Baseball's Whitewash: Sportswriter Wendell Smith Exposes Major League Baseball's Big Lie." *Nine: A Journal of Baseball History and Social Policy Perspectives* 18 (Fall 2009): 1–20.

———. *Blackout: The Untold Story of Baseball's First Spring Training*. Lincoln: University of Nebraska Press, 2004.

———. "I Never Want to Take Another Trip Like This One." *Journal of Sport History* 24 (Summer 1997): 177–91.

———. "Jackie Robinson Plays His First Game for the Montreal Royals." *National Pastime: A Review of Baseball History* (1999): 20–23.

———. "'What's Wrong with Baseball?': The *Pittsburgh Courier* and the Beginning of Its Campaign to Integrate Baseball." *Western Journal of Black Studies* 26 (Winter 2002): 189–92.

Lamb, Chris, and Glen Bleske. "Democracy on the Field: The Black Press Takes on White Baseball." *Journalism History* 24 (Summer 1998): 51–59.

Lanctot, Neil. *Negro League Baseball: The Rise and Ruin of a Black Institution*. Philadelphia: University of Pennsylvania Press, 2004.

Laucella, Pamela. "Jesse Owens, a Black Pearl amidst an Ocean of Fury: A Case Study of Press Coverage on the 1936 Berlin Olympic Games." Paper presented at the Association for Education in Journalism and Mass Communication, 2002.

Lenthall, Bruce. "Covering More than the Game: Baseball and Racial Issues in an African-American Newspaper." In *Cooperstown Symposium on Baseball and American Culture, 1990*, ed. Alvin L. Hall. Westport CT: Meckler, 1991.

Lester, Larry. *Black Baseball's National Showcase: The East-West All Star-Game, 1933–1953*. Lincoln: University of Nebraska Press, 2001.

———. "Can You Read, Judge Landis?" *Black Ball: A Negro Leagues Journal* 1 (Fall 2008): 57–82.

Levitt, Daniel R. *Ed Barrow: The Bulldog Who Built the Yankees' First Dynasty*. Lincoln: University of Nebraska Press, 2008.

Lewis, David Levering. *W. E. B. Du Bois: The Fight for Equality and the American Century, 1919–1963*. New York: Henry Holt, 2000.

Lieb, Fred. *Baseball as I Have Known It*. New York: Coward, McCann, and Geoghegan, 1977.

Lindholm, Karl. "William Clarence Matthews." *National Pastime: A Review of Baseball History* 17 (1997): 67–72.

Lindsey, Howard. *A History of Black America.* Secaucus NJ: Chartwell Books, 1994.

Lipman, David. *Mr. Baseball: The Story of Branch Rickey.* New York: G. P. Putnam's Sons, 1966.

Logan, Rayford W. "The Negro and the Post-war World." In vol. 4 of *A Documentary History of the Negro People in the United States*, ed. Herbert Aptheker. New York: Citadel, 1974.

——. *The Negro in the United States.* Vol. 1, *A History to 1945: From Slavery to Second-Class Citizenship.* Reinhold NY: Van Nostrand, 1970.

Lovell, John, Jr. "Washington Fights." In vol. 4 of *A Documentary History of the Negro People in the United States*, ed. Herbert Aptheker. New York: Citadel, 1974.

Lowenfish, Lee. *Branch Rickey: Baseball's Ferocious Gentleman.* Lincoln: University of Nebraska Press, 2007.

——. "The Gentleman's Agreement and the Ferocious Gentleman Who Broke It." *Baseball Research Journal* 30 (Summer 2009): 33–34.

Macht, Norman L. "Does Baseball Deserve This Black Eye?" *Baseball Research Journal* 38 (Summer 2009): 26–30.

Mann, Arthur. *Branch Rickey: American in Action.* Boston: Houghton Mifflin, 1957.

——. *The Jackie Robinson Story.* New York: Grosset and Dunlap, 1950.

Mardo, Bill. "Robeson-Robinson." In *Jackie Robinson: Race, Sports, and the American Dream*, ed. Joe Dorinson and Joram Warmund. Armonk NY: M. E. Sharpe, 1998.

Martindale, Carolyn. *The White Press and Black America.* Westport CT: Greenwood, 1986.

Milkman, Paul. *"P.M.": A New Deal in Journalism.* New Brunswick: Rutgers University Press, 1997.

Moore, Leonard J. *Citizen Klansmen: The Ku Klux Klan in Indiana, 1921–1928.* Chapel Hill: University of North Carolina Press, 1991.

Morgan, Ted. *Reds: McCarthyism in Twentieth-Century America.* New York: Random House, 2003.

Myrdal, Gunnar. *An American Dilemma: The Negro Problem and Modern Democracy.* Vol. 2. New York: Harper and Row, 1944.

Naison, Mark. "Lefties and Righties: The Communist Party and Sports during the Great Depression." *In Sport in America: New Historical Perspectives*, ed. Donald Spivey. Westport CT: Greenwood, 1985.

Norwood, Stephen H., and Harold Brackman. "Going to Bat for Jackie Robinson: The Jewish Role in Breaking Baseball's Color Line." *Journal of Sport History* 26 (Spring 1999): 115–41.

O'Connor, Richard. *Heywood Broun: A Biography*. New York: G. P. Putnam's Sons, 1975.

Orodenker, Richard, ed. *Twentieth-Century Sportswriters*. Detroit: Gale Research, 1993.

———. "Westbrook Pegler." In *Twentieth-Century American Sportswriters*, ed. Richard Orodenker. Detroit: Gale Research, 1993.

Overmyer, James. *Effa Manley and the Newark Eagles*. Metuchen NJ: Scarecrow, 1993.

Patterson, William L. "Against Jim Crow in Professional Baseball." In vol. 4 of *A Documentary History of the Negro People in the United States*, ed. Herbert Aptheker. New York: Citadel, 1974.

———. *The Man Who Cried Genocide*. New York: International Publishers, 1971.

———. "We Charge Genocide." In vol. 4 of *A Documentary History of the Negro People in the United States*, ed. Herbert Aptheker. New York: Citadel, 1974.

Peterson, Robert. *Only the Ball Was White*. New York: Oxford University Press, 1970.

Pietrusza, David. *Judge and Jury: The Life and Times of Judge Kenesaw Mountain Landis*. South Bend IN: Diamond Communications, 1998.

Polmer, Murray. *Branch Rickey: A Biography*. New York: Signet, 1982.

Pride, Armistead S., and Clint C. Wilson II. *A History of the Black Press*. Washington DC: Howard University Press, 1997.

Rader, Benjamin. *Baseball: A History of America's Game*. Urbana: University of Illinois Press, 1992.

Rampersad, Arnold. *Jackie Robinson*. New York: Alfred A. Knopf, 1997.

Reidenbaugh, Lowell. *The "Sporting News'" First Hundred Years, 1886–1986*. St. Louis: Sporting News, 1986.

Reisler, Jim. *Black Writers/Black Baseball*. Jefferson NC: MacFarland, 1995.

Reynolds, Grant. "What the Soldier Thinks about This War." In vol. 4 of *A Documentary History of the Negro People in the United States*, ed. Herbert Aptheker. New York: Citadel, 1974.

Ribowsky, Mark. *A Complete History of the Negro Leagues, 1884–1955*. New York: Birch Lane, 1995.

Rice, Grantland. *The Tumult and the Shouting*. New York: Dell, 1954.

Riley, James A. *The Biographical Encyclopedia of the Negro Baseball Leagues*. New York: Carroll and Graf, 1994.

Roark, Eldon. "How Dixie Newspapers Handle the Negro." *Negro Digest* (June 1946): 34–35.

Roberts, Gene, and Hank Klibanoff. *The Race Beat*. New York: Vintage Books, 2006.

Robinson, Jackie, and Alfred Duckett. *I Never Had It Made*. New York: Fawcett, Crest, 1974.

Roeder, Bill. *Jackie Robinson*. New York: A. S. Barnes, 1950.

Rogosin, Donn. "Black Baseball: The Life in the Negro Leagues and Professional Negro Baseball Players." PhD diss., University of Texas, 1981.

———. *Invisible Men: Life in the Negro Leagues*. New York: Kodanshu International, 1995.

Rose, Arnold, ed. *The Negro in America: The Condensed Version of Gunnar Myrdal's "An America Dilemma."* New York: Harper and Row, 1964.

Rowan, Carl, and Jackie Robinson. *Wait Till Next Year*. New York: Random House, 1960.

Rusinack, Kelly. "Baseball on the Radical Agenda: The *Daily* and *Sunday Worker* on the Desegregation of Major League Baseball, 1933–1947." Master's thesis, Clemson University, 1995.

Rusinack, Kelly, and Chris Lamb. "'Demand the End of Jim Crow in Baseball!': The *Communist Daily Worker*'s Crusade against the National Pastime." *Cultural Logic: An Electronic Journal of Marxist Theory and Practice* 2 (Fall 1999).

Rust, Art, Jr. *"Get That Nigger Off the Field": The Oral History of the Negro Leagues*. New York: Delacorte, 1992.

Schaffer, Alan. *Vito Marcantonio: Radical in Congress*. Syracuse: Syracuse University Press, 1966.

Schapp, Jeremy. *Triumph: The Untold Story of Jesse Owens and Hitler's Olympics*. Boston: Houghton Mifflin, 2007.

Seymour, Harold. *Baseball: The Early Years*. New York: Oxford University Press, 1960.

Shane, Ted. "Chocolate Rube Waddell." *Saturday Evening Post*, July 27, 1940.

Sheehan, Tom. "The Boston Red Sox: Are They Racist?" *Boston Phoenix*, August 17, 1976.

Silber, Irwin. *Press Box Red: The Story of Lester Rodney, the Communist Who Helped Break the Color Line in American Sports*. Philadelphia: Temple University Press, 2003.

Simmons, Charles. *The African American Press: A History of News Coverage during National Crisis, with Special Reference to Four Black Newspapers, 1827–1965*. Jefferson NC: MacFarland, 2006.

Simon, Rita James, ed. *As We Saw the Thirties: Essays on Social and Political Movements of a Decade*. Urbana: University of Illinois Press, 1967.

Simons, William. "Jackie Robinson and the American Mind: Journalistic Perceptions of the Reintegration of Baseball." *Journal of Sport History* 12 (Spring 1985): 39–64.

———. "Jackie Robinson and the American Zeitgeist." In *The Cooperstown Symposium on Baseball and American Culture*, ed. Peter M. Rutkoff. Jefferson NC: MacFarland, 2000.

Sternsher, Bernard, ed. *The Negro in Depression and War: Prelude to Revolution, 1930–1945*. Chicago: Quadrangle Books, 1969.

Stevens, John. *Shaping the First Amendment*. Beverly Hills: Sage, 1982.

Stout, Glenn. "Tryout and Fallout: Race, Jackie Robinson, and the Red Sox." *Massachusetts Historical Review* 6 (2004): 11–38.

Thorn, John, and Jules Tygiel. "Jackie Robinson's Signing: The Untold Story." In *The Jackie Robinson Reader: Perspectives of an American Hero*, ed. Jules Tygiel. New York: Dutton, 1997.

Tuttle, William M., Jr. *Race Riot: Chicago in the Red Summer of 1919*. New York: Atheneum, 1984.

Tye, Larry. *Satchel: The Life and Times of an American Legend*. New York: Random House, 2009.

Tygiel, Jules. *Baseball's Great Experiment*. New York: Oxford University Press, 1997.

———, ed. *The Jackie Robinson Reader: Perspectives of an American Hero*. New York: Dutton, 1997.

———. "Revisiting Bill Veeck and the 1943 Phillies." *Baseball Research Journal* 35 (2006): 109–14.

Veeck, Bill, and Ed Linn. *Veeck — as in Wreck*. New York: Ballantine Books, 1962.

"View from Left Field: Interview with Lester Rodney." *Political Affairs* (July 24, 2004).

Voigt, David Quentin. *American Baseball: From Gentleman's Sport to the Commissioner System*. University Park: Pennsylvania State University Press, 1979.

———. *American Baseball: From the Commissioners to the Continental Expansion*. Vols. 2–3. University Park: Pennsylvania State University Press, 1979, 1983.

Ward, Geoffrey C. *Unforgiveable Blackness: The Rise and Fall of Jack Johnson*. New York: Alfred A. Knopf, 2004.

Ward, Geoffrey C., and Ken Burns. *Baseball: An Illustrated History*. New York: Alfred A. Knopf, 1994.

Washburn, Patrick. *The African-American Newspaper: Voice of Freedom*. Evanston IL: Northwestern University Press, 2006.

———. "New York Newspapers and Robinson's First Season." *Journalism Quarterly* 58 (Winter 1981): 640–44.

———. "The *Pittsburgh Courier*'s Double V Campaign in 1942." *American Journalism* 3 (1986): 73–86.

————. *A Question of Sedition: The Federal Government's Investigation of the Black Press during World War II*. New York: Oxford University Press, 1986.

Weaver, Bill L. "The Black Press and the Assault on Professional Baseball's 'Color Line,' October 1945–April 1947." *Phylon* 40 (Winter 1979): 303–17.

Weinbaum, Willie. "Rodney Pushed for MLB Integration." ESPN.com, February 24, 2010.

Westbrook, Deeanne. *Ground Rules: Baseball and Myth*. Urbana: University of Illinois Press, 1996.

White, Sol. *Sol White's History of Colored Base Ball*. Ed. Jerry Malloy. Lincoln: University of Nebraska Press, 1995.

White, Walter. "Chicago and Its Eight Reasons." In vol. 3 of *A Documentary History of the Negro People in the United States*, ed. Herbert Aptheker. New York: Citadel, 1974.

————. *A Rising Wind*. Garden City NY: Doubleday, 1945.

————. "A Rising Wind." In vol. 5 of *A Documentary History of the Negro People in the United States*, ed. Herbert Aptheker. New York: Citadel, 1974.

————. "Supremacy in World War II." In vol. 4 of *A Documentary History of the Negro People in the United States*, ed. Herbert Aptheker. New York: Citadel, 1974.

Wiggins, David K. "Wendell Smith, the *Pittsburgh Courier-Journal*, and the Campaign to Include Blacks in Organized Baseball." *Journal of Sport History* 10 (Summer 1983): 5–29.

Williams, Nat D. "Beaten Half to Death." In vol. 4 of *A Documentary History of the Negro People in the United States*, ed. Herbert Aptheker. New York: Citadel, 1974.

Williams, Peter. *The Joe Williams Reader*. Chapel Hill: Algonquin Books, 1989.

Wilson, Henry. "Jim Crow Army." In vol. 4 of *A Documentary History of the Negro People in the United States*, ed. Herbert Aptheker. New York: Citadel, 1990.

Wilson, W. Rollo. "They Could Make the Big Leagues." In vol. 4 of *A Documentary History of Negro People in the United States*, ed. Herbert Aptheker. New York: Citadel, 1974.

Winchell, Mark Royden. "Grantland Rice." In *Twentieth-Century American Sportswriters*, ed., Richard Orodenker. Detroit: Gale Research, 1993.

Winterich, J. T. "Playing Ball: Negroes in Organized Baseball." *Saturday Review*, November 24, 1945.

Wolseley, Roland E. *The Black Press, U.S.A.* Ames: Iowa State University Press, 1971.

Woodward, C. Vann. *The Strange Career of Jim Crow*. New York: Oxford University Press, 1974.

Yergan, Max. "Democracy and the Negro People Today." In vol. 4 of *A Documentary History of the Negro People in the United States*, ed. Herbert Aptheker. New York: Citadel, 1974.

Zang, David W. *Fleet Walker's Divided Heart: The Life of Baseball's First Black Major Leaguer*. Lincoln: University of Nebraska Press, 1995.

Zirin, Dave. "More than a Sportswriter: Lester 'Red' Rodney." *Nation*, December 23, 2009.

——. *A People's History of Sports in the United States: 250 Years of Politics, Protest, People, and Play*. New York: New Press, 2008.

INDEX

140, 185; opposition to baseball desegregation, 5, 8, 11
McKechnie, Bill, 99, 139
McKeever, Steven, 99
McLaughlin, George V., 225
McNew, Frank, 128
Meany, Tom, 6
Mehlman, Jerome, 260, 269
Memphis Free Speech, 64
Memphis World, 241
Méndez, José, 5, 11, 41, 147
Messenger, 167
Metcalfe, Ralph, 6
Meyers, John "Chief," 41, 45
Miami FL, 317
Miami Herald, 301
Michigan Chronicle, 172, 197, 232
Miller, Bing, 45
Miller, Buster, 191, 208, 219
Miller, Dorie, 167–68, 177
Mills, Bill, 102
Milwaukee Journal, 101
Mintz, Morris, 200
Monroe, Al, 59, 149; on Powell affair, 121, 122, 126–27, 151
Montreal Gazette, 303
Montreal Royals: Robinson as player for, 314–15, 317, 319–20; Robinson signing with, 16, 128, 276, 283–84, 293, 303; Wright and, 309–10, 319
Montreal Star, 283, 303
Moore, Leonard J., 48
Moore, Richard B., 164
Moreland, Nate, 175–76, 206–7, 224
Morton, Charlie, 33–34
Moses, Alvin, 8
Muchnick, Isadore, 247–48, 261–63

muckraking journalism, 46–47
Mulcahy, Hugh, 142
Mullane, Tony, 34, 193
Murphy, Carl, 80
Murphy, Howard H., 234
Myer, Buddy, 112
Myers, Billy, 139, 140
Myrdal, Gunnar, 22, 165–66, 174, 240, 332

Nation, 110, 118
National Association for the Advancement of Colored People (NAACP), 64, 115, 172, 174, 221, 285
National Maritime Union, 181, 220
National Negro Congress, 105, 115, 164, 165, 167
National Pastime, 227, 228
Nazi-Soviet pact, 160–61
Negro American League, 76, 202, 239, 268, 298
Negro Baseball, 272
Negro Digest, 300
Negro League Baseball: The Rise and Ruin of a Black Institution (Lanctot), 15
Negro leagues: and absorption by Major Leagues, 8, 148–49; and baseball centennial, 135; baseball desegregation as end of, 59, 62, 149, 201–2, 204, 278, 287, 298; baseball establishment denigration of, 138, 287; black owners of, 13, 201, 202, 231; black sportswriters and, 10–11, 61, 73, 74–75, 77, 239, 268–69; *Daily Worker* coverage of, 97, 98; early history of, 66–68; East-West all-star